American Cinema and
the Southern Imaginary

Series Editors

Jon Smith, Simon Fraser University

Riché Richardson, Cornell University

Advisory Board

Houston A. Baker Jr., Vanderbilt University

Jennifer Greeson, The University of Virginia

Trudier Harris, The University of North Carolina, Chapel Hill

John T. Matthews, Boston University

Tara McPherson, The University of Southern California

Scott Romine, The University of North Carolina, Greensboro

American Cinema and the Southern Imaginary

edited by
DEBORAH E. BARKER and
KATHRYN MCKEE

The University of Georgia Press   Athens and London

© 2011 by the University of Georgia Press
Athens, Georgia 30602
www.ugapress.org
All rights reserved
Set in Sabon by Graphic Composition, Inc.,
   Bogart, Georgia
Printed digitally in the United States of America

Library of Congress Cataloging-in-Publication Data
American cinema and the southern imaginary / edited by Deborah E. Barker
   and Kathryn McKee.
      p. cm. — (The new southern studies)
   ISBN-13: 978-0-8203-3380-9 (hardcover : alk. paper)
   ISBN-10: 0-8203-3380-8 (hardcover : alk. paper)
   ISBN-13: 978-0-8203-3710-4 (pbk. : alk. paper)
   ISBN-10: 0-8203-3710-2 (pbk. : alk. paper)
      1. Southern States—In motion pictures. 2. Motion pictures and history.
   3. Race relations in motion pictures. 4. African Americans in motion pictures.
   5. Memory in motion pictures. I. Barker, Deborah, 1955– II. McKee,
   Kathryn B. III. Series.
   PN1995.9.S66A44 2010
   791.43'65875—dc22   2010020388

British Library Cataloging-in-Publication Data available

For Anna, Molly, and Malcolm

Contents

III. Crossing Borders

Acknowledgments

We would like to thank all the contributors who made this collection possible. We also are indebted to Jay Watson, Annette Trefzer, Jack Pendarvis, Theresa Starkey, and Matthew Bernstein for their willingness to read and comment on the introduction. A special thanks goes to Ivo Kamps, who has been instrumental throughout the entire project. We are especially pleased that the collection was included in the New Southern Studies series and want to thank the series editors, Jon Smith and Riché Richardson, for their input and faith in the project. At the University of Georgia Press we thank our editor, Erika Stevens; the design team; our amazing copyeditor, Susan Silver; and all those who helped us see the project through from start to finish. Thanks also to UM graduate student Vincent Rotkiewicz for his help in compiling the index. Most importantly, we are grateful to the University of Mississippi students in the South in Film classes who inspired us to put together this volume.

American Cinema and
the Southern Imaginary

Introduction

The Southern Imaginary

Deborah E. Barker and Kathryn McKee

All movies smell of a neighborhood and a season.
—Walker Percy, *The Moviegoer*

In Walker Percy's *The Moviegoer*, the movies tell people who they are and where they are: suspended in a South that is as much imagined and represented as it is concrete, as much created and performed as it is organic. The neighborhoods and the seasons Binx Bolling smells borrow their scents, at least in part, from the movies that have themselves shaped his expectations for ordinary, non-Hollywood space. In *Ordering the Façade: Photography and Contemporary Southern Women's Writing*, Katherine Henninger maintains that the U.S. South's visual legacy is as strong as or stronger than its fabled oral tradition.[1] Henninger's argument focuses primarily on the South's rich photographic history, but likewise in film the "South" takes on a variety of sometimes contradictory meanings that nonetheless converge to locate it as a primarily visual and visualized place that may shape all subsequent encounters of it for the moviegoer. Yet the last collection of essays devoted exclusively to the topic, *The South in Film*, was published in 1981.[2] Since that time, crucial changes have occurred in both southern studies and film studies that call for a re-evaluation and rethinking of what we mean when we talk about southern film.

Capitalizing on innovations in media studies, southern cultural studies, and the global South, *American Cinema and the Southern Imaginary* is an exploration of the various ways in which the southern imaginary is constitutive of American cinema and of the ways in which the makers of movies—from Hollywood films to independents and documentaries, and from silent films to the latest technological innovations—have imagined the "South" both to construct and to unsettle national narratives.[3] In bringing together the authors in this collection our purpose is to publish new essays that help to theorize and contextualize the evolving and expanding field of southern film. The essays included here complicate the foundational term "southern," in some places literally stretching the traditional boundaries of regional identification until they all but disappear, while in others limning a persistent and sometimes self-conscious performance of place that only intensifies its power. The authors in this collection, then, contribute to what Houston Baker and Dana Nelson first called the "new Southern Studies" by "construct[ing] and survey[ing] a new scholarly map of 'The South'" as it pertains to cinematic representations of the region and the decided sway they hold over the national and international imaginary.[4]

The collection is not, however, an attempt to define what makes a film southern or to categorize the southern as a genre comparable to the Western (a filmic type that represents region to the nation and uses it as emblematic of particularly American qualities, such as the wide-open sky of limitless individualism).[5] By invoking in our title the southern imaginary and its relation to American cinema, we do not mean to suggest that we have access to a real, historically knowable South or an authentic southernness that has somehow been corrupted or romanticized by Hollywood. The southern imaginary (and the cultural work it performs) is not contained by the boundaries of geography and genre; it is not an offshoot or subgenre of mainstream American film but is integral to the history and the development of American cinema. Therefore, we use the term "southern imaginary" precisely because of its evocative, overdetermined, and contradictory impulses and its many critical and theoretical resonances. For the purposes of this essay collection, we can think of the southern imaginary as an amorphous and sometimes conflicting collection of images, ideas, attitudes, practices, linguistic accents, histories, and fantasies about a shifting geographic region and time. Some of the essays in this volume mine the southern imaginary in places traditionally associated with the geographic or literary South, but others examine inflections of the southern imaginary that emerge in far less likely places.

An expanded concept of the southern imaginary is necessary because never more so than today has the South failed to call forth a set of stable defining features. The site of dramatic demographic shifts, transnational industry, and fissured red state power, the South has, if anything, become a more complicated and necessary idea to examine in assembling national, hemispheric, and global narratives of power and identity. U.S. southern studies has likewise undergone a paradigm shift away from the model of regional exceptionalism, once the discipline's bread-and-butter justification for its existence. The South was, ran this intellectual trajectory, distinct from the rest of the nation and by extension the rest of the world in nearly every manifestation: history, literature, economics, politics, food, religion, and education.[6] Recent scholarship is not invested in denying the particularities of place or in disavowing the contributions of earlier work. Rather than identify the factors isolating locations, it seeks to plumb the nexus of the local, the national, and the global to track the resonances linking them. Beginning most notably with Michael Krey-ling's 1998 study, *Inventing Southern Literature*, scholars have called into question foundational terms including "South" and "Faulkner" as the region's persistent literary synecdoche.[7] The result has been a critical recognition of the U.S. South as fully implicated in the process of national self-creation. That southerners themselves have been active participants in alternately rejecting and embracing, and continually reinventing, understandings of themselves likewise complicates any effort to offer a fixed summary of what it means to claim a southern identity today.

At the same time, scholars have recognized that the South bears the imprint of hemispheric and global affiliations that wrench its notoriously self-absorbed gaze outward, beyond the confines of nation.[8] Interdisciplinary and comparative literary studies are a further means of studying the hemispheric forces that unite locations over and around the boundaries of the nation-state that demarcate them, spilling into Latin America, the Caribbean, and Africa.[9] In a broader framework, scholars have begun tentatively situating portions of the Deep South, most particularly the former "Black Belt," within the paradigms of the Global South, a configuration that cares for literal direction only insofar as it identifies areas subordinated to an internal or external Global North that withholds from it the economic and political means to achieve parity of standards. As Jon Smith and Deborah Cohn assert, the U.S. South is "a space simultaneously (or alternately) center and margin, victor and defeated, empire and colony, essentialist and hybrid, northern and southern (both in the global sense)."[10] Yet particular *images* or ways of *seeing* the South persist alongside these expanded approaches to its study, in no small part due to the way the South has been represented in film.

Just as a more complex notion of "southern" is critical to this collection, so too is a consideration of the term "imaginary" in its many variations, not only in its more common association with creativity, fantasy, and the production of images, but also in the contexts of film, postcolonial, psychoanalytic, and Marxist theory, and especially as it has been employed in analyses of regional and national narratives. The two terms taken together open up rather than close down or define a single approach to the South in film. The southern imaginary, therefore, is not a false representation that must be stripped away to see the real South but a multifaceted, multivalent concept that informs our understanding of U.S. culture, especially in relation to ideas about race, gender, and region.

Although we lack the time and space in this introduction to attempt a comprehensive history of the many uses of southern imaginary in cinema, we would like to sketch out at least some of the more visible theoretical and thematic confrontations and permutations among southernness, race, gender, and cinema, many of which will be developed further in the essays in this collection.[11] In 1903 W. E. B. Du Bois famously pronounced, "The problem of the Twentieth Century is the problem of the color-line."[12] That Du Bois's insight appeared the same year as the first cinematic *Uncle Tom's Cabin* (1903) suggests its applicability to cinema, one of the most influential media of the twentieth century; moreover, in the history of American cinema, the color line has been conspicuously placed below the Mason-Dixon line.[13] As Linda Williams suggests, dramatic adaptations of *Uncle Tom's Cabin*, called traveling Tom shows, were instrumental in developing not only cinematic melodrama but also the racial melodrama that is "a central *mode* of American popular culture" and that inspired and influenced other cinematic milestones.[14] But this early melding of a twentieth-century technology with nineteenth-century subject matter also exemplifies one of the early and persistent invocations of the southern imaginary. In part, the southern imaginary in American cinema began as a construct predicated on the past. The U.S. film industry did not come into existence until well after the Civil War, and consequently American cinema's initial engagement with southernness was rooted in a form of southern tradition that, as Scott Romine asserts, comes out of "a selective, fetishized set of icons and memories culled from the messiness of history and consigned forever to a past irretrievable except through representation."[15] Many of these "icons and memories," whether in the form of a nostalgic ideal or a blistering condemnation, populate the world of early cinema. For example, *Uncle Tom's Cabin* depicts the ruinous effects of slavery through the image of Simon Legree's iconic Gothic plantation house. Like many of the subsequent versions of *Uncle Tom's Cabin*, Edwin S. Porter's 1903 film reimagines the story's antebellum narrative in the context of the Civil War and its aftermath. When Uncle Tom dies, a superimposed image of an angel precedes a series of iris-framed drawings depicting the stages of the Civil War, including an image of Lincoln freeing a kneeling slave, and Lee and Grant shaking hands at Appomattox. This narrative of future events reinscribes Legree's gothic mansion with the image of the antebellum ruined plantation house, while the final shot of Lee and Grant confirms the restoration of the Union and the end of slavery.

The fallen plantation, in particular the ruined house at its center, has undeniably served as a national symbol of unrepentant pride and the failure to recognize defeat and as such, it has served as a mythic repository for the shifting specters of our national wrongs, the historical legacy of U.S. slavery, and the persistent blight of poverty. In a national narrative of limitless opportunity and unrestricted resources that validated the present and looked to a bright future, the cinematic South often served in terms of both place and time (the past) as a repository for the nation's unresolved problems and contradictions.[16] This outsider's mythic version of the southern imaginary, based on the projections and needs of the rest of the country and imposed on the South, suggests Edward Said's notion of "imaginative geography and history," which "help the mind to intensify its own sense of itself by dramatizing the distance and difference between what is close to it and what is far away."[17]

An alternate construct of the southern imaginary, similar to Benedict Anderson's national "imagined community," is predicated on the active identification of the community members themselves.[18] However, the South as an "exceptional" region disrupts what Anderson refers to as the "meanwhile," synchronic time of the "imagined community": a national narrative of homogeneity and anonymity, which, as Homi K. Bhabha contests, requires an obligation to forget "the anteriority of the nation."[19] In opposition to Anderson's "imaginary community," Bhabha explains, we need "to rearticulate the sum of knowledge from the perspective of the signifying position of the minority that resists totalization—the repetition that will not return as the same."[20] Thus, to maintain a U.S. national narrative we are also obliged to forget the regional and ethnic differences that disrupt that narrative. But, of course, some southerners also had their own national "imagined community" of the Confederate States of America (CSA), which was predicated on the need to forget or distort the voices, lives, and histories that are left out of both the U.S. and the CSA national narratives.

Twelve years after the first *Uncle Tom's Cabin*, and only one year after Sam Lucus became the first African American to play Uncle Tom on film, D. W. Griffith's *The Birth of a Nation* (1915) was heralded as the first feature-length film. Whereas Anderson focuses on the importance of the novel as a genre in the formation of a modern national narrative of "homogenous empty time," Gilles Deleuze asserts that cinema creates its own version of time through what he calls the "movement-image" and the "time-image." According to Deleuze, Griffith conceives of the movement-images as "a great organic unity," and it is "the nature of the organic set that it should continually be threatened: the accusation raised against the Negroes in *Birth of a Nation* is that of wanting to shatter the newly-won unity of the United States by using the South's defeat to their own advantage."[21] Applying Deleuze, we can see that D. W. Griffith's use of the movement-image—crosscutting and montage—in *The Birth of a Nation* (as its name implies) precisely attempts to regain a cinematic homogeneous, synchronous national "meanwhile" by depicting a series of scenes of whiteness, northern and southern, threatened by what he portrays as the destructive force of a "new black empire."[22] Griffith reimagined the failure of Reconstruction as a triumphant restoration of antebellum order and racial hierarchies, positing a new national identity of whiteness that illustrates, in Leigh Anne Duck's words, how "racism and regionalism have converged perhaps most prominently in the white supremacist account of Reconstruction."[23] In *The Birth of a Nation* an iconic cabin reminiscent of the one in *Uncle Tom's Cabin* becomes the haven for white northerners and southerners against the threat of armed, black troops; at the end, the inhabitants of the plantation house are restored to their "rightful" place as leaders of the nation.

To justify the Ku Klux Klan's violent enforcement of racial subjugation, Griffith invokes the southern rape complex, predicated on an endangered, engendered whiteness and the fear of "race mixing." The persistent and powerful image of rape in Hollywood versions of the South suggests another aspect of the southern imaginary, which combines the highly charged mix of both racial and sexual politics. The southern rape complex, later defined by W. J. Cash in his influential *The Mind of the South* (1941), brutally limits the freedom of black men but also paternalistically limits the freedom of white women, while totally ignoring white male sexual violence against black women (both during and after slavery) and all other forms of intraracial sexual violence. Significantly, the rhetorical yoking of the southern belle, the vessel of purity, and the black "brute" in the southern rape complex reinforces nineteenth-century theories of the inferiority of both blacks and women as childish, morally weak, easily manipulated, and in need of protection and guidance from superior white males; yet despite its applicability to widespread notions of racial and gender inferiority, the complex and its cinematic depictions are typically localized within a southern imaginary.

Before the Tom shows or their more violent inheritors, music and comedy provided another less obvious way to contain African American culture. White northern and southern appropriations and exaggerations of southern slave culture in the form of the minstrel show permeated vaudeville and not surprisingly informed later cinematic depictions of African American culture. With the advent of sound, the first "talkie" show features just such an appropriation: Al Jolson's blackface rendition of "Mammy" in *The Jazz Singer* (1927). The continuing impact of African American blues and spirituals on Broadway helped to pave the way for early film musicals and the first all-black casts in *Hearts in Dixie* (1929) and in King Vidor's *Hallelujah!* (1929), which featured the Jubilee Singers and was filmed in Arkansas and Memphis, Tennessee.[24] As the three versions of *Show Boat* (1929, 1936, 1951) indicate, the southern musical, with its ties to African American music, would be a recurring staple of Hollywood in films such as *The Green Pastures* (1936), *Cabin in the Sky* (1943), *Song of the South* (1946), *Carmen Jones* (1954), and *Porgy and Bess* (1959). Despite the many variations among the filmic adaptations of *Show Boat*, they all maintain the use of music as a racial and regional marker. The plot centers on the discovery that Julie (the lead singer for the Cotton Blossom, a Mississippi River showboat) passes as white and is married to a white man. Her "dark secret" is exposed when Julie sings "Can't Help Lovin' Dat Man," a southern folk song that "only colored people" sing, but which was actually written by the songwriting team of Jerome Kern and Oscar Hammerstein.

With the onset of the Depression, the ruined plantation house became a symbol, not only of ravages of the Civil War, but of the economic devastation of an already struggling South, the area that FDR would famously refer to as "the nation's number one economic problem."[25] The Depression may have hit the South hardest, but it also hit Hollywood. In the same year that Paramount went into receivership, the studio released a low-budget adaptation of Faulkner's scandalous *Sanctuary*. Turning the dilapidated plantation mansion into a backdrop for the utter degradation of the southern belle, *The Story of Temple Drake* (1933) is the first cinematic version of the Gothic South and one of the films that Joseph Breen refused to rerelease when he tightened the enforcement of the Motion Picture Production Code.[26] Cinematographer Karl Struss used the style of German expressionism and the U.S. horror film to shoot the Americanized form of Dracula's castle and the sinister, vampirelike gangster/rapist, Trigger. Subsequent southern horror films such as *Hush . . . Hush, Sweet Charlotte* (1964), *Two Thousand Maniacs!* (1964), its 2005 sequel *2001 Maniacs*, *The Beguiled* (1971), *Angel Heart* (1987), and *Skeleton Key* (2005) draw on the legacy of the southern Gothic in its many manifestations, including run-down plantation houses, deranged belles, voodoo rituals, dark family secrets, and lost-cause revenge. Equally important to this cinematic Gothic South is the portrayal of the anemic, Depression-era poor "white trash" who came to occupy the dilapidated plantation house and who would continue to inhabit the imagined space of literary and cinematic southern whiteness in films including *Tobacco Road* (1941), *Deliverance* (1972), and *Southern Comfort* (1981).

The Depression-era gloom of *The Story of Temple Drake* gave way to musical comedies like *Mississippi* (1935) and period dramas like *So Red the Rose* (1935) and *Jezebel* (1938), culminating with the Technicolor epic, *Gone with the Wind* (1939), a lush return to the romantic South that broke all box-office records. The southern imaginary invoked by *Gone with the Wind* is predicated on an irretrievable and idealized past, which, as the rolling titles in the film suggest, can be alluded to only through language because it can be found "only in books, for it is no more than a dream remembered." As such, the film seems to invoke a more specific psychoanalytic Lacanian imaginary in which identity is based on a misrecognition of wholeness and unity. In the late twentieth century, film theorists employed Jacques Lacan's mirror stage to articulate the ways in which the spectator identifies with the camera's act of looking and is therefore "sutured" into the ideological work of the film.[27] The nation's ongoing fascination with "a dream remembered" in *Gone with the Wind* seems rooted in a willingness to look past what Toni Morrison terms "the Africanist presence" to focus on a story about the ups and downs of white people left to demonstrate their all-American tenacity and determination as they rebuild their world—quite literally—with the tools of sharecropping and Jim Crow segregation.[28] The question of labor—who performs it, who owns its result—is then quietly excused, and what remains is a South free of racial tension, ensconced in a narrative of peaceful, antimodern allure. The film, therefore, invites the viewer to share in its aristocratic hierarchy of wealthy planters as well as its story of the plucky daughter of an immigrant who claws her way back to the top with hardheaded, capitalistic determination.

In more recent application of Lacanian film theory, Slavoj Žižek argues that rather than being seamlessly sutured into a film's ideology, its very mechanism indicates the gaps in the symbolic through which the "stain of the real" is made manifest. Žižek argues that in a "post-ideological" world the film critic's role is not to reveal the "hidden" ideological apparatus but instead to detect "beneath the deceiving openness of post-ideological cynicism" the fetish that is the "embodiment of the Lie which enables us to sustain the unbearable truth."[29] In *The Real South* (2008) Scott Romine examines the commodity fetishist role of Tara not only in the narrative of *Gone with the Wind* but also in reference to its many material and cultural manifestations, arguing that it constitutes "the commodification of southern culture, reproducing the South not as *home* (inhabited place), but as *homesickness*, as an object of nostalgia in both the spatial and temporal senses of the word." Within this commodification, "Tara is the sim-plantation that all real plantations of the tourist industry strive to reproduce . . . a platonic ideal that quotidian objects of all sorts, from wedding cake toppers to Barbie dolls, strive to represent."[30]

After the romantic sweep of *Gone with the Wind*, a grittier South reemerged during and after World War II. Hollywood—influenced by postwar Italian neorealism with its documentary visual style, bombed-out ruins, and postwar poverty—turned again to the ruined South as a symbol of poverty, racism, and resistance to the forces of change, in such black and white social problem films as *Pinky* (1949), *Lost Boundaries* (1949), *Intruder in the Dust* (1949), *All the King's Men* (1949), and *A Streetcar Named Desire* (1951).

The decaying, black and white South persisted, and despite a few musicals, period pieces, and two strangely upbeat Technicolor adaptations of Faulkner novels—*The Sound and the Fury* (1959) and *The Long, Hot Summer* (1958)—the southern cinematic 1950s and 1960s were dominated by Tennessee Williams's impotent men, sex-starved women, and dominating patriarchs and matriarchs. From 1950 to 1970, Hollywood made fifteen filmic adaptations of Williams's works, including *The Glass Menagerie* (1950), *A Streetcar Named Desire* (1951), *Baby Doll* (1956), *Cat on a Hot Tin Roof* (1958), *Suddenly, Last Summer* (1959), *The Fugitive Kind* (1960), *Sweet Bird of Youth* (1962), *This Property Is Condemned* (1966), and *Boom* (1968). In the sinful South, the image of the decadent southern aristocrat, especially the southern belle (the nucleus of segregationist rhetoric), was multivalent. Depending on the audience's attitude toward segregation, the downfall of elite white southerners could be seen either as a fit form of retribution for their association with the wrongs of slavery or as punishment for their failure to win the Civil War and to defend "their way of life." The decadent belle is depicted as both victim and aggressor, and her fall as both tragic and just, as exemplified in Williams's Blanche Dubois.

The counterpoint to the decadent southern elite was the southern "cracker." While depictions of the former focused on past wrongs, racism in the present was systematically localized in the lower classes, as "*intra*racial confrontation assumed interracial connotations." According to Allison Graham, the celluloid redneck "perform[ed] his time-honored, generic duty: roar the hatred that his betters will only whisper, and then die at their hands in a near-mythic purgation of the race."[31] Thus, ironically, the southern redneck's expulsion from the film was presented as the solution to racism and as the symbolic cleansing of white blood to achieve a new form of white, middle-class racial purity in films such as *To Kill a Mockingbird* (1962), with its reaffirmation of a class structure that links vengeance with economics. The racial reversal of the southern rape complex, as depicted in *The Story of Temple Drake*, became the model for "redneck menace," in which working and lower-class white men embodied the threat to white womanhood, as in *To Kill a Mockingbird*, *A Streetcar Named Desire*, and both versions of *Cape Fear* (1962, 1991), or the threat to white southern masculinity as in *Deliverance* (1972), *Come Back to the Five and Dime, Jimmy Dean, Jimmy Dean* (1982) and *Prince of Tides* (1991).

After the political successes of the civil rights movement, the dignity of the African American family in *Sounder* (1972) seemed to herald a new era of Hollywood depictions of African Americans. However, it was the made-for-TV movies and miniseries, not Hollywood, that produced some of the most important representations of African American life, most notably the adaptation of Alex Haley's *Roots* (1977), as well as several adaptations of Ernest Gaines's works, *The Autobiography of Miss Jane Pittman* (1974), and later *The Sky Is Gray* (1980), *A Gathering of Old Men* (1987), and *A Lesson before Dying* (1999). In the post–civil rights 1970s, Hollywood largely avoided films that dealt seriously with race. In *Smokey and the Bandit* (1977), the overweight southern cop—so long an image of racialized abuse and white supremacy, and played brilliantly by Rod Steiger in *In the Heat of the Night* (1967)—became a comic figure who pursued white bandits, not black men or civil rights workers. *Smokey and the Bandit* was one of the highest grossing films in 1977 (second only to *Star Wars*), and its popularity would continue into the 1980s and 1990s with two sequels (1980 and 1983) and a series of television movies in the 1990s. The success of the Smokey films led Warren French to speculate in 1981 that the "South's best chance of rising again—this time cinematically—appears to be in resourceful producers finding new challenges for the 'bandits' who have traded their stallions for thundering wheels," establishing "a new kind of 'road' film" that mobilizes regional identity and difference.[32]

The most notorious 1970s films that depict southern racism—*Mandingo* (1975) and *Drum* (1976)—tend to use the abuses of slavery as an excuse for sensationalized, sadistic sex and violence. The popular 1970s blaxploitation films relocated African Americans from the rural South to the urban north as the Great Migration had done earlier and staged the destructive force of black-on-black violence and drugs in the inner city. The rise of urban African American filmmakers in the 1990s, John Singleton (*Boyz N the Hood*, 1991) and Mario Van Peebles (*New Jack City*, 1991), reinforced this geographic shift. As Riché Richardson argues in *Black Masculinity and the U.S. South*, the black southern male of popular culture was both pathologized and emasculated: "the earliest national ideological scripts of black masculinity in the United States" depend on the figures of Uncle Tom and the black rapist and link the South inextricably to these competing versions of black masculinity.[33] Screenwriters and directors turned to urban settings, whether in the north or on the West Coast, to dramatize the dangers to and potential for black masculinity. However, even though African American directors produced these films, predatory black males, gang culture, and drugs, rather than white racism, remain the predominant threat to the black community and to the survival of other, respectable, black males.

As post–civil rights films took the black male out of the South, Hollywood whitened the southern past. The civil rights movement was recast from the perspective of white officers and lawyers in *Mississippi Burning* (1988), *A Time to Kill* (1996), and *Ghosts of Mississippi* (1996) as the comic officer of *Smokey and the Bandit* was transformed into a hero of justice. In a similar yet depoliticized vein, the late 1980s and 1990s also saw a whitening of the female-centered cinematic South (especially the prefeminist, pre–civil rights South). One of the first films to be called a "chick flick" was the southern-based *Steel Magnolias* (1989), and the film's popularity helped to generate a series of white southern films, which stretch into the twenty-first century: *Fried Green Tomatoes* (1991), *Thelma and Louise* (1991), *Hope Floats* (1998), *Where the Heart Is* (2000), and *Divine Secrets of the Ya-Ya Sisterhood* (2002).[34] By setting these early chick flicks in the South, filmmakers invoked the region's general resistance to politicized feminism and helped to establish the genre by facilitating the nonpolitical impulse of an emerging 1990s postfeminism. Southern chick flicks provide, then, a traditional and often comic backdrop against which to examine the unresolved conflicts generated by the feminist movement, while avoiding issues of race by focusing mainly on the lives of white southern women.

The precursor and exception to the white southern chick flick was the strongly African American female-centered *The Color Purple* (1985), which seemed to mirror the crossover appeal of prominent African American women writers. Yet despite the box-office success of *The Color Purple*, again it was the made-for-TV movies—especially those produced by Oprah Winfrey—that featured adaptations of African American women writers' books in *The Women of Brewster Place* (1989), *The Wedding* (1998), and *Their Eyes Were Watching God* (2005).[35] The most critically significant exception to the whitening of the cinematic South is the compelling independent film *Daughters of the Dust* (1991), written, directed, and produced by Julie Dash. Ironically perhaps, it is a story of an African American family on the eve of their departure from the South; furthermore, despite the critical acclaim of the film, the majority of Dash's subsequent work is in television. More recent southern chick flicks, however—most notably *Beauty Shop* (2005) and *The Secret Life of Bees* (2008)—incorporate racial and gender politics by exploring the lives of southern African American women. Significantly, these films feature prominent African American stars who also serve as producers. Tyler Perry's Atlanta-based films incorporating his cross-dressing performance as Madea—*Diary of a Mad Black Woman* (2005), *Madea's Family Reunion* (2006), *Madea Goes to Jail* (2009)—draw on, yet further complicate, the southern chick flick and the urban gangster films, infusing them with a strong Christian message and attracting a large African American audience.

A salient feature of so many of the films we have discussed thus far is that they are adaptations of literary works, primarily those of southern writers. It would be only a slight exaggeration to say that the majority of prominent films set in the South have been literary adaptations and even less of an exaggeration to say that the works of most prominent southern writers have been adapted for the screen. However, it is much less common for the producers and directors of these films to be from the South. For example, two of the most important directors to adapt southern literature to the screen are Elia Kazan, who directed Williams's *Streetcar* and *Baby Doll* and other adaptations such as *Pinky* (1949) and *Wild River* (1960); and Martin Ritt, who directed the film versions of Faulkner's *The Long, Hot Summer* (1958) and *The Sound and the Fury* (1959), and others such as *Hud* (1963), *Sounder* (1972), and *Norma Rae* (1979). Within the framework of a southern imaginary that often envisioned the South as an exotic "other" for the nation, southern authors served as intermediaries or tour guides, taking us into the fictional world of the South and at the same time ensuring its authenticity.

Even when prominent southern writers refused to participate in the adaptation—most noticeably Margaret Mitchell—the studios still conspicuously used their names to sell and validate the Hollywood South: in the opening titles of *Gone with the Wind* over the first image of the South (a row of slaves hoeing the field), the title reads, "Margaret Mitchell's South." However, with greater popularity and visibility through the Spirit Award, the Independent Film Channel, and festivals such as Sundance, there has been a steady increase in independent films set in or directly dealing with the South, many of which feature original screenplays as well as directors and/or writers who grew up in the South: *Sex, Lies, and Videotape* (1989), *Mississippi Masala* (1991), *Slacker* (1991), *Ruby in Paradise* (1993), *Ulee's Gold* (1997), *Rosewood* (1997), *Down in the Delta* (1998), *Cookie's Fortune* (1999), *George Washington* (2000), *All the Real Girls* (2003), *Junebug* (2005), *Hustle and Flow* (2005), *Forty Shades of Blue* (2005), *Black Snake Moan* (2006), *Come Early Morning* (2006), and *Ballast* (2008), to name only a few.[36]

The Independent Film Channel, as well as HBO and PBS, has also aired a wealth of documentaries, many of them independently produced, which provide a new look at the South. In addition to acclaimed documentaries of the twentieth century on topics most associated with the South—such as the Civil War (Ken Burns's *The Civil War*, 1990); the Great Depression (*The River*, 1938); and the civil rights era (*Eyes on the Prize*, 1987, 1990; *At the River I Stand*, 1993; and Spike Lee's *4 Little Girls*, 1997)—Ross McElwee's offbeat *Sherman's March* (1986) presents a very different look at a seemingly traditional region. The twenty-first century continues to produce such new takes on the South in *Southern Comfort* (2001), *Searching for the Wrong-Eyed Jesus* (2003), and *Prom Night in Mississippi* (2009). Furthermore, Hurricane Katrina has drawn attention to New Orleans in documentaries such as *When the Levees Broke* (2006), *Trouble the Water* (2008), and *A Village Called Versailles* (2009). Documentaries have also looked at contemporary legal and moral ramifications of the civil rights period in *Mississippi Cold Case* (2007) and *Neshoba* (2008). And, finally, a new take on the plantation emerges in *Moving Midway* (2007), a documentary about the moving of a plantation to make way for a mall, and the family secrets it uncovers. Many indie movies and documentaries have produced new cinematic ways to view the region, which undercut or complicate traditional iconic elements. Mirroring critical debates about postsouthernism and the global South, these movies unsettle the conviction that there is a "real," definitive South lodged somewhere just beyond our reach.

To facilitate the range of approaches and subject matter in this collection, we have divided the essays into three sections, which are roughly chronological: 1) Rereading the Hollywood South, 2) Viewing the Civil Rights South, and 3) Crossing Borders. The essays in the first section reassess Hollywood films that incorporate the South, in light of new critical perspectives and insights, beginning with the early silent era before *The Birth of a Nation*, moving to the height of the studio system with *Gone with the Wind*, and ending with the social problem films of the 1940s and 1950s. The second section examines films from the civil rights period— both low-budget drive-in movies and lavish productions—as well as later films that document the era. And the last section reflects the explosion of films, especially indies, that confront and dismantle earlier forms of the cinematic South, many of which fulfill Bhabha's "aim of cultural difference," to rethink or revision the South through an alternative perspective that "resists totalization": repetition with a difference.[37]

In the first essay in "Rereading the Hollywood South," Robert Jackson examines pre-Hollywood films in "The Celluloid War before *The Birth*: Race and History in Early American Film." Jackson elucidates the racial dimensions of the pre-1915 film industry in relation to Civil War memory, the rise of Jim Crow segregation, and modern mass culture, arguing that *The Birth of a Nation* is not an originating moment, as often conceived of, but a pivotal, transitional point in American cinema.

Just as southern studies has undergone a transformation, cinema studies has broadened to include media studies and, even more broadly, visual culture, acknowledging the interplay between film and other forms of media. In "Mammy's 'Mules' and the Rules of Marriage in *Gone with the Wind*," Riché Richardson demonstrates the ongoing cultural impact of Mammy's code of conduct in *Gone with the Wind*, which still holds sway in various forms of popular culture, including the self-consciously sophisticated and New York–centered TV series *Sex and the City*, the best-selling contemporary conduct book *The Rules*, and even the Hollywood star system. At a performative level, Mammy, as a nurturer and caretaker in the film, represents and enforces the "law," exposing Scarlett's violations of the very racial codes that should define and legitimate her status as a white, elite southern woman, thus unsettling the notion of inherent superiority and femininity that the rules are meant to codify.

The next two essays in this section place film in the context of the larger forces of capitalism and politics. In "Bodies and Expectations: Chain Gang Discipline," Leigh Anne Duck builds on well-established arguments that *I Am a Fugitive from a Chain Gang* (1932) exoticizes the South. Although the film focuses on regional penal abuses and even naturalizes Jim Crow injustice, Duck argues that it nonetheless situates these models of constraint in a critique of the larger national culture. Observing how the film uses the chain gang as both an extreme case and a metaphor for depicting the structures that impede individuals' access to the mobility promised by capitalistic society, Duck views it as representing an essentially carceral nation. Thus, although the film's understanding of the chain gang is flawed in many respects—misperceptions that persist, she argues, in contemporary commentary—*Fugitive* also engages productively with the then still developing notion of the prison-industrial complex.

In "The Postwar Cinematic South: Realism and the Politics of Liberal Consensus," Chris Cagle demonstrates the confluence of aesthetics and politics in the late 1940s prestige pictures and social problem films that addressed the ideology of liberal consensus, which was dominated by political and cultural elites in postwar America. While the ideology of liberal consensus cuts across regions, the problems it addresses are often cinematically localized in the aesthetically "realist" South in race problem films such as *Pinky* (1949) and *Intruder in the Dust* (1949) or through the mixture of fictional and documentary styles in political-conflict films including *All the King's Men* (1947), *The Southerner* (1945), and *Wild River* (1960).

An important addition to understanding the influence of the southern imaginary on films is Hollywood's formation of the southern audience as censor. Matthew H. Bernstein in "A 'Professional Southerner' in the Hollywood Studio System: Lamar Trotti at Work, 1925–1952" examines how screenwriter Lamar Trotti's own sense of southernness shaped the cinematic South he created and influenced his representation of that region to Hollywood insiders who consulted him about the preferences of an imaginary and perhaps overvalued southern audience. Focusing particularly on Trotti's work for *Judge Priest* (1934), *Young Mr. Lincoln* (1939), and *The Ox-Bow Incident* (1943), Bernstein concludes that this "professional southerner" willingly tackled seemingly taboo issues, including race and lynching, with both an insider's knowledge of the white southern mindset and a social conscience that outweighed the misgivings of Hollywood studios reluctant to alienate a regionally specific audience.

Just as the Civil War profoundly shaped our image of the South in the nineteenth century, the civil rights movement was the catalyst of change in the twentieth century. The essays in "Viewing the Civil Rights South" analyze the attempts to document and dramatize the impact of changes in race and class before, during, and after the civil rights movement. In "Black Passing and White Pluralism: *Imitation of Life* in the Civil Rights Struggle," Ryan DeRosa reads the issue of passing in *Imitation of Life* (1959) as a potentially subversive gesture in keeping with the political struggles of the civil rights movement: the daughter's passing can be read as the vehicle for symbolically destroying not her mother but *mammy* (as ideology), as the melodrama unites, not separates, black mother and daughter. Contemporary white reviewers, on the other hand, praised the plot of passing for its realism (as opposed to the artificiality and melodrama of the white mother/daughter conflict), stressing the authenticity of the black community, especially as presented in the climactic funeral scene, which builds on narrative hints of the South as a culture separate from the North and of black culture as hidden from the white mainstream. De Rosa links these readings of the black community to a new cultural pluralism that seeks to contain or deny the activism and depth of black integrationist discourse through the logic of cultural difference, a logic that is evident in historian Stanley Elkins's influential *Slavery: A Problem in American Institutional and Intellectual Life* (1959). Elkins's revision of history asserts the slave's lack of fitness for full citizenship and the need for gradual reforms, which reinforces the new cultural pluralism's resistance to a fully integrated society.

Turning to civil rights documentaries, Valerie Smith in "Remembering Birmingham Sunday: Spike Lee's *4 Little Girls*" demonstrates the ways in which Spike Lee's 1997 documentary about the bombing of the Sixteenth Street Baptist Church contributes to critical revisions of a popular, self-congratulatory understanding of the southern freedom struggle, characterized by sentimentalized iconic martyrs, whose sacrifices, like racial injustice itself, are in the past. Lee's documentary—through interviews with the girls' friends and families—"dislodges the 'four little girls' from their symbolic status as a collective icon," thus presenting them as individuals precisely through the ordinary and even typical elements of their daily lives. Similarly, Lee's interviews document the movement, as well as the white response to it (which indirectly and directly in some cases led up to and provided cover for the bombing) as it played out in day-to-day life in the city of Birmingham.

In "Exploitation Movies and the Freedom Struggle of the 1960s," Sharon Monteith examines a small but significant number of 1960s low-budget movies, *Free, White and 21* (1963), *Girl on a Chain Gang* (1964), and *Murder in Mississippi* (1965). Almost completely unstudied, these films exploited actual contemporary events, depending on southern anxiety about miscegenation and northerners and presenting the region as completely disassociated from any sort of recognizable racial or civil justice. Ultimately, Monteith finds these films to be simultaneously fascinated by and critical of the region they take as their setting. Their lurid violence, later domesticated in more mainstream films, here "pinion[s] the grotesque at the heart of the southern civil rights story in an apocalyptic pantomime of social breakdown."

The last section, "Crossing Borders," includes readings of more recent films that chart the influence of postmodernism, postcolonialism, and media studies on southern films. These newer films most directly investigate and problematize the very idea of the South as a self-contained geographic and cultural entity, as well as look at the convergence of southern film with other forms of media. To draw out the cinematic implications of the postsouthern—a concept that, as Jay Watson points out, has been "slow to make its way into the burgeoning field of southern film studies"—"Mapping out a Postsouthern Cinema: Three Contemporary Films" focuses on two very different films from 1991: *Slacker* and *Mississippi Masala*, neither of which has typically been analyzed from that critical perspective. As Watson articulates, *Slacker's* distinctive, disjointed narrative style and disaffected consumer culture with "media-molded" characters wandering aimlessly through a placeless, urban landscape exemplify Fredric Jameson's analysis of postmodernism as "the cultural logic of late capitalism." The film's fragmented narratives provide a postmodern/postsouthern deconstruction of paradigmatic southern themes: family, storytelling, community, history, and place. *Mississippi Masala*, on the other hand, relocates postcolonial confrontations in the Deep South, shattering the racial and regional binaries of white/black and North/South that have dominated southern representations. Both films implicate the South in a larger global sphere that remains hidden through the singular lens of region.

In "The Native Screen: American Indians in Contemporary Southern Film," Melanie R. Benson argues that in the contemporary U.S. South in particular, Native American figures are used to symbolize the region's own cultural dispossession under northern, political, and industrial pressures. Benson presents *The Education of Little Tree* (1997), based on the

1976 novel by Alabama white supremacist Forrest Carter, as a striking example of the white southern tendency to romanticize and inhabit stereotypical Indian identities. Similarly, in Julie Dash's acclaimed *Daughters of the Dust* (1991), southern African Americans use Native cultures and characters as props in their own (more sympathetic but equally self-serving) chronicles of dispossession. Finally, in *The Doe Boy* (2001), Benson examines the possibilities for Native American self-representation in the work of Randy Redroad, a Cherokee filmmaker from Texas. Redroad depicts a young mixed-blood Indian man suffering from hemophilia, whose "uncontrollable blood loss becomes an urgent, evocative sign of both biological and cultural erasure."

While there has been much serious discussion of Spike Lee's compelling documentary about Katrina, *When the Levees Broke: A Requiem in Four Acts*, Briallen Hopper in "The City That *Déjà Vu* Forgot: Memory, Mapping, and the Americanization of New Orleans" argues for the need to examine *Déjà Vu* (2006), the first Hollywood film set in post-Katrina New Orleans, too hastily dismissed by many critics. Hopper reads the film as a revisionist reimagining of the Bush administration's handling not only of Katrina but also of 9/11 and the war on terror. The film is predicated on a futuristic, time-bending government surveillance device, which gives government agents superhuman powers that, while totally destroying all rights of privacy, allow them to stop terrorism before it happens. By depicting a white, domestic terrorist from the Ninth Ward and limiting the surveillance power to the French Quarter, the film visually denies the destruction of Katrina and remaps New Orleans as an uncomplicatedly national rather than international city "in the service of a revisionist national narrative."

In "Humid Time: Independent Film, Gay Sexualities, and Southernscapes," R. Bruce Brasell first examines the limitations of previous attempts to define southern cinema or a southern genre. While not attempting to create a new definition of the "southern," Brasell draws on genre theory and applies Mikhail Bakhtin's concept of the chronotype to a "mutual southernscape," which he calls "Humid Time," "a retroactively constructed framework" for "understanding a dominant trend in films set in the South." The salient feature of Humid Time is the correlation between the oppressiveness of the weather and the concomitant societal oppression. While oppression in southern films has typically been likened to issues of racial discrimination, Brasell uses his framework of Humid Time to analyze four fictional feature-length independent gay films—*The Delta* (1997), *Red Dirt* (2000), *Strange Fruit* (2004), and *Loggerheads* (2005)—that deal overtly with multiple forms of oppression, but which feature gay sexualities that in classic Hollywood films are presented covertly. Humid Time, as expressed in these four films, "contains a nihilistic component as a result of the existential angst expressed by the main characters and the fatalistic narrative conclusions."

Christopher J. Smith, in "Papa Legba and the Liminal Spaces of the Blues: Roots Music in Deep South Film," analyzes the filmic use of the blues, asserting its liminality as a construction, a goal, and an expectation of the filmic blues experience in *Crossroads* (1986), *O Brother, Where Art Thou?* (2000), *Lackawanna Blues* (2005), and *Black Snake Moan* (2006). Smith, employing techniques from ethnomusicology, literature, film, and drama theory, argues that Delta blues virtuosity exists precisely in the creation and manipulation of the "space in-between"— the dichotomy between Jesus and the Devil, between Sunday morning and Saturday night—which the blues both manifest and resolve in southern culture.

Finally, in "Revamping the South: Thoughts on Labor, Relationality, and Southern Representation," Tara McPherson examines the television series *True Blood*, one of popular culture's latest plunges into the world of vampires, this time as "southern gothic gone more than a little goth." McPherson identifies but then reads beyond *True Blood*'s engagements with and incorporations of images traditionally linked to the South to locate its filming within the schema of global capital and patterns of labor production that have propelled Hollywood into Louisiana. By introducing the notion of "expansive relationality," McPherson finally argues that *True Blood* animates a broader human desire to escape those capitalist constraints, one for which rural Louisiana provides a particularly appropriate backdrop.

The South that emerges from these fourteen essays and the more than thirty films they treat is a complicated one, made denser by the conflicting images that the essays trace and interrogate. Many other movies, both well known and little known, might have been discussed here, either for their head-on confrontations with southern place and identity or for their subtle, unacknowledged evocation of those same elements. The South in film remains an understudied, undertheorized dimension of American cinema, but one of increasing relevance to the way in which the nation understands its contemporary self within a global context. The essays in this collection illustrate that the earlier ruin-versus-romance plantation narrative is too simple to account for the myriad ways the U.S. South shapes the national imagination. As Jon Smith and Deborah Cohn point out, the plantation "—more than anything else—ties the South both to the rest of the United States," as a model for the national penal system, and "to the rest of the New World," through plantation colonialism.[38]

Yet as indicated by Tara McPherson's notion of the "lenticular logic" of race and gender, films have typically summoned only one South at a time, either a wistfully romantic idyll or a damaged and ruinous stain on the nation's progress; either a white world where African Americans are present only in menial roles or a world that directly confronts issues of racial strife and then projects the resulting anxiety onto black(nes)s. McPherson encourages readers to understand the lenticular as more than "a mere visual strategy"; in addition to its representational quality, the lenticular applies as well to ways "of organizing knowledge about the world," in this case to organizing knowledge about how a particular region has functioned in relation to a national whole. In a similar vein, Deleuze's emphasis on the movement-image and the time-image, rather than on the representation of images, provides a way of seeing and knowing the world that is constitutive of the framework and expectations of the cinematic apparatus. As Kira Keeling explains, Deleuze's cinema "challenge[s] demands for 'positive,' 'negative,' or 'accurate' representations—demands that assume the coherence of an indexical relationship between image and 'reality' that has never cohered for blacks and other groups who consistently have claimed to be misrepresented." With the increased pervasiveness of the moving image in our media-saturated age comes an increase in its power and reach, one that requires ongoing scholarly attention to its impact on how individuals assemble their perceptions of places and of the people who inhabit them.[39]

NOTES

1. Katherine Henninger, *Ordering the Façade: Photography and Contemporary Southern Women's Writing* (Chapel Hill: University of North Carolina Press, 2007).

2. Warren G. French, ed., *The South in Film* (Jackson: University Press of Mississippi, 1981).

3. Our collection profits from important innovations in critical approaches to film and media studies such as R. Barton Palmer and William Robert Bray, *Hollywood's Tennessee: The Williams Films and Postwar America* (Austin: University of Texas Press, 2009); Riché Richardson, *Black Masculinity and the U.S. South: From Uncle Tom to Gangsta* (Athens: University of Georgia Press, 2007); Tara McPherson, *Reconstructing Dixie: Race, Gender, and Nostalgia in the Imagined South* (Durham, N.C.: Duke University Press, 2003); Linda Williams, *Playing the Race Card: Melodramas of Black and White from Uncle Tom to O. J. Simpson* (Princeton, N.J.: Princeton University Press, 2001), and Allison Graham, *Framing the South: Hollywood, Television, and Race during the Civil Rights Struggle* (Baltimore: Johns Hopkins University Press, 2001). There have been significant collections on southern studies and the global South, most particularly Jon Smith and Deborah Cohn, *Look Away! The U.S. South in New World Studies* (Durham, N.C.: Duke University Press, 2004), and on southern cultural studies, such as Richard H. King and Helen Taylor, eds., *Dixie Debates: Perspectives*

on Southern Cultures (New York: New York University Press, 1996), which includes several essays on film. Larry Langman and David Ebner compiled an extensive 2001 filmography of southern films in *Hollywood's Image of the South: A Century of Southern Films* (Westport, Conn.: Greenwood, 2001), in which they attempt to establish the "southern" as a genre, but there have been no essay collections that focus exclusively on film and media studies since the early 1980s. The most recent collection about southern film is Warren French, ed., *The South and Film* (Jackson: University Press of Mississippi, 1981), published the same year as Edward D. C. Campbell Jr.'s *The Celluloid South: Hollywood and the Southern Myth* (Knoxville: University of Tennessee Press, 1981).

4. Houston Baker Jr. and Dana D. Nelson, "Preface: Violence, the Body, and 'The South,'" *American Literature* 73, no. 2 (June 2001): 243.

5. For an excellent analysis of attempts to define the "southern," see R. Bruce Brasell, "Humid Time: Independent Film, Gay Sexualities, and Southernscapes" in this collection.

6. The mission of the original *Encyclopedia of Southern Culture* (Chapel Hill: University of North Carolina Press, 1989), for example, was to document the cultural particularities of the southern United States, just as *The History of Southern Literature* (Baton Rouge: Louisiana State University Press, 1985) aimed to chart a regionally specific set of narratives focused primarily on conjoining ideas of place, home, and South.

7. Michael Kreyling, *Inventing Southern Literature* (Jackson: University Press of Mississippi, 1998).

8. A nonexhaustive list of books and essays in literary and cultural studies that exemplify this paradigm shift and thus are foundational to the work the present essay collection is able to do includes the following titles: Melanie R. Benson, *Disturbing Calculations: The Economics of Identity in Postcolonial Southern Literature* (Athens: University of Georgia Press, 2008); Scott Romine, *The Real South: Southern Narrative in the Age of Cultural Reproduction* (Baton Rouge: Louisiana State University Press, 2008); Jessica Adams and Michael Bibler, eds., *Just below South: Intercultural Performance in the Caribbean and the U.S. South* (Charlottesville: University of Virginia Press, 2007); Houston Baker, *I Don't Hate the South: Reflections on Faulkner, Family, and the South* (New York: Oxford University Press, 2007); Baker, *Turning South Again: Rethinking Modernism/Re-reading Booker T* (Durham, N.C.: Duke University Press, 2001); Annette Trefzer, *Disturbing Indians: The Archaeology of Southern Fiction* (Tuscaloosa: University of Alabama Press, 2007); Leigh Anne Duck, *The Nation's Region: Southern Modernism, Segregation, and U.S. Nationalism* (Athens: University of Georgia Press, 2006); Martyn Bone, *The Postsouthern Sense of Place in Contemporary Fiction* (Baton Rouge: Louisiana State University Press, 2005); Gary Richards, *Lovers and Beloveds: Sexual Otherness in Southern Fiction* (Baton Rouge: Louisiana State University Press, 2005); Keith Cartwright, *Reading Africa into American Literature: Epics, Fables, and Gothic Tales* (Lexington: University of Kentucky Press, 2002); Suzanne Jones and Sharon Monteith, eds., *South to a New Place: Region, Literature, Culture* (Baton Rouge: Louisiana State University Press, 2002); George Handley, *Postslavery Literatures in*

the Americas: Family Portraits in Black and White (Charlottesville: University Press of Virginia, 2000); Patricia Yaeger, Dirt and Desire: Reconstructing Southern Women's Writing, 1930–1990 (Chicago: University of Chicago Press, 2000); Deborah Cohn, History and Memory in the Two Souths: Recent Southern and Spanish American Fiction (Nashville, Tenn.: Vanderbilt University Press, 1999); Jennifer Greeson, "The Figure of the South and the Nationalizing Imperatives of Early United States Literature," Yale Journal of Criticism 12, no. 2 (1999): 209–48; José Limón, American Encounters: Greater Mexico, the United States, and the Erotics of Culture (Boston: Beacon, 1998); and Kreyling, Inventing Southern Literature. In addition a number of journals have hosted special issues devoted to recent developments in southern studies, including Larry J. Griffin and Harry L. Watson, "The Global South," Southern Cultures 13, no. 4 (Winter 2007): 1–149; Kathryn McKee and Annette Trefzer, "Global Contexts, Local Literatures: The New Southern Studies," American Literature 78, no. 4 (December 2006): 677–924; David McWhirter, "'Southern Literature' / Southern Cultures: Rethinking Southern Literary Studies," South Central Review 22, no. 1 (Spring 2005): 1–149; Denise K. Cummings, Anne Goodwyn Jones, and Jeff Rice, "Souths: Global and Local," Southern Quarterly 42, no. 1 (Fall 2003): 2–153; Jon Smith, Scott Romine, and Kathryn McKee, "Postcolonial Theory, the U.S. South, and New World Studies," pt.1, Mississippi Quarterly 56, no. 4 (Fall 2003): 487–691, and ibid., pt. 2, Mississippi Quarterly 57, no. 1 (Winter 2003–4): 1–194; Baker and Nelson, "Violence," 231–458; and Pearl McHaney and Thomas L. McHaney, "The Worldwide Face of Southern Literature," South Atlantic Review 65, no. 4 (2000): 1–249.

9. In the same year that Kreyling offered a means of defamiliarizing "southernness," Limón published American Encounters, an interdisciplinary study in which he explored the U.S. South's connection to the formation of Greater Mexico and the placement of Texas within that scheme. Cohn's comparative literary study History and Memory followed the next year, and Handley's 2000 monograph, Postslavery Literatures in the Americas, posited the conceptual "Plantation America," while Keith Cartwright's Reading Africa into American Literature proposes yet another complicated lineage for much of U.S. Southern literature by tracking its narrative sources and influences in a different direction. Such work in cultural and literary studies naturally complements the projects in other disciplines that have worked to embed the U.S. South within global crosscurrents of economic flows, most particularly in the collections assembled by James L. Peacock, Harry L. Matthews, and Carrie R. Matthews, The American South in a Global World (Chapel Hill: University of North Carolina Press, 2005), and James C. Cobb and William Stueck, Globalization and the American South (Athens: University of Georgia Press, 2005).

10. Jon Smith and Deborah Cohn, introduction to "Uncanny Hybridities," in Smith and Cohn, Look Away, 8.

11. For a more detailed historical overview of southern film up to 1980, see Campbell, Celluloid South.

12. W. E. B. Du Bois, The Souls of Black Folk, ed. Brent Hayes Edwards (Oxford: Oxford University Press, 2007), xxxvi.

13. *Uncle Tom's Cabin* (1903) appeared several months before *The Great Train Robbery*, although the latter is often incorrectly cited as the first narrative film.

14. Williams, *Playing the Race Card*, xiv.

15. Scott Romine, "Things Falling Apart: The Postcolonial Condition of *Red Rock* and *The Leopard's Spots*," in Smith and Cohn, *Look Away*, 176.

16. Traces of that iconic, ruined South emerged as recently as November 2008 when Barack Obama's historic election as the nation's first African American president transformed from possibility to certainty. Earlier media narratives of southern racial progress, prompted by the changes at the University of Mississippi—site of the first presidential debate—gave way on election night to television commentators lamenting the failure of the "Confederacy" to keep up with a forward-looking nation's bid for change.

17. Edward Said, *Orientalism* (New York: Vintage Books, 1979), 55. Said is, of course, referring to the European construction of "Orientalism," but such a construct is also applicable to South-North imagined geographies.

18. For a discussion of Benedict Anderson's "imagined community" and film, see Ella Shohat and Robert Stam, eds., "The Imperial Imaginary," in *Unthinking Eurocentrism: Multiculturalism and the Media* (New York: Routledge, 1994), 100–136.

19. Homi K. Bhabha, *The Location of Culture* (1994; London: Routledge, 2006), 230. For Bhabha's critique of Anderson, especially concerning the issue of racial difference, see 226–35, 356–60.

20. Ibid., 233.

21. Gilles Deleuze, *Cinema 1: The Movement-Image* (Minneapolis: University of Minnesota Press, 1986), 31.

22. In Griffith's "convergent montage," as various actions come to a single conclusion, the interval between the shot accelerates, "reaching the site of the duel to reverse its outcome, to save innocence or reconstitute the compromised unity" (Deleuze, *Cinema 1*, 31).

23. Duck, *Nation's Region*, 37.

24. For a discussion of early African American musicals, see Thomas Cripps, *Slow Fade to Black: The Negro in American Film, 1900–1942* (New York: Oxford University Press, 1977), 236–62.

25. Franklin D. Roosevelt, "The President Discusses Political Principles, Social Objectives, and Party Candidates with His Fellow-Georgians" (address, Barnesville, Ga., August 11, 1938), in *1938 Public Papers and Addresses of Franklin D. Roosevelt* (New York: Random House, 1941), 464, Hein Online, http://www.heinonline.org/HOL/Page?handle=hein.presidents/ppafdr0007&id=1&size=2&collection=presidents&index=presidents/ppafdr (accessed December 29, 2009).

26. The Production Code was an industry-generated censorship guideline that was not rigorously enforced until 1934. For a discussion of the Production Code in relation to *The Story of Temple Drake*, see Mark A. Vieira, *Sin in Soft Focus: Pre-code Hollywood* (New York: Abrams, 1999), 196. For a more extensive reading of this film, see Deborah Barker, "Moonshine and Magnolias: Whiteness and the Essential Quality of *The Story of Temple Drake*," *Faulkner Journal* 22, no. 1–2 (Fall 2006/Spring 2007): 140–75.

27. See Jacques Lacan, *Ecrits: a Selection*, trans. Alan Sheridan (New York: Norton, 1997). Lacan's theory of the imaginary and the mirror stage have had a profound impact on film studies; see Christian Metz, *The Imaginary Signifier: Psychoanalysis and Cinema*, trans. Celia Britton, Annwyl Williams, Ben Brewster, and Alfred Guzzetti (Bloomington: Indiana University Press, 1982). For a discussion of more recent uses of Lacan's work, see Todd McGowan and Sheila Kunkle, eds., *Lacan and Contemporary Film* (New York: Other Press, 2004): xi–xxix.

28. Toni Morrison, *Playing in the Dark: Whiteness and the Literary Imagination* (Cambridge, Mass.: Harvard University Press, 1992), 17.

29. Slavoj Žižek, *Enjoy Your Symptom! Jacques Lacan in Hollywood and Out* (New York: Routledge, 1992), x.

30. Romine, *Real South*, 28–29.

31. Graham, *Framing the South*, 13. Graham's work provides a thorough examination of southern film during the civil rights era.

32. French, introduction to *South and Film*, 13.

33. Richardson, *Black Masculinity*, 4.

34. For a discussion of the southern chick flick, see Deborah Barker, "The Southern Fried Chick Flick: Postfeminism Goes to the Movies," in *Chick Flicks: Contemporary Women at the Movies*, ed. Suzanne Ferriss and Mallory Young (New York: Routledge, 2007), 92–118.

35. However, Winfrey's cinematic production of Nobel Prize–winning Toni Morrison's *Beloved* (1998) was a critical and box office disappointment.

36. In *Rosewood* (1997) John Singleton turns to the South as a director, and as a producer he backed Greg Brewster in *Hustle and Flow* (2005) and *Black Snake Moan* (2006).

37. Bhabha, *Location of Culture*, 233.

38. Smith and Cohn, *Look Away*, 2, 6.

39. McPherson, *Reconstructing Dixie*, 25; Deleuze, *Cinema 1*, 8; Kira Kelling, *The Witch's Flight: The Cinematic, the Black Femme, and the Image of Common Sense* (Durham, N.C.: Duke University, 2007), 5.

 PART ONE

Rereading the
Hollywood South

The Celluloid War before *The Birth*

Race and History in Early American Film

Robert Jackson

The Anxiety of Teleology

By the time D. W. Griffith's *The Birth of a Nation* arrived on the big screen in 1915, cinematic representations of the Civil War had been around for nearly two decades, virtually the entire lifetime of the young medium. The early twentieth-century America into which the film was released was marked not just by the memory of that war but also by complex forces of progressive reform, Jim Crow segregation, the woman suffrage movement, the maturation of popular culture and its realist critiques, and perhaps most importantly at mid-decade, the fiftieth anniversary of Robert E. Lee's surrender at Appomattox coupled with anxieties about possible American involvement in the Great War. Yet because of the blockbuster status of Griffith's three-hour epic, because of the exceptionalism of its massive scales of production, promotion, and reception, and because of its claims to authority both as a historical document and as a definitive text from the entire three-decade silent film era, *The Birth of a Nation* has sometimes resisted such contextualizations. Instead, until recently it has functioned more commonly for film scholars and social historians alike as a generic reference point, a monument of sorts, with more limited connotations of technical inventiveness, economic success, and racism.[1]

The discussion of *The Birth of a Nation* in William K. Everson's *American Silent Film* (1978), which stood as a standard text in film history for many years, reveals two simultaneous desires on the part of its author that were characteristic of much of the criticism surrounding the film. Everson seeks first to celebrate Griffith's mastery of narrative and emotional effect and second to distance himself, as a right-thinking, post–civil rights egalitarian, from Griffith's problematic racial politics. Everson settles on the Manichaean course of dismissing (or at the very least, bracketing) race from any critical consideration of Griffith's achievement, while fetishizing his stylistic innovations to the effect that they hover in a kind of aesthetic vacuum.[2] Both in his sense of the original contribution of Griffith's film to the art of the motion picture and in his pedagogical impulse to transmit the brilliance of Griffith's vision without the blurring lens of racism, Everson struggles to keep form and content separate. Everson's approach represents an impasse that much film historiography, from Lewis Jacobs's classic 1939 study *The Rise of the American Film* to work by many of Everson's contemporaries, has faced.[3] Everson's enthusiastic appraisal of *The Birth of a Nation* leaves no doubt about his approval of the film's aesthetic merit and long-term impact on the medium, nor about his resentment of what he called the "often artificially created and sustained" controversy over its portrayal of race that had tempered the film's chorus of support for many decades.[4] Only the most recent generation of scholarship has begun to challenge the very assumption that these two elements, form and content, are to the last separable; indeed, much recent work has offered substantial evidence of an early-cinema context in which form and content, particularly in racial matters, were mutually constitutive across a wide range of American film institutions and screen practices.[5]

Everson's flawed teleology, like his aversion to discussing race, is representative in a historical narrative that regards 1915 as a starting point for American cinema, a foundational moment of inspired transcendence from "primitive" early silent film.[6] But the tangled roots of early cinema—marked by two decades of extraordinary formal experimentation as well as social and historical change from its commercial debut in 1894 to its feature-length consolidation around 1914—tell another story, in which *The Birth of a Nation* is no beginning at all. In this story, which lacks the revisionist impulse of the post–civil rights era to save the triumphant "form" but jettison the "content" of racial oppression, the body of early American film in the years before *The Birth of a Nation* provides a diverse historical and aesthetic record that differs in important ways from the received wisdom of Griffith's epic summation. Representations of race in some of the earliest motion pictures (along with Griffith's own diverse and sensitive treatments of the Civil War in several of his earlier one-reel films between 1908 and 1912) provide for a critical, historically grounded perspective from which to glimpse *The Birth of a Nation* in particular and American film history in general.

The Myth of Black Exceptionalism

American culture circa 1900, although never entirely focused on race, was nevertheless committed to a social vision based on racial inequality and injustice. The roots of popular culture reach back to nineteenth-century traditions of blackface minstrelsy and local color fiction (dominated after 1865 by the so-called plantation school of literature), and spectacle lynchings were mass-mediated, well-attended popular entertainments.[7] As American military and economic imperialism in Cuba and the Philippines rationalized a cultural imperialism based on the "four stages of civilization"—a blatantly racist hierarchy moving upward from barbarism and savagery to civilization and enlightenment—racial segregation in the United States was consolidated in legal, economic, and social forms by the turn of the century.[8] As a result of these conditions, the first twenty years of American cinema happened to coincide with what were among the most difficult years for African Americans in the United States at any time since the end of slavery. In this historical milieu, where U.S. patriotism and whiteness reinforced one another, filmmakers were hardly immune to the same racism that pervaded American society and had little reason to feel any need to apologize for producing racist images for the screen. Aside from a handful of black filmmakers who began producing films around 1910 (the beginning of the vital but poorly funded "race film" countertradition that would last for decades), most early filmmakers were white and simply participated in the life of their culture, absorbing and reflecting the racism—casual or vitriolic, unconscious or intellectualized—of the era.

Arriving in forms already firmly established by the minstrel stage, derivative racial stereotypes were themselves the subject of a large number of very early American films. Between 1896 and 1905, for example, at least ten—and likely many more—short films depicted black people eating watermelon. Such films as the American Mutoscope and Biograph Company's *A Watermelon Feast* (1897), Lubin's *Watermelon Contest* (1897), and Edison's *Watermelon Contest* (1900) typically consist of a single shot of several (usually male) blacks gorging themselves on the fruit, often in exaggerated and desperate fashion. Another Lubin film, *Who Said Watermelon?* (1902), was summarized in an advertisement to exhibitors as follows: "The usual watermelon picture shows darkey men eating the luscious fruit. We have an excellent one of that kind of which we have sold quite a number, but the demand for new watermelon pictures has induced us to pose two colored women in which they are portrayed, ravenously getting on the outside of a number of melons, much to the amazement of the onlookers."[9]

This mention of "the usual watermelon picture" suggests that such films were considered a discrete genre and probably existed in greater numbers than surviving records indicate. Also clear from this summary is the popularity of these films. The prevailing style of film presentation before about 1904 was not narrative but what film historian Tom Gunning has termed the "cinema of attractions." This cinema was, as Gunning describes it, "an exhibitionist cinema, a cinema that displays its visibility, willing to rupture a self-enclosed fictional world to solicit the attention of its spectator."[10] Even so, it is important here to apprehend a watermelon picture such as *Who Said Watermelon?* as something quite distinct from what would later come to be known as documentary film, because Lubin was at pains to draw attention to the careful composition and portrayal of its subject and because the film conformed neatly to the expectations of the watermelon-eating film genre. The emphasis on spectacle and visuality in this early cinema makes it clear that such gestures as Everson's to separate form from content would be fruitless. Lack of narrative movement in these early films simply foregrounds their subject matter itself, revealing the inescapably racist images as nothing more or less than themselves, posed and composed for the camera's gaze. The real subject of such seemingly "primitive" single-shot films is not the stated cultural or biologic inferiority of blacks but the raw racism of this cinematic practice in its historical milieu.

A pair of later watermelon pictures reveals the ways that the presentation of racist images would gradually be incorporated into narrative filmmaking styles, identified by Gunning as the "cinema of narrative integration" that Griffith's one-reel films would help to succeed the "cinema of attractions."[11] Lubin's *Eating Watermelons for a Prize* (1903) is, at fifty feet, no longer than *Who Said Watermelon?* and continues to rely on the primacy of spectacle for its effect. In addition, however, the film generates a kind of narrative movement within its static frame, in the form of a food fight that lifts the earlier racial stereotypes to a new level of absurdity, as this advertisement to exhibitors reveals:

> This is one of the most ludicrous films ever shown. Three young coons are first seen eating "watermillion" and the fellow in the middle is seen to dive forward several times and bury his face in the watermelon of his companions. The three are finally joined by four others who attack the remains of the luscious fruit with a vengeance. Mr. Anthony Rastus Jackson, who also loves chicken, is the ringleader and manages to swipe all there is in sight. They wind up the affair by throwing the rind at each other and they wash their faces with it, and seem to enjoy it. This is really funny and exciting, the action is perfect.[12]

The traditional stereotype of blacks—shiftless, animalistic, ravenous, completely at home on the plantation, and so on—takes on added weight here because of an increasing differentiation of characters and the added action of the struggle. In *The Watermelon Patch* (1905), produced by Edison and directed by Edwin S. Porter, who gained fame with his early narrative film *The Great Train Robbery* (1903), this stereotype is fully integrated into a narrative that advances the watermelon genre to its most complex dimensions yet. The comic film includes several scenes. At the outset, "a number of darkies are sneaking through the vines and picking out the best melons" in "a typical Southern watermelon patch." After the patch's scarecrows remove their garments and reveal themselves as "animated skeletons," the frightened thieves escape to a cabin, where a gathering of blacks includes music and "buck and wing and other styles of negro dancing." After the thieves arrive with their watermelons, everyone proceeds to "enjoy the melons as only Southern 'coons' can." As this occurs, farmers with bloodhounds close in on the cabin, nail its doors and windows shut, and seal off the chimney to "smoke the merry-makers out." When they can ignore the smoke no longer, "all hands make a mad rush from the building." As each one flees, he or she is given "a kick or a clout over the head to vary the monotony."[13]

A similar series of films including *Chicken Thieves* (1897), *Who Said Chicken?* (1901), *Dancing for a Chicken* (1903), and *The Chicken Thief* (1904) parallels the watermelon-eating pictures in both the facile assumption of racial stereotypes and the movement toward a greater narrative involvement. The last of these, an early American Mutoscope and Biograph film photographed by G. W. Bitzer, Griffith's future collaborator, includes a chase scene and final administration of justice at a cabin very similar to the one in *The Watermelon Patch*. "From the opening of the picture," its Biograph summary advertised, "where the coon with the grinning face is seen devouring fried chicken, to the end where he hangs head down from the ceiling, caught by a bear trap on his leg, the film is one continuous shout of laughter."[14]

Comic films such as *The Chicken Thief* and *The Watermelon Patch*, which feature armed white farmers trailing black fugitives, do not conclude with lynchings (though they gesture ominously in that direction), but a number of early films portray lynchings and other racially motivated violent acts in explicit ways. A Lubin film called *Fun on the Farm* (1905) weaves together scenes of a rustic farm setting, including plowing, dairy milking, hay rides, a husking bee, and a love story, all performed by white characters. Among these bucolic pleasures is the punishment—"after one of the best chases ever seen, they catch him, tar and feather him and carry him riding on a rail down to the water when he gets a good ducking"—of a black man who has stolen several chickens from the coop.[15] *Fun on the Farm* provides a useful bridge between the comic plantation pastoralism of films such as *The Watermelon Patch*, a pastoralism that was heir to both minstrelsy and local-color writing, and the stark intensity of a number of silent films that depict lynchings and dramatically averted near-lynchings.[16] Some of these lynching films, such as *Tracked by Bloodhounds; or, A Lynching at Cripple Creek* (1904), have western rather than southern settings. *Tracked by Bloodhounds* features a wandering tramp who strangles a woman in view of her little daughter after a robbery attempt in a western mining town, followed by a series of chase scenes and his final lynching "with a howling mob of bloodthirsty miners and cowboys surrounding him" and as the film's summary notes, "before life is extinct bullets from their revolvers pierce the body."[17]

Another lynching film from 1904, *Avenging a Crime; or, Burned at the Stake*, raises interesting questions about the western setting of *Tracked by Bloodhounds*. *Avenging a Crime* features a virtually identical plot, complete with the attempted robbery and successful strangulation of a white woman (witnessed not by a daughter but by a little girl hiding in the bushes) and an elaborate chase sequence that culminates in a lynching. But *Avenging a Crime* is set in "a typical Southern scene" rather than a western mining town, and its villain is a "very sulky" black man who commits his crimes after losing his money in game after game of craps. He is not hanged, as in the western variation; instead, his lynchers burn him at the stake, though other similarities persist: "Lashing him to a tree, they gather brushwood, and, stacking it around him, set it on fire. He is soon enveloped in flames, the angry mob fire shot after shot at him and the vengeance is complete."[18]

The resemblance of these two films—*Tracked by Bloodhounds* produced by the Selig Polyscope Company and released in April 1904 and *Avenging a Crime* produced by Paley and Steiner and released in November 1904 (the later date suggesting its debt to the other film)—is evidence not primarily of the rabidly racist southern influence in early cinema but more generally of the shared generic conventions of films produced during the same historical moment. It is certainly true that despite the numerous lynching films set in the West during this period, the South far exceeded the rest of the country in the number of lynchings between 1880 and 1930, and thus a case might be made for the displacement of such connotatively southern subject matter on other regions.[19]

But in this cinematic tradition, the similarities of *Tracked by Bloodhounds* and *Avenging a Crime* also reflect shared influences of melodrama and suspense, gender roles, community values, and a progressive social critique of poverty and vice. Along with the watermelon-eating and chicken-stealing genres, these films finally provide a severe but valuable insight into the racial views of mainstream American popular culture in the first years of the cinema.[20] What is most distressing, and perhaps most instructive looking ahead to the career of D. W. Griffith, is not that the racism of these and many other films constitutes the central and defining content of the early American cinema, but that it could so seamlessly merge into the broad matrix of early filmmaking practices and that filmmakers, distributors, and viewers could so easily appropriate and celebrate the derivative racial codes—violent as well as comic—of the era. In this historically grounded context, as in the pastoral *Fun on the Farm*, blackness was anything but exceptional in early film. And therein lay the offense.

Life to Those Other Civil Wars

Embarking on a phenomenally prolific directing career at American Mutoscope and Biograph in 1908, D. W. Griffith adopted the broad racial assumptions of early cinema for his own work. Over the next five years he would make nearly five hundred one-reel films—roughly two a week—before moving on to the multireel films that would culminate in the twelve-reel *The Birth of a Nation* in 1915. Griffith would eventually direct ten Civil War films, produce three, and supervise one.[21] Most of these films' blacks—exemplified by Old Ben, a loyal house slave in *Swords and Hearts* (1911) who clairvoyantly "anticipates the bushwackers' attack" on his old master's home and secretly buries the family's valuables in the woods—do not voraciously consume watermelon; instead, they play all-important roles, subscribing unstintingly to the paternalism of white patriarchy at its most beleaguered hour and thus revealing the synthesis of Griffith's implicit racism within his larger cinematic and social visions.

Griffith's Civil War films represent a fraction of his total output during these years, suggesting that the war was not as urgent a topic for his attention as it would seem to generations of film scholars and historians after 1915. During the same period, for example, he made no fewer than thirteen temperance films, revealing an awareness of his contemporary audience and the culture at large in those pre-Prohibition years.[22] Film historians, following Griffith's own comments later in his career, have variously pointed to the filmmaker's native Kentucky roots, his father's service as a Confederate colonel, and the stories of war and home front he absorbed as a young boy as possible influences on his films. But one striking aspect of these short films is their overall generic conformity. Dramatically, they remain as faithful to the popular melodrama of the late Victorian novel and stage—Griffith's training ground as a young actor—as Old Ben remains to his master's model of racial codes. Griffith rarely ventured beyond the standard myths and legends of white southern chivalry and honor, heroic women on the home front, and loyal slaves that predominated in the popular memory of the war during this period. This more or less official memory was widely propagated in memorial societies, mainstream fiction, legitimate theater, and pageantry of the late nineteenth and early twentieth centuries. It also prevailed in scholarly history, indelibly shaped by the work of Columbia University's William A. Dunning and his cohort of graduate students—the so-called Dunning

School of southern history, whose work validated these myths and lent them intellectual justification. Considering these short films as a collective group, Griffith's fidelity to a more narrowly southern perspective of the war is even less marked than one might expect. The fact that he produced so many other films on countless other topics between 1908 and 1913 also places these few war films solidly within his overall cinematic practice and maturation. Like the watermelon-eating, chicken-stealing, and lynching films of the early silent era, Griffith's Civil War films are significant not so much for their divergence from contemporary filmmaking as for their very embeddedness within that larger system.

Nor was Griffith alone in perceiving the cinematic potential of the war. Nonnarrative films on Civil War topics had been made since at least 1899, when Lubin produced *Unveiling of Grant Monument* in Philadelphia, a film whose greatest attraction at its time was the image of President McKinley in the reviewing stand. Representative later films include *U.S. National Cemetery* (1901), which pictures children strewing flowers on the graves of unknown dead soldiers at Gettysburg, and the elaborate, somewhat longer battle reenactments in *Military Maneuvers, Manassas, Va.* (1904) and *Scenes from the Battlefield of Gettysburg, the Waterloo of the Confederacy* (1908). In 1908, the year Griffith directed *The Guerrilla*, a dozen other fictional films about the war were released. From there, the number increased annually to twenty-three in 1909, thirty-four in 1910, and close to one hundred each year thereafter to 1916.[23] The year 1913, the widely memorialized semicentennial of Gettysburg, saw two important longer films about the war: Lubin's melodramatic four-reel *The Battle of Shiloh* and more importantly, Thomas H. Ince's five-reel *The Battle of Gettysburg*, which presaged the epic treatment Griffith would bring to the war two years later in *The Birth of a Nation*. According to historian Bruce Chadwick, many southern moviegoers surprised film producers with requests for films about the war. Genuinely upset that most of the earliest films about the war advanced a pro-Union perspective, the occasional viewer from Dixie seems to have thought, a bemused Chadwick points out, "that the South had won the war."[24] Just as surprising to producers was the warm reception of pro-Confederate Civil War films in the North. In general, though, and in a faithful adaptation of the popular reconciliationist literature and memory that had emerged during Reconstruction, early Civil War films tend to portray the heroism of both sides and often include friendships and love stories between enemies.[25] Chadwick summarizes the winning formula utilized by many of these films: "Most involved some kind of prewar friendship between men divided by the war, a girl of the North or the South, perhaps a mother or father fearful of a son's battlefield death, and some sort of device whereby a former friend, now an enemy, helps an enemy, saves an enemy, or survives an enemy. The girl, usually quite young, always winds up being swept into somebody's arms, war or no war."[26] Griffith's films are located in this tradition even as they can be seen as revealing elements of his own filmmaking style and emotional texture. They focus a great deal of attention on the special plight of women during and after the conflict. Slaves, portrayed by white actors in blackface, are also featured both as background figures and, in several key instances, as protagonists.

The most recognizably reconciliationist of these films are set in border regions that allow for indecision and disagreement among family members or neighbors about which side, the Union or the Confederacy, they should support. That these films' major battles are often fought in what seems like the backyard of the principal characters' homes exploits the dramatic potential of this situation even more. *In Old Kentucky* (1909), *In the Border States* (1910), and *The Fugitive* (1910) reveal the common concern of early Civil War films to negotiate the complex allegiances of the fratricidal conflict. The first film dramatizes the argument between a Unionist father and his headstrong son, who exits to fight for the Confederacy. Later, after his cowardice has driven him to desert the army and return home, the son's mother hides him in her bed, after which he leaves. At the end of the war he returns home and embraces the Union flag in a scene of reunion with his father. *In the Border States* and *The Fugitive* both feature female characters who help fugitive enemy soldiers to hide. The former depicts a little girl, daughter of a Union soldier, who saves a wounded Confederate by hiding him in a well and sending Union troops to search for him elsewhere; later, she successfully appeals to the Confederate to spare her own father, who lies wounded inside the house. The enemy soldiers even shake hands, and the Confederate salutes the little girl as he departs. In *The Fugitive*, the mother of a Confederate harbors a Union soldier, protecting him even after she learns that he killed her own son. Realizing that the Union soldier's mother would grieve for him if he were to die, she overcomes her desire to turn him over to his enemies and allows him to escape back to his own mother and sweetheart. These films encourage sympathy for the Union as well as for the Confederacy by emphasizing the heroism of soldiers and civilians on both sides of the struggle and by depicting with melodramatic sentiment the human contact between individuals that transcends political and military allegiances. In doing so they are representative of the reunion tradition of Civil War memory that had been flourishing in literature since at least the 1880s and would flourish in American film for decades to come.

In his first film about the war, *The Guerrilla* (1908), Griffith does not indulge in any sort of Lost Cause mythology, but he subtly nods to southern honor even in the absence of heroic Confederates. The film's hero is a Union soldier who poignantly leaves his sweetheart to fight in the war. After the soldier has left, a wily guerrilla posing as a Confederate (he wears a stolen uniform) presents himself to the girl, is rebuffed, and attempts to force himself on her. The girl manages to pass a written note to her black servant, who delivers it to her lover but loses his life completing his mission. The film concludes after a parallel-edited chase sequence in which the Union soldier narrowly escapes several Confederates (again, not regulars but guerrillas with stolen uniforms) and arrives just in time to rescue his girl from the drunken guerrilla. In this film Griffith had for the first time utilized parallel editing for more than two subjects at a time, a considerable innovation in his narrative repertoire. The film also complicates Griffith's reading of the Civil War and its legacy in *The Birth of a Nation*, by reversing the connotations of North and South so popular in the Lost Cause, such that the North is feminized victim and chivalrous hero and the South (albeit a counterfeit one) is intimidating aggressor.[27] Perhaps at this early date Griffith, like others, remained skeptical of the fortunes of a prosouthern film and simply had a northern audience in mind as he assigned the soldiers' roles as he did. Or perhaps, cranking out film after film, he gave the matter little thought. Tellingly, however, he could not bring himself to attribute evil deeds to actual Confederates, only to opportunistic imitators pretending to be the real thing; the stolen uniforms provided a sly escape clause for tarnished southern honor.

One of Griffith's last Civil War films before *The Birth of a Nation* also features a Union soldier as protagonist, though in more ambivalent terms than those offered in *The Guerrilla*. In *The Battle* (1911), it is not the color of his uniform but the decisions he makes during the heat of the fighting that shape the character of the soldier. After panicking and deserting the frontlines, the soldier summons his courage with the help of an attractive girl who lives nearby and goes on to complete a dangerous mission that ensures a Union victory in the battle. Receiving both a commendation from the wounded general and a kiss from the girl, the soldier reaps the rewards of conquering his own cowardice. *The Battle* also includes the most elaborate battlefield sequences Griffith had attempted to that date, including the devastating Union repulsion of a Rebel charge that resembles a miniaturized Pickett's Charge, a kind of trial run for what was to come in *The Birth of a Nation*.

The protagonist's unreliable courage in *The Battle* had precedents in several other films, including *In Old Kentucky*, discussed earlier, as well as *The Honor of His Family* (1909) and *The House with Closed Shutters* (1910). In each case, a young man proves himself unworthy of his uniform (which in these films is gray) and brings shame to his family. In *The Honor of His Family*, a Confederate officer identified as Colonel Pickett shoots his own son, George Pickett Jr., and secretly delivers the body to the battlefield to preserve the family name. This film's beginning shows the father regaling his son with stories and images of family forebears who distinguished themselves as soldiers and giving the advice, "My son, emulate those gone before you. Be fearless and fight, fight." It is tempting to reflect on the autobiographical echoes of this father-son tableau and to consider *The Honor of His Family* as a statement about Griffith's ambivalent relationship to the war, which he was experiencing not in battle, as his own father had, but merely in the make-believe world of celluloid. Returning almost compulsively to the same theme in several of his Civil War films, Griffith makes it clear that expectations of family honor constitute quite a heavy burden for a young man.

The House with Closed Shutters features an opening intertitle that reads, "Our flag—fight, fight for it, and the honor of our name." Cutting to a shot of the protagonist, who is helping himself to a drink, and his energetic sister, who sews an enormous Rebel flag, Griffith conflates the Confederate cause and family honor. Unfortunately for this family, however, the young man of the house proves himself "a drink-mad coward," as an intertitle bluntly puts it, from the moment he sees military action. Returning home to the surprise of his mother and sister, he cowers disgracefully and reveals a total inability to fulfill his duty as a soldier. Even the family's slave seems ashamed by this behavior. It is the sister, finally, who cuts her long hair, dons her brother's uniform, and goes out to fight the war. She survives a dangerous mission to deliver key information to a ranking Confederate officer but is shot down "endeavoring to save the flag" in the fierce battle. The letter that arrives to announce the death makes it clear that the Confederate army believes it was the girl's brother who died, adding the ironic condolence, "His death was an added honor to his family name." The mother, aware of the shame that will come to the family if anyone learns that her son is such a coward that his sister died in his place, orders the slave to close all the house's shutters and tells her son: "You stay here forever for the good of the family name that the world may not know your sister died protecting a coward." Twenty-five years later, the son continues to ignore his mother's entreaties to stop drinking (an interesting echo of the temperance polemics in other Griffith one-reelers) until he cannot contain the secret of his shame any longer and throws open the shutters to reveal himself to several amazed neighbors. A moment later he dies.

Griffith emphasizes the man's ironic demise to lend authority and pathos to the women in the family. Women here are far stronger and braver than men, and they stand to suffer at least as much by the uncertain fortunes of the family's reputation. In an important sense it is their Civil War Griffith seeks to portray in *The House with Closed Shutters*, as well as in such films as *The Fugitive* (1910), *His Trust* (1911), *His Trust Fulfilled* (1911), and the aforementioned *Swords and Hearts*. Women in these films personify the home front, that complex network of communal values, customs, and expectations so crucial to understanding what the war—that is, the military engagements—really means in the daily terms of human experience. Insisting on the nonnegotiable nature of this system of values, the parents who enact such harsh penalties on their children in these films—the colonel's killing of his own son in *The Honor of His Family*, the mother's order that her cowardly son remain shuttered for the rest of his life in *The House with Closed Shutters*—do so with a reverence for honor that finds its ultimate expression in the inviolability of the female. A few years later, of course, the violation of white womanhood would push this sense of honor to assert itself with a vengeance in *The Birth of a Nation*.

But if these parents understand the necessity of preserving family honor in the face of the Civil War's ravages, it is the loyal slave in *His Trust* and *His Trust Fulfilled* who best preserves the white female apotheosis of this honor in Griffith's early Civil War films. Released three days apart in early 1911, these two films constitute Griffith's first two-reel production, though his wish to have them exhibited as a single film was overruled by his Biograph bosses. In the first film, which is subtitled "The Faithful Devotion and Self-sacrifice of an Old Negro Servant," the war brings down a wealthy southern family when a planter dies in battle and his beautiful home is burned to the ground by marauding Yankees. Risking his own life to save both his master's young daughter and, just as important, his master's saber, the slave George (played by a white actor in blackface, to less than realistic effect) brings the girl and her disconsolate, widowed mother—struggling to bear up under "the southern woman's heavy burden," in the words of a particularly melodramatic intertitle—to live in his own cabin. The film ends as he goes to sleep on a blanket outside the front door of the cabin, preserving their privacy and taking up his own role as their guardian. At the outset of *His Trust Fulfilled*, several years have elapsed. The family's slaves have abandoned the plantation, and the girl's mother dies of a broken heart. George miraculously comes up with enough money for the girl's education, which he finances secretly with the grudging assistance of a white lawyer. When she returns from finishing school a young woman, an English cousin arrives to court her, and they are married. She pauses before departing on her honeymoon to shake the now elderly George's hand, and he returns to his cabin to gaze mystically at his master's Confederate saber on the wall. As he does so, the lawyer appears in the cabin and in an unprecedented gesture, shakes George's hand as an acknowledgment of the latter's "trust fulfilled."

These films provide a compressed version of the events of *The Birth of a Nation*, narrating both the Civil War and Reconstruction from the point of view of a southern hearth that is irrevocably disrupted by history itself. Military matters are dispatched in a few short minutes, and in any case rendered meaningless without the home front to endure, interpret, and give context and consequence to their events. The crisis of *His Trust Fulfilled* is not black political dominance and sexual predation, which cries out for white vigilante justice in *The Birth of a Nation*; more simply, but no less urgently, it is the precarious position of a young white girl whose family has been ravaged by the cosmic forces of a war she is too young and innocent to understand. In shepherding the girl through these hardships and delivering her to the wedding altar, George single-handedly reassembles the shattered dream of the Old South for modernity. In his steadfast fealty to his master, George foregoes personhood in favor of continued submission to the familial—and by extension in this context, social and political—vision of his long-deceased owner and to the slave era that expired in law but not in spirit in 1865. George is not a person so much as a wistfully desired force of stability, designed to counter the chaotic sundering of white southern order by the war and its harrowing aftermath. George's self-sacrifice fashions the white girl as the heir to a temporarily interrupted but at long last restored and redeemed lineage of the southern family.

Griffith endows George with a strong measure of pathos here; his paternalistic portrait of the slave (or legally if not practically, the ex-slave) seems quite ingenuous and blind to the irony in the lawyer's final handshake with George. Rather than understanding the handshake as a hearty endorsement of the ongoing servility and inferiority of the black man—which on a fundamental level it most certainly is—Griffith invests the gesture with affection and respect, with a disarming sense of the lawyer's profound appreciation of the black man's honor. It is this vision of honor that the film so fully celebrates. George's attainment of such a rarefied status is the result of his own sense of the white girl's sacredness in the profane milieu of radical Reconstruction. Reflecting on the racial implications of *His Trust* and *His Trust Fulfilled*, film historian Scott Simmon returns to the familial hearth so aptly depicted by George's slave cabin: "Griffith fostered a dream of Reconstruction that maintained the pre-'alienated' racial harmony under the sort of 'honor' usually reserved exclusively for relations among Southern white men. The adjective 'childlike' attached to 'Negroes' that is woven through various Dunning school histories places blackfolk, after all, in a family structure. Preceding race, the family remains Griffith's touchstone. Would anyone, black or white, not yearn for its nurture?"[28]

This characterization of southern honor makes the point that, in Griffith's eyes, films such as *His Trust* and *His Trust Fulfilled* are not consciously racist or antiblack; rather, they are pro-family. Simmon's formulation, focused as it is on familial harmony rather than the obvious motives of racial stability and social control, is perhaps a bit too generous to Griffith, but it gets at a crucial insight. Griffith's immediate strategy is not to victimize blackness but to fix it into a larger constellation of family sentiment, that most powerful weapon with which to wage his cinematic Civil War.

The Tragedy of American Film History

This insight should not be understood to mitigate or rationalize the disturbing racism of *His Trust* and *His Trust Fulfilled*. If anything, it only deepens an appreciation of Griffith's intractably hierarchical racial assumptions and illustrates how intuitively Griffith made blackness work in the service of his overall aesthetic agenda, an agenda for which white supremacy was axiomatic. But perhaps the same insight also helps to explain why Griffith was so genuinely astonished and hurt by the massive, organized protests and charges of racial antagonism leveled at him during the general release of *The Birth of a Nation*.

Throughout Griffith's early Civil War films, white men repeatedly reveal frail faces of humanity behind the burnished facade of honor. If a single theme runs through these films, it is the failure of these men to transcend their fears, to prove themselves worthy of a mythical code of chivalry that seems increasingly superhuman and unattainable. White men die in battle and leave their wives and children defenseless. They flee from the battlefield in disgrace, shaming their fathers or, even worse, their mothers. They bring about suffering instead of happiness, shame instead of pride, and sometimes even the deaths of their family members. As Griffith makes explicit in *The Informer* (1912), his last Civil War film before *The Birth of a Nation*, these men are emasculated: the wounded and missing limbs of veterans connote impotence, loss of one's very identity and potentiality as a man. In these films, it is only the females—the proud mother and brave sister in *The House with Closed Shutters*, the selfless poor white girl in *Swords and Hearts*, the fearless daughter in *In the Border States*, and so on—and the unwaveringly dedicated slaves and ex-slaves like George in *His Trust* and *His Trust Fulfilled* and Old Ben in *Swords and Hearts* who consistently rise to the challenges of heroic action. Women do so by necessity of circumstance; blacks do so, it seems, by nature, by a kind of mechanistic instinct. Thus women and to an even greater degree blacks are necessary figures in this world because the white men have simply failed. Their heroism, however, is always only a completion of the pattern established but abandoned by white men. They are the "content" with which white men's "form" will be restored, the hands with which white men's lands will be set in order.

Griffith's early Civil War films thus offer a tentative solution to the critical ruptures of history and society represented by the war and

Reconstruction. Closer to short stories than novels, these films seek more limited ends, resonate with sometimes deeply ambivalent emotions, and revel in insights more private and domestic than public and explicitly political. In these ways, the films sit comfortably within what has come to be called the "transitional era" in early cinema, a period roughly covering the decade from 1908 to 1917. These years saw many of the shifts exemplified by Griffith's work: greater formal and narrative complexity, the emergence of multireel films across the industry, the migration from the East Coast to the West, the concomitant consolidation of the studio system, and the rise of state and private censorship advocates.[29] Important in this context, however, is the intermediate state of Griffith's representation of the meaning of the Civil War and Reconstruction for a besieged white patriarchy. For it is only in his collaboration with Thomas Dixon, the North Carolina–born author of a trilogy of obsessively racist novels about the war and its harrowing effects on southern whites, that the loyal slaves who serve Griffith in the earlier films are revealed as transitional figures who ambiguously and only partially redeem the world of the old masters. Only in *The Birth of a Nation* did Griffith envision the logical end point to his impulse to bend black service to white ends and identify at last the most perfect symbol of the elusive backbone of those films: the Ku Klux Klan.

Dixon's novels *The Leopard's Spots* (1902), *The Clansman* (1905), and *The Traitor* (1907) narrate the hypocritical deceptions of northern racial liberalism, expose Reconstruction as an outrage against the white South, and apotheosize the Klan as savior of the region and the white race. Dixon's sheer paranoia about the risk of racial amalgamation pushed him to portray the blacks in his novels as a savage, incompletely evolved species of beasts. The description of the black man offered by Dr. Cameron, a white paterfamilias who has impotently watched the unfolding of Reconstruction in *The Clansman*, is typical:

> "He lived as his fathers lived—stole his food, worked his wife, sold his children, ate his brother, content to drink, sing, dance, and sport as the ape!
>
> "And this creature, half-child, half-animal, the sport of impulse, whim and conceit, 'pleased with a rattle, tickled with a straw,' a being who, left to his will, roams at night and sleeps in the day, whose speech knows no words of love, whose passions, once aroused, are as the fury of the tiger—they have set this thing to rule over the Southern people—"
>
> The doctor sprang to his feet, his face livid, his eyes blazing with emotion. "Merciful God—it surpasses human belief!"[30]

Dixon himself had no trouble believing in both the innate inferiority of blacks and the veracity of the doctor's historical narrative. His commitment to the truthfulness of *The Birth of a Nation*, in which Griffith actually toned down the racist rhetoric of the novels to a considerable degree, led him publicly to offer *New York Evening Post* editor and NAACP vice president Oswald Garrison Villard five thousand dollars if Villard could identify any historical inaccuracy of the film.[31] Griffith shared Dixon's belief in the film's historical truth, often citing the "historical facsimilies" sprinkled throughout the film and footnoted on intertitles with textual and photographic sources, as proof of his pure intentions. Neither Dixon nor Griffith, however, drew attention to certain more problematic facts—for example, that the film's notorious depiction of black dominance and corruption in the South Carolina State House of Representatives had been based not on government records or still photography from the period but on a series of political cartoons that caricatured black political participation as inherently absurd.

Most extraordinary, though, and most revealing of how Dixon and Griffith themselves saw the fruit of their collaboration is the fact that neither man made the least effort to distinguish between the historical record, contested though it might be, and the generic form of melodrama and its framing of all the purportedly historical events in the film. Indeed, Dixon had given *The Clansman* the subtitle "An Historical Romance of the Ku Klux Klan" with no apparent sense of the problematic authority of the hybrid genre "historical romance," and Griffith revealed a fundamental continuity of method with the novel in *The Birth of a Nation*, even as he softened Dixon's insatiable "half-child, half-animal" blacks into more stock blackface figures. Dixon's rapist Gus is a beast "with an ugly leer, his flat nose dilated, his sinister bead-eyes wide apart gleaming ape-like" as he breaks into a prominent white family's home and mercilessly corners his victims, mother and daughter; the next day, the women fling themselves from a cliff, but only after having a conversation that serves to polemically justify their deaths in light of the black presence in their world. "We could not escape ourselves!" cries the daughter, Marion. "The thought of life is torture. Only those who hate me could wish that I live. The grave will be soft and cool, the light of day a burning shame."[32] Griffith's Gus, by contrast, interrupts Flora Cameron's pastoral idyll with a kind of humility, with intentions of marriage rather than rape. "You see—I'm a Captain now—and I want to marry," he tells her; when she runs away, he calls out after the fleeing girl, "Wait, missie, I won't hurt yeh." At the top of the cliff, Gus seems to be entreating Flora to step back from the precipice, and there is more fear than fury in his eyes. But such distinctions, as well as the fact that the actor playing Gus was obviously a white man in blackface, seem picayune considering the very real terror Flora exhibits and the peroxide-induced foaming at the mouth discernible for flickering moments in several shots of Gus. While a marriage proposal may seem a considerable upgrade over an imminent rape, Gus's approach to Flora in the solitude of the piney woods teeters ambiguously and dangerously between his seemingly genuine stated intentions and the more foul possible implications of his pursuit. And finally it was Griffith, not Dixon, who dramatized Gus's castration at the hands of the Klan—a sequence later cut to appease censors.

Despite their subtle differences in this sequence, novel and film share fundamental intentions that are anything but subtle. Both narratives, in the end, guide the young white girl through "the opal gates of death." Griffith's comparative humanization of Gus cannot change this fact any more than Griffith considers acquitting Gus of his crime. Both incarnations of Gus—the one degenerating into a wild animal, the other expressing, if not exactly remorse (for he did not, after all, want Flora to die), then a pretty human sense of fear—must be lynched for their crimes. And the lynchings are necessary to establish that the reassertion of white manhood, exemplified by the Klan, represents the culmination of both melodramatic narratives.

Griffith undoubtedly perceived a difference between his own racial attitudes and those of Dixon. In the early months of 1915, when protesters and a handful of critics defied the upsurge of popular support and clamored for the film's suppression, Griffith tended not to defend the racism of the film, as Dixon did, but attempted to take the higher ground in defense of free expression and, even more pointedly, in defense of the medium's enormous aesthetic potential. On March 12, after considerable public demonstration against the film by the NAACP, Griffith inserted an intertitle immediately before the film's title to express these ideas succinctly but without explicitly addressing race:

A Plea for the Art of the Motion Picture
We do not fear censorship, for we have no wish to offend with improprieties or obscenities, but we do demand, as a right, the liberty to show the dark side of wrong, that we may illuminate the bright side of virtue—the same liberty that is conceded to the art of the written word—that art to which we owe the Bible and the works of Shakespeare.[33]

This sentence reveals something of the narrative basis of Griffith's work. Returning for a moment to the one-reel Civil War films *His Trust* and *His Trust Fulfilled*, it becomes clear that Griffith's shift to feature-length filmmaking was marked by a consistent fidelity to both melodrama and the technical innovation of "the art of the motion picture." In the early films, "the dark side of wrong" consists of the forces of chaos unleashed by Reconstruction and the threat to white patriarchy inherent in that historical moment. Without that established presence, "the bright side of virtue"—that is, George's loyal service—cannot be fully appreciated. Race is simply part of the film's vocabulary in effecting this "illumination." By the same token, as Griffith implies in his "plea," those elements considered improper or obscene in *The Birth of a Nation* are simply the narrative antecedents over which "virtue" will ultimately triumph.

In likening film to print, Griffith sought both to protect motion pictures from censorship and to show that his medium, still considered a merely popular amusement by most people in 1915, deserved the same respect as that accorded to the literary canon. The first claim would be rejected by the U.S. Supreme Court later in the year, in the case of *Mutual Film Corporation v. Ohio*; distinguishing between the commercial motives of film and the supposed economic disinterest of print, the court likened motion pictures more to carnival performances and vaudeville skits than to *Othello* and *King Lear*.[34] The second claim, certainly the more audacious in 1915, would not be settled so quickly.

In the short term, Griffith sought to appear a gentleman and offered occasionally to appease his critics by trimming a scene or two from the film. But this very impulse, and the very idea that anyone could isolate and excise the offending frames from a film as fundamentally, pervasively racist as *The Birth of a Nation*, suggest that Griffith himself did not perceive the nature of the problem. For in making "the dark side of wrong" and "the bright side of virtue" pivot in his melodramatic narrative on a deterministic, hierarchical model of race, Griffith had ensured that form and content would be utterly inseparable. Without the racist assumptions at the heart of the story, there would be no film whatsoever to argue over. And once the trimming began, where would it end? Griffith's opposition to censorship, and his disappointment with the *Mutual* decision later in 1915, constituted in a sense the only consistent stance he could take to evade this line of questioning, which seems properly deconstructionist today but likely would have appeared nothing short of nihilistic—like Reconstruction itself, as it was then understood—to Griffith in his day.

The historical irony in Griffith's untenable position, of course, is that the young medium he inherited and did so much to transform into one of the most dominant institutions of American popular culture in the twentieth century was already tainted with racism when he arrived in 1908 to try his novel hand at directing. Far beyond the explosive genre of melodrama, the early American cinema shared in its culture's overextended investment in whiteness as a primary grounding of narrative, humanity, history, and citizenship. In his success Griffith brought this racist presence into a clearer light and deepened the commitment of the medium and the culture at large to its assumptions. He also spurred others to success and in doing so extended an influence on American film history far beyond his own films. Among the many members of his cast and crew who went on to prominence within the industry, for example, a pair of less noted actors in *The Birth of a Nation*—Raoul Walsh as John Wilkes Booth and John Ford as a hooded Klan rider—would themselves enjoy long, influential directing careers during and beyond the classical era. This period would be marked not by the startling, vicious racism of the 1915 blockbuster so much as by the comfortable assimilation of its racist ideas into the seductive body of mainstream American film, from musicals to gangster films to Westerns like Ford's *Stagecoach* (1939). One of the film's distributors, the ambitious Louis B. Mayer, would make a personal fortune on *The Birth of a Nation* in New England's theaters, putting him in excellent position to establish his own studio—later to become MGM—in the wilds of southern California. But all this, and so much more, lay in the future, not the restive past of Jim Crow's birth and adolescence.

The middle ground that William Everson and so many others were once eager to occupy has become less tenable in recent years as new Griffith scholarship has emerged. Among the best examples of this work are Linda Williams's *Playing the Race Card* (2001), a valuable cultural history of melodrama that situates *The Birth of a Nation* at a midpoint between Uncle Tom and O. J. Simpson, and Clyde Taylor's *The Mask of Art* (1998), with its radical insistence that the entire architecture of Western aesthetic values be reevaluated to better contextualize the racial motives of Griffith's art.[35] As a field, film history since *American Silent Film* has likewise been motivated by a generation of poststructural literary and cultural theory to consider the proposition that those old categories of form and content are not so easily segregated after all, both in films themselves and in the relations between films and their producers and viewers.[36] A more sophisticated integration of theory and history points the way to an ongoing, rigorous questioning of the ways that early cinema both reflected and shaped the social world of its genesis. The teleological assumptions of cinema's linear progress from "primitive" to "classical" have been subjected to greater scrutiny in recent years, suggesting a richer and more resonant community of cultural forms and practices helping to shape an overall historical moment.[37] As in other fields, film history will continue to benefit from the knowledge that the results of historical change cannot be known to those in the midst of a movement. Yet film history, like so many other areas in American life, continues to show a reluctance to accept the embeddedness of race in its very being. In doing so, it still views *The Watermelon Patch* and its genre as marginal rather than normative and looks to D. W. Griffith as a major innovator of the medium who just happened to be a certain kind of racist southerner, whose racism and southernness could be neatly divorced, or perhaps just politely and paternalistically segregated, from his greatness as a filmmaker.

As in so many other areas of American life, it is the struggle to imagine viable alternatives that limits film history in its racial self-conception. After all, what might American film, and Griffith within it, look like with the centuries-old problem of racism acknowledged and privileged rather than denied and repressed? The most promising recent work that speaks to this open-ended question examines, not surprisingly, other kinds of black agency in film than those ascribed by Griffith. Both in studies of early silent film's connection to African American social history and in studies of the "race film" industry that produced such visionary works as Oscar Micheaux's powerful antilynching film *Within Our Gates* (1920), this work demands a reconsideration of the historical origins of American film as well as of the problematic critical position necessitated by any vision of citizenship grounded in constructs other than an exclusionary whiteness.[38]

And then there is Griffith, the great and small man himself. For perhaps, when we finally understand the rippling implications of setting race at the center of a film history made not just of cinematic genres and schools but of broad regions of social and cultural history, we will apprehend the filmmaker and the man anew. Perhaps we will come to see that Griffith's genius lay not just in devising the narrative vocabulary that enabled him to tell his stories so fluidly and subtly but also, and inseparably, in dramatically exposing America's founding flaw and Original Sin—its crisis of racial identity, its tragedy of racial oppression—in the official language of the American Century. With a renaissance of southern letters just a few years off, coming on the heels of World War I, which would gradually spell the end of the filmmaker's inspired run, Griffith would not be the last southerner to render such a service to his nation. Amid his screenwriting assignments for the big studios in the mid-1930s, William Faulkner would shape the modernist narrative to incredibly complex and profound ends in his greatest novel, the tale of a white man named Thomas Sutpen who designs his own glorious vision of empire—a vast slave plantation in north Mississippi—pursues it relentlessly all his life, and loses everything because the design has been flawed all along without his knowing it. Faulkner set *Absalom, Absalom!* (1936) in a South that endured the upheavals of the Civil War and Reconstruction, but he pitched it to a twentieth-century America that had never fully acknowledged its crippling legacy of race and thus struggled mightily to make sense of so much of its own history and identity. The novel's design, of course, is Greek, but the flaw is only too American. D. W. Griffith, too, pursued a flawed dream in *The Birth of a Nation*. His tragedy is film history.

1. See, for example, William P. Everson, *American Silent Film* (1978; New York: Da Capo, 1998), 72–89; Richard Schickel, *D. W. Griffith: An American Life* (New York: Simon and Schuster, 1984), 267–302; David W. Blight, *Race and Reunion: The Civil War in American Memory* (Cambridge, Mass.: Harvard University Press, 2001), 394–97.

2. Scott Simmon, *The Films of D. W. Griffith* (New York: Cambridge University Press, 1993), 106–8, provides an excellent treatment of this trend in the context of *The Birth of a Nation*'s famous chase sequence involving Flora Cameron and the black soldier Gus, exposing some of the bizarre and tortured logic utilized by sophisticated critics to defend Griffith against charges of racism. Simmon's overall study represents an important exception to the critical tradition to which I am drawing attention here; Simmon resists any recourse to such logic, more appropriately noting that Griffith's 1915 film "is not an isolated anomaly. Rather, it drew from, and helped codify, a pair of overlapping traditions that were developing into genres: the Civil War film and the 'Southern' (to use that word in a generic sense, like the 'Western')" (114). Locating Griffith's aesthetic in this generic form, Simmon effectively highlights both its ambivalence and its debt to Griffith's earlier work: "To engage in a Civil War is to be divided against oneself, something that comes to mind in more than one context with *The Birth of a Nation*. Yet it would be a mistake to let that epic obscure Griffith's earlier success during his Biograph period with the very issues and patterns for which it is famous" (125).

3. See Lewis Jacobs, *The Rise of the American Film* (New York: Harcourt, Brace, 1939); Kevin Brownlow, *The Parade's Gone By* (New York: Knopf, 1968); Eric Rhode, *A History of the Cinema: From Its Origins to 1970* (London: Lane, 1976); and Jack Spears, *Hollywood, the Golden Era* (South Brunswick, N.J.: Barnes, 1971).

4. Everson, *American Silent Film*, 77.

5. See notes 33–36 for more on these scholarly traditions.

6. The teleological connotations of the term "primitive" have been questioned by several scholars, including Noel Burch, whose *Life to Those Shadows* (Berkeley: University of California Press, 1990) represents one sustained attempt to provide an alternative historical frame for this period in film history. See also note 36.

7. On these traditions, see, for example, Michael Rogin, *Blackface, White Noise: Jewish Immigrants in the Hollywood Melting Pot* (Berkeley: University of California Press, 1996); Lucinda MacKethan, *The Dream of Arcady: Place and Time in Southern Literature* (Baton Rouge: Louisiana State University Press, 1980); W. Fitzhugh Brundage, ed., *Under Sentence of Death: Lynching in the New South* (Chapel Hill: University of North Carolina Press, 1997); Amy Louise Wood, *Lynching and Spectacle: Witnessing Racial Violence in America, 1890–1940* (Chapel Hill: University of North Carolina Press, 2009).

8. On the regional and national implications of segregation, especially in political and economic contexts, see, for example, C. Vann Woodward, *The Strange Career of Jim Crow* (New York: Oxford University Press, 1955), and

Edward L. Ayers, *The Promise of the New South: Life after Reconstruction* (New York: Oxford University Press, 1992). Grace Elizabeth Hale provides a thorough analysis of the cultural artifacts, including *The Birth of a Nation*, generated by segregation in *Making Whiteness: The Culture of Segregation in the South, 1890–1940* (New York: Pantheon, 1998).

9. *Who Said Watermelon?* summary, *Lubin's Films* catalog (Philadelphia: Lubin, 1907), J3, 36, http://gateway.proquest.com/openurl?ctx_ver=Z39.88-2003&xri:pqil:res_ver=0.2&res_id=xri:afi-us&rft_id=xri:afi:film:31514 (accessed August 30, 2007).

10. Tom Gunning, *D. W. Griffith and the Origins of American Narrative Film: The Early Years at Biograph* (Urbana: University of Illinois Press, 1991), 41.

11. For the general shift between these styles and for more on Gunning's conception of narrative integration, see Gunning, *D. W. Griffith and the Origins*, 6–7.

12. *Who Said Watermelon?* summary, *Lubin's Films* catalog (Philadelphia: Lubin, 1907), J3, 48, http://gateway.proquest.com/openurl?ctx_ver=Z39.88-2003&xri:pqil:res_ver=0.2&res_id=xri:afi-us&rft_id=xri:afi:film:42557 (accessed August 30, 2007).

13. *The Watermelon Patch* summary, Edison catalog (New York: Edison, 1906), J6, 39–40, http://gateway.proquest.com/openurl?ctx_ver=Z39.88-2003&xri:pqil:res_ver=0.2&res_id=xri:afi-us&rft_id=xri:afi:film:30107 (accessed August 30, 2007).

14. *The Chicken Thief* summary, Biograph catalog (New York: American Mutoscope and Biograph, 1904), December 27, B1, 140–43, 209, http://gateway.proquest.com/openurl?ctx_ver=Z39.88-2003&xri:pqil:res_ver=0.2&res_id=xri:afi-us&rft_id=xri:afi:film:32516 (accessed August 30, 2007).

15. *Fun on the Farm* summary, *Lubin's Films* catalog (Philadelphia: Lubin, 1907), 29–30, http://www.afi.com/members/catalog/DetailView.aspx?s=&Movie=29660 (accessed April 28, 2010).

16. A Biograph film from this period is *Miss Jewett and the Baker Family* (1899), described by the Biograph summary: "The young Boston philanthropist, and the family of negroes whom she rescued from a lynching party in the South." This film is interesting not least because it was photographed by G. W. Bitzer, who would collaborate with Griffith on his short Civil War films and *The Birth of a Nation*, among many others. *Miss Jewett and the Baker Family*, listed at 28 or 153 feet (probably to offer exhibitors the choice of running times), provides evidence of the alternative approaches of the cinema to contemporary films that simply utilized lynchings as an appropriate and just narrative climax. See *AMB Picture Catalog*, November 1902, 242, http://gateway.proquest.com/openurl?ctx_ver=Z39.88-2003&xri:pqil:res_ver=0.2&res_id=xri:afi-us&rft_id=xri:afi:film:44317 (accessed August 30, 2007).

17. *Tracked by Bloodhounds*, Selig summary, Kleine Optical Company catalog (Chicago: Kleine, 1904), November 5, 222, http://gateway.proquest.com/openurl?ctx_ver=Z39.88-2003&xri:pqil:res_ver=0.2&res_id=xri:afi-us&rft_id=xri:afi:film:32983 (accessed August 30, 2007).

18. *Avenging a Crime* summary, *Lubin's Films* catalog (Philadelphia: Lubin, 1907), O7, 114–15, http://gateway.proquest.com/openurl?ctx_ver=Z39.88-2003&

xri:pqil:res_ver=0.2&res_id=xri:afi-us&rft_id=xri:afi:film:32446 (accessed August 30, 2007).

19. This process of displacement seems even more curious in light of the preponderance of lynchings in the South by 1900, a divergence between the South and the rest of the country that had been widening for some time. Brundage writes in *Under Sentence of Death*: "Lynching, like slavery and segregation, was not unique to the South. But its proportions and significance there were unparalleled outside the region. Drawing on traditions of lawlessness rooted in slavery and the turmoil of Reconstruction, lynch mobs continued to execute alleged wrongdoers long after lynching had become a rarity elsewhere in the nation. By the late nineteenth century, mob violence had become a prominent feature of race relations in the South that for many symbolized black oppression. Lynching also came to define southern distinctiveness every bit as much as the Mason-Dixon line marked the boundary of the region" (4). If lynching indeed had become both distinctively southern and overwhelmingly aimed at black victims, why the overrepresentation of the West and white victims in this genre of films? The classical era's two greatest studio-produced antilynching films, *Fury* (1936) and *The Ox-Bow Incident* (1943), both take place in the West (the latter staged as a traditional Western, although clearly borrowing conventions from the "social problem" films of the 1940s as well) and feature white men as victims (*The Ox-Bow Incident* does include one Mexican among its three lynched cowboys, enabling the killers to indulge a strain of xenophobia en route to the gallows, but that serves only to emphasize their more generalized indifference to the identities, and innocence, of the victims). For a more comprehensive treatment of these issues and of the prolific presence of lynching in American film history more generally, see Robert Jackson, "A Southern Sublimation: Lynching Film and the Reconstruction of American Memory," *The Southern Literary Journal* 40, no. 2 (Spring 2008): 102–20.

20. For more on the historical contexts that gave rise to lynching films during the silent era, see Jackson, "Southern Sublimation."

21. Bruce Chadwick, *The Reel Civil War: Mythmaking in American Film* (New York: Knopf, 2001), 44.

22. Schickel, *D. W. Griffith*, 182.

23. Chadwick, *Reel Civil War*, 41.

24. Ibid.

25. For a more synthetic treatment of the reconciliationist culture and the alternatives to its memories of the war in the half-century after 1865, see Blight, *Race and Reunion*. Blight's narrative, which culminates ominously with the explosive critical and popular reception of *The Birth of a Nation* in 1915, portrays the triumph of this reconciliationist memory of the war, in which northern and southern whites eschew their prior enmity and fuse in mutual respect and admiration, advancing a belief in both sides' heroism during the war and common purpose looking forward into modernity, at the expense of the competing "emancipationist" memory, in which black humanity and citizenship might finally be recognized in fulfillment of the long-deferred American promise.

26. Chadwick, *Reel Civil War*, 40.

27. For an elaboration of the editing patterns of *The Guerrilla* and the important placement of the film amid Griffith's other early innovations in narrative style, see Gunning, *D. W. Griffith and the Origins*, 133–34.

28. Simmon, *Films of D. W. Griffith*, 127.

29. For a diverse collection of approaches to this period, see Charlie Keil and Shelley Stamp, eds., *American Cinema's Transitional Era: Audiences, Institutions, Practices* (Berkeley: University of California Press, 2004).

30. Thomas Dixon, *The Clansman* (1905; New York: Wessels, 1907), 292–93.

31. Schickel, *D. W. Griffith*, 287.

32. Dixon, *Clansman*, 304, 306.

33. For more on this episode, see Schickel, *D. W. Griffith*, 282.

34. For more on the *Mutual* decision, see Garth Jowett, *Film: The Democratic Art* (Boston: Little, Brown, 1976), 119–22. Lee Grieveson provides the best recent study of film censorship in early American film in *Policing Cinema: Movies and Censorship in Early-Twentieth-Century America* (Berkeley: University of California Press, 2004).

35. Linda Williams, *Playing the Race Card: Melodramas of Black and White from Uncle Tom to O. J.* (Princeton, N.J.: Princeton University Press, 2002); Clyde Taylor, *The Mask of Art: Breaking the Aesthetic Contract: Film and Literature* (Bloomington: Indiana University Press, 1998). Perhaps the most important single critical statement in the development of this body of work is Michael Rogin, "'The Sword Became a Flashing Vision': D. W. Griffith's *The Birth of a Nation*," *Representations* 9 (Winter 1985): 150–95. For a more recent treatment of many of the same concerns, a consolidation of much of the more recent scholarship, and a particular focus on the life of Jim Crow segregation as a tenacious historical and discursive phenomenon, see Michele Wallace, "The Good Lynching and *The Birth of a Nation*: Discourses and Aesthetics of Jim Crow," *Cinema Journal* 43, no. 1 (2003): 85–104.

36. Representative examples in the now sizable literature advancing more sophisticated theoretical paradigms are Robert Stam, *Film Theory: An Introduction* (Oxford: Blackwell, 2000), and Robert Stam and Toby Miller, eds., *Film and Theory: An Anthology* (Oxford: Blackwell, 2000). Miriam Hansen, *Babel and Babylon: Spectatorship in American Silent Film* (Cambridge, Mass.: Harvard University Press, 1991), pursues a theoretically subtle, historically grounded model of how "the emergence of cinema spectatorship is profoundly intertwined with the transformation of the public sphere" across the entire silent period from the late 1890s to the late 1920s (2).

37. See, for example, Burch, *Life to Those Shadows*; Tom Gunning, "'Primitive' Cinema—A Frame-up? or The Trick's on Us," *Cinema Journal* 28, no. 2 (Winter 1989): 3–12; and Charles Musser, *The Emergence of Cinema: The American Screen to 1907* (Berkeley: University of California Press, 1990).

38. A flurry of scholarship on the "race film" industry and its major figure, Oscar Micheaux, has given strong impetus to this critical line of investigation. Following the pioneering efforts of Thomas Cripps, *Slow Fade to Black: The Negro in American Film, 1900–1942* (New York: Oxford University Press,

1977), and Henry T. Sampson, *Blacks in Black and White: A Source Book on Black Films* (Metuchen, N.J.: Scarecrow, 1977), more recent—and in general more theoretically sophisticated—work includes Pearl Bowser and Louise Spence, *Writing Himself into History: Oscar Micheaux, His Silent Films, and His Audiences* (New Brunswick, N.J.: Rutgers University Press, 2000); Pearl Bowser, Jane Gaines, and Charles Musser, eds., *Oscar Micheaux and His Circle: African-American Filmmaking and Race Cinema in the Silent Era* (Bloomington: Indiana University Press, 2001); Anna Everett, *Returning the Gaze: A Genealogy of Black Film Criticism, 1909–1949* (Durham, N.C.: Duke University Press, 2001); and Jacqueline Najuma Stewart, *Migrating to the Movies: Cinema and Black Urban Modernity* (Berkeley: University of California Press, 2005). Foregrounding a greater consciousness of the effort to document the complex experience of race in American film history, both in the efforts of its essayists and in African Americans' films themselves, Phyllis R. Klotman and Janet K. Cutler's edited collection, *Struggles for Representation: African-American Documentary Film and Video* (Bloomington: Indiana University Press, 1999), represents another group of theoretical and historical approaches to the ongoing reorientation of American film history to this consciousness of race.

Mammy's "Mules" and the Rules of Marriage in *Gone with the Wind*

Riché Richardson

Ellen Fein and Sherrie Schneider's 1995 runaway bestseller, *The Rules: Time-Tested Secrets for Capturing the Heart of Mr. Right*, questions and even self-consciously resists the prevailing logic of second-wave feminism concerning gender relations and marriage and emphasizes more conventional approaches to dating for contemporary women to meet and marry their dream guy. Fein and Schneider argue that career-oriented, take-charge "[n]ineties women simply have not been schooled in the basics— *The Rules* of finding a husband or at least being very popular with men." While the authors suggest their support of feminism, the book implicitly concedes biologic differences between male and female genders, including inherent characteristics of masculinity and femininity typically questioned by scholarship in feminist and gay and lesbian and queer studies. To achieve the goal of marriage, they offer thirty-five rules, such as "Be a Creature Unlike Any Other," "Don't Call Him and Rarely Return His Calls," and "Always End Phone Calls First." They reveal in the opening pages that their philosophy of dating, courtship, and marriage is inspired by a friend they call Melanie, who assures them that "plain-looking women who followed *The Rules* stood a better chance of being happily married than gorgeous women who didn't."[1] Because of their own proven success with such strategies, they feel motivated to write them down and share them with women everywhere.

The authors acknowledge that they became motivated to record and clarify their rules precisely when they realized that this legendary arsenal for succeeding in dating and marriage had crisscrossed the nation and passed among networks of women from New York to California.[2] The U.S. South does not register ostensibly in the geography across which the rules are said by the authors to have circulated cross-country, a particularly surprising omission when we consider some of the courtship protocols of young white women of the Old South, including those to which Margaret Mitchell alludes in her 1936 epic novel *Gone with the Wind*. In acknowledging changes that emerged among the southern elite during the post–Civil War period, Mitchell's novel invokes a custom of declining a marriage proposal three times before accepting: "But men [in the Civil War] who expected to die within a week or a month could not wait a year before they begged to call a girl by her first name, with 'Miss,' of course, preceding it. Nor would they go through the formal and protracted courtships which good manners had prescribed before the war. They were likely to propose in three or four months. And girls who knew very well that a lady always refused a gentleman the first three times he proposed rushed headlong to accept the first time."[3] Indeed, Mitchell's plot itself is set in motion by anxieties related to the topic of marriage—a subtext sustained to the bitter end.

In her study titled *Scarlett's Sisters: Young Women in the Old South*, Anya Jabour provides a detailed historical discussion that examines courtship and engagement among the young white southern female elite in the antebellum era. As she points out, they were keenly aware of the social responsibilities and expectations that came with marriage. While often relishing the attentions that came with courtship and marriage proposals, they were reluctant to rush into engagement and tended to delay marriage as long as possible: "Some women subjected their lovers to a series of tests. Like the heroines of the 'double proposal plot' romance novels to which many southern girls were addicted, young women might initially reject a suitor—or call off a wedding—only to resume the relationship once they had received assurances of undying love and devotion, which might result in a more egalitarian match." Jabour acknowledges that power in a relationship shifted to the suitor when a young woman accepted a marriage proposal, and so young women valued the power that they could claim during the courtship stage. In her words, "When young women yielded their hearts, they relinquished much of their ability to negotiate for a favorable position in marriage—and to resist their subordinate position in southern society." Furthermore, Jabour points out that "[s]outhern women used long engagements as final testing grounds that gave them time to come to terms with their fears of marriage—or, if that failed, to end the relationship. It was not uncommon for engagements to be broken in the antebellum South." The approaches to courtship and marriage in the Old South, Jabour suggests, were shaped by a visceral understanding of the expectations of marriage and by the aim of young women to make prudent decisions.[4]

The exclusion of the U.S. South from Fein and Schneider's narrative is something that a popular work such as Lisa Bertagnoli's *Scarlett's Rules: When Life Gives You Green Velvet Curtains, Make a Green Velvet*

Dress and 23 Other Life Lessons Inspired by Scarlett O'Hara attempts
to rectify. Mitchell's eponymous character Scarlett O'Hara, Bertagnoli
suggests, is an ultimate "rules girl." In Bertagnoli's words, "There's no
shortage of women in today's media-saturated world who have captured
our collective attention, and fictional and real characters from Carrie
Bradshaw to Paris Hilton keep us entertained and amused. Yet true role
models are scarce; for that we need more than entertainment and amusement. My dear, we need Scarlett."[5]

Anyone carefully and truthfully watching the David Selznick film made
in 1939 and based on Mitchell's novel *Gone with the Wind* might say
otherwise, for the film suggests that who we really need is Mammy, revealing in numerous scenes that *she* is the one who knows such rules best.
Indeed, one irony in the case of both the book and the film is Mammy's
salient role in regulating and monitoring Scarlett's social encounters with
men, in spite of Mammy's subjection as a slave. Some of the most time-
honored scripts and protocols of southern social life for Scarlett, including rules for getting a husband, are articulated and policed by Mammy.
The film *Gone with the Wind* dramatizes these dialectics in a range of
scenes that feature the two characters together. Mammy is the *rule* model
to whom we need to look for a thorough epistemology of the character
Scarlett.

Vivien Leigh epitomized Mitchell's character Scarlett on-screen, alongside Clark Gable's portrayal of Rhett Butler and Hattie McDaniel's of
Mammy. Scarlett as a character is provocative and becomes utterly infamous because she repeatedly flouts a range of cherished southern social
conventions and values for which Mammy is positioned as the primary
advocate, custodian, and judge; Mammy voices and establishes the laws
that Scarlett breaks. *Gone with the Wind* reveals nostalgia for the Old
South and its attendant hierarchical and polarized paternalistic social
order grounded in slavery, along with a widespread view of people of
African descent as passive, childlike, and inferior to whites in intelli-
gence. Yet the film offers through the interplay of Scarlett and Mammy
a dynamic that unsettles such notions of black inferiority, racial hierarchy, white supremacy, and racial purity and illustrates the impact of
blackness on some aspects of white racial and social identity. The performative role that Mammy plays in regulating Scarlett's proprieties on
the road to an initial marriage and successive marriages becomes all the
more complicated if we consider the exclusion of slaves from notions of
citizenship and the barriers that prohibited them from legal marriage.
Yet the character Mammy's authority in this area is precisely what facili-
tates her abstraction and lack of subjectivity (a fact emblematized in her
namelessness) and helps to sustain her relation to the myth of mammy.
As Kimberly Wallace-Sanders acknowledges in her study titled *Mammy:*

A Century of Race, Gender, and Southern Memory, "'Mammy' is part of the lexicon of antebellum mythology that continues to have a provocative and tenacious hold on the American psyche."[6]

Such racialized and gendered ideologies of black femininity as mammy are important and useful contexts for understanding how and why some public dialogues in this nation in recent years have featured black women prominently and accorded them a motherly and moralizing voice in television and media advertisements, affirming the sanctity of traditional marriage to critique and oppose same-sex marriage. Yet virtually no energies of the reactionary sectors that appropriate black female bodies for these purposes have been invested in addressing the kinds of social and economic conditions that have contributed, for instance, to black women being the least likely to marry, the most likely to divorce, and least likely to remarry if they divorce.[7] Such ads position black women to promote social prerogatives and choices they are not positioned to share widely. They also foreclose discussions of state-based policy making related to family that might nurture the livelihood of a broader demography beyond the white and middle-class sectors tacitly invoked in public dialogues on protecting and promoting marriage.

Sex and the City and the U.S. South

An episode of the popular HBO show *Sex and the City*—which had devoted one of its early episodes to a "rules" book akin to Fein and Schneider's—alludes to the Old South marriage proposal custom that Mitchell describes. When the character Charlotte York attempts to convert to Judaism, her boyfriend Harry informs her that it is customary to be turned down three times before being taken seriously as a prospective convert. Charlotte has an epiphany precisely because a rules dating manual has familiarized her with such strategies. Yet Fein and Schneider never mention such a protocol about marriage in their first book or, for that matter, in any of their sequels.[8] *Sex and the City* typically excluded the representation of southern bodies even as it appropriated discourses and traditions conventionally associated with the region in developing characters such as Charlotte York, who was portrayed by Kristin Davis. Davis was born in Boulder, Colorado, and grew up in Columbia, South Carolina. Many articles and interviews have indicated that she was raised as a "Southern belle," and in the media, qualities such as charm, elegance, and refinement have been associated with her and suggested to be an outgrowth of her southern background.[9] They are the very same qualities of her *Sex and the City* character. On the other hand, Charlotte is urbanized and scripted as a young, wealthy New York woman who lives on the Upper East Side of the city. With her long, conservative hairstyle and classic clothes and shoes, she is a modern-day version of "ladies who lunch," which seems all the more appropriate because she does lunch so often with her three closest friends—Carrie, Miranda, and Samantha.

Often, Davis's marketing as an actor has emphasized that she can portray such an elegant and refined type of woman on television because she *is* one in real life. When planning a line of clothes for the North Carolina–based Belk department store, Davis explained, "I feel like I understand what the Southern woman wants to wear—it's influenced my personal style so much, growing up in the South."[10] The pedagogy of womanly behavior and propriety to which she was exposed and that she internalized while growing up in the South shapes Davis's demeanor on the show to some degree. It is a pedagogy that makes her more reserved, sexually and socially, than some of the other characters, especially the promiscuous Samantha, often implied to be her alter ego. The show portrays Charlotte as an ex-sorority girl, which evokes the stereotypical association of middle- and upper-class women in the South with sororities. Furthermore, it consistently depicts her as the most sentimental of all the women characters about marriage, motherhood, and friendship. A racially conservative southern tenor in Charlotte's characterization may be subtly evident in the fact that she, unlike Samantha or Miranda, is never featured in an intimate sexual encounter with a black man on the show. Davis's character is implied to be too socially reserved for such a racial crossing, notwithstanding her close friendship with a gay man, marriage to a Jewish man, and adoption of a Chinese baby.

Paradoxically, the character Charlotte is not ostensibly associated with the South at all. While we can argue that there is an allusion to a southern city in the name "Charlotte," the surname "York," at a linguistic level, crystallizes the association of this character with New York. The decontextualization of Charlotte's femininity from the South reinforces a narrative logic that associates the Northeast with U.S. national subjectivity.

Indeed, the erasure of the South in Charlotte's characterization can be interpreted as a symptom of the show's more general strategies of representing the region. Southerners tended to be portrayed stereotypically on *Sex and the City*, if at all. In the fifth season, when Carrie and her boyfriend Jack Burger debate whether New York women wear scrunchies as hair accessories, Carrie categorizes such accessories as tacky ones that no New York woman would ever wear. One night, she presumes that there might be exceptions when she sees a woman boldly wearing one in a hip restaurant. She prepares to make a concession to Burger, but wins the argument hands down when the woman turns around and begins to speak in a southern country drawl (which the show exaggerates for comic effect) and excitedly exclaims to her husband that someone actually thought she was from New York City. Similarly, in the final season, a white couple from North Carolina coded as working class (or even as "white trash") fails to inform Charlotte and her husband that they have had a change of heart about giving up their baby for adoption. They admit that they held up the pretense so they'd have a chance to visit New York City. The formal setting of Charlotte's dining room in which they are presented in this episode is telling too, for the suggestion is that such luxuries are as foreign to them as New York City itself; it magnifies their poverty, "country" background, and awkwardness. Significantly, this action unfolds as the character Carrie Bradshaw explores life in Paris, another major contemporary global city from which such characters, by implication, stand worlds apart.

In these instances, *Sex and the City* highlights such "country" characters as visitors to New York City to make the city look all the more modern, big, energetic, and overwhelming. In their awkwardness and foreignness, the southern visitors make New York look like the chic and fashionable place to be and like the ultimate place to visit, although the implication is always that they are not quite fit to endure life there. Such characters clarify the show's association of supreme cultural authority in the nation with the city. It is a city that never even has to be named explicitly in the title of the show because in the United States, it is the consummate city. Indeed, the show's New York City setting, like the high-fashion clothing for which it is well known, has sometimes been regarded as another character. (Over its six-year run on HBO, episodes set in Los Angeles and Paris make the point that there's no city on earth like New York City.)

There are southern allusions on *Sex and the City* that may be even more specific and directly related to the epic film *Gone with the Wind*. The tenor of the show and its emphasis on sex boldly contrast with the conservatism and decorum that are often associated with the U.S. South, particularly given the region's persisting traditionalism and prevailing religious conservatism. Yet if Carrie Bradshaw, as Bertagnoli suggests, manifests some of Scarlett's qualities in the contemporary era, then the inexhaustibly wealthy and gallant "Big," her tall, dark, on-again, off-again lover throughout the series, has many qualities of Rhett Butler. Carrie's youth and idealism, coupled with Big's maturity and sophistication, and their volatile relationship resonate in some ways with the continuing angst between Scarlett and Rhett.

But the Carrie/Big relationship can be said to reverse the Scarlett/Rhett saga as well. Whereas Scarlett marries twice in *Gone with the Wind* before marrying Rhett and resolves at the end of the novel that she will have to find a way to get him back, Big is the one who marries another woman on the road to uniting with Carrie, a woman who is his second wife.

Ultimately in the series, he makes a desperate trip to Paris to reclaim Carrie before all is lost. In *Gone with the Wind*, Rhett admits that he knows Scarlett is the woman for him when he first lays eyes on her at Twelve Oaks. Indeed, in her initial interest in marrying Ashley Wilkes, and in her literal marriages to Charles Hamilton and Frank Kennedy prior to the union with Rhett, Scarlett unconsciously revises the Old South rule that Mitchell invokes of turning a man down three times.

All of the four main characters on *Sex and the City* are white women; minority women are entirely absent within this nexus of primary characters, a structure premised on the idea of cross-racial friendships between women as nonnormative and unrealistic. The all-white cast reinforces the notion of a pure and homogeneous white identity and the racial separation (even segregation!) of white women from ethnic and minority women in private and social (i.e., nonwork) settings. In the antebellum era, legal prohibitions against slaves marrying reflected a lack of black citizenship and were premised on notions of black inhumanity and the categorization of blacks as property. Contemporary popular representations that exclude or marginalize blacks reinforce ideologies of blackness as pathological and socially inferior. Furthermore, such representations ideologically suggest that minority women are alien from matters of love, romance, marriage, and family and conflate such concerns with whiteness. They reinforce the notion highlighted in the title of a March 26, 2006, *Washington Post* article by Joy Jones, which was inspired by a statement from an eleven-year-old African American boy in her class: "Marriage Is for White People." Yet the popular television show *Girlfriends*, which features black female friends as a foursome, provides one of several illustrations that such themes related to relationships are as much of a concern for some women in the African American context. Indeed, this formula shaped the success of the film *Waiting to Exhale*, which was based on a novel by Terry McMillan and released in 1995 (*before* the premier of *Sex and the City* as a series).

The 2008 film adaptation of *Sex and the City*, which presents the actor Jennifer Hudson as the personal assistant to the character Carrie, nevertheless fails to significantly alter the racial homogeneity that was evident at this level in the original series. Indeed, it arguably revises the servant/mistress relation of Mammy and Scarlett. It is a representation premised on the kind of "lenticular" logic that Tara McPherson—who has exponentially expanded possibilities for thinking about southern identity and femininity in film studies—theoretically associates with the film *Gone with the Wind* in her analysis of characters such as Scarlett and Mammy. She emphasizes how technologies of representation, including lighting, reinforce notions of separateness and polarity, with Scarlett as superior and Mammy as inferior.[11]

From the Old South to the New Hollywood and American Sweethearts

On *Sex and the City*, Charlotte York's complex characterization illustrates the U.S. South's role in constituting gender typologies that undergo abstraction and signify in a national context. Nowadays, it is commonplace for feminine codes originally cultivated in the South to be emptied of any regional specificity when translated and repackaged for Hollywood audiences in the national mainstream. There have been some noteworthy exceptions, however. For instance, in the 1980s, the actor Jasmine Guy admitted that her interpretation and portrayal of Whitley Gilbert on the *Cosby Show* spin-off *A Different World* (1987–93) was informed by southern girls she had met at school while growing up. At the fictive Hillman College, Whitley was an elite, black, spoiled southern student from Virginia who spoke with a thick southern accent and even had a building on campus named after her family.

The phenomenon of appropriating characteristics and qualities that are often recognized as southern and feminine also partly explains why southern-born actors such as the Georgian Julia Roberts are so frequently abstracted and beloved as "America's sweetheart." Roberts's rise in popularity for her national audiences, especially in the early years of her career, partly had to do with the allure of qualities that her fans associated with her (such as being naturally beautiful, genuine, and ladylike) and that were sometimes presumed to be a reflection of her early cultivation in the South. Some of her key film roles, from *Steel Magnolias* (1989) to the more recent *Charlie Wilson's War* (2007), have presented Roberts as an embodiment of southern femininity on-screen. Similarly, New Orleans native Reese Witherspoon's popularity as an emblem of sweet, youthful, blonde, and beautiful American womanhood also feeds on southern aspects of her identity and the perception of southern womanhood as more authentically feminine. Witherspoon's roles in films such as *Sweet Home Alabama* (2002) draw on her southern significations, which she also seemed to evoke purposely and strategically in her acceptance speech at the 2006 Academy Awards, where she emphasized June Carter Cash, whom she had portrayed in *Walk the Line* (2005), as a "real woman" who, like herself, believes in family. Witherspoon's upbringing in Nashville, Tennessee, the nation's premier epicenter for country music production, also informed her portrayal of the singer. In her publicity, Witherspoon has sometimes identified herself as "a girl from the South" and, in 1998, had a very traditional southern wedding to the actor Ryan Phillippe at the Wide Awake Plantation in Charleston, South Carolina. Examples such as Roberts and Witherspoon illustrate how some of the familiar and cherished models of Hollywood cinematic feminine icons with widespread national currency in the contemporary era have sometimes gained (and sustained) popularity in their audiences through embodiments of varied abstractions and dispersals of southern femininity.

The silent film actor Lillian Gish, while not a southerner by birth, helped to inaugurate the Hollywood cinematic trope of the nation's ideal womanhood as southern in D. W. Griffith's epic 1915 film *The Birth of a Nation*, a paean to the Old South. By ideologically linking the fate of the region to the fate of the nation, while simultaneously feminizing and southernizing it, the film helped to establish a basis for such national abstractions of southern femininity within the Hollywood machine. In light of her popularity, the actor Lillian Gish, cast in the film as "the very flower of femininity; the linchpin of the chivalric code by which Southern gentlemen live," crystallized the movie's thesis about a feminized nation and centrally positioned the U.S. South in measuring and shaping the status of that nation.[12] Furthermore, it helped to make the scenes involving her would-be black rapist Silas Lynch all the more incendiary.

The transformation of a southern woman such as Julia Roberts into "America's sweetheart" needs to be understood in a continuum with the iconic popularity of Lillian Gish in early U.S. cinema history. Through *Birth of a Nation*, the U.S. South was foundational in establishing a form of national cinema within the global schema, including a range of ideologies related to femininity and race that have had continuing effects. That the film could conceivably produce enduring racialized and gendered formulas in Hollywood for white feminine icons becomes more understandable if we recognize the continuing ideological impact of its black characterizations. As Manthia Diawara argues, *Birth of a Nation* set the foundation for and in effect nationalized the range of stereotypes of blacks that continues to be salient in Hollywood films: "*Birth of a Nation* constitutes the grammar book for Hollywood's representation of Black manhood and womanhood, its obsession with miscegenation, and its fixing of Black people within certain spaces, such as kitchens, and into certain supporting roles, such as criminals, on the screen."[13] All of the key racial stereotypes established in this film, whose dispersals have been national, were birthed originally in the U.S. South.

What Southern Belles Have to Do with the Red Carpet

In *David O. Selznick's Hollywood*, Ronald Haver acknowledges that *Gone with the Wind* costume designer Walter Plunkett "loved discovering the details of craftsmanship, the look and feel of the past as expressed by the styles, the fabrics of clothing and its accessories."[14] Similarly, in an essay titled "From Innocence to Grandeur: The Costumes of *Gone with the Wind,*" Cynthia George notes that "Plunkett spent five weeks visiting southern cities at his own expense. In Atlanta, Margaret Mitchell introduced him to notable women of the community who permitted Plunkett to snip material from the seams of old garments. George goes on to observe that

> [t]he costumes were instrumental both in dramatizing individual character and in revealing the fortunes of an entire region. Scarlett's nature was particularly well portrayed through her gowns. Introduced in a white organza dress accented with ruffles, which Selznick thought gave her a youthful, virginal quality, Scarlett quickly dispelled this innocent image when she insisted on wearing a low-cut, green-sprigged muslin afternoon dress to a morning barbecue. Like her behavior, Scarlett's costumes were frequently unsuitable for the occasion.[15]

George contends that the green velvet dress best symbolized Scarlett's character. That Mammy designs and sews this dress also speaks symbolically to her impact on Scarlett's development. Achieving unprecedented mastery in costuming, George suggests, was crucial to delineating the temporalities of the film ranging from the antebellum period to Reconstruction and to making it a visually stunning capstone film. Alan David Vertrees argues that *Gone with the Wind* represents the "zenith" of David O. Selznick's filmmaking career and that his role as producer was most pivotal in the film's achievement of status as "the most successful motion picture of the classical age."[16] In content, *Gone with the Wind* epitomizes the elaborate costuming techniques that distinguish the classic era of Hollywood filmmaking. The Old South so masterfully recuperated in its costuming aesthetics may have some residual traces among Hollywood actors in the contemporary era.

Southern belles of the antebellum period, the product of vast wealth and privilege generated in relation to the South's plantation economy, were primarily mythologized through their association with a rarified beauty and femininity symbolized in the elaborate and colorful gowns they wore trimmed with lace and ribbons and made from expensive and often imported fabrics. Even in contemporary popular contexts, such attire seems indispensable for their visual representation, which is typically contextualized in the plantation as a space. In *Gone with the Wind*, lavish sets that showcase plantation homes such as Twelve Oaks and Tara, particularly in the opening scenes awash with southern belles and southern gentleman, and the casting of established stars such as Clark Gable and Vivien Leigh to embody such types, brought the mythic Old South and the glamour of Hollywood together. If the defining representations of the Old South were popularized in plantation literature that emerged in the late nineteenth century, film gave us the defining images of Old

South mythology in the twentieth century. No film did that more decisively than *Gone with the Wind*. Indeed, like forms of feminine icons in the nation, and through films such as *Birth of a Nation* and *Gone with the Wind*, the U.S. South is one early context that helped to popularize and nationalize Hollywood as an industry, and arguably, as an ideology.

In *Hollywood's Image of the South: A Century of Southern Film*, David Ebner and Larry Langman remark, "In their portraits of the 'Old South,' creators of literature and films often 'followed the money' and the money led to the wealthy planter class. This offered more fascination and entertainment when compared to the simple, prosaic lives of the numerous poorer planters and independent Southern farmers."[17] The authors document the continuing fascination with the U.S. South in film during its first century, highlighting the interest in southern romance, aristocracy, and figures such as the southern belle. As its role as a powerhouse within the capitalist system consolidated, by inaugurating traditions such as the Red Carpet in 1922, Hollywood also powerfully demonstrated its fascination with notions of aristocracy. Ebner and Langman reveal how profoundly and how long the U.S. South has helped to shape themes in visual representation in Hollywood.

A most classic and memorable image from the film *Gone with the Wind* is that of the character Mammy corseting Scarlett and helping her get into one of her many fancy and colorful gowns in preparation for the barbecue at the Twelve Oaks plantation. Mammy's assistance in Scarlett's dressing rituals and protocols reflects the notions of aristocracy that inflected the Old South. Indeed, in thinking about whatever happened to this stylistic aspect of the Old South, with its belles and balls, body servants and elaborate dress protocols, we might look to contemporary Hollywood and the aspects of its "star system" related to the pampered lifestyles of the most revered female actors. They are frequently fashioned in keeping with dress protocols that evoke aspects of aristocratic femininities, including the variety associated with the Old South. Labor on the part of stylists, designers, personal assistants, trainers, hairstylists, makeup artists, and jewelers is necessary to prepare stars for a walk down the red carpet and an evening at award ceremonies such as the Academy Awards, the Golden Globes, the Emmys, and the Screen Actors Guild. Actors must consult with designers to select a dress before a major event and be meticulously fitted and suited with the proper undergarments, shoes, and accessories, including (often borrowed) jewels worth thousands—and sometimes millions—of dollars. It takes tremendous wealth, of course, to sustain such lifestyles and this range of goods and services. This wealth has come for some leading female actors with the rise of a few who now make millions of dollars per film, after a hard-won fight for salaries on par with those of top leading male actors in the industry.[18] The money that film stars amass reflects the vast wealth and influence of Hollywood in this nation and, for that matter, in the world. Hollywood women are part of a socially elite and highly privileged class who have access to the best couture products of fashion design. There is intense competition among top designers to dress the most beautiful and popular actors, who can then advertise their work on the red carpet. Given the fascination with celebrities, actors can even give couture designs more media exposure than models on fashion runways. Hollywood actors, who often live on sprawling estates in vast mansions, rank among the most pampered and revered models of femininity in society. The protocol for fashioning female actors for events such as movie premieres and award ceremonies in the contemporary era recalls the protocol that helped to fashion the southern belle for social events in the Old South and that structured her daily life. On the other hand, most women in the United States and in the world wear "ready to wear" items, and the majority never set foot in a designer shoe or wear a couture piece of fashion. The demands of modern life and work, with the rise of mass-produced goods and the industrial growth of synthetic fabrics, moved most women even further from the kinds of special touches in clothing design that were evident in handmade and homemade items when sewing skills were widespread.

On *Sex and the City*, the indulgences of Carrie Bradshaw in clothing and shoes are what help to give the show its appeal at a visual level and make the actor who portrays Carrie, Sarah Jessica Parker, a fashion icon. While most viewers are aware that this character could not afford her expensive and inexhaustible designer wardrobe of clothes and shoes on her salary as a columnist, her audience is able to savor such fine products, and the possibility that an ordinary woman could conceivably possess them, through their relationship to the show as spectators. The designer clothing, shoes, and accessories highlighted on the show are fundamental to sustaining the spectatorship of its mainly female audience. One show focuses on Carrie's sobering realization, as she faces eviction from her apartment, that her cherished collection of signature stiletto designer shoes, Manolo Blahniks, which on average cost four hundred dollars a pair, had totaled forty thousand dollars. The desirability of fashion clothing and accessories typically escalates when such items are featured on the show. Indeed, as a popular phenomenon, *Sex and the City* illustrates how television and film have come to play a more and more salient role in helping to shape consumer tastes.

In *Hollywood and the Culture Elite: How the Movies Became American*, Peter Decherney acknowledges the ideological roots of Hollywood and its function at a national level, remarking that "the overwhelming identification of film with Hollywood and American culture is the result of commercial tactics and government intervention as much as it emanates from something in the films themselves" and that "the star system and the genre system are perhaps the only two (relatively) consistent methods producers have adopted to give Hollywood's product some stability in the marketplace."[19] Ultimately, we need to remember that workers in the United States help to finance the lavish lifestyles in Hollywood. Their purchasing power of movie tickets generates the millions and millions that are, in this day and age, linked to the success of films and their box office, particularly during crucial premiere weekends. Significantly, most of Hollywood's profits come from whatever Americans can afford nowadays to see a film, whether at home or at a theater, once they cover their living expenses. Some of the most glamorous stars make their money from extra pocket change. The patronage of U.S. workers has historically helped to *make* Hollywood—one manifestation of the nation's inherent capitalist system—as Hollywood in turn impacts consumer tastes and aspirations. Films' success and escalating profits are to some extent premised on the despair of a labor force that "needs" such forms of popular entertainment. Film, of course, was the new art genre that emerged and predominated throughout the twentieth century. Although conventional forms of consumption are expanding and transforming in light of the rise of new Internet and information technologies, film continues to occupy a salient space for entertainment. As film production is transformed and made more accessible through technology, it is intriguing to ponder how Hollywood itself will change in response to such new developments and to imagine where film will go in the future.

Hollywood has been historically associated with an ideal of glamour that peaked during the 1930s when dominated by studio-based actors, with female actors especially revered for their sophistication and elegant dress. Such actors shaped Hollywood's golden era and helped to consolidate its star system. Close-up facial shots with the camera were a primary technique that emerged during this era to highlight these stars on-screen. Ironically, the ideal of Hollywood glamour crystallized during the Great Depression. In subsequent decades, such stars have been nostalgically associated with "old" or "classic" Hollywood, an era that declined with the coming of World War II.

By the late twentieth century, imagining the period of classic Hollywood as an ideal time gone by was in some ways akin to the representation of the Old South in the late nineteenth century. Such continuities make it seem quite fitting, in retrospect, that a filmic feast such as *Gone with the Wind*, which was released at the very end of the 1930s, recast feminine dress conventions of the Old South at the height of an era of Hollywood glamour. Contemporary Hollywood stars are also often linked to a classic notion of Hollywood. One of the most iconic examples of recent years is Gwyneth Paltrow's pink dress and upswept hairdo on the runway the night she won the Academy Award for her performance in *Shakespeare in Love* in 1999. For many, her look recalled the style of the legendary actor who became a princess of Monaco, Grace Kelly. Some contemporary actors see Old Hollywood as a primary reference point and seek to reinvent or recall it in their fashions on the red carpet.[20]

Was Scarlett Black?

In "How Black Was Rhett Butler?" Joel Williamson discusses factors such as a darker skin color and attitudes about sex and work to examine Rhett Butler, ultimately immortalized on-screen by Clark Gable, and his complex racial significations in Mitchell's novel.[21] Similarly, Diane Roberts considers the racial aspects of Scarlett in *The Myth of Aunt Jemima: Representations of Race and Region*, by examining the question "How white is Scarlett?" She emphasizes Mammy's role in enforcing Scarlett's whiteness and the novel's profuse red imagery, including Scarlett's name, that link her with a physical hyperembodiment, transgression, and sexuality.[22]

Shelley Fisher Fishkin's *Was Huck Black? Mark Twain and African American Voices* advances such critical methodologies by arguing that a black boy whom Mark Twain encountered in a Chicago hotel and chronicled in a piece titled "Sociable Jimmy" provided the linguistic energies for the title character in *The Adventures of Huckleberry Finn*, so often identified as the quintessential American novel. In *Playing in the Dark: Whiteness and the Literary Imagination*, Toni Morrison widens the critical space for thinking about how much blackness, whether or not it is acknowledged, has shaped narration in literary works in the American canon. She examines such questions within the critical and theoretical context of poststructuralism, which stresses antiessentialism and emphasizes race as a social construct with no inherent biologic basis.[23]

In the Selznick film, which builds on Mitchell's novel, many of the social protocols that Mammy attempts to enforce for Scarlett are specifically related to the issue of marriage, itself one of the key legal and linguistic frameworks for enacting the performative and the legal ramifications of Mammy's status as a slave. Many of these protocols further reveal her agency in Scarlett's fashioning as a woman and have the potential to deepen our understanding of Scarlett's racial instability as a character.

Margaret Mitchell's Scarlett, the product of an Irish father and French-descended mother, is presented as an ethnic hybrid. Her volatile personality is suggested in some ways to be a result of this admixture, notwithstanding her mother's mild manner, elegance, and grace. The 2001 novel *The Wind Done Gone*, Alice Randall's provocative revision of *Gone with the Wind*, plays on Scarlett's complex family background.[24] The novel, whose release was suspended as a result of recriminations by the Mitchell estate in the months before its publication, not only casts Scarlett as a character of mixed ethnicity but also scripts her as mixed race. A purloined letter of sorts holds the evidence that Ellen Robillard had black blood, which would of necessity mean that Scarlett, by the conventional rules of hypodescent, inherited this racial status from her mother. Revising the Scarlett story so that she has inherited black ancestry in her family tree is truly provocative and makes Scarlett an unlikely bedfellow with a character such as William Faulkner's Quentin Compson (who, for instance, Ben Railton compellingly compares to Rhett Butler), or even Faulkner's Joe Christmas.[25]

On-screen, the film *Gone with the Wind* thoroughly embodies the linguistic energies that the novel associates with the character Mammy. The force of the character, as many critics have pointed out, owes a great debt to Hattie McDaniel herself as an actor. In his now classic study of black actors in Hollywood film, Donald Bogle notes that Hattie McDaniel's "Mammy also feels confident enough to express anger toward her masters. She berates and hounds anyone who goes against *her* conception of right and wrong, whether it be Mrs. O'Hara or Scarlett and Rhett. Not once does she bite her tongue." Bogle goes on to say that Mammy "becomes an all-seeing, all-hearing, all-knowing commentator and observer. She remarks. She annotates. She makes asides. She always opinionizes."[26]

As Bogle suggests, Mammy stands above the other characters and does not hesitate to judge them, a point of view Rhett Butler is keenly aware of when he identifies her as "one of the few people whose respect I'd like to have." The opening scene of the film—along with some others—highlights Mammy sanctioning Scarlett about flouting aspects of social decorum. Mammy is concerned that Scarlett has gone out without a shawl in the night air and failed to invite the Tarletons for dinner as a proper girl would. Indeed, her appearance in the opening scene of the film, along with her forceful speaking, helps to establish Mammy's authority. The camera shot of Mammy from below and the framing of her face and upper body in an upstairs window of Tara make her look even more authoritative.

Recurrently in the film, Mammy underscores Scarlett's lack of propriety by likening her behavior to that of a range of people who are her social inferiors. In the opening scene, for instance, Mammy rebukes Scarlett by telling her, "You ain't got no more manners than a field hand."

As Scarlett runs off to investigate Ashley's intentions to marry Melanie Hamilton, the immediate cut to Tara's field hands, in a pastoral scene as the sun sets and it's "quittin' time," dramatizes this contrast. In associating Scarlett with the crude behavior of field hands, Mammy highlights her behavior as the most extreme contradiction of the delicacy and femininity befitting proper young, wealthy white women in the South. Such analogies, which ironically recall ways in which white women in the nineteenth century were often likened to slaves, effect a symbolic blackening of Scarlett in the film. More generally, they can also be understood in relation to the film's release during the years of the Great Depression. As Marian J. Morton points out, "Scarlett returns to Tara to find her mother dead, her sisters ill, her father insane, and the plantation in ruins. . . . Scarlett works, literally like a slave, even picking cotton which the servants refuse to do, and learns to do for herself what others used to do for her."[27]

Gerald O'Hara's later chiding of his daughter for making a spectacle of herself running after a man when she might "have any of the beaux in the county" reinforces the criticism of Scarlett's lack of propriety that Mammy begins. Later on, Mammy's criticism of Ellen O'Hara, whom she had also nursed as a child, for "wearing herself out" by serving as a wet nurse to the poor white woman Amy Slatterly, in effect extends the link of a lack of proper decorum as a southern woman to Scarlett's mother. Ellen O'Hara first appears in the film as she returns from the birth of Jonas Wilkerson and Amy Slatterly's out-of-wedlock stillborn child. Amy, the obverse of Scarlett and her sisters Suellen and Careen, is a girl whom Gerald O'Hara ostensibly classifies as "white trash." Significantly, the opening scenes of the film emphasize notions of southern propriety and stress the proper protocols and boundaries for the southern elite. The close sequential timing (i.e., on the same day) and the repetitions of all Mammy's quips and chides related to proper behavior for southern girls and ladies are performative and emphasize her role as a gatekeeper of such values.

Moreover, in the early and now classic scene that features Mammy tightening Scarlett's corset prior to the picnic at Twelve Oaks—a ritual that recurs later in the film once Scarlett marries Rhett—Mammy continues her rebukes of Scarlett, warning her that she can't wear the dress she prefers because "you can't show your bosom before three o'clock!" When Scarlett refuses food that has been brought to her and expresses her intention to Mammy to eat at the picnic, Mammy replies, "You can always tell a lady by the way she eats in front of people like a bird," and likens Scarlett's eating habits to a field hand. Scarlett tells Mammy that Ashley Wilkes, whose family is hosting the barbecue, says that he likes a girl with a healthy appetite. But Mammy wins the argument with

Scarlett, forcing her to accept her tray and eat at home, by pointing out that "what gentlemans says and what they thinks is two different things" and by reminding her that Ashley had not asked for *her* hand in marriage. The scene implies the protocols of southern social female decorum designed mainly for getting a husband, a ritual to which Mammy is far more attuned than Scarlett, a point confirmed in Scarlett's question, "Why does a girl have to be so silly to catch a husband?"

The content of their dialogue initiates one of the film's reigning themes: it reinforces Mammy's subversion of her own legal subordination as a slave at the same time that it establishes her voice and authority on the topic of marriage. The film intensifies this tension, for instance, when Mammy chides Scarlett about the impropriety of going to Atlanta to intrude on the relationship of Melly and Ashley or, later, when she restrains Scarlett from interrupting this couple's reunion when Ashley returns home from the war (saying, "He's her husband"). Here, while the emphasis is on Scarlett, we see more generally how vigilantly Mammy guards the reputation of the O'Hara family. Ironically, as a slave Mammy cares more than Scarlett about the O'Hara name and regards herself as a custodian of its reputation, exclaiming, "If you don't care what folks say about this family, I does!" As Scarlett leaves, Mammy warns her to take her shawl to protect her skin from developing freckles, skin to which Mammy had applied buttermilk all winter. Mammy's sanctioning continues at the barbecue, where she reminds Scarlett that "well-brought-up young ladies take naps at parties" and that she and her sisters should act like Ellen O'Hara's daughters, not like the children of "poor white trash."

The film presents the opulent Twelve Oaks plantation, even more so than Tara, as the emblem of the Old South's wealth, where the paternalism of the slave system was fully and fairly actualized. Through the eyes of the characters Melly and Ashley, it appears on-screen in all its glory as a beautiful and peaceful world that is in every way ideal. The Civil War is the greatest and most immediate threat to the sanctity of this place. Yet the sign at Twelve Oaks on which the camera zooms in as Scarlett and her sisters arrive at the plantation, reading "Anyone Disturbing the Peace on This Plantation Will Be Prosecuted," teases viewers with the idea that *Scarlett* represents its most imminent threat. Her indiscriminate flirting with beaux at the barbecue, her refusal to take a nap, her clandestine pursuit of Ashley, her breaking of a vase, and her harsh words to Rhett attest to this possibility. In this setting, the knowledge that Rhett Butler took a girl out without a chaperone in the late afternoon and refused to marry her is scandalous information that points to his social aberrance. It represents him as extreme in his lack of social decorum. But the film makes it clear that Scarlett is not too far behind him. Rhett's question to her—"Has the war started?"—after she throws the vase in anger, seems to play on and revise Abraham Lincoln's legendary reference to Harriet Beecher Stowe as "the little woman who started the big war," in light of the impact of her 1852 novel *Uncle Tom's Cabin*.

Indeed, the negotiation and procurement of marriage is a dimension that gives the film thematic coherence and continuity from the very beginning, evident in the pronouncement of Ashley and Melly's betrothal; Ashley's lecture to Scarlett on what makes a successful marriage; the connection of Mammy's rebukes about the protocols of getting a husband; Scarlett's serial marriages to Charles Hamilton, Frank Kennedy, and Rhett Butler; and Rhett's final rejection. Costuming is used effectively at the barbecue, particularly for women, to create a festive atmosphere and to emphasize the lavish lifestyles and luxuries associated with the Old South. It also sets up a subtle contrast, if we notice the juxtaposition of Scarlett's bright-colored gowns with Melly's more reserved attire. Melly's brownish and more demure gown, with black gloves, emphasizes her mature, matronly qualities and her readiness to marry Ashley, setting her in contrast with Scarlett's girlishness and flirtatiousness. That Scarlett overhears other belles talking about her and remarking, "Men may flirt with girls like that but they don't marry them," and the encounter with Ashley and his imminent marriage to Melly prompt her to marry Charles Hamilton hastily.

Some of Scarlett's most egregious deceptions are connected to the reigning marriage plot in the film. Scarlett's sadness when she learns that the war has begun is related to the fact that Ashley will be going off to the battlefield, though the naive Charles thinks that she is sad because he will be leaving her. Similarly, her tears at her wedding relate to the fact that she is mortified over the kiss on the cheek by Ashley after having married Charles, a man she does not love, although Charles thinks that she is lamenting his imminent departure. That Scarlett shows all the "right" emotions at the right times but for the wrong reasons points to her insincerity and makes her all the more suspect and improper as a woman—and as a wife. Moreover, the scorn of her sister Suellen and other belles at the barbecue, and repeated missteps thereafter, such as the dance with Rhett Butler when she is in mourning as the widow of Charles Hamilton, put Scarlett on the path to becoming a veritable pariah. Other women, with the exception of Melly, loathe Scarlett. As the film continues, the marriage theme is sustained as Melly and Scarlett are juxtaposed as wives, mainly through the eyes of Rhett Butler as a character, who regards the former as a "great lady." His acts of reclaiming Melly's wedding ring after she has made a donation of it to support the war because "it will do my husband more good off my finger" and then returning Scarlett's ring as an afterthought dramatize the distinctions he makes between them as women in his mind. While Rhett says that he is not attracted to "ladies" when he meets Scarlett and chides her for attempting to flirt with him like a southern belle, he is captivated by Melly's kindheartedness and femininity and seems to lament Scarlett's failure to measure up to it.[28] After all, as Mammy has said, "what gentlemans says and what they thinks is two different things."

We should remember that Scarlett's failure to be a proper wife and then widow, or to respect the marriage of Ashley and Melly, is at the heart of the scorn heaped on her, including Mammy's criticism. Mammy chides Scarlett about failing to honor mourning attire and, unlike Ellen O'Hara, is aware of Scarlett's true motives for going to Atlanta to see the Hamiltons: to await Ashley when he comes home on furlough from the war. As wise and perceptive Mammy puts it, Scarlett will be "sittin' there waiting for him just like a spider." In Atlanta at the Hamiltons', Scarlett's indiscretions continue as she disregards her status as a widow and dances in the Virginia reel with Rhett Butler, who has placed a bid for her with $150 in gold, an action that causes Melanie and Charles's aunt Pittypat to faint. The socialite Dolly Merriwether labels the activity a "slave auction" before she learns that Melly approves of it.

Indeed, this colorful scene extends the film's metaphorical connections between Scarlett and slaves. This time, however, the analogy is more feminine than masculine. Slave women were most frequently purchased on the auction block, sometimes for the express purpose of sexual exploitation. As Patricia Hill Collins has pointed out, the public touching and stripping of slave women at auction was inherently pornographic.[29] There is a prior scene, even, that establishes the foundation for this purchase of Scarlett at the ball; Scarlett feels very uneasy as Rhett intensely eyes her as she ascends the stairs at Twelve Oaks because she feels he is undressing her with his eyes. Such derisive invocations of slavery to regulate the social behavior and conserve the privilege of its elite members such as Scarlett show the ubiquity of the institution in the consciousness of the Old South as a defining feature of social life. They also speak to the degree to which slaves were subordinate within the social hierarchy in which the planter class held the most power. Moreover, this scene links Scarlett to prostitution. Rhett indicates that he expects a return on his money at the same time that he indicates his lack of interest in marriage, and her acquiescence to dance with him anticipates her visit to the jail to see him, where she expresses willingness to exchange sex for the three hundred dollars that she needs to pay the taxes on Tara. We know, from Rhett's scandalous relationship with Belle Watling, that he is intimately related to prostitution. The intense irony in her name is telling, for she is no "belle" at all in the conventional sense. Similarly, Ashley implies Scarlett's willingness to prostitute herself when he suggests that in uniting with Frank Kennedy, she has married a man she does not love to get the three hundred dollars for the taxes.

After the war ends, when Scarlett goes to Atlanta to see Rhett, Mammy insists on going with her to keep Scarlett out of trouble. Significantly, Rhett comments that Scarlett's hands are not the hands of a lady but of a field hand. Mammy accuses her of visiting "white trash." But once Reconstruction begins, the comparisons between slaves and Scarlett shift to comparisons to carpetbaggers, in light of her economic endeavors that reflect her determination to beat the Yankees at their own game. Scarlett gains more disapproval when she begins to drive around in her own buggy alone, in spite of her status as a woman. This last choice leads to an attack on her and ultimately to a raid on the Old Sullivan Place to defend her honor, which angers women like India who feel that Scarlett has brought the attack on herself.

The prostitute Belle Watling, who at Rhett's behest supplies an alibi for the men, including Ashley, notably refers to Scarlett as lower class and unfit in a clandestine dialogue with Melly. Even she feels fit to judge Scarlett and look down on her. The film's highlighting of gentlemen versus rabble, South versus North, and ladies versus prostitutes—and the comparison of Scarlett to "white trash" and "field hands"—is the larger context in which to recognize Scarlett's abjection as a southern woman, along with some bitter ironies. For she has all of the right stuff to get what she wants, yet she plays her cards miserably and carelessly.

Throughout the film, Mammy turns the most critical eye on both Scarlett and Rhett as characters and sees their behavior as inappropriate and excessive. Her scathing estimation of the both of them is epitomized in her assessment of their marriage and of their effort to dress up and hobnob among the elite in New Orleans as an attempt to dress up like racehorses when they are really "mules in horse's harness." In essence, this is another allusion to the slave class, for Mammy accuses them of attempting to do a cakewalk in reverse by pretending to have the refinement and pedigree of the elite. Mammy's reference to horses is particularly significant here, because she is ultimately commenting on their failure to manifest the social behavior in keeping with the breeding that they have had in the Old South. The word "horses" also links them to racial instability if we remember that "mulatto," an epithet whose etymology is unclear, is sometimes linked to the mule, a hybrid of the horse and donkey.

Though she is black and subordinate, Mammy is the best custodian of the Old South's values and protocols in the film. This role continues after the birth of Rhett and Scarlett's daughter Bonnie. That she has played such a salient role in fashioning females in the family is emphasized when she says, "I done diapered three generations of this family's girls." As Bonnie gets older, Mammy chides Rhett for the blue color of Bonnie's riding outfit, which is not the traditional black broadcloth that a little girl should wear, and for her riding with her dress flying up. From the time that he returns Melly's wedding ring, Rhett, in spite of his blockading, seems to have a deep-seated desire for the approval of southerners in the old guard. Indeed, when he and Scarlett are taking Bonnie for a ride in her buggy, a ride that Rhett insists will remedy their position as social outsiders, the camera significantly remains on them. They are the focus in this scene, and we see none of the neighbors to whom they speak strolling down the sidewalk. Such a technique emphasizes their behavior as a performance and an awkward, ill-fitting one at that; in fact, they appear to be on stage.

That the character is not given any name beyond "Mammy" in *Gone with the Wind* suggests her invisibility and subjection as a slave, a status that persists once she becomes a free servant. Hattie McDaniel famously remarked, "I can be a maid for $7 a week . . . or I can play a maid for $700 a week," a comment that responded in part to the black civil rights establishment's concern about perpetuating stereotypes of subservience on-screen.[30] Jill Watts, who has written a masterful biography of McDaniel, remarks, "She not only was commonly accorded screen credit, her name was increasingly identified with black cinematic female servants." Watts observes that McDaniel, who had read the novel and become fascinated with the role of Mammy, reinterpreted the character, built on her past experiences in acting, and constructed the version of Mammy that she portrays in the film, in effect "breaking new cinematic ground."[31] Even so, McDaniel separated herself from the servant characters that she portrayed. This perspective clarifies her acumen as an actor and her actions on-screen as a performance. Watts helps us to understand that McDaniel's appearance in *Gone with the Wind*, while distinctive, was the outgrowth of a very complex journey for her as an actor who had portrayed either mammies or maids in films throughout the 1930s. In a time when Jim Crow governed the southern social order, that the actor McDaniel was not allowed to attend the premiere of the film in Atlanta, Georgia, was a poignant illustration of one way in which her subordination on-screen was manifested in life.

Critical readings have most typically focused on the prototypical mammy's limitations and her lack of agency. In her classic study *From Mammies to Militants: Domestics in Black American Literature*, Trudier Harris, through a lens that juxtaposes northern and southern geographies, reminds us of the eruptive and subversive potential in a figure such as the mammy as represented in literature.[32] Similarly, artists of the black liberation era in the 1960s, including Joe Overstreet, Murray N. DePillars, Betye Saar, and Jeff Donaldson, evoke such subversion at a visual level in their preoccupation with producing radical images of Aunt

Jemima, a logo inaugurated in 1889 and the first national trademark in U.S. advertising history. McDaniel's understanding that there was some power in portraying servant characters like maids and mammies also perhaps explains the subversive qualities with which she infused her *Gone with the Wind* character, paving the way to some of her more revolutionary incarnations in literature and art in later years. Indeed, McDaniel's performance of the role on film becomes all the more significant if we recognize how much it undermines the stereotypical and dehumanizing imagery associated with Mammy as a character throughout Mitchell's novel, which refers to blacks repeatedly as "darkies." This character is nameless but not necessarily lacking in power. Characteristically, the mythic mammy was plump, asexual, and a nurturer ever at the service of her beloved white charges, with the willingness to neglect caring for her own children. Yet, McDaniel's portrayal of Mammy in *Gone with the Wind* invests this character with an agency that belies and critiques such stereotypes. Though she refers to her sometimes as "my lamb," Mammy is hardly *affectionate* where Scarlett is concerned; continually, she is Scarlett's harshest critic in the vast majority of the scenes in which they appear together. In the authority that she wields, as well as through her repeated comparisons of Scarlett to field hands, Mammy in effect challenges and unsettles the polarity of their positions within the hierarchy of mistress and slave.

Such authority as Mammy wields in *Gone with the Wind* might seem ironic for black characters in the antebellum South during a time when slavery reigned. Yet, the Mitchell novel portrays this paradox and how it was enabled within the racial hierarchy that governed the Old South even more poignantly than the film, despite the novel's sanctioning and propagation of gross black stereotypes. The character Uncle Peter, who is mainly responsible for the care of Melly and her brother Charles, makes the decisions in the Hamilton household, in many ways compensating for the indecisiveness of Aunt Pittypat. Charles admits to Scarlett that Uncle Peter practically raised him and Melly and made all decisions, including sending Charles to attend Harvard and deciding when it was time for Melanie to "put up her hair and go to parties." Uncle Peter is clearly the man of the house and in charge. This authority is clearest when he rebukes Melly for speaking with the prostitute Belle Watling in public: "And when he saw who was with me, he—Scarlett, he hollered at me! Nobody has ever hollered at me before in my whole life. And he said, 'You git in dis hyah cah'ige dis minute!' Of course, I did, and all the way home he blessed me out and wouldn't let me explain and said he was going to tell Aunt Pitty." Even Scarlett, on her arrival in Atlanta, perceives the depth of his authority: "Scarlett, who had hoped for a freer rein when she escaped Mammy's supervision, discovered to her sorrow that Uncle Peter's standards of ladylike conduct, especially for Mist' Charles' widow, were even stricter than Mammy's." Yet, in the novel's translation to film, while Mammy's authority continues to be evident, all of the power associated with Uncle Peter disappears. The main scene in which he appears, making a clumsy attempt to catch a chicken in the yard for Christmas dinner for "the white folks" (which even seems in some ways to revise the stereotype of black men as chicken thieves), seems designed for comic relief. The film implies that he has been hiding wine in the household away from the Hamilton family for his own benefit. Melanie Hamilton, the most quintessential, refined, and revered model of southern femininity and the main custodian of Old South values, was not molded so much by the temperamental and erratic Aunt Pittypat as she was by Uncle Peter; she is chiefly *his* invention and as she grew up he set the standards and rules for her.[33]

The plump body form and an intimate association between food and the mammy figure have been established as spectacle in American film. For instance, the mammy in the inaugural film epic *Birth of a Nation* helped to establish the type's stereotypical representations on-screen. The emphasis on the body was a signpost of the mammy figure's powerlessness and underscored her vulnerability and accessibility. In *Gone with the Wind*, Mammy comes across as wise and disruptive, challenging Western philosophy's classic association of rationality with a disembodied white masculinity. The wealth of Rhett Butler and the security that it brings, along with the birth of Bonnie, who extends Mammy's role of nurturing in Scarlett's family to three generations, are the main factors that change her perspective on Rhett. After Melly, Rhett cares most about what Mammy thinks of him. Notwithstanding her racial subordination, Mammy, like Melly, sets a very high standard in determining what—and *who*—is respectable. When it comes to other blacks and when it comes to Scarlett, and even to Rhett, Mammy is the boss, so to speak.

The popularity of servant figures like Mammy on-screen, of course, must be understood as a nostalgic paean to a traditional domestic culture that was collapsing during the Great Depression. By the 1940s, with World War II and the entry of more white women into the workforce, the circulation of items featuring mammy figures in U.S. material culture signaled nostalgia for a time gone by. In *Gone with the Wind*, though she is not the feminine ideal sanctioned in the Old South, Mammy comes across as the wiser in attempting to tutor Scarlett in the art of femininity. Scarlett's emergence as a pillar of strength in the film, ultimately vowing that she will never go hungry again, marks her coming of age via the traumas of the war and the ruptures, temporally and geographically, that have defined her identity. Yet, the factor that seems to remain most stable for Scarlett in the film is Mammy's circumscription and shadowing of her behavior and social comportment. It is a shadowing so profound that it is more enduring and pronounced, perhaps, than the impact of either of Scarlett's parents.

Incidentally, Alice Randall's aforementioned novel, *The Wind Done Gone*, seems perceptive and subversive in describing Scarlett as Mammy's child and reveals that Mammy deliberately taught Scarlett how to manipulate men and hurt them as a way of avenging her servitude: "I wonder what she would feel now if she ["Other"/Scarlett] knew, if I told her, if she ever come to understand that Mammy used her, used her to torment white men. Other was Mammy's revenge on a world of white men who would not marry her dark self and who had not loved her Lady [Ellen O'Hara]. Did Other see how she had been weaned to pick up hearts and trained to dash them down, both with casual ease? Who convinced her to conquer?"[34] The film's Atlanta scene in which Scarlett attempts to seduce the unwitting Frank Kennedy and lure him away from her sister Suellen poignantly illustrates such dialectics; it is an impropriety about which Mammy remains silent and fails to chide Scarlett. By the film's narrative, we must also remember that Mammy in effect designed and sewed the lavish green dress that Scarlett is wearing at the time. Scarlett lives the very life and has the possessions, such as beautiful dresses, that southern racism will not allow Mammy, making the noticeably erotic gift that Mammy receives from Rhett, a red taffeta petticoat, all the more provocative. Mammy was more in control than Scarlett ever knew or, for that matter, anybody around them ever perceived.

Ultimately, domestic authority to sanction the propriety of marriage is not the same as having the privilege oneself. Hence, in some ways, that the desexualized and hyperembodied Mammy is given salience as the guardian and gatekeeper of the social prerogative of conjugal union legally reserved for whites in the antebellum era emphasized her own subordination and exclusion from such privileges. Her exclusion and dissociation from notions of femininity was an unspoken premise of revered types such as the southern belle, who eventually grew into the southern lady. After all, there is not much use in knowing the rules if one cannot play (and win) the game.

NOTES

1. Ellen Fein and Sherrie Schneider, *The Rules: Time-Tested Secrets for Capturing the Heart of Mr. Right* (New York: Warner Books, 1995), 2, 13.

2. The authors elaborate on the rules in a range of sequels such as *The Rules II: More Rules to Live and Love By* (New York: Warner Books, 1997), *The*

Rules for Marriage: Time-Tested Secrets for Making Your Marriage Work (New York: Warner Books, 2001), and *The Rules for Online Dating: Capturing the Heart of Mr. Right in Cyberspace* (New York: Pocket Books, 2002).

3. Margaret Mitchell, *Gone with the Wind*, Special Commemorative Sixtieth Anniversary Edition (New York: Warner Books, 1993), 216.

4. Anya Jabour, *Scarlett's Sisters: Young Women in the Old South* (Chapel Hill: University of North Carolina Press, 2007), 169, 170, 162; Helen Taylor richly reveals the impact of the film on female audiences in *Scarlett's Women: Gone with the Wind and Its Female Fans* (New Brunswick, N.J.: Rutgers University Press, 1989).

5. In this phrasing, Bertagnoli riffs on one of Rhett Butler's penultimate and most provocative lines in the 1939 David Selznick film *Gone with the Wind*, "Frankly, my dear, I don't give a damn." *Scarlett's Rules: When Life Gives You Green Velvet Curtains, Make a Green Velvet Dress and 23 Other Life Lessons Inspired by Scarlett O'Hara* (New York: Villard, 2006), xviii. In this millennial era, a range of popular books highlights southern women as distinct and exceptional models of femininity who possess a unique charm. Among such works are Loraine Despres, *The Southern Belle Handbook: Sissy LeBlanc's Rules to Live By* (New York: Morrow, 2003); Marilyn Schwartz, *A Southern Belle Primer: Princess Margaret Will Never Be a Kappa Kappa Gamma* (New York: Broadway Books, 1991), and *New Times in the Old South, or Why Scarlett's in Therapy and Tara's Going Condo* (New York: Harmony Books, 1993); Ronda Rich, *What Southern Women Know (That Every Woman Should)* (New York: Berkeley, 1999), and *What Southern Women Know about Flirting* (New York: Penguin, 2005); Deborah Ford, *The Grits Guide to Life: Girls Raised in the South* (New York: Penguin, 2003), and *Puttin' on the Grits: A Guide to Southern Entertaining* (New York: Plume, 2006).

6. Kimberly Wallace-Sanders, *Mammy: A Century of Race, Gender and Southern Memory* (Ann Arbor: University of Michigan Press, 2008), 2.

7. Matthew D. Bramlett and William D. Mosher, "Cohabitation, Marriage, Divorce, and Remarriage in the United States," National Center for Health Statistics, *Vital and Health Statistics* 23, no. 22 (2002): 1–103.

8. The closest that Fein and Schneider come is an acknowledgment in an interview for an article on Carolyn Bessette Kennedy titled "Crazy for Carolyn: She Has What It Takes to Be a True Style Icon in the New Millennium: A Look That's Both Raunchy and Regal—and JFK Jr. at Her Side." The authors explain that Carolyn was a natural rules girl and did not just play hard to get but was hard to get. They note that the first time JFK Jr. proposed, she said, "I'll think about it." *Newsweek*, October 21, 1996, 67.

9. InStyle.com describes her as a "scandal-free" "Southern belle," who "could probably be called boring by Hollywood standards." "Kristin Davis," *Transformation*, http://www.instyle.com/instyle/package/transformations/photos/0,20290121 _1167880_1024185,00.html (accessed April 23, 2010).

10. Natalie Finn, "Kristin Davis in Style Down South," June 2, 2008, http://www.eonline.com/uberblog/b1560_kristin_davis_in_style_down_south.html (accessed April 23, 2010).

11. Tara McPherson, *Reconstructing Dixie: Race, Gender and Nostalgia in the Imagined South* (Durham, N.C.: Duke University Press, 2003).

12. Robert Lang, ed., *The Birth of a Nation: D. W. Griffith, Director* (New Brunswick, N.J.: Rutgers University Press, 1994), 16.

13. Manthia Diawara, "Black American Cinema: The New Realism," in *Black American Cinema*, ed. Manthia Diawara (New York: Routledge, 1993), 3–25, quote on 3.

14. Ronald Haver, *David O. Selznick's Hollywood* (New York: Knopf, 1980), 243.

15. Cynthia George, "From Innocence to Grandeur: The Costumes of *Gone with the Wind*," *Library Chronicle of the University of Texas at Austin*, no. 36 (1986): 34, 45.

16. Alan David Vertrees, *Selznick's Vision: Gone with the Wind and Hollywood Filmmaking* (Austin: University of Texas Press, 1997), 185.

17. David Ebner and Larry Langman, *Hollywood's Image of the South: A Century of Southern Film* (Westport, Conn.: Greenwood, 2001), 2.

18. Hollywood's top leading men have often been paid millions per film, but these prerogatives have been extended to top female actors only in recent years.

19. Peter Decherney, *Hollywood and the Culture Elite: How the Movies Became American* (New York: Columbia University Press, 2005), 3.

20. The increasing popularity and cultural authority of the entertainment industry in the contemporary era is one context, of course, in which it is also important to understand the obsession among U.S. women, especially teenage girls, with achieving the beauty and body ideals associated with Hollywood's stars. In recent years, procedures such as breast implants and plastic surgery have skyrocketed, even among teens, along with eating disorders. In this culture, and as more and more information circulates, many people observe the red carpet and images on-screen and want what the stars have. The goal, for some at least, is to look like a star, and women tend to be inordinately impacted by media pressures to appear so. What we have witnessed within contemporary culture, really, is a reflection of the nationalization and, in some sense, the democratization of Hollywood in areas related to beauty, style, and femininity.

Notably, even in *Gone with the Wind*, Scarlett's obsession with remaining thin and keeping an eighteen-inch waistline, to the point of refusing food and, later, sex with her husband to avoid pregnancy, anticipates many of the eating problems that have been pervasive among women in the nation in more recent years. Later in the film, one of Scarlett's fears is that she will become as big as Aunt Pittypat. Rhett even warns her while they are honeymooning that she will become as "fat as Mammy." Indeed, Scarlett's vow in the climactic scene of the film that she will never go hungry again is a bitter and ironic contradiction of her food and weight panic that are evident in the film.

21. Joel Williamson, "How Black Was Rhett Butler?" in *The Evolution of Southern Culture*, ed. Numan Bartley (Athens: University of Georgia Press, 1988), 87–107.

22. Mitchell's Rhett Butler, interestingly enough, is dangerously dark, with a pirate's skin tone. It is in some ways provocative to link it to his social otherness,

given that he has been cast out by his wealthy Charleston family and "isn't received" in respectable homes because of his flouting of southern codes of masculine honor. This infamy only intensifies with his work as a blockade runner during the war. Diane Roberts, *The Myth of Aunt Jemima: Representations of Race and Region* (New York: Routledge, 1994). For discussion of questions related to race, see also Elizabeth Young, *Disarming the Nation: Women's Writing and the American Civil War* (Chicago: University of Chicago Press, 1999), 232–86, and Lauren S. Cardon, "'Good Breeding': Margaret Mitchell's Multi-ethnic South," *Southern Quarterly* 44, no. 4 (2007): 61–83.

23. Shelley Fisher Fishkin, *Was Huck Black? Mark Twain and African American Voices* (New York: Oxford University Press, 1993); Toni Morrison, *Playing in the Dark: Whiteness and the Literary Imagination* (Cambridge: Harvard University Press, 1992).

24. Alice Randall, *The Wind Done Gone* (Boston: Houghton Mifflin, 2001).

25. Ben Railton, "'What Else Could a Southern Gentleman Do?': Quentin Compson, Rhett Butler, and Miscegenation," *Southern Literary Journal* 35, no. 2 (2003): 41–63.

26. Donald Bogle, *Toms, Coons, Mulattoes, Mammies, and Bucks: An Interpretive History of Blacks in American Films* (New York: Continuum, 1991), 88.

27. Marian J. Morton, "'My Dear, I Don't Give a Damn': Scarlett O'Hara and the Great Depression," *Frontiers: A Journal of Women Studies* 5, no. 3 (1981): 53.

28. In *Scarlett*, a 1991 sequel to Mitchell's *Gone with the Wind*, Alexandra Ripley draws on these dimensions of Rhett as a character, whose second wife, after he and Scarlett divorce, is reminiscent of Melly. In the end, however, he and Scarlett reunite (New York: Warner Books).

29. Patricia Hill Collins, *Black Feminist Thought: Knowledge, Consciousness, and the Politics of Empowerment* (New York: Routledge, 1990).

30. Quoted in Jill Watts, *Hattie McDaniel: Black Ambition, White Hollywood* (New York: HarperCollins, 2005), 139.

31. Jill Watts, *Hattie McDaniel: Black Ambition, White Hollywood* (New York: HarperCollins, 2005), 131, 166. Victoria Sturtevant provides a compelling discussion of McDaniel's approach to her Hollywood roles in "'But Things Is Changin' Nowadays an' Mammy's Gettin' Bored': Hattie McDaniel and the Culture of Dissemblance," *Velvet Light Trap* 44 (Fall 1999): 68–80.

32. Trudier Harris, *From Mammies to Militants: Domestics in Black American Literature* (Philadelphia: Temple University Press) 1982.

33. Mitchell, *Gone with the Wind*, 143, 247, 157.

34. Randall, *Wind Done Gone*, 47, quote on 54.

Bodies and Expectations

Chain Gang Discipline

Leigh Anne Duck

In overviews of film history, *I Am a Fugitive from a Chain Gang* (1932) is known chiefly for its Depression-era success as a "social problem" film, popular with audiences and influential in penal reform. In its day, the film benefited from the charismatic lead performance of Paul Muni and a notoriously chilling conclusion: *Variety* warned, "It leaves the women limp."[1] It also received substantial publicity from the continuing legal travails of Robert E. Burns, the actual fugitive on whose autobiography the film was based. Thus, in its aesthetic appeal and topicality, director Mervyn LeRoy's work promoted Warner Brothers' reputation as a studio with a social conscience. Critics often note, however, that the film's claim to political progressivism is limited by its treatment of both region and race: its penal critique is directed toward a South that explicitly defies the larger nation, and while focusing on this regional carceral injustice, the film obscures the most fundamental feature of that subjugation. Concentrating on the abuses meted out on a white prisoner, *Fugitive* naturalizes those against African Americans, who were far more vulnerable to a government that accorded them neither political nor juridical representation. Indeed, within the film, African American prisoners seem to constitute a model of American unfreedom—residents to whom the nation's promise of mobility and fulfillment in labor do not apply.

But while identifying the chain gang as strictly southern and largely black, *Fugitive* also positions this institution amid a multitude of obstacles that impede the white northern protagonist's efforts to achieve normative masculine citizenship. Seeking individual opportunity and achievement in an economy that relies largely on monotonous work, the protagonist James Allen finds himself in a region that has historically resolved this tension between capitalist ideals and actualities by coercing labor from a designated category of persons—first through slavery and in subsequent decades through convict leasing and labor. Because James's experience suggests that the condition of unfreedom cannot be contained by the boundaries of race and region, the film's repeated insistence on the security of these categorical differences exposes both its desire to believe that northern white men should have limitless opportunities and its dismay over that disappointed dream.

This latter aspect of the film has received much less attention than its relatively conventional representations of race and region, issues that remain crucial to my argument. The United States' continuing carceral expansion has been facilitated by problems exemplified in *Fugitive*, specifically the tendencies to naturalize abusive practices in the case of certain categories of persons and to detach local penal practices from the nation-state that condones them. In the case of this film, however, these representational logics are complicated by a committed critique of a nation that, while promising opportunities for geographic and economic mobility, nonetheless seeks to keep all workers in their literal and metaphoric place. Rather than simply and sentimentally portraying the experiences of a white man who travels to a backward region where he is treated as a black man, the film goes so far as to suggest that containment and coercion—so brutally and overtly exercised against black southerners—may be, in other forms, axiomatic in U.S. society. Through both plot and metaphor, the film describes the chain gang as an intensification of the many social constraints—including class, business-oriented theology, and the heterosexual family—that isolate white men throughout the country, like southern black men, from the possibility of choice and satisfaction in their labor. In this way, the film questions the meaning of freedom in a carceral nation—one in which an array of institutions require and seek to inculcate docility and constancy.[2]

Thus, *Fugitive* remains instructive not only for its unproductive insistence on regional and racial difference but also for its more encompassing exploration of the relationship between freedom and enchainment. Ironically, the faults so widely noted in the film remain prominent in journalistic and liberal commentary on the chain gang. For example, when this penal institution was revived in the 1990s—briefly in the cases of Alabama and Florida and continuing in Maricopa County, Arizona—many national media observers treated these not as potential indicators of intensifying abuse in the nation's penal systems but as interesting or even amusing local solutions to crime, while critiques of these chain gangs focused on regional and racial aberration.[3] Meanwhile, in film, as in other discourses, the demonization of prisoners continues apace.[4] In contrast, *Fugitive*, while focusing on a white and relentlessly normative man, resists what Avery F. Gordon describes as the increasingly prevalent idea that convicts constitute "an inferior race in and of themselves" and instead links the chain gang to broader forms of "socioeconomic abandonment."[5]

"A living Hell": Chain as Aberration

In the continuing effort to understand whether and how popular film may be used to challenge rather than cement hegemonic ideologies, *Fugitive*, though influential and broadly viewed, serves in some ways more to caution than to inspire. Formalist approaches to film history and genre studies of prison films admire its "ineffable" and "revelatory" power.[6] But critics also suggest that by containing this problem within the U.S. South, *Fugitive* serves to stereotype the region in a manner comforting to residents elsewhere in the nation.[7] In the film, after all, nonsouthern voices and texts challenge the region's penal system: after the protagonist has escaped the chain gang and become a successful engineer in Chicago, *Fugitive* indicates the city's outrage at and Illinois officials' defiance of his potential extradition through a series of headlines and editorials. These protests are rebuffed by southern elites, who are represented through an editorial that demands "states' rights," reminding Depression-era audiences of the region's historical (and, as it would happen, future) willingness to defy the larger nation for the purposes of oppression. More problematically, the film's explicit reference to "medieval torture"—which is pictured in a newspaper editorial under a headline asking, "Is This Civilization?"—misleads as to the chain gang's relationship to modernity.

Though complaints of "backwardness" are often used to critique unjust or abusive institutions, the beneficent intent of such temporal arguments is impeded by their implication that "the modern" is, in contrast, just and humane. Familiar from accounts of convict leasing since the late nineteenth century, such claims of archaism obscured the fact that convict labor, whether applied to private or public projects, was vital to the region's efforts to modernize after emancipation.[8] In Georgia, for example, postbellum labor for mining minerals and tapping turpentine came from leased convicts; when this practice was abolished in 1908 due to complaints about brutality, corruption, and competition with free laborers, these convicts were chained and put to work on public roads and highways, a system vaunted for greater efficiency.[9] Far from an antimodern relic, the chain gang was developed, as Alex Lichtenstein explains, as a source of cheap labor for building "a transportation infrastructure which might contribute to the expansion of the manufacturing, consumer and commercial sectors" of the South's economy.[10]

Perceptions of the historical chain gang as anachronistic have persisted, however, in part because its modernizing strategies and effects appear incongruous with its accoutrements and practices. Literal shackling and torture—including solitary confinement (often in "sweat-boxes"), limited and unsanitary food (in one county, a diet of corn bread, water, and raw fish), flogging (sometimes to death), and hanging from stocks— practically compel such labels as primitive and barbaric.[11] Theoretical discussions of carceral modernity often rely heavily on Michel Foucault's *Discipline and Punish*, which provides an exacting critique of how such institutions as prisons, schools, and charitable institutions produce the conformity and passivity that prove useful to an industrial economy and a bureaucratic state. Observing Foucault's model of increasing rationality and decreasing public violence in state punishment, scholars often emphasize how the southern chain gang diverged from national models of penal development.[12] But as suggested even in the twenty-first century by the U.S. military's treatment of detainees at Abu Ghraib and Guantánamo Bay, as well as in continuing debates within branches of the U.S. government concerning the definitions and appropriateness of torture, what Foucault called "exorbitant . . . punishment" has hardly been expurgated from U.S. modernity.[13] Rather, it has been condoned through claims of "abnormalcy"—simultaneously "aberration[al]" (the province of a "few bad apples") and "necessary" when responding to "extraordinary" circumstances.[14]

In this sense, the development of the southern chain gang exemplified one aspect of modern statecraft, in which exceptions constitute an emblematic justification for practices that enable "the physical elimination not only of political adversaries but of entire categories of citizens who for some reason cannot be integrated into the political system"; such brutality can thus be simultaneously embraced and disavowed by national governments.[15] In the post–Civil War South, the very presence of large numbers of free black laborers was, from the perspective of previous economic and governmental systems, exceptional, but penal practices effectively returned many members of this new category of persons to their previous circumstances. As Alex Lichtenstein explains, "the ex-slaves who were emancipated from the dominion of the slaveholder" continued to provide "forced labor" to mines and factories through "the authority of the state"; many states even "enact[ed] a battery of new criminal laws designed to entrap the freedpeople."[16] Even decades after emancipation, chain gang labor on public roads was justified as a regional and racial exception. Citing the South's "radically different" "human material," staff for the U.S. Office of Public Roads opined in memos that "the negro is accustomed to outdoor occupations[,] . . . experienced in manual labor," and "compelled by the chain-gang to live a regular and healthful life."[17] Such arguments not only demarcated African Americans as a distinct category of human beings, particularly conditioned to outdoor labor and enchainment, but also, ironically, institutionalized the belief that torture was crucial for disciplining and extracting labor from them.[18] Here again, as in more recent instances of penal violence, the viciousness of state practice was typically attributed to the deficiencies of individuals employed as guards, who were deemed "usually ignorant, often of low mentality and low moral standards."[19] But such arguments obscured the fact that flogging and other forms of abuse were prescribed for infractions and also that any racist or other violent predilections that penal employees brought to their jobs could only be exacerbated by the fact that they were hired by the state to punish bodies distinguished from their own not only often by color but also uniformly by chains.

Some contemporary accounts of the chain gang—responding, understandably, to the bifurcated spaces and justice systems of the segregated South—collapse that latter distinction between prisoner and guard into a racial distinction between black and white, but such descriptions elide the way in which the chains and stripes worn by convict laborers demarcated their bodies for particular forms of exceptional control.[20] While, in its earliest manifestation, the chain gang subjugated chiefly African Americans, it expanded to include numerous whites as well. In 1908, for example, 90 percent of Georgia's convict laborers were black, but twenty years later, 27 percent were white, such that the chain gang constituted one of the South's few integrated institutions.[21] Racial inequities continued: most of these laborers were convicted only of "petty crimes such as gambling, carrying a concealed weapon, drunkenness, fighting, disorderly conduct, loitering and vagrancy," many of which depended heavily on the definitions of a segregated justice system, and disfranchised African Americans had no juridical recourse when unjustly charged.[22] Guards subjected black prisoners to a greater frequency and intensity of physical violence, and yet the deaths of white prisoners occasioned far greater public protest.[23] Nonetheless, the chain gang presented the public with the image of a contained, multiracial "criminal class" or, for more discerning observers, a sense of how criminal law might function to disfranchise and dehumanize the poor.[24]

To read the chain gang in this way is to observe its role amid an array of penal practices that not only rely on but also produce distinct forms of "othering, denigration, stigmatization and vulnerability," and *Fugitive* gestures toward this problem with rather inchoate anxiety.[25] On the one hand, the danger of losing all civic recognition constitutes a source of unquestionable tragedy, as the conscientious James Allen, rendered jobless by a shrinking economy, is wrongly convicted; unable to overcome his legal status as prisoner even after two escapes and a successful career (under the pseudonym Allen James), he becomes a kind of anticitizen, spectral and isolated. But this inexorable decline aligns James's final position with that of black southerners more generally, a similarity intimated (though perhaps inadvertently) in the film's final shot, as James's image vanishes into literal blackness. Overtly suggesting a shadowy realm in which not-quite citizens are forced to reside without political and economic rights—a form of existence paradoxically produced by and antithetical to U.S. statehood—the film nonetheless refrains from criticizing Jim Crow injustice in any way. Instead, while protesting the dreadful fate of its protagonist, *Fugitive* represents the chain gang's black convicts—though no less burdened or abused than James—as relatively well adjusted to their circumstances.[26]

Lichtenstein rightly links this naturalization of black enchainment to the film's focus on one normative individual's spectacular story.[27] Far from revealing the extraordinary intensity with which African Americans were convicted and abused by this system and seemingly hesitant even to acknowledge that—though to differing degrees—this injustice confronted both blacks and whites, the film focuses strictly on the wrongness of its protagonist's conviction, providing no backstory for any other prisoners. (James Allen is tricked by a new acquaintance into participating in a holdup during which the chief perpetrator and victim are apparently killed, leaving no one to corroborate James's story.) This focus on a single juridical failure exemplifies the film's individualism. Burns's autobiography was, after all, initially serialized in *True Detective Stories* and repeatedly proclaims his "honesty, adherence to ideals . . . courage and real worth of character."[28] But Burns's work at least observes the abuses to which other prisoners have been subjected, and though he uses racial stereotypes, he protests against the torture inflicted on black convicts. One, for instance, is consigned to forty years of chain gang labor, and his term is unabated even after his first winter results in frostbite so severe that all his toes must be amputated.[29] In contrast, as the film streamlines and alters Burns's narrative, it fails to individuate black prisoners.

Instead, most of the African American figures in the film serve merely to illustrate the conditions of chain gang life, providing visual or aural details to establish the setting. For example, when James submits himself to southern authorities near the close of the film, he is sent to the "last word" in chain gangs—reserved for convicts deemed uncontrollable in other units—and the image of a chalkboard tally notes that roughly one-third of these convicts are white. Nonetheless, their pickax swings are synchronized to an African American work song, notably absent from James's previous, less "tough" camp. Subsequent images represent a racially integrated workforce, but the sound track insists that, though they are overseen by white men with guns, the rhythm and arguably the nature of the convicts' labor is established by a black baritone.

The one African American character who is individuated within the film serves more to underscore than to disrupt the way in which the film naturalizes black enchainment: he is presented as the iconic chain gang worker. Tall and consistently shirtless so that audiences can see how well his body accommodates the severe heat, strenuous work, and menu of "slime" bemoaned by white prisoners, Sebastian is singled out by another white prisoner who seeks to explain the chain gang's function during James's first day. Using racist language, Bomber nonetheless elucidates the combined function of the chain gang and the segregated justice system: "Look at that big buck handle a sledge. He never misses. . . . You could lay down a nickel and he'd knock the buffalo's right eye out. They like his work so much they're going to keep him here the rest of his life." But in its visual suggestion that Sebastian thrives under this exploitation, *Fugitive* confirms the judgment of the bureaucrats and apologists who argued that outdoor chained labor suited black prisoners.[30] The character's words are also enlisted to this purpose: when James asks Sebastian to bend his shackles with the sledgehammer, the latter helpfully responds, "I'd certainly like to see you get away from this misery." (The film omits the "boss" and "suh" attributed to Sebastian in the screenplay.)[31]

Indeed, the film suggests that, for James, part of the horror of imprisonment on the chain gang is that it disrupts the racial boundaries that had previously secured for him a more privileged form of citizenship. Hardly a modernist exploration of fragmented or shifting consciousness, LeRoy's visual narrative diverges from conventional realism only to clarify his linear biography—using superimposition, for example, when he must condense periods and movements in James's life. But this visual logic switches from chronological development to juxtaposition precisely at the moment when James, in his first morning on the gang, moves from segregated living quarters to the relatively integrated yard. These shots initially produce an equivalence that dehumanizes black and white: chains are applied, in a series of shots, to the white prisoners on James's truck, the mules who accompany the trucks, and the black prisoners on another truck. The concluding shot in this series returns to James's anxiously shifting gaze, but the following and more chaotic series of faces renders this equivalence more destabilizing: James looks around, but no one looks back, and the camera wanders extensively before returning to James's face. Two of the characters pictured, Bomber and Red, have already appeared in the narrative, encouraging viewers to wonder whether other prisoners featured here will also reemerge (they do not); further, in this series of black and white faces, none look at the camera, and each seems rather to contemplate his own misery in a kind of mental isolation. At this point in the narrative, it appears, James recognizes himself as one in a chained mass of laborers who lack any relationship with the world outside the gang. That point is reiterated in the following shot of the quarry, as the workers, on a guarded break, constitute a barely distinguishable set of tired bodies—all wearing stripes—in a barren landscape.

In terms of the film's social critique, these shots produce contradictory effects. On the one hand, in suggesting James's anxiety at his loss of social status, the film implicitly acknowledges the relative privilege he has previously been granted as a white man, and it has become customary in scholarly commentary to describe such awareness as progressive.[32] On the other hand, James responds to these events not by wanting to learn more about how such systems of social hierarchy function to oppress others but by wanting his privilege back. Rather as the film exploits images of African Americans to indicate the particular depths of James's suffering, the character himself exploits African Americans to achieve his freedom. (Although Sebastian agrees to help James, the screenplay specifies that his first act after his escape is to steal regular clothing from a "Negro shack."[33] Because the dwelling is uninhabited at that moment, however, viewers would know nothing about its owners' racial identification.) Thus, the film does not manifest antiracist consciousness, but it powerfully registers anxiety that white men may be subjected to the same kinds of vulnerability and even noncitizenship that it naturalizes for black men.

Situated within the broader narrative of the film, in fact, the horror of James's enchainment emerges not only from its seeming abnormality but also from its confirmation of his fear that he will always be consigned to banal and compulsory labor for the benefit of others. Critics have rightly noted that this focus on James's goal of individual success precludes attention to the systematic injustice of the actual chain gang.[34] But it is precisely through this bourgeois narrative, with its shocking subversion of a Horatio Alger–style plotline, that the film manages to suggest some nonaberrational relationship between the southern chain gang and the U.S. polity and can thus be seen, as Mike Nellis notes, as "a far more radical film than almost any of its makers intended."[35] In this respect, James's moment of social vertigo on the truck exemplifies the film's central, and most embedded, argument: perhaps perversely analogizing the misery of the chain gang to the deep disappointment of everyday life, the film depicts the latter as so constraining that the vulnerability of southern African Americans to coerced labor seems less a regional and racial exception than a particularly brutal exemplar of the national norm.

"You're trying to harness me": Chain as Axiom

Comparisons of free but largely unrewarding labor to unfree chained labor are often clichéd in contemporary parlance, and they also run the danger of making "real-world prisoners or prison conditions seem to fade into insignificance."[36] But *Fugitive*'s vigorous insistence on the brutality of the actual chain gang effectively obviates such possibilities here: historically, in fact, press materials and reviews tended to focus on the film's documentary and propagandistic importance, and this publicity contributed to the movement for a state investigation and eventual change in Georgia's prison system.[37] *Fugitive* is unstinting in its depiction of violence against both black and white prisoners: guards punch them in the face and beat them with even greater vigor when they are ill, and convicts are shown stumbling and bleeding after being flogged. Though these beatings are not depicted directly, the shadow of the moving whip and the frozen expressions of observing convicts are justly famous for their unnerving effect.

But the film devotes even more screen time to the routines of chain gang life—the hour when the trucks arrive to collect and deliver the workers, the monotony of the diet, the repetitiveness of the work itself, the incessant inspection by guards, and the endlessly reiterated deprivation of agency, as prisoners are unable even to wipe away sweat without permission, let alone move their legs freely. These aspects of chain gang labor are emphasized further through juxtaposition with the opening scenes of the film, in which James vehemently declares his desire to exercise greater freedom and ingenuity in his work. In this way, despite its emphasis on the cruelty specific to the chain gang, the film links the bodily immobility imposed by the southern penal system to the class immobility imposed by the national economy.[38]

This surprising linkage suggests the film's critique of the carceral discipline that suffuses national society; indeed, James's resentment toward the control exercised by the chain gang differs only in intensity from his feeling toward any obstacles to his goal of creative and self-directed work. Returning from World War I with new skills and expectations, James seeks from the film's opening to escape his previous life of factory labor, which he describes as "a drab routine—cramped, mechanical, even worse than the army." His concern revolves less around class identification or even type of labor—he moves, after all, from an office position to manual labor on construction sites and eventually to more creative office work—than his sense of entrapment and alienation; he wants a greater sense of control over the circumstances and goals of his labor.

Carefully constructed as industrious and conscientious, this protagonist differs significantly from that of the film's source material, *I Am a Fugitive from a Georgia Chain Gang!* In his autobiography, the historical fugitive, Robert E. Burns, is unable to remain in one vocation before the war and is also more cynical than his fictional counterpart. Troubled by posttraumatic stress when he returns from World War I, Burns immediately comprehends that his options would be limited anyway, explaining, "An ex-soldier with the A.E.F. service was looked upon as a sucker.

The wise guys stayed home—landed the good jobs—or grew rich on war contracts."[39] The film's protagonist, in contrast, is presented as a previously loyal son and worker who now seeks individual advancement. His face alight with visible idealism, he claims that "being in the Engineering Corps has been swell experience" to prepare him for construction work and wants his family to understand that his experiences in the armed forces have granted him new ambition.

In a trope familiar from a variety of post–World War I narratives, the film attributes this change not only to James's experience of soldiering but also to that of contemplating broader possibilities. Now, he is committed to the project of mobility—both literal (as suggested by his desire to work on bridges) and metaphorical (his desire for economic advancement).[40] In a sense, this change is analogized to shell shock. When he first tells his family that he wants to find a new job, his brother sanctimoniously intones, "He's tired, mother—excited," and later, when James arrives back at the factory, he ducks when he hears an explosion. Nonetheless, he is immediately excited to learn that these sounds come from a nearby construction site; ultimately, he is less an anxious or alienated veteran than a desiring one. Told that soon "you'll be doing [your job] again with your eyes shut," he instead shuffles papers while gazing at the bridge being built outside his window, the bars of which serve to accentuate his sense of entrapment.[41]

While arguing that this transformation renders James incomprehensible to his preexisting social network, *Fugitive* nonetheless features explicitly national contexts in which his ambition is viewed as a valuable trait. He is first seen on a ship full of returning veterans as he comes below deck in his uniform to interrupt his unit's craps game. Presented in the center of the screen, awash in light, he smiles down on the men whose pleasure he is disrupting, and the ensuing dialogue reveals that they admire his aspiration and sense of purpose. As others lounge awaiting "bunk inspection," wondering—and also worrying—about the next stage of their lives (one vaudevillian plans to return to his "lion-taming act"), James sits on the stairs expressing confidence that he will not go "back to the old grind of a factory." His motivation is renewed after he first escapes from the chain gang. Where Burns, at this moment in his narrative, initially develops capital through collaborating with a woman in an overtly (albeit mutually) exploitative relationship, James's eventual success is attributed to more individual and principled efforts: the film pictures him studying as he becomes successful in his long-cherished profession. His conformation to national ideals is corroborated when the Chicago Chamber of Commerce supports his bid for clemency by proclaiming him a "reputable engineer of this city, veteran of the World War, and citizen of the United States of America."

In his quest for professional success, this character resonates with concerns about national masculinity—both in contrast to femininity and in possible transition in terms of its racial and ethnic implications—pertinent to both the period of its early setting and that of its release. The decades before World War I had featured apprehension over men's declining opportunities for economic advancement, the increased number of women in the workforce, the concomitant blurring of gender roles (often expressed as concerns about the feminization of men's bodies or personalities), the relative decline in white men's agrarian pursuits (not only in terms of work but also in terms of leisure—the hunting and exploration that had provided earlier models of frontier masculinity), and the emergence of immigrant men and labor unions as potent economic forces; it also revealed contradictory and vehement opinions concerning whether black men and stereotypical black manhood constituted antitheses to, models for, or competitors with white men and stereotypical white manhood.[42] During the war itself, the meanings of masculinity and male citizenship were complicated further by anxieties over "shell shock"—a newly coined term often understood as male "hysteria," or simply "men who acted like women"—and by the increased activism of African Americans, who briefly had new leverage in their efforts to procure full rights from the U.S. government, as their labor was needed both in the armed forces and in domestic war industries.[43] By the early years of the Depression, when *Fugitive* was produced, economic anxieties were profound and often psychologically devastating for men who had defined themselves through ideas of work and economic prowess; Christina S. Jarvis notes that oral histories, letters, and even suicide notes indicate that "the impulse to equate manhood with successful breadwinning remained strong throughout the 1930s."[44]

Fugitive's protagonist is situated among these tensions in ways that seem designed to grant him broad "manly" appeal. He is simultaneously middle-class, as indicated by the spaciousness and furnishings of his family home, and working-class, as suggested by his previous position and the tendency of others to dismiss his chances for advancement. He is both physically vigorous, as evidenced by his World War I medal and his early construction work, and mentally astute, in that he becomes a successful civil engineer. Despite the character's apparent whiteness, the film uses subtle, extratextual cues that might link him with immigrant and black men. On the one hand, Muni famously began his career in New York's Yiddish theater, and on the other, James's argument that the war has "changed him" and led him to demand greater opportunity aligns with arguments made by African Americans who participated in World War I—a resonance augmented by the film's insistence that the larger society abandoned its veterans, which was certainly the government's response to black soldiers after the war.[45] (When James becomes desperate for money, he seeks to pawn his medal and is told that it is worthless; the pawnshop owner then reveals a large box of similar medals.) Perhaps particularly important for Depression-era viewers, James exhibits humor amid hardship. When he does leave the factory to seek a new career, he discovers that very few jobs are available, and he is always, as the newest hire, the first to be laid off. When he finally becomes a hobo, he explains, "I took to walking the ties when my Rolls-Royce broke down."

Establishing James's identification with multiple models of masculinity, the film never lets viewers forget that he is struggling to assert that manhood against the constraining institutions of the heterosexual family and the hypocritical church and state, each of which wants male workers to stay where they are. This objective is, of course, obvious on the part of the southern penal system, and in emphasizing the state's desire to retain workers, the film again aligns itself with African American critiques: the *Chicago Defender* charged that arrest and enchainment were southern strategies for maintaining a labor force during the Great Migration.[46] But James's brother, a minister, also seeks to discipline James's lack of enthusiasm for his factory job. After hearing that James has been late returning from lunch, Clint accuses his younger brother of "loitering," a charge for which black southerners could notoriously be placed into forced labor. James explains that he cannot bring himself to devote energy and attention to a position he finds confining, but his brother argues that he should forego his goals and desires to fulfill his "duty toward [his] job." Controlling as this figure appears in the film, he was, in a previous treatment for the screenplay, depicted as a kind of corporate lackey, preaching to his congregation, "Our work may seem dull . . . but we must . . . obey our orders—respect our business generals—each a cog in a cosmic platoon that ever advances forward in the name of civilization and progress."[47] Though these more explicit critiques of capitalism are generally omitted from the eventual film, their echoes remain in James's sense that his desire to exercise greater creativity is simultaneously upheld as a norm and denied as an opportunity.

James responds to his brother's speeches as if they themselves constituted a kind of metaphoric chain: "You're trying to harness me and lead me around to do what *you* think is best for *me*!" This comparison, if strained, nonetheless reveals how *Fugitive*'s chain gang functions as both a literal, spatially limited, and appalling institution and a metaphoric, broad, and looming threat to individual—and especially masculine—independence. The film does not address the circumstances of women on chain gangs, though they were presumably subjected to a similar degree of control; rather, *Fugitive* is particularly concerned with the problem of male citizenship and agency, figuring women as foils in that difficult project.[48] Thus, when James's family argues that his plans are unsuitable, their rejection constitutes not merely a lack of support but, more deeply, a lack of esteem; James is disturbed to learn that they might not think him worthy of a "man's job." Notably, and in keeping with Depression-era anxieties about how the demands of women unsatisfied with their husbands' earnings might affect gender roles, James is most deeply concerned over his mother, who has no husband (no details are provided) and has faithfully awaited her son's return.[49] She initially pleads for him to sacrifice his individual desires to stay close to home (and, one gathers, to continue to support the household). When James tells her he wants not "to be cooped up" and rather "to do something worthwhile," she responds by saying, "Why, Jim, how can you talk like that?" It is only after she acknowledges the depth of his desire and encourages him to "find himself"—explore a more individualistic and less filial and traditional model of manhood—that he departs for his ill-fated search.

But James leaves home only to discover that his domineering brother was right to suggest that "a job in the hand's worth two in the bush": the national economy has no place for his expanded goals and talents. After traveling northeast and southeast, as well as through the Midwest, he is imprisoned on the chain gang "for looking at a hamburger," as he wryly complains, and is visibly appalled when other convicts, one of whom has killed his wife and female in-laws, assure him that he is "among friends." This moment, as he is imprisoned with a misogynist murderer, would seem to constitute a sufficiently ironic close to his earlier desire "to start a new life . . . to be free." Neither mobile nor successful, he has joined a group of men who appear—at least from one example—to have flaunted society's norms in particularly ignoble ways.

And yet this theme of "friendship" is subject to yet another ironic reversal, as prisoners do seem to feel a degree of solidarity. James finds his gangmates' advice vital to his survival and eventual escape, after which he is initially and generously aided by Barney, who has previously been released from the gang.[50] More even than in the countercultural *Cool Hand Luke* (1967) (billed as "The man—the motion picture—that simply will not conform"), the ultimate cause for alarm here is plainly the penal system itself. The later picture features convicts who refer to entering prisoners as "new meat"; though they can be friendly and supportive toward each other, they are also deceptive, exploitative, and violent. Such characterizations are stock for contemporary prison films, which overwhelmingly depict other prisoners as the institution's chief source of violence and fear, and occasionally suggest that the very experience of prison serves to render an individual incapable of functioning in ways that are not criminal or even brutal.[51] But while *Fugitive*'s chain gang does not prevent recidivism—Barney returns to running a brothel—neither does it render convicts vicious.[52] Rather, they are excluded from and eventually return to a society that, despite its purported valuation of male professional creativity and supportive female heterosexuality, allows for full expression of neither, such that Barney's labor is both criminal and aligned with the revered institution of marriage.

For just as the chain provides a metaphor for the professional obstacles James faces in the free world, it is also compared to coercive heterosexual relations. The prostitute instructed by Barney to "take good care of" James admires his escape from the chain gang; in the screenplay, she expresses her "envy" of someone resourceful enough "to get away from a spot you hate . . . and forget it . . . and start all over again!"[53] In this scene, as with convicts on the gang, Linda's assertion that James is "among friends" seems to indicate less his immersion in a criminal class than his association with those deeply familiar with the frustration of imposed restraint; she and James kiss (and, implicitly, have sex) only after he has refused the sex promised by Barney, thus guaranteeing that Linda is offering on her own behalf. Later, James is coerced into marriage by Marie, who learns that he is a fugitive by intercepting his mail and then threatens to report him. When she refuses to divorce him, he argues that finishing his sentence on the chain gang would be "no worse than serving out" his time with her. Recognizing his potential "to be a big shot someday, with plenty of sugar," she argues, "I'd be a sucker to let you go now." The plot device of blackmail serves not only to set James up for a return to the chain gang but also to include marriage among a list of constraints—particularly the expectations allotted by natal family, church, community, and class—that prevent a man from working for his own satisfaction.

Interestingly, though the film imagines no vocation for women other than the gratification of men, it nonetheless insists—within these highly patriarchal limits—that women, too, should be able to enjoy their work. In this regard, an early screenplay pushed the metaphor of chained labor to a remarkable degree, as James's main love interest, Helen, is depicted as a chorus girl performing in "a kinky chain-gang number with silver chains and a skimpy costume." Following producer Darryl Zanuck's note that this relationship should be "kept on a high plane," the film removes any information regarding her financial resources (which appear, given her clothing, to be ample).[54] But while this character is no longer literally paid to entertain anonymous men, the film includes a conversation describing heterosexual interaction as her career, which she now undertakes voluntarily:

HELEN: You're a strange, moody person. You need someone to pull you out
   of those doldrums.
JAMES: Are you applying for that job?
HELEN: I might consider it.
JAMES: You're hired.
HELEN: When do I start?

Helen has just pronounced her ability to make such choices—"There are
no musts in my life. I'm free, white, and 21"—but James wryly notes
that she is "lucky" to have such independence, as his other relationships
are marked by the presence of metaphorical chains.

In so vigorously emphasizing James's normative goals of professional
success and a companionate heterosexual relationship, the film manages
to link its critique of the chain gang to a more sweeping indictment of the
nation's social structure. Clearly, Georgia's carceral policies, rather than
punishing crime, initiate it by precluding James from earning a living.
A year after his second escape, he briefly appears to Helen, explaining
that he lives on the run, unable to keep a job for fear of being revealed:
"I hide in rooms all day and travel by night . . . no rest, no friends, no
peace! . . . I steal!" But though the forces that have led to this travesty
are, in important and obvious ways, regional, the film continues, even
at this bleak conclusion, to link James's plight to the challenges facing
the nation's men more broadly. The final headline in the film, featured
immediately before the dialogue between Helen and James, ties his mis-
fortune to a familiar trope of Depression-era masculinity: "What has become of James Allen?—Is he, too, just another forgotten man?"

Through this reference, the film notes how individual workers can
become the "remainders of a social system," a phrase used by Lindsay
Holmgren to describe the convicts on the chain gang in Carson McCullers's 1951 novella "Ballad of the Sad Café." As Holmgren argues, these
chained laborers represent particularly stark exemplars of an experience
shared by other of McCullers's regional characters, who are denied any
agency in the nation's economy.[55] Though the chain gang serves, in Mc-
Cullers's narrative, as a kind of aesthetic counterpoint to relieve the frus-
trations of excruciatingly bored locals ("you might as well walk down to
the Forks Falls Road and listen to the chain gang"), this very proposition
implicitly links seemingly divergent forms of constraint: the limited mobility of free bodies exhausted from grueling and poorly paid mill work
or tenant farming and the utter immobility of the chained.[56] The concept of "remainder" nicely articulates how the chain gang can readily
be described as either aberrant (not fitting into economic equations) or
axiomatic (the inevitable extremity resulting from typical socioeconomic

processes). This concept also suggests a paradoxical continuity between the social context of LeRoy's film—which recoils at the alleged backwardness it records—and our own era. For while today's convicts are rarely used to build public infrastructure and are only contracted for corporate labor on a limited scale, Ruth Wilson Gilmore argues that California's incarceration boom, for example, has been driven in part by the effort to contain the "relative surplus population" that cannot be employed by a fluctuating economy.[57]

Fugitive at Large

Analysis of "prison films" has become a vigorously interdisciplinary activity, the work not only of film scholars but also of activists and criminologists who seek to understand the expanding role of the penal system in contemporary society.[58] Accordingly, to examine Fugitive today is to engage a new field of penal discourses, influenced by the sheer rate of imprisonment in the contemporary United States—now more than 1 percent of adult residents, with significantly higher percentages for racial minorities—as well as the resurgence of the chain gang.[59] This historical convergence underscores the need to analyze the chain gang not simply as an anachronistic regional anomaly but rather as a penal practice significant within the history of the world's most vigorously incarcerating nation.[60]

Like other carceral institutions, after all, historical and contemporary chain gangs elicit and enact judgments concerning the meaning of excessive violence, the standards of appropriate discipline, and whether or how these definitions might be applied differently across various imprisoned populations. These groups may, for example, be delineated by conviction (felon, misdemeanant), perceived manageability (minimum to maximum security facilities), alleged associations (gangs, syndicates, terrorist groups), gender, age, and—implicitly or explicitly—race.[61] Certainly, the chain gang is distinct in many ways; unlike the contemporary "supermax" prison, for example, it does not "disappear" prisoners' bodies.[62] On the contrary, chained convicts, with their "armed guards and prisoners in stripes," were "a familiar sight on the highways of the majority of the Southern states" in the early twentieth century, and in present-day Arizona, convicts are conspicuous in pink shirts and signs.[63] But despite the invisibility imposed by one institution and the intentionally humiliating visibility imposed by the other, each seeks to function as an instrument of "absolute social exclusion," isolating convicts from others and, by strict control of their movements, precluding their opportunity to act as "rational, self-regulating human being[s]." And just as the "character" of long-term control unit prisoners is viewed "as a perfect fit with—and perfect reason for—the environment in which they are held," as Lorna A. Rhodes explains, contemporary convicts on the chain gang are described, from the perspective of at least some workers in the corrections industry, as "scum."[64]

In this context *Fugitive*'s critique may be more relevant than ever. Prison films have tended, since the beginning of the twentieth century, to depict convicts as "dehumanized other[s] . . . deserving of harsh treatment."[65] *Fugitive*—which inadvertently initiated Hollywood's fascination with the experiences of white men on chain gangs—effaces this seeming "species boundary" by attributing its protagonist's enchainment to the disconnect between the purportedly national ideals of individualistic opportunity and achievement and a social structure that offers few opportunities to fulfill such goals.[66] Of course, some of its followers, particularly *Sullivan's Travels* (1942) and *Oh Brother, Where Art Thou?* (2000), treat the chain gang chiefly as a source of aesthetic inspiration, and others—from *The Defiant Ones* (1958) to *Black Mama, White Mama* (1973)—explore the chain gang as a site of forced interracial interaction. But *Cool Hand Luke* (1967) and *Take the Money and Run* (1969)— each, ironically, from the decade when the chain gang was eradicated nationwide—implicitly return to the question of what kind of white man becomes enchained and in doing so diverge notably from *Fugitive*'s characterization of its protagonist.[67] Where James Allen is, in some critics' assessment, almost annoyingly normative, later convicts seem driven to defy laws and norms.[68]

Though such films could be seen to mock the very idea of crime—from the eponymous "Cool Hand" Luke's decapitation of parking meters to the charges of "assault, armed robbery, and illegal possession of a wart" against Woody Allen's character in *Take the Money*—they simultaneously naturalize the idea of persons essentially unable to cope with authority. This pattern holds even for seemingly subversive moments. When the "captain" in *Cool Hand Luke*, for example, proclaims, "What we've got here is a failure to communicate," he simultaneously appalls—in that beating hardly qualifies as an effort to communicate thoughtfully—and articulates an inevitability, for Luke himself proclaims his deep-seated inability to comprehend messages in which he is not interested. When the narrator of *Take the Money* intones that "the jungle . . . is no place for a cellist," he simultaneously mocks and affirms the idea that, in his words, "the violence and poverty of the slums" yield habitual criminals.

Used to generate pathos in *Cool Hand Luke* and laughs in Allen's madcap comedy, this belief in characterological criminality has been associated, in recent years, with the zeal for retributive sentencing to which the chain gang's resurgence is often attributed.[69] Such fervor for punishment is expressed, for example, in political races at state, local, and even presidential levels, as evidenced in 1988 by George W. Bush's attacks against Massachusetts governor Michael Dukakis over the crimes of furloughed black prisoner Willie Horton, and in 1992 by Gov. Bill Clinton's return to Arkansas to affirm the execution of brain-damaged black prisoner Rickie Ray Rector. Such eagerness to kill, humiliate, and pain prisoners is not always expressed in racial terms but is familiar from more unambivalently racist periods in U.S. history. Accordingly, the *Harvard Law Review* argues that legislation for the Florida chain gang "either ignores the racially divisive nature of this symbol or, more insidiously, attempts to take advantage of it by subtly scapegoating one segment of society."[70]

Notably, however, critiques of the chain gang that focus on race often repeat one of *Fugitive*'s main conceptual errors: that is, the tendency to treat the chain gang chiefly as an anachronism. For example, Douglas A. Blackmon's popular *Slavery by Another Name* (2008) dismisses the 27 percent of chained white convicts who served as "forced labor slaves" in Georgia during the early 1930s as "peripheral and inconsequential"— a statistical interpretation driven by his effort to describe the chain gang as a second period of slavery. Though such a reading, in accord with Blackmon's stated goal, usefully disrupts the nation's "mythology" surrounding Emancipation in 1865, it asserts that the "Age of Neoslavery" ended in 1945 and thus dismisses "the fissures that still thread our society"—which might be attributed to continuing political and economic injustice—as "ephemera" from this earlier era.[71] Such refusal to acknowledge the present-day temporal coordinates of penal abuse creates perhaps even more significant distortions in critiques focused on the contemporary chain gang. Tessa M. Gorman, for example, argues that chained labor is "cruel and unusual" specifically because it "invokes an historical association with slavery" and that "chain gangs are particularly repugnant in Alabama, a state infamous for its history of civil rights atrocities."[72] This analytic framework explicitly disregards the abuses inflicted on Arizona convicts or on convicts of other races anywhere in the United States. Perhaps most importantly, such an approach neglects to develop or affirm any synchronic framework through which to proclaim chain gangs "cruel and unusual."

Meanwhile, governmental sponsors of chain gangs appear to be attuned to and prepared for racial critiques, as they carefully demonstrate their willingness to punish white people similarly. When Alabama reinstituted the chain gang in 1994, for example, it required that participants' racial demographics correspond to those of the state's broader prison population, which was roughly 60–70 percent black and 30–40 percent white.[73] Thus, though both the physical and rhetorical practices of the chain gang suggest racism and are directed with vast disproportionality against black people, they explicitly target a group not identified as racial: "the criminal." And public support for these policies seems, at least to some extent, to reflect such understandings.[74] This form of demarcation might underpin, for example, the attitudes of the 43 percent of Alabama's African American residents who expressed approval for the chain gang.[75]

Such concepts of recalcitrant criminality are abundantly visible in Xackery Irving's documentary *American Chain Gang* (1999), which focuses on the late twentieth-century revival of chain gangs in Alabama and the women's chain gang in Arizona. Here, the racial tensions that undoubtedly shaped the sentencing of black and white men in Alabama are also conspicuous among chained convicts, but guards describe inmates as a group defined by their legal status. Warming to his subject, one white guard explains that convicts are people "who can't cope with society . . . the worst scum God ever allowed to walk this green earth," a dehumanizing contempt that may well constitute what Angela Y. Davis calls "camouflaged racism" but nonetheless extends to dismiss all inmates as "sorry individuals."[76] Notably, after listing various crimes for which convicts have been sentenced, the guard pauses and adds, "Child rapists—we've got 'em all in here," as if eager to support his previous claim of "scum." This moment corroborates Adolph Reed's claim that the categories "habitual criminal" and "sexual predator" have become forms of "ascriptive differentiation" or "consensually commonsensical Other[s]."[77]

As the guards and even prisoners featured in Irving's documentary describe the purported crisis of ingrained criminality said to justify the return of the chain gang (titled in Alabama "The Alternative Thinking Unit"), they blame inmates' "mamas," the "rush" of "breaking the law," and the failure of inmates to "learn" how to stay out of prison. Only one convict asks, "How can you learn something when the system is designed for you to come back?" His question correctly refers to not only what Davis describes as "the skyrocketing punishment industry" and "racist arrest and incarceration practices," but also a more mundane feature of each: the explicit demand for sentences to intensify with subsequent arrests, which brand ex-convicts as recidivist criminals, such that any injustice inflicted on the prisoner in an earlier encounter with the criminal justice system is viewed, instead, as the sign of a flaw within the prisoner.[78]

Ironically, it is this largely individualistic approach to criminality—which seeks to diagnose and contain the aberrance within the prisoner—that the individualistic narrative of *Fugitive* avoids, precisely by observing various forms of containment at work outside the penal system. (To be clear, the film does not diverge from the continuing and self-fulfilling tendency to associate incarceration with blackness but rather disrupts associations between incarceration and criminal character.) More metaphoric than analytic and more impressionistic than structural, *Fugitive*'s critique of the southern penal system is nonetheless linked to a critique of the nation's capitalism, a form of analysis that has since practically abated in all discourse except that produced by movements to reform or abolish U.S. prisons.[79] Through this argument, the film suggests some unwelcome fungibility (as the exchange takes place against the wishes of the party whose conditions are being traded) between the gloom and confusion of free citizens, who are encouraged to seek what they are unlikely to achieve, and the disfranchisement and stasis of the unfree. Rather than depicting carceral abuses as deprivations of freedom and humane treatment necessary for securing nonconvicts' safety, *Fugitive* presents the chain gang as an extreme form of a shared constraint. Reflecting on the fate of his own early dreams to "build bridges and roads for people to use when they want to get away from things"—a goal he later thwarts when his second escape requires him to destroy a bridge between himself and the chain gang guards—James concludes that failure is inevitable: "But they can't get away; nobody can."

NOTES

I thank Lindsay Holmgren and Kathy Lou Schultz for their comments on an earlier version of this essay; I am also grateful to Holmgren and Adolph Reed Jr. for sharing their manuscripts, which were unpublished at the time of writing.

1. Abel Green, review of *I Am a Fugitive from a Chain Gang*, *Variety*, November 15, 1932, rpt. in *Variety Film Reviews*, vol. 4 (New York: Garland, 1983), n.p. For examples of film overviews, see Joan Cohen, *I Am a Fugitive from a Chain Gang*, in Frank N. Magill, ed., *Magill's Survey of Cinema: English Language Films*, 1st ser. (Englewood Cliffs, N.J.: Salem, 1980), 2:803–5; Daniel Leab, *I Am a Fugitive from a Chain Gang*, in *International Dictionary of Films and Filmmakers*, vol. 1., ed. Christopher Lyon (Chicago: St. James, 1984), 404–5.

2. Michel Foucault, *Discipline and Punish: The Birth of the Prison*, trans. Alan Sheridan (1977; New York: Vintage, 1995), 295.

3. When Super Bowl XVII was held in Phoenix, for example, sportswriters described this institution as "chain-gang lite" and polled prisoners on their picks for the game; see Scott Ostler, "Game's Not Main Focus of Arizona Chain Gang," *San Francisco Chronicle*, February 2, 2008, *SFGate*, http://www.sfgate .com, http://articles.sfgate.com/2008-02-02/sports/17140303_1_joe-arpaio-tent -city-super-bowl (accessed June 23, 2008), and Stan Grossfield, "Moving the Chain Gang: Innovative Maricopa County Reform Aims to Keep Area Clean— and Sober," *Boston Globe*, February 2, 2008, http://www.boston.com/sports/ football/patriots/articles/2008/02/02/moving_the_chain_gang/ (accessed April 15, 2010). For descriptions of positive television coverage concerning Florida and

Alabama chain gangs, see Randolph Lewis, "Black and White on the Chain Gang: Representing Race and Punishment," *Borderlines: Studies in American Culture* 3, no. 3 (1996): 242–44.

4. Paul Mason, "Prison Decayed: Cinematic Penal Discourse and Populism 1995–2005," *Social Semiotics* 16, no. 4 (December 2006): 607–26.

5. Avery F. Gordon, "Methodologies of Imprisonment," *PMLA* 123, no. 3 (May 2008): 652, 651.

6. N. Roy Clifton, *The Figure in Film* (Newark, N.J.: University of Delaware Press, 1983), 346; David Wilson and Sean O'Sullivan, "Re-theorizing the Penal Reform Functions of the Prison Film: Revelation, Humanization, Empathy and Benchmarking," *Theoretical Criminology* 9, no. 4 (November 2005): 482; Mel Gutterman, "Abuse, Racism, Torture, Savagery: Hollywood Pictures the Dark Side of American Prisons," *Humanist* 65, no. 5 (2005): 24.

7. Peter A. Soderbergh, "Hollywood and the South, 1930–1960," *Mississippi Quarterly* 19, no. 1 (Winter 1965–66): 2, 9; Jack Kirby, *Media-Made Dixie: The South in the American Imagination*, rev. ed. (Athens: University of Georgia Press, 1986), 57; Mike Nellis, "Notes on the American Prison Film," in *The Prison Film*, ed. Mike Nellis and Christopher Hale (London: Radical Alternatives to Prison, 1982), 44–45; Saverio Giovacchini, *Hollywood Modernism: Film and Politics in the Age of the New Deal* (Philadelphia: Temple University Press, 2001), 55.

8. Matthew J. Mancini, *One Dies, Get Another: Convict Leasing in the American South, 1866–1928* (Columbia: University of South Carolina Press, 1996), 218.

9. Ibid., 226; Martha A. Myers, *Race, Labor and Punishment in the New South* (Columbus: Ohio State University Press, 1998), 20–28.

10. Alex Lichtenstein, *Twice the Work of Free Labor: The Political Economy of Convict Labor in the New South* (New York: Verso, 1996), 178, quote on 181.

11. Ibid., 183; Jesse F. Steiner and Roy M. Brown, *The North Carolina Chain Gang: A Study of County Convict Road Work* (1927; Montclair, N.J.: Patterson Smith, 1969), 89–95.

12. Lewis, "Black and White," 226–28; Mark Colvin, *Penitentiaries, Reformatories and Chain Gangs: Social Theory and the History of Punishment in Nineteenth-Century America* (New York: St. Martin's Press, 1997), 259–60.

13. Foucault, *Discipline and Punish*, 301.

14. Michelle Brown, "'Setting the Conditions' for Abu Ghraib: The Prison Nation Abroad," *American Quarterly* 57, no. 3 (2005): 974, 976–78.

15. Giorgio Agamben, *State of Exception*, trans. Kevin Attell (Chicago: University of Chicago Press, 2005), 2.

16. Lichtenstein, *Twice the Work*, 3, 29.

17. Ibid., 179–81.

18. Ibid., 181–85; Steiner and Brown, *North Carolina Chain Gang*, 101; Vivien M. L. Miller, "Murder, 'Convict Flogging Affairs,' and Debt Peonage: The Roaring Twenties in the American South," in *Reading Southern Poverty between the Wars, 1918–1939*, ed. Richard Godden and Martin Crawford (Athens: University of Georgia Press, 2006), 94–95.

19. Steiner and Brown, *North Carolina Chain Gang*, 83, 100, 89.

20. For examples of this approach, see Lewis, "Black and White"; Douglas A. Blackmon, *Slavery by Another Name: The Re-enslavement of Black Americans from the Civil War to World War II* (New York: Doubleday, 2008).

21. Lichtenstein, *Twice the Work*, 189–90.

22. Ibid., 169; Miller, "Murder," 96.

23. Steiner and Brown, *North Carolina Chain Gang*, 101; Miller, "Murder," 88, 86; Lichtenstein, *Twice the Work*, 190.

24. Miller, "Murder," 88–89.

25. Gordon, "Methodologies of Imprisonment," 652.

26. Lewis, "Black and White," 235–37; Alex Lichtenstein, "Chain Gangs, Communism, and the 'Negro Questions': John L. Spivak's *Georgia Nigger*," *Georgia Historical Quarterly* 74, no. 3 (Fall 1995): 654.

27. Lichtenstein, "Chain Gangs," 652.

28. Ibid.; Robert E. Burns, *I Am a Fugitive from a Georgia Chain Gang!* (1932; Athens: University of Georgia Press / Brown Thrasher, 1997), 103.

29. Burns, *I Am a Fugitive*, 157.

30. Replicating such arguments, coverage of contemporary chain gangs notes that some commentary presents the outdoor labor as "therapeutic." See Grossfield, "Moving the Chain Gang"; Marylee N. Reynolds, "Back on the Chain Gang," *Corrections Today* 58, no. 2 (April 1996): 180–84.

31. Howard J. Green, Brown Holmes, and Sheridan Gibney, screenplay of *I Am a Fugitive from a Chain Gang* (Madison: University of Wisconsin Press, 1981), 110.

32. Sally Robinson, *Marked Men: White Masculinity in Crisis* (New York: Columbia University Press, 2000), 3.

33. Green, Holmes, and Gibney, *I Am a Fugitive*, 116.

34. Lichtenstein, "Chain Gangs," 654; Pare Lorentz, review of *I Am a Fugitive*, in *Movies 1927 to 1941: Lorentz on Film* (New York: Hopkinson and Blake, 1975), 99.

35. Nellis, "Notes on the American Prison," 45.

36. Monika Fludernik, "Metaphoric (Im)prison(ment) and the Constitution of a Carceral Imaginary," *Anglia* 123, no. 1 (2005): 23.

37. Nellis, "Notes on the American Prison," 14; John E. O'Connor, "Warners Finds Its Social Conscience," introduction to screenplay of *I Am a Fugitive from a Chain Gang* (Madison: University of Wisconsin Press, 1981), 41–42.

38. David Laderman, *Driving Visions: Exploring the Road Movie* (Austin: University of Texas Press, 2002), 24–25.

39. Burns, *I Am a Fugitive*, 38.

40. Laderman, *Driving Visions*, 24–25.

41. Ibid., 25.

42. Gail Bederman, *Manliness and Civilization: A Cultural History of Gender and Race in the United States, 1880–1917* (Chicago: University of Chicago Press, 1995), 12–42; Michael S. Kimmel, *The History of Men: Essays in the History of American and British Masculinities* (Albany: State University of New York Press, 2005), 97–101.

43. Elizabeth Lunbeck, "American Psychiatrists and the Modern Man, 1900 to 1920," *Men and Masculinities* 1, no. 1 (1998): 82; William Cohen, "The Great Migration as a Lever for Social Change," *Black Exodus: The Great Migration from the American South*, ed. Alferdteen Harrison (Jackson: University Press of Mississippi, 1991), 73–76.

44. Christina S. Jarvis, *The Male Body at War: American Masculinity during World War II* (DeKalb: Northern Illinois University Press, 2004), 16–17.

45. Cohen, "Great Migration as a Lever," 76–77.

46. Cited in Miller, "Murder," 90–91.

47. Quoted in O'Connor, "Warners Finds Its Social Conscience," 29.

48. Lichtenstein notes the presence of female convicts on Georgia chain gangs in 1904 (*Twice the Work*, 169). Steiner and Brown's statistical analysis of the North Carolina chain gang, published in 1927, includes no categories of women and speaks only of men (*North Carolina Chain Gang*). Joe Arpaio, the sheriff of Arizona's Maricopa County, boasts that his are the first chain gangs solely for women in history. "Sheriff Runs Female Chain Gang," *CNN.com/U.S.*, October 29, 2003, http://www.cnn.com/2003/US/Southwest/10/29/chain.gang.reut/ (accessed June 28, 2007).

49. Jarvis, *Male Body at War*, 17–18.

50. As suggested earlier, any solidarity between black and white prisoners is limited to that between James and Sebastian, but there is no apparent racial conflict, either. Interestingly, white convicts refer to attempted escape as "hanging it on a limb," as if in undertaking the risk of escape they are preparing for their own lynching.

51. Mason, "Prison Decayed," 611–19.

52. In an unscripted echo, in the documentary *American Chain Gang* (1999), a member of an Arizona chain gang declares her impatience to get back to work, by which she means her career as a prostitute.

53. Green, Holmes, and Gibney, *I Am a Fugitive*, 128.

54. O'Connor, "Warners Finds Its Social Conscience," 24, 29.

55. Lindsay Holmgren, "McCullers's Others" (paper presented at the annual meeting of the Space between Society, Evanston, Ill., June 2006), 9, 1–2, 9–10.

56. Carson McCullers, *The Ballad of the Sad Café, and Other Stories* (1951; New York: Houghton Mifflin / Mariner, 2005), 4; Holmgren, "McCullers's Others," 9.

57. Ruth Wilson Gilmore, *Golden Gulag: Prisons, Surplus, Crisis, and Opposition in Globalizing California* (Berkeley: University of California Press, 2007) 21, 64–77; see also Angela Y. Davis, "Race and Criminalization: Black Americans and the Punishment Industry," in *The Angela Y. Davis Reader*, ed. Joy James (Malden, Mass.: Blackwell, 1998), 67. To suggest that convict labor has become less significant in maintaining infrastructure is not to argue that it has ceased; rather, its purpose seems to have changed. The Web site for the Mississippi Department of Corrections, for example, chronicles the amount of agricultural products generated by Parchman's convicts and the number of labor hours provided by prisoners at other facilities; the presentation of this data suggests an effort at public relations, and the explicit objective is to provide inmates

"meaningful work." See "Division of Institutions State Prisons," *Mississippi Department of Corrections*, October 9, 2009, http://www.mdoc.state.ms.us/division _of_institutions%20State%20Prisons.htm (accessed October 14, 2009).

58. Wilson and O'Sullivan, "Re-theorizing the Penal Reform Functions," 471–74.

59. According to the Pew Center for the States, "one in 36 Hispanic adults is behind bars, based on Justice Department figures for 2006. One in 15 black adults is, too, as is one in nine black men between the ages of 20 and 34." Adam Liptak, "1 in 100 U.S. Adults behind Bars, New Study Says," *New York Times*, February 28, 2008, *NYTimes.com* http://www.nytimes.com/2008/04/23/us/23prison .html?pagewanted=all (accessed February 28, 2008).

60. Roy Walmsley, "Global Incarceration and Prison Trends," *Forum on Crime and Society* 3, no. 1–2 (December 2003): 65–78, *United Nations Office on Drugs and Crime* www.unodc.org/pdf/crime/forum/forum3_Art3.pdf (accessed June 23, 2008).

61. Brown, "Setting the Conditions," 987; Joy James, *Resisting State Violence: Radicalism, Gender, and Race in U.S. Culture* (Minneapolis: University of Minnesota Press, 1996), 29–43.

62. Lorna A. Rhodes, *Total Confinement: Madness and Reason in the Maximum Security Prison* (Berkeley: University of California Press, 2004), 10.

63. Steiner and Brown, *North Carolina Chain Gang*, 4; Grossfield, "Moving the Chain Gang."

64. Rhodes, *Total Confinement*, 7, 15, 164; see also the documentary *American Chain Gang.*

65. Mason, "Prison Decayed," 611, 623.

66. Lewis, "Black and White," 235.

67. Ibid., 239.

68. Giovacchini, *Hollywood Modernism*, 59; O'Connor, "Warners Finds Its Social Conscience," 29.

69. Reynolds, "Back on the Chain Gang"; "Criminal Law. Prison Labor. Florida Reintroduces Chain Gangs. Act of June 15, 1995, ch. 283, 1995 Fla. Sess. Law Serv. 2080, 2081 (West)," *Harvard Law Review* 109, no. 4 (February 1996): 876–79; Tessa M. Gorman, "Back on the Chain Gang: Why the Eighth Amendment and the History of Slavery Proscribe the Resurgence of Chain Gangs," *California Law Review* 85, no. 2 (March 1997): 455–56.

70. "Criminal Law," 878.

71. Blackmon, *Slavery by Another Name*, 371–72, 384, 401–2.

72. Gorman, "Back on the Chain Gang," 443, 472, 476; see also "Criminal Law."

73. Lewis, "Black and White," 225; Gorman, "Back on the Chain Gang," 442; "Criminal Law," 88n26.

74. Davis, "Race and Criminalization," 65.

75. "Frugal Alabama Still Chained to the Past," *Journal of Blacks in Higher Education* 8 (Summer 1995): 19.

76. Davis, "Race and Criminalization," 61.

77. Adolph Reed Jr., "The 'Color Line' Then and Now: *The Souls of Black Folk* and the Changing Context of Black American Politics," *Renewing Black Intellectual History: The Ideological and Material Foundations of African American Thought*, ed. Kenneth W. Warren and Adolph Reed Jr. (Boulder, Colo.: Paradigm, 2010), 260.

78. Davis, "Race and Criminalization," 70.

79. Ibid., 67.

The Postwar Cinematic South

Realism and the Politics of Liberal Consensus

Chris Cagle

In a critical early scene in *Panic in the Street* (Elia Kazan, 1950), a representative from the U.S. Public Health Service challenges the New Orleans mayor's office and police on their failure to acknowledge the potential for a dangerous epidemic in the city. The narrative is a contagion story cloaked in a crime thriller, but it is equally a psychological drama between the men trying to stop the disease. The relationship between Lt. Cdr. Clint Reed (Richard Widmark) and police captain Tom Warren (Paul Douglas) represents allegorically a new political arrangement of the postwar years, with the film's three-act structure pivoting around the moments of conflict and resolution between local authority and the federal government. Reed, after all, understands the public-health dimension of contagion and the need for assertive federal powers. Ideologically, the film rebukes conservative attempts to reel back the New Deal's strengthened role of the federal government and also challenges the "states rights" platform of 1948's Dixiecrats. In other words, the film endorses what historians diagnose as an ideology of liberal consensus hegemonic in the postwar years—a belief that large-scale intervention by the federal government can ameliorate national problems.[1]

Through a complicated and at times diffuse development, the politics of liberal consensus became intimately connected to cinematic realism. *Panic in the Streets* exemplifies this confluence. Stylistically, this city hall confrontation, the first plot point of the narrative, is equally remarkable for its realist aesthetic in the fast film stock, crisp and contrast-laden cinematography, and even the distinct echo of the location sound recording. All of *Panic* was filmed on location in New Orleans; many of the actors were nonprofessionals. Producer Darryl Zanuck had sought a "semi-documentary melodrama" in the vein of *Boomerang!* (Kazan, 1947) and *Call Northside 777* (Henry Hathaway, 1947), but unlike other entries in this cycle, *Panic in the Streets* lacked voiceover or much of the narrational apparatus of documentary filmmaking.[2] As such, it represents Hollywood's final sublation of the pseudodocumentary impulse into a generalized narrative realism, dominant by the early 1950s.

Filmographies of the cinematic South, popular or scholarly, rarely keep *Panic in the Streets* in their purview, but the film succinctly points out the distinctiveness of Hollywood's representations of the U.S. South in the two decades after World War II. Location shooting would soon become a conventionalized component of much of the major studios' fiction filmmaking, but in a transitional period in which location footage's newness lent it a special signifying weight, the new realist style drew attention to *place*, with a social and political resonance rarely granted studio footage. In the context of films about the South, *place* took on particular significance. One generation of scholars writing on the cinematic representations of the South have critiqued a "mythology" of the South in classic Hollywood and opposed it to socially and historically "realistic" images. For these scholars, the postwar years represent a move away from this mythology, a "reform" and "reinterpretation" in Edward D. C. Campbell Jr.'s words.[3] From this perspective, the commonplace "realism" (less romanticized, closer to verisimilitude, and including a broader view of social classes) dovetails with a more properly cinematic realism that began to mark Hollywood's prestige products in the 1940s and 1950s.

Hollywood studios repeatedly employed a distinctively realist form for what it offered as social and political serious content and, reciprocally, privileged the political and social realism of dramas set in the contemporary South for the new postwar style of prestige film. The causes of this connection are multiple, but crucial to the development were two overlapping historical changes. First, the changing political alignment of the United States after the New Deal led to a constitution of the South as a *political* problem for Northern liberals. Second, the political culture of the Keynesian Welfare State led to the constitution of the South as a *social* problem. These twin discourses on the U.S. South translated the historical currents of liberal consensus into the representational forms of realism that were proliferating in the postwar years.

South as Political Problem: Narratives of Liberal Consensus

National cinemas, Pierre Sorlin has argued, often fixate on national historical origins; in the American context, the Civil War, even more than the Revolutionary War, has been the "original shock," a "major split, the end of a wonderful, brotherly life for some people, the dawn of an egalitarian, democratic society for others."[4] The "mythology" historians have already given a credible picture of the politics of nostalgia that drove the Northern reception of the presplit nation. Sorlin's historiographic framework further emphasizes that the nostalgia corresponded to a particular political moment, in which party alignments were beginning to realign in response to industrialization and in which open immigration policy was being opposed by nativist Protestant white votes, North and South. Hollywood's Old South (with its aristocratic milieu and view of slaves as blissfully subservient) therefore was at least in part an ideological retreat away from ethnic, labor, and class divisions in early twentieth-century America.

If this oblique reading of Old South mythology and the North's fascination with it is accurate, then the postwar turn to a contemporary South, pathologized rather than idealized, spoke to an underlying political configuration of the nation as a whole. Within a generation the dynamic Sorlin describes had reversed. Where Civil War idealization had allowed an imagined community between white Protestant North and South, currents of political realignment eventually highlighted regional discontinuity. The South both helped constitute a national liberal consensus and challenged the political longevity of that consensus. As the peculiar role the South played in national political arrangements shifted in the postwar years, northern political and cultural elites came to see the South as a political problem. Many of the new realist films therefore commented thematically on the New Deal political coalition between ethnic power blocs in northeastern cities and the solid South.

To apply the label "liberal" to a period popularly remembered for its conservatism may seem counterintuitive. After all, in the immediate postwar years, the liberal-left New Deal coalition was increasingly on the losing end of the major political battles, and the Fair Deal was defeated; although New Deal policies were not reversed, the pace of introduction for new liberal policies was rapidly decelerated, posing what historian Alan Brinkley calls the "end of reform."[5] Moreover, many histories, both academic and popular, depict the following decade as one of *conservative* consensus, in which dominant, even regressive, social ideals reestablished hegemony.[6] While undoubtedly forces of conservatism and reaction did exert significant force in the postwar economy and culture, the "ideology of liberal consensus" as coined by Godfrey Hodgson refers less to the beliefs of the general population and more to the political attitudes of the postwar elites toward U.S. economic strength and global dominance. "Historical logic," Hodgson argues, "made some form of consensus likely. . . . But the basis for the consensus was something more than a vague mood or a reaction to passing events."[7] This "something more" comprised at least three basic tenets: free market capitalism combined with certain welfare state and "crisis management" measures; anti-

Communism at home and especially abroad; and an enlarged role of the state and corporate sector alike in fixing economic and cultural problems.

These tenets defined the central political thought of the period, the work of major corporate foundations, and the parameters of domestic and foreign policy.[8] The left and right of the U.S. political spectrum mostly accepted them, and a combination of Keynesian mixed economy and anti-Communist containment formed the platform and policy of both Democratic and Republican parties. Hodgson writes of this combination, stretching

> from Americans for Democratic Action . . . as far into the board rooms of Wall Street and manufacturing industry as there could be found a realistic willingness to accept the existence of labor unions, the rights of minorities, and some role in economic life for the federal government. Since the consensus had made converts on the Right as well as on the Left, only a handful of dissidents were excluded from the Big Tent: southern diehards, rural reactionaries, the more *farouche* and paranoid fringes of the radical Right, and the divided ramparts of the old, Marxist, left.[9]

In essence, the partisan rancor and political battles of the latter part of the 1940s set the stage for a narrowing of the political spectrum in the 1950s. "To be conservative did not mean to be reactionary," historian James Patterson remarks of Dwight Eisenhower, whose acceptance of Keynesian macroeconomic policy, New Deal tenets, and social welfare expenditure signals how entrenched liberal consensus was across the two political parties.[10]

As Hodgson's words suggest, another problem arises from reading Hollywood's South against a historical backdrop of liberal consensus. The South, historically, has been by many measures the most conservative region of the country. One Virginia newspaper editor could write in 1957, with a perceptive sense of the stakes for conservative philosophy, "If the conservative cause is to survive at all in the United States, as a political philosophy, as an approach to the perplexing problems of our restless and edgy civilization, it will be largely because a body of tradition exists within the South and will not lie down."[11] In formulating a history of liberal consensus, Hodgson downplays not only what Richard Hofstadter calls the "paranoid style in American politics" but also the reactionary strain in southern politics from 1948 through the 1960s. However significant these developments were in the medium run, though, Hodgson usefully points out how marginal they were to the party system and policy decisions of the period. If status politics would eventually vie with interest politics, to borrow Hofstadter's distinction, the politics of ressentiment lived a sub rosa existence in the 1940s and early 1950s.[12]

Still, the political parties *were* undergoing a significant transformation in these years. The liberal consensus did not simply map onto the Democratic party because a moderate Republicanism held dominance despite the significant exception of McCarthyism; yet the continued electoral strength of the Democratic party established a climate of liberal consensus lasting through the Great Society. Under Al Smith, Hofstadter notes, "The Democratic party became the coalition party of the new urban polyglot America. What Smith had begun, Roosevelt completed; F. D. R.'s consolidation of the ethnic and working-class elements in the country into an effective political force was almost as important as his economic reforms."[13] One half of this coalition, moreover, was the "solid South," whose loyalty to the Democratic party allowed the continuity of the New Deal coalition. The postwar period saw increasing strains placed on Democratic solidarity, but these strains did not cohere into a full break in the intraregional unity.[14]

Against this backdrop, the narratives Hollywood set in the postwar South comment on the formation and dissolution of the New Deal coalition. The crisis of party alignment serves as both the explicit and implicit subject of *All the King's Men* (Robert Rossen, 1949). Adapted from Robert Penn Warren's political novel, it fictionalizes the Huey Long governorship in Louisiana in the character of Willie Stark (Broderick Crawford), a firebrand populist. While the solid South's participation in the New Deal was not always populist—southern legislators in Congress often exercised their power to contain New Deal and prounion measures as well as civil rights legislation—Long (and Stark) foreground the home-grown political coalition behind the New Deal's mixed economy. Two central thematic strains intertwine: one juxtaposes the ideal of political ethics with the reality of political machinery ("you can't get good without bad," Willie Stark tells the old-moneyed Burden family); the other suggests the impossibility of clinging onto a gloried past indefinitely. In voiceover narration, protagonist Jack Burden (John Ireland) criticizes the local elite's romanticism: "Home was Burden's Landing, only 130 miles from Kanoma City. It was separated from the mainland by a body of water. For the first time I wondered if it wasn't separated by more than that." By the end, however, Stark's corruption proves the voices of the "past" partly correct. Ultimately, the film ends up being a resigned tribute to the achievements of the New Deal while hinting of the southern ressentiment to come.[15] Corroborating the theme, the film alternates three distinct styles: a high-contrast combination of studio and location shooting with controlled, even lighting for much of the film's action; a relatively high-key style for some of the Burden's Landing scenes; and rougher, documentary-style montages of what Stark calls the "hick vote," shot with faster film stock, existing light, and framing unconventional

for a feature narrative. On the level of style, then, *All the King's Men* suggests the separate political realities of the South's class constituencies and
moreover thematizes its own presentation of a contemporary South as a
break from Hollywood's romanticized South.

In 1960's *Wild River* (Elia Kazan), the counterpart to *All the King's
Men*'s sense of tragic loss, is a nostalgic picture of the New Deal's past.
The film's narrative centers around the efforts of Tennessee Valley Authority (TVA) engineer Chuck Glover (Montgomery Clift) to evacuate,
by eminent domain, the last of the inhabited land to be flooded from
the constructed dam, in this instance inhabited by an obstinate old
woman, Ella Garth (Jo Ann Fleet). As in *Panic in the Street*, the battle
between federal authority and local control becomes the structuring conflict of the film, yet *Wild River*'s thematic treatment of the national/local
battle pushes toward the terrain of political philosophy: the film asks,
how much should the greater good balance against personal property
and liberty? Whereas *Panic* imagines only shortsightedness in local control, *Wild River* articulates libertarian objections to New Deal statism
while thematically seeking to overcome those objections. However, this
change in tone gives its historical look at the New Deal a nostalgic sense
of loss. Chuck is an outsider northerner, who meets opposition from
townspeople hostile to his intervention in Jim Crow hiring practices.
Set in the 1930s but citing 1960, the film's ambiguous historical reference creates a larger ambivalence about liberalism's heritage. The Second
Reconstruction–era split of the Democratic party figures as a fatal flaw in
the New Deal coalition's origins.

A color film a decade removed from postwar pseudodocumentary
realism, *Wild River* nonetheless adopts two realist strategies to further its
theme. First, the film begins with a documentary segment about the Tennessee River floods and the formation of the TVA. Archival footage depicts
flooding and includes an interview with a man who had lost his children
to the flood; voiceover narration segues between this black and white
archival footage and the color aerial photography of present-day Tennessee. This aerial perspective is repeated at the film's end, as Chuck flies
over the completed dam. Second, the film foregrounds the East Tennessee
location shooting; not only do the establishing shots take a long view of
the landscape but also the unusual composition and blocking frame characters against their environment. In the cemetery scene in which Chuck
talks with Ella and Carol Garth about the necessity of abandoning her
property, a shot/reverse-shot pattern alternates high angles that place the
land around Chuck's figure with low angles that link the women with
the hardwood trees; the latter equation is made more explicit later with
a symbolic shot of a large oak falling on the flooding island. Meanwhile,
a traveling shot looking up straight up into the sky and framing a view

of the trees passing suggests the point of view of the walking characters without taking their literal perspective. Later, an interior scene set inside Carol's house across the river frames the characters in widescreen against the exterior visible through the doorway. The connection between the dual themes of the film—the nostalgic narrative of gain and loss in the New Deal and the importance of the land in people's lived historical connection to place—do not map onto each other perfectly, but, tellingly, the film bolsters the purported authenticity about region by emphasizing location shooting as historical and geographic place.

Perhaps the tightest synthesis of political allegory and realist aesthetic comes in Clarence Brown's *Intruder in the Dust* (1949). As literary critic Noel Polk notes of the source novel, "William Faulkner wrote *Intruder in the Dust* in the winter and early spring of 1948, seasons during which the Mississippi Democratic party geared itself for a vital confrontation with the national Democratic party at the summer convention in Philadelphia, over the report of President Truman's Commission on Civil Rights."[16] Polk reads the novel as a statement of the white southern moderate mentality as well as a critique of the moderate. The protagonist, Gavin Stevens, is both a mouthpiece of the moderate viewpoint and a character prone to be blind to the social upheaval behind postwar race relations. The film, too, balances an explicit moderate message (the South must solve the race problem on its own) with an implicit, more radical one (a shift in black consciousness is overdue).

Metro-Goldwyn-Mayer (MGM) filmed *Intruder* on location in Oxford, Mississippi, borrowing from new postwar cinematic vocabularies of realism. The cinematography emphasizes a harsh contrast and flat surface cast by daylight or, alternately, the low-key effects of day-for-night shooting. The narration, moreover, shares stylistic traits with the cycle of pseudodocumentaries that Twentieth Century Fox produced. The opening scene begins with a tilt down the steeple of a chapel in extreme long shot, a shot of a church bell ringing, and a slow pan revealing Oxford's town square. The cinematographic emphasis on the tilt and pan is reminiscent of other pseudodocumentaries, whose use of pans and tilts over more emphatic camera movements speak to a narration about showing (what André Gaudreault calls "monstration") rather than telling.[17] After a dissolve to a long shot from inside a barber shop, the editing adopts the montage-oriented form of the expository documentary: shots of men gathered around the town square, a church congregation worshipping, and patrons waiting at a barber shop connect through a logic as much social as spatial-temporal and without the montage sequence's conventions of voiceover or dissolves. Only slowly, through cross-cutting, does a more traditional analytic storytelling editing insert itself into the narrative, until the narration hides the identity of Lucas Beauchamp with a point-of-view shot. Again, at the end of the film, this pseudodocumentary monstration returns. Whereas the novel ends on Lucas Beauchamp's retort to Stevens ("What are you waiting for?" "My receipt"), the film follows this dialogue and scene with a denouement, again panning to follow Lucas and cutting to a long shot reminiscent of the start. This framing reinserts a sense of location into a narrative whose generic elements could just have easily transposed into another location, real or imagined.

In these examples, realist style converges with an allegorical presentation of the political problem of the solid South. The region stood as a separate political entity, yet one whose fate determined the coherence of the national liberal power base. Meanwhile, its difference was presented as a stylistic difference, and the realism developed in other postwar films took on a special function in narratives that stressed the contemporary role the region played in the national political stage.

The South and the Social Problem Discourse

Intruder in the Dust suggests that alongside the political drama, the postwar social problem film also depicts the region as distinctive. In "race problem" films like *Pinky* (Kazan, 1949), *Intruder in the Dust*, and *The Defiant Ones* (Stanley Kramer, 1956), the Jim Crow South is both setting and problem, although the exact "problem" in each film could be left open to the viewer's interpretation. Their contemporary setting provides an alternative generic template to the historical film and the antebellum melodrama. While Hollywood studios had reasons of their own to produce social problem films, they shared with the broader national culture a tendency to understand the South as a social problem. In the postwar years, this mentality behind a successful cycle of films matched neatly a national tendency among policy elites to approach the South as a social problem in itself. The very nature of the social problem in U.S. culture therefore is at the heart of Hollywood's postwar South.

Americans had long considered the South distinct as a region and often saw its peculiarity as problematic for the nation as a whole. Starting with Reconstruction and into the Gilded Age and the twentieth century, the sense of distinctiveness coalesced increasingly into a conception of the "southern problem" and, correspondingly, the "Negro problem." Social problem sociology has at times stressed the definitional problem of who constitutes a social problem and how.[18] Sociologist Larry J. Griffin applies this self-reflexivity to the national discourse on the South: "In no other case," he argues, "were social problems so intimately related, even equated, in the public mind to a particular region for so sustained a period of time that the region itself—rather than the objective conditions—became commonly understood as the 'real' problem."[19] The objective conditions of the South, Griffin maintains, were necessary but insufficient conditions for the ideas that influential "social problem operators" formed and circulated about the region.

This sociological impulse has been paralleled by scholarship on the social problem film that interrogates the "social problem" of its moniker. The genre, Charles J. Maland notes, "presupposes power: an individual or group must have enough power in society to get the matter into public debate. . . . [I]mplicit in the very notion of the term *social problem* is the belief that something can be done about it—that the problem has a solution."[20] Similarly, John Hill posits a "social problem discourse" in his study of the British problem film of the 1950s. In an attempt to read the ideology behind the rubric of social problem filmmaking, Hill views the definition of a social problem as a matter of power:

> [A] social problem is the product of discourse rather than the property of any particular condition in itself. What then becomes accepted as a social problem is not in any way inevitable but a consequence of the ability to have any particular definition legitimated, be it via the media, or other "accredited agencies." . . . To this extent, the "social problems" so defined are not so much the problems of "society" as a whole as the "problems" of those who enjoy the ability to universalize their particular point of view as the point of view of all in society.[21]

Hill's notion of a social problem discourse stresses, in Marxian fashion, the power relations underlying social legitimation, but if we are to take seriously the *discourse* of the social problem discourse, we cannot ignore the definitional half of the equation. How social problems were defined in mid-century America was as important as who was defining them. The power relationships behind a political and cultural elite speaking for the poor, rural, or regionally marked areas of the country did change between, say, 1919 and 1949 but not as rapidly as social science language and understanding. Survey research, statistical sampling, and a new sense of an aggregate social self fostered a collective sense of a mass public.[22] Meanwhile, the shift from progressive-era and Chicago School sociology to the new postwar functionalism brought an emphasis on anomie and the pathology of social relations; small-scale social dysfunctions, not class conflict or individual morality, were at the center of the postwar research agenda. By 1950 a visible subfield of social problem sociology had established itself.

The spread of either functionalism or the aligned social problem sociology into more popular discourse was a complicated process. Howard W. Odum complained that sociologists used the term "social problem" with little consistency or clarity; in popular usage, it was even less precise.[23]

By the time the discourse filtered into the realm of popular-press and even trade-press film criticism, its referent often seemed contradictory or confused. Nevertheless, the reception of the postwar social problem dramas reveals one key tenet of the social problem discourse: a tendency to look beyond the individual for causes of phenomena. *Variety*, for instance, warned that *Lost Weekend* (Billy Wilder, 1945) "isn't a pretty story for more than one reason. Its moral, of course, crusades against alcoholism, but to casual readers of the book and patrons of the picture there may well be a wholesale condemnation of the suppliers of spirits." Even when criticizing the films, journalistic critics often did so on the grounds that they did not illuminate better the deeper sociological causes of the problem. In a judgment mirrored by the *New Yorker*, Bosley Crowther's review of *Gentleman's Agreement* complained that protagonist Phil Green's "explorations are narrowly confined to the upper-class social and professional level to which he is immediately exposed. And his discoveries are chiefly in the nature of petty bourgeois rebuffs, with no inquiry into the devious cultural mores from which they spring." Similarly, a *Commonweal* reviewer complained that given *Crossfire's* (Edward Dmytryk, 1947) Manichaean characterization of the villain and the multiple murders in the narrative, "it is hard to consider the first killing (committed only because the victim was a Jew) with the sociological import the film intends." The discourse had diffused enough that some educated consumers of Hollywood's product wished for narratives that could suggest social causation.[24]

The setting of problem films in the South also brought this pop-sociological attitude, a disposition shared by filmmakers and critics alike. Instructively, *Pinky* repeats and reformulates the ideas circulating from public discussion of a specific sociological work, Gunnar Myrdal's *An American Dilemma*. Howard Winant suggests that U.S. sociology's understanding of race comprised four distinct phases, organized around central paradigms of race: biologist, including Herbert Spencer–influenced work; pragmatist, primarily the sociology of the Chicago School; structural-functionalist, which gained dominance in the postwar decades; and social, tied either to new social movements or the neoconservative movement.[25] An ambitious sociological study of race relations, *An American Dilemma* shifted the framework for understanding them by ushering in a structural-functionalist paradigm, tied to white liberalism and the U.S. government. Understanding race, that is, meant diagnosing a social problem whose dysfunctions threatened American society as a systemic whole: "the structural-functionalist view of race consistently stressed the integrative qualities of U.S. society; thus the overlap of the two uses of the term *integration*—one that summarized the key civil rights demands of the era, and one that frames sociological explanation in terms of social unity and commonality."[26] Moreover, *An American Dilemma*'s readership exceeded a merely academic one, reaching into policy circles, the clergy, police forces, and newsrooms; directly and indirectly it popularized this functionalist and liberal understanding of race as social problem.[27]

This popularization extended to Hollywood. *Pinky* screenwriter Philip Dunne's "behind the scenes" discussion suggests an explicit inspiration from Myrdal's work: "Every American citizen, white or Negro, has his own ideas on the subject of race in America. Few Americans have been able to approach it without passion or prejudice. (It is significant that the only truly dispassionate and unprejudiced appraisal of the problem is the work of a foreigner, Gunnar Myrdal, in his monumental *An American Dilemma*.)"[28] *An American Dilemma* gave *Pinky* a high-minded justification for its message about prejudice but also shaped the film's depictions of the black community and conception of the social problem. In story conference memos, one producer at Fox, Michael Abel, wrote of the script:

> Striking with the skill and daring of the surgeon's knife it lays open the foulest cancer in the American way of life, and by exposing, paves the way, let us hope, for its eventual eradication. The wretched condition of the Negroes in our southern states—the poverty, ignorance, fear and humiliation they suffer at the hands of the "superior" whites are hammered here in powerful blows to the shame of the people in this country. It is high time the facts were faced openly and honestly; there has long been a crying need for a picture of this type.[29]

Throughout their deliberations the film's writers and producers acknowledged Jim Crow, discrimination, and segregation as the backdrop for the social message of the film, yet they emphasized the conditions of black life and so maximized the black southerner's status as object rather than subject.

An American Dilemma's project registers in the text itself. Myrdal writes, "If a Negro commits a crime against another Negro, and no white man is involved, and if the crime is not a serious one, white policemen will let the criminal off with a warning or a beating, and the court will let him off with a warning or a relatively light sentence."[30] Compare this observation with the climactic courtroom scene. When the defense attorney asserts in cross-examination that the police officer let Pinky off without any charges, the policeman replies, "You generally always let 'em off with a good talking to, like you give her. You know how it is." Furthermore, the Manichaean characterization of the "good" and "bad" African Americans in the film sets up an objectified "Negro condition." While *American Dilemma* explicitly warns against moralizing variants of prejudice, it does read "the Negro community as a pathological form of an American community."[31] Subproletarian character Jake stands in for this pathologized black experience; in Darryl Zanuck's words, "[Jake] is supposed to be a shifty, dishonest, low-class Negro, a sort of agitator."[32]

Additionally, as much as *Pinky* owes its narrative of passing to literary and filmic precedents, it also moves passing from mere categorical ambivalence (the "caught between two worlds" trope of the tragic mulatto) to social and political conflict. "As a social phenomenon," *An American Dilemma* notes, "passing is so deeply connected with the psychological complexes—built around caste and sex—of both groups that it has come to be a certain theme of fiction and of popular imagination and storytelling."[33] By presenting the protagonist's dilemma as a choice between self-affirmation and freedom of economic oppression, *Pinky* combines the thematic preoccupations of fiction and cinematic storytelling with the social understanding of caste and sex.

Intruder in the Dust likewise adopted themes presented in Myrdal's publication. *An American Dilemma* organizes its quilt-work composite of qualitative and social findings around a central conceit: that racial segregation and stratification affronts core American ideals for freedom and equality and therefore poses a challenge to the American conscience.[34] In *Intruder in the Dust*, the protagonists' exchange at the end lays out a comparable message:

> CHICK [referring to Lucas Beauchamp]: They don't see him, as though it never happened.
> JOHN STEVENS: They see him.
> CHICK: No, they don't even know he's there.
> STEVENS: But they do. The same as I do. And they always will as long as he lives. Proud, stubborn, insufferable. But there he goes. Keeper of my conscience.
> CHICK: Our conscience, Uncle John.

This social problem tendency bounced against the more straightforwardly generic murder-mystery material of the narrative, as well as the film's complicated status as a semifaithful adaptation of William Faulkner's novel. These contradictions inflected the marketing of the film across regional lines. *Intruder in the Dust* features two trailers, one the studio designated for southern audiences, another for northern audiences:

Southern Trailer
TITLE: The faith of this BOY. . . . The courage of this MAN. . . . The heart of this Lady. . . . Fighting against what unholy violence?
TITLE: *INTRUDER IN THE DUST* [over CU of book]

VOICEOVER: Boiling like hot lava from the angry pen of one of the world's greatest storytellers, *Intruder in the Dust* brings to the screen the most striking characters you've ever met. Filmed on location to authenticate its raw, rugged, realistic background, *Intruder in the Dust* tells its story in tense terms of men of action and women of courage, of the furtive whine of a bullet fired from the shadows . . . the baying of hounds at the edge of a pool of quicksand. . . . Of the smoldering hate in a carven heart . . . of the silent terror of a man who waits alone in the night for he knows not what. . . . Of the sullen fury that grips a town and whips it to the brink of violence.

Intruder in the Dust, an outstanding American novel, is from the same studio which gave you *The Yearling*. And like that distinguished film, has been made with force, fire, and fidelity. MGM presents a faithful dramatization of one of the great novels of our time.

Northern Trailer

[CU of book] TITLE: INTRUDER IN THE DUST. [dissolve to] "You can't film *that* novel . . . but we did! Metro-Goldwyn-Mayer announces the savage story of one man . . . [CU of Lucas] . . . this man . . . against the weight of the world!

DIEGESIS / DAVID CLARKE: "You crummy, bigoted, burr-headed . . ." (attacks Lucas) . . .

TITLE: NO BEATING AROUND THE BUSH! NO SIDESTEPPING! NO DOUBLE-TALK!

DIEGESIS / DAVID CLARKE: ". . . Nigger!"

TITLE: INTRUDER IN THE DUST [over CU of book]

VOICEOVER: The seething fury that grips a town and whips it to the brink of violence . . . a mystery drama that quivers with suspense . . . the burning fever that spawns reckless, ruthless action—that's *Intruder in the Dust*. The strong force of pride and decency, which thrives even in the midst of terror. . . . The faith of this boy. . . . The courage of this man. . . . The heart of this lady. . . . That, too, is *Intruder in the Dust*, a faithful dramatization of the superb novel by William Faulkner, one of the world's greatest living authors.

[Trailer excerpts four scenes of confrontation, emphasizing racial conflict]

TITLE: *INTRUDER IN THE DUST* [over CU of book][35]

The southern trailer whitewashes the racial conflict in the film, playing up the genre, the character traits of the white protagonists, and the film's status as adaptation. The national-release trailer, meanwhile, emphasizes the social problem content, lending sensationalism to depictions of southern racism. The combination of liberal didacticism and virtuosity that producer Dore Schary had adopted in *Crossfire* takes on a specific regionalized appeal to a northern spectator.

Social problem discourse was not confined to the problem of race relations. *The Southerner* (Jean Renoir, 1945), for instance, extended a parallel notion of the South as an economic problem. The narrative follows a yeoman farmer, Sam Tucker, attempting to work his way from tenancy to self-sufficiency; at every turn he faces hardships that threaten with starvation and bankruptcy. Much like the government documentary *The River* (Pare Lorentz, 1938), the film points to the economic organization of the South's agricultural economy as pathological. As sensible as this thesis may sound, Robert A. Margo points out that while the South undoubtedly was poor for the century after the Civil War, its economic backwardness was mostly the result of insufficient capital, not an economic disease. "What really made the postbellum South unique as an economic problem was the size of the shock that the region had experienced, not an unusual inability to cope with such a shock."[36] However, today's economic historians tend to take a perspective not shared by contemporary economic observers and policy makers. For contemporaries, the South's economic hardship flowed from its distinctiveness.

A Historiography of Elites

The window for the convergence of realist cinematic style, political liberalism, and the conception of South as problem was historically finite. The implosion of the Democratic party beginning in 1968 and the multiple economic and political crises of the 1970s signaled a decline in liberal consensus and a new role of the South in U.S. political party coalitions. With liberalism's decline, the social problem discourse faced contestation and critique from the left and the right. Too, the South itself changed rapidly under the dual transformations of the civil rights movement and the Sunbelt economic boom. Regional distinctions still mattered and vestiges of the Old South stubbornly remained, but increasingly the region assimilated into a national culture, while racial and economic problems hit other parts of the country. From the vantage of the early twenty-first century, the social problem culture and Hollywood's postwar depictions of the American South appear to be an artifact: dated, naive, misguided, or ideological.

At the same time, the social problem culture was not mere artifact but also an attempt by many citizens to make sense of changing historical circumstances. Putting "social problem" in scare quotes does not solve the problem that film scholars continue to use concepts, like culture and social conflict, that are not too different. The structuring paradox of collective definition perspectives on social problem formation is that underlying social conflicts exist whether people recognize them or not, yet the cultural and discursive definitions of the problem are conventional and historical in nature. Racial division, economic backwardness, and political conflict were all real problems for many people in midcentury America, yet people understood, interpreted, and talked about these problems differently, depending on their social position.

Between the sociological, the political, and the economic constitution of the South as problem, Hollywood's way of talking about the South dovetailed remarkably with the way that the northern bourgeoisie, what we might call the political and cultural elite, talked about the region and its relation to the national body. This elite voice was hardly the only constituency for the social problem films, which after all had a mass audience. Thus, the problem-discourse model of Hollywood's portrayal of the postwar South leaves aside several possible determinants for the change in representation. How did ordinary filmgoers' attitudes about the South change around World War II? How did African Americans of the 1940s and 1950s tend to view these dramas and problem films? What did southerners in general make of this turn to the contemporary South? What about intraregional difference within the South? All of these questions are worth asking and exploring, but they should not obscure the remarkable synchronization during this period of elite attitudes (of journalists, social scientists, and artists) with those in Hollywood (writers, directors, and producers, among others). The contemporary South appeared not in generic output—which in the late 1940s concentrated in sentimental dramas, musicals, B Westerns, crime films, and Bob Hope–style parodic comedies—but rather in the prestige dramas the studios made with an eye to political and cultural seriousness. The prestige aspirations suggest how a cinematic style seen as opposing mass entertainment spectacle matched social content seen as opposing mass entertainment formula; the resulting films were "non-Hollywood" Hollywood films.

The new postwar emphasis on a type of prestige film gives perhaps the best explanation for the rapid shift of Hollywood's South from romanticized plantation films to a modern New Orleans, TVA dam, or Oxford. The prestige film's non-Hollywood reputation derived from the realist aesthetic. Additionally, popular press critics called "realistic" any qualities defined against the idea of "Hollywood."[37] As with social problem definition, realism is at once objective and conventional. *Panic in the Streets* constructs a fictional portrait of New Orleans and uses pseudodocumentary style as a means to market its authenticity; at the same time, due to the indexicality of cinema and the practice of location shooting, New Orleans really does appear in *Panic in the Streets*, but not in *Jezebel*. So the turn from antebellum to contemporary South marked real changes in Hollywood's filmmaking. Nonetheless, both versions were cultural fictions tied to particular *national* political configurations.

Northern discourse on and anxiety about the South as a problem for the nation drove Hollywood's postwar realist turn, as the "southern problem" preoccupied one of the key postwar genres. To put it another way, the realist cinematic South was a privileged occasion for the seriousness characterizing a changing Hollywood in the postwar years. Regional politics, therefore, are central to the historical trajectory of the American film industry in the middle of the twentieth century.

NOTES

1. I credit Karl Schoonover for suggesting I take a closer look at *Panic in the Streets* as a drama about local government.

2. Darryl Zanuck to Sol Siegel, conference memo, August 8, 1949, box 2408.5, Twentieth Century Fox Script Collection, Doheny Library, University of Southern California, Los Angeles.

3. Edward D. C. Campbell Jr., *The Celluloid South: Hollywood and the Southern Myth* (Knoxville: University of Tennessee Press, 1981), 141.

4. Pierre Sorlin, *The Film in History: Restaging the Past* (Totowa, N.J.: Barnes and Noble Books, 1980), 42.

5. Alan Brinkley, *The End of Reform: New Deal Liberalism in Recession and War* (New York: Knopf, 1995).

6. A prime example is Elaine Tyler May, *Homeward Bound: American Families in the Cold War Era* (New York: Basic Books, 1988).

7. Godfrey Hodgson, *America in Our Time* (New York: Vintage Books, 1976), 75.

8. Arthur Meier Schlesinger Jr., *The Vital Center: The Politics of Freedom* (Boston: Houghton Mifflin, 1949); Seymour Martin Lipset, *Political Man: The Social Bases of Politics* (Garden City, N.Y.: Doubleday, 1960); and Daniel Bell, *The End of Ideology: On the Exhaustion of Political Ideas in the Fifties* (Glencoe, Ill.: Free Press, 1960). On the increased role of foundations in problem solving, see Martin Bulmer, "The Growth of Applied Sociology after 1945: The Prewar Establishment of the Postwar Infrastructure," in *Sociology and Its Publics: The Forms and Fates of Disciplinary Organization*, ed. Terence C. Halliday and Morris Janowitz (Chicago: University of Chicago Press, 1992), 317–45.

9. Hodgson, *America in Our Time*, 73.

10. James Patterson, *Grand Expectations: The United States, 1945–1974* (Oxford: Oxford University Press, 1996), 271–72.

11. James Jackson Kilpatrick, "Conservatism and the South," in *The Lasting South*, ed. Louis J. Rubin Jr. and James Jackson Kilpatrick (Chicago: Regnery, 1957), 188.

12. Richard Hofstadter, *The Paranoid Style in American Politics, and Other Essays* (New York: Knopf, 1965), 86.

13. Ibid., 78.

14. O. Douglas Weeks, "The South in National Politics" in *The American South in the 1960s*, ed. Avery Leiserson (New York: Praeger, 1964), 221–40.

15. F. Garvin Davenport Jr. makes a more explicit argument about the relation the novel's vision of history held to white Southern reaction. *The Myth of Southern History: Historical Consciousness in Twentieth-Century Southern Literature* (Nashville, Tenn.: Vanderbilt University Press, 1967), esp. 169–70.

16. Noel Polk, "Man in the Middle: Faulkner and the Southern White Moderate," in *Faulkner and Race*, ed. Doreen Fowler and Ann J. Abadie (Jackson: University Press of Mississippi, 1987), 130.

17. André Gaudreault, "Narration and Monstration in the Cinema," trans. Paul Attallah and Tom Gunning, *Journal of Film and Video* 39, no. 2 (1987): 29–36

18. See, for instance, Howard Becker, ed., *Social Problems: A Modern Approach* (New York: Wiley, 1966), 7. Becker's admonition about the variegated nature of the "Negro problem" is not too different from the introduction to Gunnar Myrdal, with Richard Sterner and Arnold Rose, *An American Dilemma: The Negro Problem and Modern Democracy* (New York: Harper and Row, 1944), 969.

19. Larry J. Griffin, "Why Was the South a Problem?" in *The South as an American Problem*, ed. Larry J. Griffin and Don H. Doyle (Athens: University of Georgia Press, 1995), 14.

20. Charles J. Maland, "The Social Problem Film," in *Handbook of American Film Genres*, ed. Wes D. Gehring (New York: Greenwood, 1988), 306.

21. John Hill, "The British 'Social Problem' Film: *Violent Playground* and *Sapphire*," *Screen* 26, no. 1 (1985): 35.

22. See Sarah E. Igo, *The Averaged American: Surveys, Citizens, and the Making of a Mass Public* (Cambridge, Mass.: Harvard University Press, 2007).

23. Howard W. Odum, *American Sociology: The Story of Sociology in the United States through 1950* (New York: Longmans, Green, 1951), 281.

24. Review of *Lost Weekend*, *Variety*, August 15, 1945, 14; John McCarten, Review of *Gentleman's Agreement*, *New Yorker*, November 15, 1947, 117; Bosley Crowther, Review of *Gentleman's Agreement*, *New York Times*, November 12, 1947, 36; Philip T. Hartung, Review of *Crossfire*, *Commonweal*, August 1, 1947, 386.

25. Howard Winant, "The Dark Side of the Force: One Hundred Years of the Sociology of Race," in *Sociology in America: A History*, ed. Craig Calhoun (Chicago: University of Chicago Press, 2007), 535–71.

26. Ibid., 561.

27. David Southern, *Gunnar Myrdal and Black-White Relations: The Use and Abuse of an American Dilemma, 1944–1969* (Baton Rouge: Louisiana State University Press, 1987).

28. Philip Dunne, "Approach to Racism," *New York Times*, May 1, 1949, X5.

29. Michael Abel to Darryl Zanuck, conference memo, *Pinky*, November 17, 1948, box 2391.12, Twentieth Century Fox Special Collection.

30. Myrdal, Sterner, and Rose, *American Dilemma*, 969.

31. Ibid., 927.

32. Darryl Zanuck, conference memo, *Pinky*, November 17, 1948, box 2391.11, Twentieth Century Fox Special Collection.

33. Myrdal, Sterner, and Rose, *American Dilemma*, 688.

34. Ibid., esp. chs. 1 and 45.

35. Descriptions are based on the screenplay transcription of these trailers. MGM Script Collection, box 5300, Doheny Library, University of Southern California, Los Angeles.

36. Robert A. Margo, "The South as an Economic Problem," in Griffin, *South as an American Problem*, 174.

37. See Chris Cagle, "Two Modes of Prestige Film" *Screen* 38, no. 3 (2007): 291–311.

A "Professional Southerner" in the Hollywood Studio System

Lamar Trotti at Work, 1925–1952

Matthew H. Bernstein

In the minds of many studio-era Hollywood talents, executives, and administrators of the 1920s through the 1950s—as in the view of many Americans—the South was a region apart, a foreign country, one whose customs and beliefs, particularly concerning race and race relations, were quite strange. Director Rowland Lee casually listed the South among foreign markets when he commented in 1927 that the studios never informed him "why his picture didn't do well in the South, why his picture didn't do well in England, why his picture could not be shown in Germany."[1] Twelve years later, this view had not changed: Howard Dietz, from the publicity division of Loews, Inc., wrote Atlanta's mayor William B. Hartsfield to thank him for treating "us foreigners" (the Hollywood entourage attending the world premiere of *Gone with the Wind*) so well.[2]

Given this mindset, and the film industry's determination, in Richard Maltby's words, "to displease as few people as little and as seldom as possible," the South had a definite place on Hollywood's roll call of groups not to alienate.[3] This list included reformers, censors, trade associations, various professions, and most notably, ethnic and racial groups, foreign countries—and domestic regions.[4] In conceptualizing their domestic audience, film industry executives might carve up the national marketplace in a number of ways: the sticks versus the city, the sophisticated versus the sentimental, New York versus the rest of the country.[5] More than any other region, the South retained a singular position in the national film marketplace as a geographic area with distinctive tastes and sensibilities.

As many essays in this volume attest, this distinction was due to Hollywood's, indeed the entire nation's, southern imaginary. Sociologist Larry J. Griffin has noted that New England (initially settled by

intolerant Puritans) and the U.S. West (where European settlers decimated Native American tribes) also have discrete identities, "yet neither
region was so thoroughly feared and censured, on the one hand, and or
so unashamedly embraced and sentimentalized, on the other, as was the
South."[6] So powerful was the Hollywood studios' fear of offending the
South, Thomas Cripps argues, that the "Myth of the Southern Box Office" dictated that films must not offend the white South by depicting
interracial or African American scenarios. This logic, Cripps claims, held
sway in spite of the evidence that southern audiences appreciated black
performers on the legitimate stage; such fears, he pointed out, were out
of all proportion to the relatively small box office percentage that the
southern market constituted for Hollywood.[7]

By no coincidence, the white South in many ways both concurred with
this view of itself as foreign and protested against it. Two years after the
Gone with the Wind Atlanta premiere, W. J. Cash opened his landmark
study The Mind of the South by stating baldly, "There exists among
us by ordinary [sic]—both North and South—a profound conviction
that the South is another land, sharply differentiated from the rest of the
American nation, and exhibiting within itself a remarkable homogeneity."[8] As Fred Hobson has shown, Cash, in writing his book, took his
place in a long line of white southern poets, novelists, journalists, and
sociologists who had been defending the South to the rest of the country
since the 1820s. They had done this so frequently, according to Hobson,
that "explaining the South is almost a regional characteristic in itself,"
an activity provoked by criticism from outside the region as well as from
an internal sense of guilt about its many flaws. In Hobson's view, the
southerner experiences a "regional inferiority complex, a recognition of
failure," combined with "a perverse and defiant pride in the southerner,
a sense of distinction, of superiority, stemming from this inferior status.
The southerner, that is to say, wears his heritage of failure and defeat as
his badge of honor."[9]

Given this ambivalent mix of pride and shame, many white southerners, like many of Hollywood's dissatisfied constituencies, often felt that
the film studios (1915's The Birth of a Nation aside) had not done their
section and their history justice. Southerners had a list of gripes against
the industry's treatment of them on screen and off. Hence those involved
in public relations and content regulation at the Motion Picture Producers and Distributors Association (MPPDA) or in film production at the
studios came to rely on their "Southern white counselors" for advice on
southern customs and particularly on the possible reception of controversial subject matter.[10]

For example, Twentieth Century Fox screenwriter (and later director/
producer) Nunnally Johnson gave David O. Selznick unsolicited advice

on handling the southern accent for *Gone with the Wind* to avoid the embarrassing raspberries with which southern audiences had greeted *Jezebel* two years before. The core of his suggestions entailed the revelation that southerners believed they had no accent. Francis Harmon, a Mississippi native who served as Will Hays's executive assistant, drew up a set of guidelines in 1937 for Joseph Breen on how African Americans should be represented in Hollywood films. In the early 1940s, Harmon urged Walt Disney to indicate in *The Song of the South* (1946) that the faithful retainer Uncle Remus was out of date. Most astonishingly, Harmon in 1948 urged Darryl F. Zanuck, in the name of historical accuracy and realism—and in stark contradiction to the miscegenation clause of the Production Code—to revise the script for *Pinky* to depict openly and directly the southern phenomenon whereby prominent politicians' black mistresses and their mulatto offspring were well-known secrets in towns, cities, and states. When asked, southern screenwriters, directors (such as King Vidor and Clarence Brown), and executives (such as Paramount's Y. Frank Freeman) offered their expertise on matters of representation and business practices.[11]

During his career in Hollywood from the mid-1920s through 1952, Lamar Trotti was consulted for his expertise many times in many ways. This essay takes a closer look at several such instances, including the 1927 *Uncle Tom's Cabin*, 1934's *Judge Priest*, 1939's *Young Mr. Lincoln*, 1943's *The Ox-Bow Incident*, and Trotti's final film as producer/screenwriter, 1952's *Stars and Stripes Forever*. These episodes enable us to chart the intriguing dynamics of this intermediate role played by one white resident southerner in Hollywood across three decades. For while Trotti sought in part to demonstrate to the rest of the country, or at least to the film industry, that the South was a civilized place and that North and South had more in common than they realized, he himself was too ambivalent to serve as a simpleminded, regional cheerleader.

Like Ben Hecht and fellow Georgia native Nunnally Johnson, Trotti came to the film industry via reporting. He was the first graduate of the University of Georgia's Henry W. Grady School of Journalism after completing his B.A. in 1921, and he wrote for several campus publications. The son of a Civil War veteran, Trotti joined William Randolph Hearst's *Atlanta Georgian* three months after graduating. In March 1925 he was promoted to the post of city editor, the youngest journalist in the Hearst organization to hold that position. Two months later Trotti left journalism to work for Col. Jason Joy, the current head of the MPPDA's Committee on Public Relations. Joy hired Trotti to publicize Hays Office initiatives, particularly with the advent of the "Open Door" policy, and Trotti's public relations work extended to editing the association's *Motion Picture Monthly* from New York.[12] Trotti moved to Hollywood

Portrait of Lamar Trotti. Courtesy of the Academy of Motion Picture Arts and Sciences.

with Joy in 1927 to assist him in running the new Studio Relations Committee through 1932.

Trotti's work for Jason Joy and Will Hays often compelled Trotti to share his knowledge of the South and explain it to film industry types. Perhaps at no time during the first half of the twentieth century did the South seem more alien to Hollywood—and more troubling to Americans' image of themselves—than during the 1920s. There were the South's official practices of segregation, its thriving Ku Klux Klan, its high volume of lynchings, its underdeveloped economies, its sharecropper system that was symptomatic of its widespread and grinding poverty, and the region's cultural and educational backwardness. Moreover, that decade witnessed what some observers called a "Northern Offensive," in which northern-based national magazines such as the *Nation*, the *New Republic*, the *Century*, and H. L. Mencken's *American Mercury* described and ridiculed the South as a region of extreme prejudice, social backwardness, artistic emptiness, and general ignorance. The 1925 Scopes trial in Dayton, Tennessee, concerning the teaching of evolution, in Hobson's words, "dramatized most forcefully the struggle between the provincial, religious South and the modern, secular world."[13] No wonder the area figured so prominently and uniquely in the minds of film industry leaders with the myth of the southern box office and all its attendant axioms. Resident white southerners like Lamar Trotti had a lot to explain.

No Hollywood film until that time had the potential to insult the South more than Universal's big-budget production of *Uncle Tom's Cabin* in the spring of 1927. When Universal first announced the project, Trotti informed Jason Joy that in his view the entire undertaking was a bad idea. When the film was completed, he wrote Gov. Carl E. Milliken, then head of the MPPDA's publicity department, that while he had been wrong in anticipating that the South held the lost cause so dear that it would never accept Buster Keaton's Civil War comedy *The General* (1926), he felt certain that distributing *Uncle Tom's Cabin* in the South would be unfortunate. Universal's film is a far cry from Keaton's gentle satire on the South and the Civil War: it features, for one thing, an unflinching and agonizing portrait of slave families torn apart at slave auctions. (Black people do not appear anywhere in Keaton's film.) It depicts Simon Legree's (George Siegeman) fanatical sadism, in which his slaves are flogged by two black underlings. There is also Legree's undisguised lust for Liza (Margarita Fischer): on the slave auction block, he sizes up her arms and runs his hands over her breasts; back home he chases her around the plantation house. Explicit in terms of their depiction of sex and violence, these scenes are not unlike those in the later blaxploitation-influenced, plantation-revisited films such as *Mandingo* (1975) and *Drum* (1976).

In commenting on *Uncle Tom's Cabin*, Trotti referred his colleagues at the MPPDA to a letter on the subject from Atlanta's censor, Zella Richardson, whom Trotti knew well from his Atlanta days and whom he characterized as "a very friendly person" (i.e., to the film industry). Richardson had expressed in no uncertain terms her view that making the film and showing it in the South "would be suicidal!"

I called three members of my Board, two of whom are Northern people—this after I had written my own opinion for I did not want to be biased. Every one agreed that to send this South would either increase sectional feeling where it already exists or create it where it does not, that the novel had no historical value, that it was founded on untruth, was written for money only, was published by Yellow Journals first, and was a precipitating cause of the war. . . . [W]hy make a picture which the masses will see and which can but increase prejudice on both sides. You know the "red rag to the bull" is a flag of truce compared to the mention of the name of Harriet Beecher Stowe to a Southerner. We feel that no one person has ever done us the injury nor has been as unfair to us, as she. However, I will see the picture with the same unbiased mind I try to see them all and will do the best I can for it, but I am sorry that it was made.[14]

Richardson's own ambivalent position is apparent from her shifting pronouns. "We" white southerners, she had written, feel Stowe has slandered the South but "I," Richardson, will try to remain unbiased (though her biases are plenty clear from this letter).

Trotti presumably shared her ambivalence, yet his response to her letter and to the film were more moderate, almost indifferent: "I think that Mrs. Richardson expresses the view of a great many Southerners. That is the wrong view, I know. It is not mine because the appearance of 'Uncle Tom's Cabin' could not possibly mean anything to me but an evening not to go to the movies. I've never seen it nor read it. It used to be a joke that no Southerner would ever admit he had anyhow. . . . [W]ith this picture I think Universal should kind of soft pedal its Southern business."[15] By 1927 Trotti was so distanced from the southern pride and heritage Richardson had upheld in her correspondence that he could repudiate her view as wrong. In fact, he may never have shared it (a difference partly attributable to their respective generations).

Still, Trotti's modest endorsement of her sentiments and her feelings as representative of "a great many southerners" were vindicated when Atlanta civic leaders decided that the film should not be shown anywhere in Georgia after a special preview of Universal's production was shown for Richardson, Atlanta Universal distribution executives, Mayor Ragsdale, and more than a thousand other curious viewers (who might perhaps have been tempted never to admit that they actually had seen it).[16] By year's end, Universal would struggle to recut the film to recoup some of its investment; its failure and its controversy became a milestone in MPPDA wisdom about the potential impact of films about the South in the southern market's sensibilities. In 1932, facing a possible production of Robert E. Burns's exposé *I Am a Fugitive from a Georgia Chain Gang*, Jason Joy reminded Darryl F. Zanuck how bitterly Southerners resented the filming of "Uncle Tom's Cabin," and how most of the States refused ever to permit the picture to be shown within their borders. . . . After all these years of reconciliation, it would be extremely unfortunate if such old wounds should be reopened. Southerners claim that in a country where there is a large Negro population the chain gang system—and even some of the worse abuses—are necessary. Though to us these methods may seem barbarous relics of the Middle Ages, still from a business standpoint we ought to consider carefully whether we are willing to incur the anger of any large section by turning our medium of entertainment to anything which may be regarded as a wholesale indictment.[17]

Richardson's judgment of *Uncle Tom's Cabin*, and Trotti's confirmation of it, proved not only prophetic but memorable.

Joy himself left the MPPDA for the Fox studio story department in September 1932, and Trotti went with him. After collaborating with Dudley Nichols in 1933 on the script for *The Man Who Dared*, Trotti shifted to screenwriting completely. His next partnership with Nichols the following year—on John Ford's *Judge Priest*, based on three short stories by Irvin S. Cobb—afforded him an opportunity, not to distance himself from attitudes fiercely held at home, but to portray and uphold an idealized version of the South to the rest of the country. This prospect, and that of working with Will Rogers, stirred Trotti's greatest enthusiasm.

Judge Priest portrays the title character as a sage Confederate veteran who deflates social pretension and certain kinds of racial prejudice at every turn while serving as judge in a small Kentucky town circa 1890. In the opening scene, completely fabricated by Nichols and Trotti, Priest refuses to find Jeff Poindexter, played by Stepin Fetchit, guilty of chicken stealing but instead reminisces with his Civil War cronies about chicken stealing during the great conflict. Priest ultimately lets Jeff off because Jeff knows a great place to catch catfish with liver as bait; Jeff eventually becomes the judge's factotum. The film establishes Priest as a lonely widower who sponsors, over the objections of his pretentious sister-in-law, Caroline (Brenda Fowler), a romance between his newly minted lawyer nephew, Jerome (Tom Brown), and the orphaned girl next door, Ellie Mae Gillespie (Anita Louise), in yet another subplot the screenwriters created. Adapting Cobb's short story "Words and Music," Trotti and Nichols rearranged several elements so that Priest's nephew, with Judge Priest's counsel, successfully defends an unfriendly stranger in town named Bob Gillis (David Landau), who is accused of murder.

Priest's key strategy arises when he learns from the Reverend Ashley Brand (a character taken from yet another Cobb story, "A Tree Full of Hoot Owls," and played by Henry Walthall) that Gillis was a chain gang prisoner who fought valiantly during a Civil War battle. Priest arranges for the reverend to recount the defendant's military achievements in court, but he also arranges for Jeff to play "Dixie" at Priest's cue just under the courtroom window. The jury's verdict—on a defendant now revealed as a valiant fighter for the Confederate cause—cannot be in doubt. Moreover, Gillis is revealed to be Ellie Mae's father. Father and daughter are reunited; Priest's sister-in-law accepts her prospective daughter-in-law with open arms (in contrast to the utter disdain in which she held Ellie Mae throughout the film); Priest's nephew Jerome has won his very first case; and Jeff gets to keep the judge's vest he so desired.

That this script was very much the handiwork of Nichols and Trotti is affirmed by Cobb himself in a letter he composed when copyright issues arose. According to Cobb, "Many of the principal scenes and incidents, with the accompanying lines, were [in addition to many characters] their product and not mine. In other words, they kept the spirit of my background but except for certain episodes and one or two sequences, they entirely departed from my work and such outstanding episodes as they did retain were by them combined and woven into their own structure in order to make a playable, dramatic version based only in part on two un-related stories."[18] Beyond freely acknowledging the screenwriters' origi-nality and hard work, Cobb expressed great satisfaction with the film. He let Trotti know that he was "crazy" about it; "that means a lot," Trotti wrote in a letter to Mildred Seydell, his former colleague at the *Atlanta Georgian*, "for authors usually have complaints and not compli-ments." As for himself, Trotti admitted, "Of course I loved every mo-ment of doing it."[19]

Trotti's excitement over what he and Nichols had wrought fairly leaps off the page of this letter he composed when the film was completed. He wrote that if *Judge Priest* "is as good as I think it is, it ought to be al-most a sensation down there." He saw the film as a corrective to all of Hollywood's previous missteps in depicting the South. "I think you and all Sputherners [*sic*] will like it a lot," he wrote Seydell. "I really believe it is the best Southen [*sic*] picture so far. No phony Southern accents by Brooklynites; no you-alls to one person; no phony baloney of any sort. The colored people, Stepin Fetchit et al [*sic*] are really negroes as we know them, played for comedy chiefly of course but human and recog-nizable."[20]

False accents and "you-alls" to single characters were a constant com-plaint about Hollywood's depiction of the South through the late 1930s, as southern criticism of *Jezebel* attests. Black stereotypes were not. That Trotti felt Fetchit's quintessential "coon" stereotype and Hattie McDan-iel's happy, singing mammy Aunt Dilsey were "of course" comedy mate-rial demonstrates his allegiance to minstrel representation of the period. (Trotti and Nichols even composed a spiritual for the black characters to sing at an ice cream social—"Massa Jesus Wrote Me a Note.") Yet, the logic of racial relations in *Judge Priest* is more complex than this would suggest. The judge sings two songs with McDaniel's character without condescension. Dilsey's first scene has her singing about hanging the judge's wash up and then switching, improbably, when the judge's nephew Jerome shows up, to singing about cooking for him in a manic, almost parodic fashion.

Of course, Priest's exchanges with Jeff are hardly progressive: When the judge, while preparing his case for the defense, asks Jeff whether he can play "Dixie" on his harmonica, Jeff replies that he can, and he volunteers to play "Marching through Georgia" as well. The judge thereupon comments that while he has saved Jeff from one lynching (a scene not used), he would join another lynching mob if Jeff played Gen. William T. Sherman's tune. Yet their conversations also display a camaraderie that may have provoked laughs in a 1934 audience by subverting racial hierarchies through expressing a sense of equality that is completely unexpected. These wrinkles in their relationship defy, if they do not rebut, one-dimensional characterizations of the film as racist. As Ford biographer Joseph McBride writes, "In his personal and professional isolation, Judge Priest finds that he has more in common with blacks than whites."[21] One of the whites Priest disagrees with most is his sister-in-law, who wishes her son to marry a senator's daughter rather than the orphan Ellie Mae. Her pretensions inspire Judge Priest to comment that the name of Priest has never stood for intolerance in Kentucky. Here Nichols and Trotti affirmed Cobb's signed prologue to the film, which asserts that Judge Priest was "typical of the tolerance of that day and the wisdom of that vanished generation." They were visualizing Cobb's new mythology for the Old South, a counter to the foreign backwardness in the national imaginary.

In his letter to Seydell, Trotti was most enthusiastic about the film's climactic courtroom scene: "The finish is as thrilling as can be—all about Dixie." In fact, he hoped the film would be called "The Band Plays Dixie," in reference to this very scene. While the filmmakers thought it a stroke of genius to cast Will Rogers as Judge Priest, Trotti considered it a major casting coup and a fine "sentimental touch" to have Henry Walthall, the "Little Colonel" from *The Birth of a Nation*, play Rev. Ashby Brand, the character who exonerates the accused father in that scene. "When you see him in his Confederate uniform," he wrote Seydell, "you will rise and shout." In other words, the stirring evocation of the Lost Cause through the reverend's testimony (and the battle footage Ford superimposed over it), combined with Jeff's music, would galvanize the southern movie audience as much as it does the courtroom jurors. And if the theater audience's memories of D. W. Griffith's epic were really strong, they might have been further thrilled to notice that Gillis's exploits on the field of battle, as described by Walthall in the courtroom, duplicate Little Colonel's combat heroics in Griffith's film: Gillis at one point provides succor to a union soldier who has fallen, and later Gillis picks up the Confederate flag to continue a forward charge when a comrade in arms had dropped it. Ford cited Griffith for a new generation of moviegoers.

Yet in depicting Judge Priest as a master of mise-en-scène who knows how to—and does—thoroughly manipulate his "audience," Trotti and Nichols's script and Ford's direction gently but definitely also satirize the South's fierce pride in its past, as embodied in the judge's friends' boastful, repetitive but argumentative recountings of their exploits in the Civil War. Thus, humor enabled the filmmakers to celebrate the heritage of southern pride at the same time that they gently mocked it. This balancing act centers on the character of Judge Priest, as McBride puts it:

> Wise, tolerant, humorous, but also a lonely and melancholy figure, the Rogers character in Ford's films is successively a healer, a judge, and a showman—and all of those at once . . . a modest and diffident man roused to fight against social injustice. Simultaneously nostalgic and progressive in his outlook, Rogers mediates between warring factions in American life, providing a human link between past and present. He manages the seemingly impossible feat of keeping tradition alive while recognizing the necessity for social change.[22]

In this sense, the traits ascribed to Judge Priest, and the narrative structure of the film, provided a template for both Trotti and for Ford when they collaborated five years later on the far more celebrated *Young Mr. Lincoln*. The later film depicts a self-deprecating, sagacious character who embodies, like Priest, the spirit of reconciliation, this time on a national scale.

Trotti's predilection for biopics about national figures dates back to his very first script, *The Man Who Dared*, about Anton Czernak, the immigrant Chicago mayor gunned down in Florida in 1932 in an assassination attempt on Roosevelt. He later won a Best Screenplay Academy Award for his script for the 1944 *Wilson*. Trotti, however, reserved the greatest tenderness and enthusiasm for his film about Lincoln. As a collector of Lincolniana and the screenwriter of *Judge Priest*, Trotti, this time writing alone and building on failed screenplays dating back to 1935, was perfectly poised to render a portrait of the president as an awkward, humane, and ordinary young man.[23] As with *Judge Priest*, the script meandered during its first half and then settled into a contentious murder trial in the second.

We can gain insight into Trotti's approach to *Young Mr. Lincoln* beyond the model *Judge Priest* provided for his screenplay. Trotti was familiar with Hollywood's previous feature-length Lincoln biopics before 1939, and he was especially fond of Griffith's 1930 sound film, starring the patrician Walter Huston (father of director John Huston). The MPPDA anticipated criticism from both the North and the South directed at Griffith's portrayal of Lincoln in his early life as, in Joy's words, "a human, ordinary individual instead of the super-man we are taught to believe that he was."[24] Trotti was, of course, called on to lend his opinion on its possible reception. In a file memo and a letter to Joy, Trotti claimed Griffith's film had "all the elements of the best things of the screen plus popular appeal." He "liked it tremendously. . . . I'm for socking everybody who criticizes it on the grounds that Lincoln was God Almighty and could not have gone barefoot or loved a lady." In his memo, he wrote in the film's defense:

> Persons ignorant of history may object to Lincoln as a fighter, drinking out of a keg, running away from his wedding, making love to Ann Rutledge, and being henpecked by Mary Todd Lincoln, but to my mind such complaints will be worth exactly the paper they are written on and no more. We should not yield a single inch to anybody in defending this picture. It depicts the very finest points in the man—his native honesty, wit, courage, devotion to ideals and duty, and his humanity.
>
> The South can have no legitimate objection to anything in it. Its part in the conflict is handled with due respect to the section's right and pride. Lee is shown as a gallant officer and Lincoln pays tribute to him and the other Southern leaders.[25]

Joy responded to Trotti's assessment with teasing gratitude, writing, "Your criticism of [the film] is more valuable than anyone's else [sic] because you are a damn rebel."[26]

Equally important, Lincoln's "humanness," as seen in Griffith's film, would become the primary emphasis of *Young Mr. Lincoln*. At all times in this film, Lincoln—as scripted by Trotti, directed by Ford, and portrayed by Henry Fonda—is a sage, careful paternal figure whose own plain speaking and physical awkwardness compensate for his authority: he is, in fact, a more youthful version of Judge Priest. Indeed, Lincoln is shown grieving for the loss of Ann Rutledge, much as Priest does for his wife and children in the earlier film. One of Ford's most emotionally stirring scenes occurs when the river running alongside Lincoln and Rutledge freezes to signify her untimely death, and Lincoln visits her graveside, subsequently deciding to pursue law by the fall of a stick. At a later dance scene with Mary Todd, Lincoln, stricken on a balcony with melancholy at the sight of a river, falls silent. The dramatic similarities between the two characters remain striking. As Tag Gallagher himself writes, "Lincoln is a paradigm of the Fordian hero of any date:

solitary, celibate, almost impotent in grief, yet of the people; independent of logic, he arrogates authority to intervene, even violently, by cheating, in order to mediate intolerance and to impress his personal convictions upon those whose thinking he faults."[27]

Equally significant from the "professional southerner" perspective, however, was that this project afforded Trotti the opportunity to revisit the near lynching of Jeff Poindexter that he and Nichols had envisioned for *Judge Priest*, an episode based on Cobb's "Mob from Massac."[28] In the short story, a group from a nearby town descends on a local jail where a black man accused of assaulting a white woman has been arrested and deposited. The deputy jailer has no desire to lose his life defending the accused. Awakened by Jeff, Judge Priest commandeers the deputy's gun in front of the jail where the deputy has left the door wide open for the avenging crowd. The judge holds off the out-of-town mob, whose members have served as jurists in his courtroom, by appealing to law: "You can't hang any man—you can't hang even this poor, miserable little darky—jest on suspicion."[29] When this doesn't persuade them, Priest brandishes the gun and promises to shoot the first man who approaches the jail door. They reluctantly withdraw. When Judge Priest enters the jail, he learns from a ringing phone that the true culprit has been caught. The judge has not only prevailed over the racially fired mob mentality and saved an innocent man's life; when election time comes a few months later, the votes from the town of Massac give him the winning edge. Even the mob members in that showdown appreciate the fact that he had prevented them from acting on their basest instincts. In Cobb's story, the southern rabble itself is capable of reform.

In their March 1934 story outline and April 1934 final shooting script for *Judge Priest*, Trotti and Nichols had reshaped Cobb's story so that Jeff becomes the black victim of the imminent lynching. While out fishing with the judge, Jeff discovers that he forgot the beef-liver bait that makes the catfish bite. Judge Priest sends him back home to retrieve it. (This much occurs in the released film.) Meanwhile, on another side of town, the sheriff has a posse and bloodhounds searching after a "negro suspected of assault." The posse loses his trail when the suspect enters a swamp. Their hounds instead catch the scent of the beef-liver bait Jeff is carrying back to the judge. The scene was envisioned as comic: Jeff, completely unaware of the dogs' ownership and even why they are out, pets them and plays with them. The bait falls from his pocket and he has to snatch it away from the dogs, which now chase him relentlessly. When the posse arrives with torches lit ("an eerie scene," the story outline directions comment), Jeff is too petrified to speak in his defense. While some of the mob want to lynch him on the spot, the sheriff brings him to the jail. Back at the river, Jeff's girlfriend (also deleted from the film) informs the judge of what has happened. He rides his horse into town where the mob surrounds the jail and grabs a gun from one of his Civil War pals. He provides his alibi for Jeff and when the crowd refuses to listen, he raises the rifle and threatens to shoot the first man who approaches the jail. According to Ford, Will Rogers's speech against lynching at this point was "one of the most scorching things you ever heard."[30] They disperse, and Jeff is exonerated the following day.

The lynching sequence was deleted from *Judge Priest*'s final script, likely because of its controversial subject and its delay in getting to the Gillis murder storyline (though it would have offered a fine contrast in the film between mob rule and the judicial system). McBride has argued that the removal of the scene provided a key motivation for Ford to re-make *Judge Priest* as 1953's *The Sun Shines Bright*.[31] Yet, like the judge in Cobb's story, Lincoln stands at the jailhouse door in *Young Mr. Lincoln* where two brothers are imprisoned, stares down the mob, embarrasses them, and reasons them into going home. His wisdom is ultimately affirmed when Palmer Cass (Ward Bond), their chief accuser, is proven guilty of the murder. That the falsely accused are white does not entirely eliminate the racist resonances of this potential atrocity.

Young Mr. Lincoln demonstrates that in the years just prior to the United States' entry into World War II, Trotti was in the forefront of the film industry's progressive liberalism. Cripps has written that as late as 1941, "the Hollywood machine ground onward with only incidental participation by black influences . . . corporately, preferring riskfree enterprises and traditionally, defining good 'race relations' as an appreciation of only the winsome, pious, or musical traits of black culture." This trend was reinforced, according to Cripps, by the industry's southern citizens: "Every studio's cadre of Southern white counselors—Lamar Trotti, Nunnally Johnson, [Y. Frank] Freeman, [Steve] Lynch [a southern theater-chain manager] and others," Cripps continues, "provided advice on local color and racial etiquette. Moreover, in every sort of routine correspondence and conference, studio personnel displayed casual racial folkways shared with the nation at large. They called for 'nigger' extras, auditioned 'dinges,' and spoke of certain set-lights as 'niggers.'"[32] Yet elsewhere, Cripps argues, Trotti and fellow Georgian Nunnally Johnson were, unlike Paramount head Y. Frank Freeman, "trusted urbane Southerners, both of whom saw blacks in other than racist terms and were no longer prisoners of traditional Southern racial attitudes."[33]

Trotti in the early 1930s had warned Darryl F. Zanuck about offending southern sensibilities with a lynching scene in *Cabin in the Cotton*; by 1942 he was prepared to indict the savage practice. Although he did not work on Warner Brothers' fictionalized Leo Frank case film, *They Won't Forget* (1937), Trotti had the opportunity to adapt Walter Van

Tilburg Clark's novel *The Ox-Bow Incident*.[34] Initially conceived as an antifascist protest against mob rule, the film, as realized, had unmistakable implications for the United States and the South as a landmark social-consciousness movie, perhaps the most influential and widely admired antilynching film Hollywood ever produced, thanks in no small part to Trotti's no-nonsense script and William Wellman's quietly effective direction. Among the film's many admirers, Trotti could count *Strange Fruit* author Lillian Smith.[35]

The film concerns a deputized posse of mostly selfishly motivated locals from a desolate, boring Nevada town in 1885 who learn secondhand that Kincaid, one of their rancher friends, has been killed by cattle rustlers. After some debate, the group heads into the mountains, where they discover three men—an elderly man (Francis Ford, Ford's brother and the expert spitter Juror No. 9 from *Judge Priest*); a Mexican (Anthony Quinn); and a white leader, Donald Martin (Dana Andrews)—sleeping by a campfire. The three have some of the victim's cattle but no bill of sale; the Mexican has Kincaid's gun; after little debate, and the men's pleading of innocence, the mob hangs the three men at daybreak. As they ride back to town, the group encounters the sheriff, who informs them that Kincaid is in fact wounded but alive and well, that the trio they lynched were innocent, and that the leaders of the lynching will be prosecuted for murder. The film concludes with cow rustler Gil (Henry Fonda) reading Martin's letter to his wife to the stunned mob members in the saloon back in town and his departure with his friend and partner Art (Harry Morgan) to deliver the letter to Martin's widow and to help raise his two surviving sons.

The powerful impact of the film derives from more than its sober subject. As with *They Won't Forget*, no one can stop the lynching and the film lacks a happy ending. Another feature is the film's straightforward rendering of events. Aside from the first ten minutes, showing Gil getting drunk and into a fight in the town saloon, the story focuses unrelentingly on the process by which the mob is formed and the tragic inevitability of their actions. Only a brief interlude with Gil's former girlfriend passing through the mountains distracts us from the unpleasant subject of the film (this sequence also functions to plant Gil's motivation for aiding Martin's widow at the end of the film). Even more admirable is the film and novel's understanding of the mixed motives underlying the gang who go into the mountains to hang anyone they can find. The lynching group is diverse: it includes a pretend Confederate officer Major Tetley (Frank Conroy) and his son Gerald (William Eythe); the drunkard Monty Smith (Paul Hurst), who jokes about lynching by doing a laughing, grotesque impersonation of a hanging victim; Jenny "Ma" Grier (Jane Darwell), the woman who runs the local boarding house; and Kincaid's good friend (since they were five) Jeff Farnley (Marc Lawrence). The group includes dissenters such as the storekeeper Arthur Davies (Harry Davenport), who nearly talks the group out of going out to the mountains; Sparks (Leigh Whipper), a black reverend; and the main characters, Gil Carter and Art Croft, who have just ridden into town after several months away on the range.

As George Bluestone notes, in the earliest sustained analysis of the novel and film, the story achieves "the devastating power of an allegory permeated with moral and social overtones," largely through "a careful balancing of moral ambiguities. Like a morality play, Clark's characters become embodiments of virtues and vices who wage rhetorical, ethical, and even physical war with each other. But unlike a morality play, Clark's characters are endowed with complex motives."[36] The differences affect each member of the group: those who pursue lynching, those who oppose it, and the victims, whose responses to their plight range from the old man's willingness to say anything to survive (blaming the Mexican) to the Mexican's contempt for Martin's fear and anger.[37] Out of the mob members, Farnley wants to avenge his friend's murder, the drunkard Monty Smith seeks amusement, and Tetley cruelly wants to make a "man" of his sensitive son by sticking his nose in the lynching business. Gil and Art need to protect themselves from suspicion in Kincaid's death and reluctantly accompany the mob into the mountains; they ineffectually try to prevent the lynching.

In addition to the complex moral sense of the film, we might add Wellman's ability to visualize different characters' point of view, particularly the horror and dread of the victims. We see details from Martin's vantage point: the horrible cackling of Ma Grier in the distance as she laughs with the drunk Monty Smith while Reverend Sparks sings a hymn, which disrupts any semblance of order, and the close-ups on Smith's and Farnley's hands as they handle and tie the lynching ropes. The most disturbing shot in the entire film is not a point-of-view shot, however, but a general view of the mob's handiwork; after the horses have ridden into offscreen space, the camera slowly pans after them, revealing the three hanged men's shadows on the ground. The mob has come upon a morally ambiguous situation and failed a test of probity in jumping to conclusions.

The ambiguous status of the accused is often taken as a feature of the superior antilynching or anti–death penalty film—hence the innovation of They Won't Forget in only suggesting Robert Hale (Edward Norris) is innocent or the uncertain status of Barbara Graham (Susan Hayward) in the anti–death penalty film I Want to Live! (1958). Even if the men were guilty, their lynching could not be condoned or justified because they were entitled to due process. Still, as Bluestone points out, the uncertainty about Martin and his men before they are murdered is crucial to the film's message: "Any one of the protagonists could have resisted Tetley if, for example, Martin had been able to produce a bill-of-sale. But the situation as it develops calls for a truly great display of courage, and no member of the posse is able to provide it." Moreover, the presence of the black Reverend Sparks reminds the audience of the overwhelming number of black lynching victims in the country. Reluctant to join the mob, Sparks is persuaded that the criminals may need a man of the cloth. His own bit of backstory gestures toward the more complex moral scheme of the best antilynching films. When the group first arrives in the mountains, Sparks and Gil confide in each other how little they like "this business." In hushed tones, Sparks reveals that his brother was lynched and that "nobody did know for sure" if he was actually guilty. As Bluestone notes of Sparks's tale, "the extension of the reference is unavoidable."[38]

Bluestone has noted a number of changes Trotti made in adapting Clark's 1940 novel; the promise of punishment of the lynchers was created for the film in response to Production Code Administration concerns. In the novel, the sheriff lets the lynchers go. He tells his friends, "I haven't recognized anybody here. We passed in a snowstorm, and I was in a hurry."[39] In the film, he plans to prosecute them: "God had better have mercy on you, because you ain't gonna get any from me." Another change was to make Gil and Art more active against the lynching. In the novel they don't vote at all; in the film, they vote against the lynching and Gil even punches Mapes before the lynching ensues. In particular, Trotti shifted some of Art's antilynching dialogue to Gil to build up Henry Fonda's character ("hanging is everyone's business").

One of the most significant changes, however, was designed to minimize southern offense at the film. Tetley in the novel is, in Bluestone's words, "unmistakably an ex-Confederate Cavalry officer," a genuine Civil War veteran, albeit one who takes charge of the mob when the three victims are found and who persistently browbeats his sensitive son into participating actively in the lynching to prove his masculinity.[40] Trotti made Tetley a poseur who had no role in the great conflict and merely pretends to be a veteran. Significantly, he appears out of nowhere as the mob is forming outside the saloon, and when we cut to him as he speaks, the camera tracks slowly in on him to emphasize that he will play a crucial role in what unfolds. With his Confederate uniform (and even with his lavish columned house, a great contrast to the mud streets and modest storefronts lining the main street in town), Tetley seems to be the genuine article, giving the commands to go forward with his raised hand and generally presiding over the proceedings. Trotti gives Gil the cutting appraisal of Tetley as a pretender: "He never even saw the South till after the war—and then only long enough to marry that kid's mother and get run out of the place by her folks. . . . what do you suppose he'd be doin' living in this neck of the woods if he didn't have something to hide."[41]

In his insistence that his son participate forcefully in the proceedings, Tetley reveals himself to be pathologically obsessed with proving his and his son's masculinity. He forces Gerald to frisk the old man and Martin, and Gerald's distaste for the task and general friendliness to Martin gives the latter the first of many false moments of hope. Similarly, Gerald falters at the sight of blood when removing the Mexican's bullet, and he cannot bring himself to smack the horses into galloping away when the three are mounted with the nooses around their necks. But Gerald is hardly alone in this: when the moment of truth arrives and Tetley asks for volunteers to smack the horses into action, the drunkard Monty Smith—who has shown amazing skill in impersonating a hanged man—has no stomach for it, and even Ma Grier, with whom Smith has shared most of the laughs, quietly looks away from the very sight of the men about to be murdered.

Tetley receives his comeuppance when the mob returns to town after realizing its mistake. In the novel, Gerald hangs himself and Tetley responds by falling on his sword; in the film, only Tetley kills himself, and Gerald seems relieved. Here, Gerald upbraids Tetley after he locks his son out of the house: he directly boasts to his father, "I'm a coward," and denounces Tetley as a "depraved, murderous sadist." When Tetley subsequently shoots himself, we are unsure if this is because of the shame of the lynchers' crime that he urged on, because of his son's repudiation of him and his values, or some combination of the two. In this final gesture we see that Tetley has been humiliated and that he ultimately acts cowardly; he is implicitly contrasted with the Mexican, who comments with contempt on the "fine company" he dies with (Martin sobs in his final moments) and who displays great courage in the face of death. Bluestone surmises this shift was made "in order not to offend Southern sensibilities," not being aware that Trotti himself was a proud southerner.[42]

As Bluestone asserts, Trotti's other major alteration of the novel concerns the reading of Donald Martin's letter to his wife. Before being hanged, Martin asks for and receives time to compose it; he entrusts Davies with it to deliver to his wife, but before the hanging Martin angrily discovers that Davies is trying to get some of the posse to read it because its fine sentiments will certainly create even more doubt about the trio's guilt. Gil refuses to read it until after the hanging. As Bluestone points out, in the novel the contents of Martin's letter are never divulged to the reader: "All we know is that the letter's statement is honest and deeply moving in its attempt to soften the shock for Martin's wife, proof enough for Davies that the writer is incapable of willful murder, and that down in the Ox-Bow the men are reluctant even afraid, to read it." However, the letter is read aloud in the film and, as Bluestone discovered, its contents had been transposed from an earlier argument in the novel between Davies and another mob member. Surprisingly unsentimental, the letter is "too urbane, too polished, too carefully thought-out for the character of Martin, as portrayed by Dana Andrews. And it is hard to believe that Martin as we see him in his last hours—distracted, fearful, outraged, desperate—could have been capable of so polished a performance, even to his wife."[43] Indeed, Martin writes little to his wife that expresses his affection for her and their children.

The letter, transcribed by Bluestone, reads in part, "Law is a lot more than words you put in a book, or judges or lawyers or sheriffs you hire to carry it out. It's everything people have ever found out about justice and what's right or wrong. It's the very conscience of humanity. There can't be any such thing as civilization unless people have got a conscience, because if people touch God anywhere, where is it except through their conscience? And what is anybody's conscience except a little piece of the conscience of all men that ever lived?"[44] Clearly, Martin's letter functions here as the rhetorical punch line to the message movie, not unlike Sybil Hale's climactic indictment of district attorney Andy Griffin (Claude Rains) and journalist Bill Brock (Allyn Joslyn) in *They Won't Forget*. One might also compare it to Fonda's delivery of Tom Joad's celebrated "I'll be there" speech near the end of *The Grapes of Wrath*, which may well have inspired Trotti to shift the letter accordingly so Fonda could read it in the film's final moments. Like those other speeches, on paper Martin's letter would threaten to sink the novel into the moralizing monologues that also frequently mar Hollywood message movies, particularly their endings. As Bluestone notes, the reading is made "partly acceptable by the line of forlorn faces along the bar, each man aghast at what he has done, and by Henry Fonda's poignantly simple reading."[45] The lynchers' faces are shown in a series of two and three shots during the reading, but earlier in the scene, a tracking movement along the saloon bar revealed their desolation even before Gil reads Martin's letter. This shot echoes the various pans and tracks along the line of men at crucial points in the story: as they are deputized, as they vote whether or not to hang the threesome in the mountains, and here, finally, as they contemplate the horror of what they have done. Wellman's framing is odd, whereby, for much of it, Fonda's eyes are obscured by the brim of Art's hat.

The impact of the letter becomes all the greater at this point because we see that Martin was not only an innocent man but the most thoughtful, compassionate, civilized, and virtuous man in the entire film. Gil's determination to look after Martin's family stems from this realization and gives the film a glimmer of hope; this ending is certainly more positive than Trotti's alternative ending, in which Gil attacks his former girlfriend Rose Mapen's new husband, the bartender Darby (Victor Kilian) again hits him with a bottle, and he comes to, looking at the painting above the bar, all indicating, through symmetry with the opening scene, that Gil hasn't learned a thing from his night in the Ox-Bow.

Even with its more hopeful chosen ending, *The Ox-Bow Incident* seems far removed from the gentle humor and celebrations of sunny Americana in *Judge Priest* and the poetic wistfulness of *Young Mr. Lincoln*; Bluestone asserts that *The Ox-Bow Incident* paved the way for adult Westerns like *Red River*, *High Noon*, and *Shane*.[46] It is also the first instance of that rare creature, a Western film noir.

Though a box office failure, *The Ox-Bow Incident* received almost unanimous critical praise. Such acclaim was fitting for the work of a screenwriter/producer who, during the war years, as Cripps puts it,

> felt his liberalism heightened by the war in small ways recorded in his diary. He found himself bristling at racist tabletalk, questioning his own regional ideological baggage, counting the numbers of blacks in parades and in the Senate galleries during debates on polltaxes, feeling their rising presence in crowded depots and making little gestures such as after reading Lillian Smith's *Strange Fruit* leaving it in a Texas bus stop for some other Southern[er] to pick up and read. By 1944, he found himself arguing at dinner that "Negroes must be permitted to vote" and that "the South will and must face it." And in an encounter thrust upon them by their respective wartime activities, Trotti and Lillian Smith met in Washington where he found that mutually *he* had liked *Strange Fruit* and she had liked *Ox Bow*.[47]

Hence, across a space of sixteen years, Trotti's work, as a professional southerner, grew from promoting regional self-consciousness to racial awareness, and from civic tolerance to a national and then international unity. Yet Trotti remained attuned to his southern roots. Near the end of his career, in the summer of 1950, he promised North Georgia residents that *I'd Climb the Highest Mountain* would not repeat the insults of *Tobacco Road* and ironically joked that "we'll hang the first Yankee actor who tries to fake a Southern accent."[48]

When Trotti's final film, *Stars and Stripes Forever*, premiered at Atlanta's Fox theater the day after Christmas 1952, Davenport Steward of the *Atlanta Journal* pronounced it the best of the week because of its frequent scenes of the bands and the music: "Few will fail to feel a tingle along the spine when the band plays 'The Stars and Stripes forever' at the finale. . . . This is one of the very few movies we intend to see a second time." Paul Jones of the *Atlanta Constitution* agreed, noting, "Few screen writers could put the homey touch into a movie with the polish achieved by the late Lamar Trotti of Atlanta." The film appeared after

Trotti's premature death from a heart attack in August 1952. The previous month he had initiated a six-month leave of absence from Fox, partly in response to the death of his elder son Lamar Jr. in a car crash in 1950. Dudley Nichols later recounted, "I was with Lamar and Louise on the tragic occasion when Lamar Jr. was killed and the younger son's life hung in the balance. They were brave people, but the shock was so great I think it was the cause, later on, of Lamar's death."[49]

The obituaries for Trotti were lavish. Charlie Chaplin spoke of his social consciousness. Susan Hayward called him "a great creative artist, but what is more, he was a great human being, blessed with the gift of perfect understanding." Anne Baxter spoke of his "wisdom and understanding . . . insight and inspiration." Nunnally Johnson spoke of Trotti's "honor, talent and personal attractiveness."[50] In 1984 the Screen Writers' Guild made Trotti the fourth recipient of the Screen Laurel Award in thirty-five years of award giving; Trotti thereby joined the prestigious company of Frank Capra collaborator Robert Riskin, comedy screenwriter/director Preston Sturges and the legendary Ben Hecht.

According to one estimate, Trotti's fifty-four films resulted in $300 million in rentals over the course of his career.[51] Beyond the bottom line, however, Trotti, in carrying out his various duties in the film industry, was a man on a mission. From his work for the (MPPDA)'s Committee on Public Relations and then the Studio Relations Committee to his shift to screenwriting in the early 1930s, Trotti actively promoted the theme of reconciliation between North and South by advising the MPPDA on films that might give offense to southerners. With 1934's *Judge Priest*, Trotti's script with Nichols could gently satirize the South's lingering devotion to the Confederate cause while simultaneously offering the southern title character as the embodiment of humane tolerance for moviegoers north and south to appreciate.[52] With his solo script for 1939's *Young Mr. Lincoln*, Trotti could broaden his conception of national reconciliation in his fictional account of the fifteenth President's early years. After *Young Mr. Lincoln*, Trotti tried to redress southern injustice from a Hollywood standpoint by scripting and producing William Wellman's *The Ox-Bow Incident*, the film for which Trotti is best remembered, and which outstripped Hollywood's self-regulating conventions and its fear of offending the South.

Lamar Trotti's career has been largely overlooked in film history. The affectionate tone and relaxed sensibility of *Judge Priest* and *Young Mr. Lincoln* have been attributed to Will Rogers in the case of the former and John Ford in the case of both films. Moreover, by the late 1930s Trotti had come to specialize in a certain type of film cranked out regularly at Twentieth Century Fox and not championed by auteur criticism: Americana films that traded on a nostalgic appeal to the country's more rural and mythically more innocent past.[53] As a loyal studio employee who wrote on assignment, Trotti was not nearly as colorful as freelancers like Ben Hecht or political activists like Dudley Nichols.[54]

Yet Trotti played a crucial role in providing Hollywood with insight into the South and in creating films that southerners could applaud. He offered visions of the South as a progressive region. Trotti told auditors at the University of Georgia in 1947, "'The Georgia that I knew was full of enlightened people, kind people, generous people, not very different from the people of other sections of the country, except that I have always contended they were nicer to have dinner with. They had a gracious way of living. They had a tradition of culture of which no other sections could boast.'"[55] At the MPPDA, Trotti encouraged the film industry to respect southerners' views, however wrong they might be. With *Judge Priest* we find Trotti working in a self-conscious mode, telling about the South with a positive portrait that did not overromanticize the region.

Beyond this film, whenever possible, Trotti inserted some business or scene involving the South and its devotion to "Dixie" and all that the music symbolized. This occurs, for example, in a brief Georgia whistle-stop during Wilson's 1916 presidential campaign. More dramatically, in *Stars and Stripes Forever*, John Philip Sousa makes a surprise appearance at Atlanta's Cotton States Exposition of 1895 (incidentally where motion pictures were arguably first projected anywhere in the world). Here Sousa conducts an all-black choir from nearby Stone Mountain singing "The Battle Hymn of the Republic" for a white audience, after marching into the park playing "Dixie" and replaying it repeatedly to the wildly enthusiastic audience not that far removed in their pride from Judge Priest's pals in Kentucky. Praising the rousing music and Clifton Webb's performance, Jones of the *Atlanta Constitution* writes, "Trotti always managed to get something about his home town or state into his films. In this picture he recreated an incident in Atlanta's history in which Sousa played an engagement at Piedmont Park. Sousa and his band march into the park playing 'Dixie.' You may be sure this sequence is getting a rousing hand from Fox patrons." However, neither Sousa's biographer nor Sousa himself, nor accounts in Atlanta newspapers of the time, mentioned such an incident as occurring. Trotti may have invented it, and in sequencing "Battle Hymn" after "Dixie," this script by a liberal southerner acknowledged the inevitability of the growing civil rights movement.[56]

Thus, to the end of his career, Trotti played the ambassador, suggesting to the South that its attitudes had to change but also serving, in the phrasing of one Atlanta obituary, as "Hollywood's 'Southern Gentleman' and . . . the South's premiere interpreter to the motion picture business."

And while the newspaper's image of the southern gentleman itself evoked a long-standing tradition within the southern imaginary, Trotti's activities in Hollywood demonstrated that the possible intersection of southern regional identity and national media was far more complex than such praise could suggest.

NOTES

This chapter is a portion of my collaborative project with Professor Dana F. White of Emory University, "Segregated Cinema in a Southern City, Atlanta, 1895–1963." Dr. White's contributions to this essay have been invaluable.

I am using the term "professional southerner" in my title in the descriptive sense in which Cripps invoked this term in his *Slow Fade to Black* (New York: Oxford University Press, 1978) and *Making Movies Black* (New York: Oxford University Press, 1989)—that is, as an expert by birth whom the Hollywood studios came to rely on for an understanding of southern culture, mores, and attitudes. My use of the term is distinct from that of the academic "professional southernist" described as "both a monumental historian and an antiquarian" by Paul Bove in his essay, "Agriculture and Academe: America's Southern Question," in *Boundary* 2 9, no. 3 (Spring 1986): 172–74.

1. Rowland V. Lee made these comments at the "Conference between Representatives of the Producers Branch and Representatives of the Directors Branch on the Subject of Economies in Motion Picture Production; Meeting Being Held and Authorized by the Academy of Motion Picture Arts and Sciences," Los Angeles, July 14, 1927, 40–41, Motion Picture Association, reel 3, Academy of Motion Picture Arts and Sciences file, quoted in Richard Maltby, "Sticks, Hicks, and Flaps: Classical Hollywood's Generic Conception of Its Audiences," in *Identifying Hollywood's Audiences: Cultural Identity and the Movies*, ed. Melvyn Stokes and Maltby (London: BFI, 1999), 23.

2. Matthew Bernstein, "Selznick's March: The Atlanta Premiere of *Gone with the Wind*," *Atlanta History* 43, no. 2 (Summer 1999): 8.

3. Richard Maltby, "The *King of Kings* and the Czar of All the Rushes: The Propriety of the Christ Story," *Screen* 31, no. 2 (Summer 1990), rpt. in Matthew Bernstein, ed., *Controlling Hollywood: Censorship and Regulation in the Studio Era* (New Brunswick: Rutgers University Press, 1999), 62.

4. For an excellent account of the MPPDA's efforts to accommodate these various groups, see Ruth Vasey, *The World according to Hollywood, 1918–1939* (Madison: University of Wisconsin Press, 1997).

5. See Richard Maltby, "Sticks, Hicks and Flaps," 23–41. See also Henry Jenkins III, "'Shall We Make It for New York or for Distribution?' Eddie Cantor, *Whopee* and Regional Resistance to the Talkies," *Cinema Journal* 29, no. 3 (1990): 32–52; Matthew Bernstein, "A Tale of Three Cities: The Banning of *Scarlet Street*," *Cinema Journal* 35, no. 1 (Fall, 1995): 27–52, rpt. in Bernstein, *Controlling Hollywood*, 157–85. For an analysis of the dichotomy of sentimentality versus sophistication, see Lea Jacobs, *The Decline of Sentiment: American Film in the 1920s* (Berkeley: University of California Press, 2008).

6. Larry J. Griffin and Don H. Doyle, eds., introduction to *The South as an American Problem* (Athens: University of Georgia Press, 1995), 11.

7. Thomas Cripps, "The Myth of the Southern Box Office: A Factor in Racial Stereotyping in American Movies, 1920–1940," in *The Black Experience in America: Selected Essays*, ed. James C. Curtis and Lewis J. Gould (Austin: University of Texas Press, 1970), 116–44. One ground for nuancing Cripps's argument is to point out his assumption that southern audiences for the stage and for film were identical. Moreover, there is unequivocal evidence that some southerners objected heavily to seeing African Americans featured on-screen at all.

8. W. J. Cash, *The Mind of the South* (New York: Knopf, 1941), vii.

9. Fred Hobson, *Tell about the South: The Southern Rage to Explain* (Baton Rouge: Louisiana State University Press, 1983), 9–12.

10. Thomas Cripps, *Making Movies Black: The Hollywood Message Movie from World War II to the Civil Rights Era* (New York: Oxford University Press, 1993), 10.

11. For Johnson's advice on accents, see Bernstein, "Selznick's March," 10. Francis Harmon to Joseph I. Breen, memo, "Suggested Guiding Principles in Connection with Motion Pictures Dealing with Negroes and Whites," accompanying Francis Harmon to Joseph Breen, letter, November 5, 1937, Motion Picture Producers and Distributors Association Collection, Special Collections, Margaret Herrick Library, Academy of Motion Picture Arts and Sciences, Los Angeles (hereafter cited as MPPDA). Thanks to Richard Maltby for sharing this material with me. Thomas Cripps discusses the advice given Disney on *Song of the South* in *Making Movies Black*, 190; Harmon's suggestions to Darryl F. Zanuck appear in his memo, March 18, 1949, *Pinky* File, MPPDA. My argument here disputes the claim of Edward D. C. Campbell Jr. that "any chance that the old South themes could or had to be determined by natives simply was unfounded. The mythology was not sustained by Southerners. The area simply lacked the clout to shape a picture's outlook." *The Celluloid South: Hollywood and the Southern Myth* (Knoxville: University of Tennessee Press, 1981), 24.

12. "Lamar Trotti Joins Public Relations Department in Hays Office: Will Head Press Division under Direction of Jason S. Joy," *Atlanta Weekly Film Review*, May 30, 1925, 10; Maynard Tereba Smith, "Lamar Trotti: The Most Prolific of Screenwriters Wrote Films about America and Americans," *Films in Review* (August–September 1958): 377–81.

13. Hobson, *Tell about the South*, 180–86, quote on 185–86.

14. Letter from Mrs. Zella Alonzo Richardson, n.d., attached to Lamar Trotti to Governor Milliken, memo, May 13, 1927, *Uncle Tom's Cabin* File, MPPDA.

15. Trotti to Milliken, memo.

16. "Atlanta Bars 'Uncle Tom' after Preview and Uproar to Mayor," *Variety*, August 15, 1928, 4.

17. Jason S. Joy to Darryl F. Zanuck, letter, February 26, 1932, *I am a Fugitive from a Chain Gang* File, MPPDA.

18. Irvin S. Cobb, statement, n.d., *Judge Priest* File, Twentieth Century Fox Productions Collection, Special Collections, UCLA Theater Arts Library, Los Angeles.

19. Lamar Trotti to Mildred Seydell, letter, July 17, 1934, Mildred Seydell Collection, Special Collections, Robert Woodruff Library, Emory University, Atlanta, Ga.

20. Ibid.

21. Joseph McBride, *Searching for John Ford* (New York: St. Martin's Press, 2001), 210.

22. Ibid., 207. See as well Gilberto Perez's excellent discussion of the film "Saying 'Ain't' and Playing 'Dixie': Rhetoric and Comedy in *Judge Priest*," *Raritan* 23, no. 4 (Spring 2004), rpt. in *American Movie Critics: An Anthology from the Silents until Now*, ed. Phillip Lopate, exp. ed. (New York: Library of America, 2006), 682–98.

23. Scott Eyman, *Print the Legend: The Life and Times of John Ford* (New York: Simon and Schuster, 1999), 210.

24. Colonel Joy, memo to file, August 15, 1930, *Abraham Lincoln* File, MPPDA.

25. Lamar Trotti, memo to file, August 7, 1930, and Trotti to Colonel Joy, letter, August 8, 1930, *Abraham Lincoln* File, MPPDA.

26. Jason Joy to Lamar Trotti, memo, August 12, 1930, *Abraham Lincoln* File, MPPDA.

27. Tag Gallagher, *John Ford: The Man and His Films* (Berkeley: University of California Press, 1986), 173–74. In 1944 Trotti's Oscar-winning screenplay for *Wilson*, Darryl F. Zanuck's portrayal of the twenty-eighth president as a man of unsullied honesty and integrity and a prophet who sought to create the League of Nations, would show a U.S. president attempting to reconcile not just North and South but America and the world. No wonder the mise-en-scène repeatedly features Lincoln's portrait.

28. The story appears in Irvin S. Cobb, *Back Home: Being the Narrative of Judge Priest and His People* (New York: Doran, 1912), 246–84.

29. Cobb, *Back Home*, 270.

30. Ford, quoted in McBride, *Searching for John Ford*, 211.

31. Ibid.

32. Cripps, *Making Movies Black*, 8–10.

33. Thomas Cripps, *Slow Fade to Black* (New York: Oxford University Press, 1978), 359.

34. For a discussion of the production history of *They Won't Forget*, see Matthew Bernstein, *Screening a Lynching: The Leo Frank Case on Film and Television* (Athens: University of Georgia Press, 2009), 60–117.

35. Cripps, *Making Movies Black*, 98.

36. George Bluestone, *Novels into Film* (Berkeley: University of California Press, 1957), 171.

37. Ibid., 172–73.

38. Ibid., 177, 195.

39. Walter Van Tilburg Clark, *Ox-Bow Incident* (1940; New York: Random House, 2001), 211.

40. Bluestone, *Novels into Film*, 184.

41. Ibid., 184.

42. Ibid., 184.

43. Ibid., 185.

44. Ibid., 185.

45. Ibid. 194–85.

46. Ibid., 171.

47. Cripps, *Making Movies Black*, 98.

48. Quoted in Frank Thompson, "Lamar Trotti," *Atlanta Weekly*, October 26, 1986, M13. Thompson's piece is a superlative profile of Trotti's screenwriting career.

49. Davenport Steward, "Sousa Film Best of New Arrivals," *Atlanta Journal*, December 26, 1952, 4; Paul Jones, "Movies in Review," 7; see also Smith, "Lamar Trotti," 377–81; Dudley Nichols, letter to the editor, *Films in Review*, August/September 1958, 475.

50. Celestine Sibley, "Atlanta Born Lamar Trotti Mourned by Movie World," *Atlanta Constitution*, August 29, 1952, 1, 8; Ernest Rogers, "Lamar Trotti Dies after Heart Attack," *Atlanta Journal*, August 28, 1952: 1, 14.

51. For a box office accounting of Trotti's films, see Maynard Tereba Smith, "A Survey of the Screenplays Written by Lamar Trotti with Emphasis on Their Acceptance by Professional and Non-professional Groups" (master's thesis, University of Southern California, 1953), 10. It is actually not clear if Tereba is referring to grosses on Trotti films (box office intake) or rentals (box office income minus theater expenses and distribution fees).

52. Trotti did not always depict the South and southerners with gentle humor and compassion; his script for the low-budget, indifferent Gene Tierney vehicle *Belle Starr* (1941) embroidered history to depict a southern female gunslinger "like a Scarlett O'Hara of the Ozarks" with "an aristocratic background" who "conducts herself on the whole with devout Confederate fervour" motivated by the Union's hanging of her father. To the New York *Herald Tribune* critic, the film was unbalanced between explaining southern guerrillas' motivations against carpetbaggers and depicting "union officers assigned to keep order [as] . . . deserv[ing] little respect." Robert W. Dana, " 'Belle Starr'—Roxy," *New York Herald Tribune*, November 1, 1941, clipping file, Lincoln Center, New York.

53. George Custen discusses Zanuck's production strategy of Americana in *Twentieth Century's Fox: Darryl F. Zanuck and the Culture of Hollywood* (New York: Basic Books, 1997), 223–24, among other places. The term "favorite" comes from Custen, *Twentieth Century's Fox*, 245, 276. Interestingly, Trotti gets very short shrift in Custen's book (he is simply "Zanuck's favorite writer" or "most trusted writer," no doubt because of his gift for Americana scripts) and in most books about John Ford (245, 276). For example, in Gallagher's study of John Ford, Trotti simply gets a footnote in the analysis of *Young Mr. Lincoln*, noting that film's plot of two brothers accused of murder and protected by their mother stems from a case Trotti reported in Atlanta during the 1920s; see *John Ford*, 162n. Peter Stowell, in *John Ford* (Boston: Twayne, 1986) is the only exception among Ford scholars.

54. Richard Corliss neglects Trotti, author of fifty-four scripts, entirely. *Talking Pictures: Hollywood Screenwriters, 1927–1973* (New York: Overlook, 1974).

55. Quoted in Thompson, "Lamar Trotti," M13; Thompson also makes the point about Trotti not being assigned to *Gone with the Wind*, 11.

56. Jones, "Movies in Review," 7; Paul E. Bierley, *John Philip Sousa: American Phenomenon* (New York: Meredith, 1973), and John Philip Sousa, *Marching Along: Recollections of Men, Women and Music*, ed. Paul E. Bierley, rev. ed. (Westerville, Ohio: Integrity, 1994); Sibley, "Atlanta Born Lamar Trotti," 1, 8, quote on 8; in Atlanta Trotti's death was front-page news.

PART TWO

Viewing the Civil Rights South

Black Passing and White Pluralism

Imitation of Life in the Civil Rights Struggle

Ryan DeRosa

In his classic essay "Tales of Sound and Fury: Observations on the Family Melodrama," Thomas Elsaesser views stylistically sophisticated films by directors such as Vincente Minnelli or Douglas Sirk as the fruition of melodrama's potential to evoke a hegemonic social structure on the brink of implosion. The import he gives to narrative cinema in the social history of melodrama derives from the musical and spatial properties of the melodramatic form: "Considered as an expressive code, melodrama might . . . be described as a particular form of dramatic *mise-en-scène*, characterized by a dynamic use of spatial and musical categories, as opposed to intellectual or literary ones."[1] Narrative conventions of cause and effect, often portraying the individual's capacity to self-transform or to realize desire, become in melodrama a stress on *affect*, on the repetitive (circular) experience of suffering, with its social causes either rendered in certain moral schemes (in escapist melodrama) or made ambiguous yet specific to the current social arrangement of power (in radical melodrama).

A moment of radical melodrama, in Elsaesser's terms, occurs in Sirk's *Imitation of Life* (1959): Sarah Jane, a light-complexioned African American who attempts to pass for white, is brutally beaten by her white boyfriend to punish her for deceiving him and, it is implied, for making ambiguous her racial identity. The scene of Sarah Jane's collapse in the street—conjuring what Elsaesser might call her "negative identity [bestowed on her] through suffering"—cuts straight to Annie, Sarah Jane's dark-skinned mother, who rubs the feet of her wealthy, white employer, "Miss" Lora.[2] The violent repulsion of Sarah Jane's crossing of racial lines, coupled with Annie's labor that defines white privilege, posits that these characters' "emotional prisons" refer not to abstract or oblique relations of liberalism and capitalism.[3] The mise-en-scène and the editing suggest what many African Americans were voicing more and more: that slavery and its effects were remembered in the racist practices and social stratification of U.S. society.

Most critics in 1959 avoided the melodramatic treatment of the black characters—the beating scene and the stylistic excess (the nakedly emotional situations crafted to border on cliché and factitiousness) that inundates the passing narrative. Film scholars have ironically followed these earlier critics in refusing to analyze the film's melodramatic construction of racial conflict, often implying that the aesthetic consideration of melodrama in prior scholarship has been too exclusively centered on the text and the director-as-author instead of on the historical context that shapes meaning.[4] This essay adapts Elsaesser's concern with textual style to historicize melodrama in this film in relation to the black freedom movement and to the ambivalent relation of white liberals to that movement.

Imitation's melodrama potentially confers an intense legitimacy on Sarah Jane's racial passing, which white critics refuted within their reviews by transposing the melodrama into realism. "Reality" is an important discourse for the critics, a way they distinguish the black characters from the white; while they laud the "lifelike" quality of the racial-passing story, they condemn the "white" storyline as melodramatic artifice, thus expressing a stark difference in visual style and narrative credulity between the representations of whites and blacks. These binary aesthetics quarantine Sarah Jane, as much as Annie, in the narrative category of "black," precluding possible discussions of class inequality and racial conflict.

If we take seriously Elsaesser's theory that melodrama can work *with* the viewer at historical moments by shifting meaning onto the emotional tactics of the form (condensing meaning into the film's look and rhythms), then we must interrogate this realism, this representational economy and clarity through which whites viewed the black characters. The realism that framed interpretations of *Imitation* illuminates an ideological position tailored for white males: at once it forecloses the film's support of class equality between races and disparages the female fan who might see Lora, Annie, and Sarah Jane as battling compulsory domesticity. Only a feminist interpretation of the film's enchantment for female viewers can fully reveal the racial discourse at work in the reviews, because this melodrama, marketed as a woman's film, represents the home as a predicament for *all* the female characters, a point not to be lost on the white male spectator.

Outside the film experience proper, this ideological position that envelops the black characters in "realism" implicitly reacted to, and against, the radical symbolism evolving within black activism. The maternal melodrama structure (along with other "personal" structures of experience, such as migration and memory) became explicitly political—and, cultural historian Adam Green argues, implicitly national—when Mamie Till Bradley in 1955 gave her lynched son a public funeral and viewing; her activism allowed millions of black Americans to witness the real and symbolic brutality of white racism through the pictures of Emmitt Till reproduced in *Jet*. Green writes that those especially moved were likely black youth identifying with Till, age fourteen; by 1959 this generation had reached the front lines of activism, ready to lead the expansive, experimental, and militant energies of the civil rights movement during the 1960s.[5]

While studies of the film generally ignore the "radical ambiguity" of the scene in which Sarah Jane is beaten (the framing, music, and editing that help make the violence symbolic of a larger crisis), another scene captures our attention without fail.[6] The funeral scene, ending the film, in which Sarah Jane asks forgiveness for passing against a didactic staging of black culture, connotes transparent truth—or lack of ambiguity—in the black image. In this funeral, Mahalia Jackson suddenly appears as the choir leader. Jackson, a migrant from the South (New Orleans) to the North (Chicago), replaces the migrant Annie, for whom she sings. In doing so she helps shift the aesthetics of the film from the melodramatic mode of Annie's and Sarah Jane's suffering—connoting racism's "emotional prisons"—to a realist mode in which whites especially could believe that racial progress depends paradoxically on identifying and verifying the social limits of integration and blackness itself rather than the racist norms and injustice that reinforce racial and class inequality.

The funeral scene's verisimilar images of black sufferance are signs of an apparently real black community, the religious and fraternal institutions to which Annie belongs. The scene elaborates narrative hints of the South as a culture separate from the North (this is a *Harlem* Baptist funeral) and of black culture as hidden from the mainstream.[7] Displaying a cultural pluralism that was becoming an essential component of how whites viewed their identity within a to-be-integrated nation, the scene elevates cultural difference as a counterweight, even counterargument, to the social forces of integration that could have been viewed as motivating Sarah Jane's passing.

I compare and connect this strategic representation of black culture with Stanley Elkins's representation of the slave in *Slavery: A Problem in American Institutional and Intellectual Life*. Elkins postulates that the antebellum South was a "closed" culture: distinct, relatively unchanging, and not needing to *rapidly* change, since the slaveholder was "benevolent" in his paternal treatment of the slave. In his theory, slavery might have ended peacefully by ending slowly, through incremental reforms, but cultural differences prevented abolitionists from knowing the true South and true psychic condition of the slave. Northerners could not see that the South, poisoned by its own cultural purity, produced a slave *in personality*, unready ("lack of fitness") for immediate, full freedom.[8]

Elkins's ideas emerged in a white liberal public sphere in which gradualism in racial politics attained the hegemonic position, helping to ensure that freedom for black Americans would require a "slow and painfully bitter struggle."[9] *Slavery* reveals to us how this gradualism, for most whites, could devalue the *meaning* of black freedom and make it more difficult to conceive and valorize the redistribution of symbolic and real wealth in the form of guaranteed job opportunities, extended social investments in minority neighborhoods, and a decisive focus on attacking inequalities of housing and education. Parallels between how whites were viewing the black characters in *Imitation* and how Elkins viewed the slave illuminate a pivotal moment when white liberals linked cultural pluralism to the delayed implementation of racial reforms, with the tragic result of naturalizing that delay by blaming it on the victim.

Elkins proposes that the docile, immature slave was a real human type created by southern culture. Pluralism became a framework for updating a racist stereotype for use by scientific-minded liberals. So, too, the funeral scene, using Mahalia Jackson as cultural metonym, suggests *how* the white viewer could have overlooked Sarah Jane's right to social opportunity and personal dignity (expressed as her need to pass) and Annie's labor as a factor in her suffering and focused instead on the "realism" of the black representations, the "naturalism" of the tragic mulatta and mammy. The scene, like Elkins's argument, pins black lower-class stasis—Annie's deification as a servant, Sarah Jane's renunciation of passing—on an emergent discourse of cultural-racial difference.[10]

This essay historicizes the use of culture as a discourse of white privilege by examining how this use allowed whites as a group to abandon the cause of racial reform. I also have a methodological agenda: to open the historiography of race in film studies to more radical, egalitarian, and class-rethinking positions than our liberalism has generally allowed, positions that have come out of analyses and experiences, the history and currency, of black activism.

The Radical Ambiguity of Passing

Sarah Jane's passing could be her solution to an "external world . . . riddled with obstacles which oppose themselves to personal ambition."[11] Passing is her rebuff of Lora's request that she help Annie serve Lora's business conference and of Annie's suggestion that Sarah Jane stop brooding and "go over to the party at the church," a party of "bus-boys, cooks, chauffeurs," which, like Lora's meeting, seems to exclude her from the social opportunities she craves. As Sarah Jane slips out to rendezvous with Frankie, we catch an image from her point of view, of Lora's *other* servant: an older black man whom the film shows only *as* a servant, framed almost as part of Lora's decor. His image connotes she is passing to escape this interpellation of identity, the linkage between blackness and servitude.

At the end she *does* go to this church party, as the black church represents the corrective to her life of willful subterfuge; yet even here the melodrama exhibits contradiction. Lora walks Sarah Jane from Annie's hearse (screen left), and when the hearse doors shut we cut to inside of Lora's limousine as Sarah Jane falls into the lower right corner of the frame. Sarah Jane's position in the car, in the white family, is thus a reflection of Annie's position in the hearse. Lora, her daughter Susie, and her fiancé, Steve, who do not often, if ever, understand Sarah Jane's (or Annie's) desires or pain, surround her: an image of racial integration that could as easily increase as assuage the tension hanging over her deferred dreams.

Most who write about this scene do not explore the possibility that the melodrama *articulates* Sarah Jane's return, however foreseen in the narrative, as going against her interests, against her freedom—and designs this articulation as a source of emotional dissonance. Richard Dyer argues that the scene's domestic values and imagined black culture underline racial and class hierarchy and the factitiousness of Lora's acting career. For Lucy Fischer, the scene reconciles narrative and ideological contradiction: "*Imitation* settles tensions by means of a conservative dénouement" that "splits female consciousness into shifting, compatible halves—good mother and bad, natural woman and perverse, black and white, lower- and upper-caste, housewife and professional—rather than imagining their potential merging." Marina Heung explores the ending as reactionary; like Dyer she posits its "pseudo-documentary effect" that helps "reinstate Annie, in her death, as the emotional and ideological center of the film." Jackie Byars affirms, "This narrative closure definitely reinforces dominant ideology, encouraging belief in the power of the individual and ignoring the necessity for social change, even at a time when social change was under way."[12]

These readings place the funeral scene within the struggles for black freedom and for women's liberation. It remains unclear, though, why we do not give more importance to the contradictions that seem in the foreground and to the passing melodrama that lingers in our memory; we might suppose that the images of black culture carry the moral weight that gives order to the entire film. But we would still need to explain, historically and culturally, how the representation of black culture carries such ideological authority. Scholars often read the film as a whole as leaning toward the conservative resolution of the funeral scene. The funeral scene seems to have this power to constitute the imagined unity of the text and to dissuade us from looking at the film as constitutive of social and ideological struggle.

Indeed, scholars frequently read the film through the eponymous binary imitation/life, a method that has disparaged the melodrama, ignored its expressive excess, and viewed the film as a fixed object. Note how these assessments use story and dialogue as evidence but do not require (as support for their ideas) an analysis of the melodrama qua melodrama: "While Lora is chastened, Annie is dead, leading us to wonder whether *any* vision of womanhood survives this cultural bifurcation"; "Everyone in her household polices Lora . . . [E]ach pronounces a monologue that catalogues explicitly Lora's inadequacy as a lover, mother, employer—in part because she really does lie and self-deceive to further her career, but mainly because public life is 'imitation' and private life is 'real,' where women are concerned."[13] The usual exegesis privileges the story and dialogue (and film title!) over the ambiguous symbolism, leaving an impression of the masterful reach of patriarchy into a popular woman's film. The women who enjoyed this melodrama may seem duped, as the film would show Lora beguiled into wanting a career: "Lora's neglect of her daughter . . . leads irrevocably to their confrontation near the end of the film, when, in answer to Lora's defense that 'It's only because of my ambition that you've had the best of everything . . . ,' Susie retorts by asking, 'And what about a mother's love?'"[14] This method must be balanced with, and sometimes superseded by, an exploration of the melodramatic form and a more inquisitive exploration of the spectator, to show the film's constitutive engagement in nascent and ongoing struggles for gender and racial equality.

Let us interpret this last-mentioned scene, which culminates "Lora's neglect of her daughter," by using more of the melodrama. The scene follows several in which Annie is shocked from Sarah Jane's disowning of her, and now Annie, sick in bed, informs Lora that Susie is in love with Steve. In their dialogue, the camera follows Lora away from Annie's bedside, graphically showing Lora's concern with herself and Susie despite Sarah Jane's "very real problem." As Lora leaves to talk with Susie, Annie leans forward and cries, "Wait!"—but too late: the camera approaches Annie and the scene ends in muteness, evoking her longing to save both mother-daughter relations, but based on her having already lost Sarah Jane. She soon repeats this helpless gesture of leaning from the bed when she pleads with Steve to find Sarah Jane.

In this scene, the editing and camera motion underscore an experiential and psychological gulf between Lora and Annie, which is also registered in dialogue and acting, as well as in the contrast between Annie's look of psychic and physical exhaustion and Lora's pastel dress, vibrant expression, and movements. As elsewhere, they are connected in their desire to be "good mothers" yet separated through the representation of race relations. Lora's exchange with Susie, coming after her ambiguous conversation with Annie, is consequential yet quotidian: Susie is going to college, what Annie wishes hopelessly for Sarah Jane. The female viewer may have merged the experiences of Annie and Lora to feel how domestic ideology exerts constant pressures, uneven rewards, and inexplicable punishments on women; this feeling works in tandem with, even within, the evocation of black struggle against white self-interest.

If melodrama banks on "the feeling that there is always more to tell than can be said," then we are drawn to the repressed voice of Annie—in her relations with Lora and in her relations to Sarah Jane's passing (repressed in the story, but expressed in the vitality and vicissitudes of the representations).[15] In the opening sequence, as Lora and Susie leave Coney Island, Sarah Jane cries, "I'm tired!" White mother and daughter hear and bring home their new acquaintances. Sarah Jane's anxiety speaks to desperate poverty (homelessness, unemployment) and migration; compare this direct indirectness of Sarah Jane with Annie's smiling, shrewd but futile, pitch to Lora—her indirect directness, her pitch of "mammy": "[Would you like] a maid to live-in, someone to take care of your little girl, a strong, healthy, settled-down woman who eats like a bird and doesn't care if she gets no time off and will work real cheap?"

Annie's desire to protect Sarah Jane runs side by side with Sarah Jane's own self-protective discourse: "I want to go home too!" Consider, in the next scene, Sarah Jane's choice of the white doll over the black. This iconography alludes to Dr. Kenneth Clark's studies of the inferiority complex caused by racism, in which black children imagined black dolls inferior to white; he famously repeated his experiments in the *Brown v. Board of Education* desegregation case (1950–54). Yet *Imitation*'s dolls symbolize more than the psychological damage of racial stigmatizing. Sarah Jane drops the black doll when Annie hushes her protest over being installed in the maid's quarters of Lora's flat; the camera tilts down and fades out on the doll, as ominous music echoes Sarah Jane's words: "I don't want to live in the back! Why do we always have to live in the back?" While the black doll at first signifies just Sarah Jane's rejection of her race, the rhythm of parallel actions that come together—Sarah Jane's rejecting the doll from Susie and Annie's accepting accommodations from Lora—helps resignify the black doll to evince Sarah Jane's rejection of second-class status, of a life of service to whites, of "always living in the back." The scene thus captures the race *and* class struggle fueling Clark's experiments, emotionally explaining racial stigma through reference to racial discourse and to a segregating class context.[16]

Melodramatic ambiguity expresses Sarah Jane's desire for social equality, which she obeys by passing; in achieving this effect, the melodrama gives Annie a voice of social desire—Sarah Jane's voice—going beyond the structure of the story. Annie's dying words—"I'm just tired, Miss Lora, awfully tired"—refuse *service* to Lora, and do so by echoing Sarah Jane's cry on the beach. When Sarah Jane masquerades as Lora's servant in front of the agent of a movie director who would remake *Lora's* image, she interprets Annie's labor as recollecting slavery—she is literally the proxy for Annie, who is working in the kitchen—and condemns Lora's casting of her and Annie into servile roles, as Lora takes a role that recalls, to Lora's mind, a nouveau plantation mistress ("the best part since Scarlett O'Hara").

Sarah Jane burlesques as a slave with a mock southern accent, serving a southern dish ("a mess o' crawdaddies") to Lora and her guests as her "mammy" once served "ol' massa." Her fawning eyes and swaying hips, highlighted by camera angles and close-ups, embellish the caricature. Black spectators might have understood Sarah Jane's parody in the spirit of the civil rights movement's serendipitous acts of memory—the call to be "free by '63," the centennial of the Emancipation Proclamation, for instance.[17] By contrast, Elkins's *Slavery*, appearing the same year as the film, harmonizes the slave's personality with submissive postures produced by "an exquisitely rounded collective creativity" called "the South": "the most congenial resources of Southern society had been available" to make the slave the master's "chef d'oeuvre."[18] In this way Elkins disciplines our knowledge of slave rebellions. Sarah Jane, by contrast, enacts and alludes to slave resistance: she throws Lora's "chef d'oeuvre," her ideal black servant, back in her face.

These opposed historical memories evoke opposing historiographies, revealing an ideological battle over the meaning of freedom that was waged at this moment through representations of the South and of the black worker.[19] Sarah Jane's performance as slave—as Lora's fantasy of Annie—supports the freedom to control one's own labor, its activity and product: a battle for social equality whose urgency connects Sarah Jane with Annie, as it would connect, for black America, 1959 to 1859.

Hence, even against the plotline's tragic course, Sarah Jane's passing relies on her ambiguous, emotional, and *social* connections to Annie. In the scene that follows the battery of Sarah Jane, Lora, her feet massaged, declares maternal contentment; she is happy to attend Susie's graduation rather than travel to Italy for her film. Annie, visibly pale, responds with *her* feeling about motherhood: weariness. When Lora asks what is wrong, Annie explains she feels "just a little tired," *remembering* (for the audience) Sarah Jane's phrase on the beach *and* Sarah Jane's current weariness (we left her lying in the gutter). The dialogue then turns to Annie's funeral plans. We can say that Sarah Jane's passing, her rejection of second-class status, is the vehicle for destroying, symbolically, not her mother but *mammy*. Lora's first misrecognition of Sarah Jane as the daughter of Annie's white employer (unintentional passing) momentarily cancels Lora's fantasy that Annie could be *her* own maid. However, it is Sarah Jane, as Annie's daughter, who voices her desire for her own home, which finally manages to procure for the black family a lodging for the night.

Melodrama and Masquerade, Realism and Mammy

As Elsaesser suggests, the subversive qualities of melodrama require a historically situated subversive viewer or, rather, viewing community.[20] Ironically, the clearest evidence for such a viewer may come from the male critics of *Imitation*, who imagined and feared the female viewer who understood the melodrama too well, enjoyed it too much. If we widen our consideration to encompass the melodrama of the film generally, we can imagine a subversive viewer through the vehemence of the opposition to her. More theoretically, if "contestation among competing publics supposes inter-public discursive interaction," as Nancy Fraser writes, then here is one instance where we can work backward to discover a yet unorganized feminist counterpublic, starting from the dominant male public's seemingly organized resistance to it.[21]

Notices for *Imitation* deride elements of the story ("contrived and obvious," "encounters are hackneyed, the dialogue is brazenly banal") but stress the *style*—the visuals, rhythm, acting, and emoting—calling it maudlin ("a lachrymose floodtide"), ersatz ("hideously false atmosphere," "manufactured"), and superficial ("somehow it's all on the surface").[22] While scholars center the story and dialogue, these critics target the melodramatic artifice: "Certainly such a situation might be handled and performed in such a way that the basic dramatic conflicts in it would have realistic quality and strength," writes *New York Times*'s Bosley Crowther, but the director Sirk and screenwriters Eleanor Griffin and Allan Scott "passed up restraint and raw-boned eloquence." Crowther coins a "raw-boned" word for the film: "muchness." "Lacking in imagination and restraint," intones *Newsweek*, it is "not a very good imitation of life."[23]

If the scholars, who invariably critique the gender politics as compromised, are versed in the style of melodrama but often avoid discussing it, the critics critique the style as a sign of women's public or consumer power. Ads for *Imitation* solicit women with a contradiction: the need to save mother-daughter ties *and* to achieve distance from men or from the "bad" home. But they invite a feminist esprit de corps by highlighting the name, words, and sometimes image of Fannie Hurst, called in a contemporary interview "one of the nation's most successful women novelists and outspoken feminists."[24] One critic bluntly states that *Imitation of Life* is "for distaff moviegoers to spend a couple of hours in a state of happy misery."[25] For Crowther, muchness ("no reluctance, no restraint") derives from the focus on women in the film: "There are two mothers in the situation—and no fathers, by the way; no parents of masculine gender to confuse the rich flow of mother love" and also in the audience: the film "contains the sort of bathos that invariably stimulates the hearts of patrons, particularly women, whose emotional resistance is low."[26]

Exceptional turnout for *Imitation*—the highest-grossing noncomedy of the year and Sirk's most popular picture—sparked fears that movie culture would cling to the film's aesthetic and moral defects.[27] To ease these fears, because "it has long been a man's world in the cinema," a writer from the *Los Angeles Times* takes issue with a report that women want their own kind of film, let alone a film "drenched in bathos like an 'Imitation of Life.'" "What they have missed most," he avers, "is some self-identification," by which he means compelling female performers. A contrary tactic, with the same upshot of rejecting the woman's film, simply disavowed the female public: "It may be a man's world, but not in a woman's picture."[28]

Lana Turner, "beautifully gowned, but seldom convincing," could serve as shorthand for the disreputable values of the melodrama: "As an actress, Miss Turner has a great deal to learn about varying her scenes since a smile and a gape constitute her gamut of expressions. She looks, of course, sleek, composed and uses her clear blue eyes with some effect."[29] Undermining the negative connotations of these remarks, while exploring their underlying fascination, I posit that many women may have understood Turner's masklike histrionics, which depart so shamelessly from the middlebrow protocols of method acting, as offering palpable resistance to patriarchal norms and proscriptions.[30]

In "Film and the Masquerade: Theorizing the Female Spectator," Mary Ann Doane argues that conventions of Hollywood cinema privileging male heterosexual desire interweave ideas of femininity: of the woman as screen, as natural object of visual pleasure, and as threatening sign of sexual difference. Yet the female spectator might discreetly turn the tables on her role as signifier of sex and gender and the cinema itself, by employing what Doane calls the masquerade: "Masquerade constitutes an acknowledgement that it is femininity itself which is constructed as a mask—as the decorative layer that conceals a non-identity."[31]

The masquerade, as a mode of viewing that appropriates a male image and narrative of Woman for women's pleasure and self-inquiry, helps us imagine how female fans may have used the imitativeness of Lora's femininity, as interpreted through Turner's performance, to valorize her contested desire. If Lora evokes to-be-married-ness through several characterizations—her faults as a single mother, her evolving nods to the binary of career *or* marriage, and the contradictions of Turner's persona that Dyer names, connoting her femininity as "ordinary," "strongly sexual," "manufactured," "ornamental," and "suffering"—then these cumulative ties to femininity as signifier of gender difference might seem excessive.[32] This excess, in the idea of masquerade, could provide cover against psychological and social repercussions for defying patriarchy; *excess*, this stuff of melodrama, would open opportunity for women to enjoy Lora subversively, clandestinely *yet publicly*, as she fulfills *all* her desires "in her own time" and according to her own frame of reference—her professional acting, precisely.

The film might thus have safeguarded feminist pauses and reflections as they sought a common tongue. In *The Feminine Mystique*, Betty Friedan connotes a thawing of postwar middle-class gender roles in the late fifties, citing a time that matches the release of *Imitation*: "[O]n an April morning in 1959, I heard a mother of four, having coffee with four other mothers in a suburban development . . . say in a tone of quiet desperation, 'the problem.' . . . Just what was this problem that has no name? What were the words women used to express it? Sometimes a woman would say, 'I feel empty somehow . . . incomplete.'"[33] Peter Brooks has described melodrama as a crisis of language, a text of muteness; for middle-class women, experiencing and inciting a crisis in the language of domesticity, the viewing of *Imitation* may have been affirming, resonant, even promising in an elusive way.[34] This viewing strategy, making use of the artifice of melodrama to acknowledge the artifice of female identity, we can call masquerade, but it would be slightly different from Doane's concept, since this masquerade would be more collective, part of the urgent dialogues between women that Friedan reports.

But would this masquerade privilege whiteness? When discussing strategies of female spectatorship, we must bear in mind the point made by bell hooks: "Black female spectators have gone to films with awareness of the way in which race and racism determined the visual construction of gender."[35] She opens spectatorship to overlapping social spheres and relations of power, positing "the oppositional gaze" that many black women bring to the representations of race and gender. Apropos of this gaze is a column by Izzy Rowe in the black *Pittsburgh Courier*, commenting on the tragic-mulatta films of the late fifties: "I don't know about you, but I'm a little sick of these pictures depicting the so-called problems of the half-breed. You know the kind, they're more white than Negro, who feels [sic] that the best way to get away from it all is to marry what the film makes you believe is a man above her station, white, of course. To me, the much-publicized 'taboo theme' is a flagrant insult to the human race. . . . Such pictures spend more time building instead of destroying a caste system." Referring to *Night of the Quarter Moon* (1959), Rowe enfolds black audiences into her personal position: "You'll walk out of the theater wondering 'Why?' and *wishing that you had seen it with an all-colored audience.*"[36]

Rowe's notion of a black audience critiquing films made in their supposed interest would challenge much of film theory that takes a model of the isolated viewer, which leaves little room to theorize popular ideological dissent. Her aside, "You know the kind, they're more white than Negro," could suggest that a major problem confronted by black viewers of *Imitation* was the casting of white newcomer Susan Kohner as Sarah Jane over prospective black-identified thespians.[37] A string of films, attacked by Rowe for promoting "a caste system," had employed big-name whites for the role of the tragic mulatta: Yvonne De Carlo in *Band of Angels* (1957), Natalie Wood in *Kings Go Forth* (1958), and Julie London in *Night of the Quarter Moon.*

Reviews in the *Chicago Defender* reveal one way black viewers could navigate, while opposing, these "blackface politics of casting."[38] The *Defender* celebrates Juanita Moore as Annie; Mahalia Jackson—who appears as choir soloist during Annie's funeral—as "a single [sic] with potency equal to [Hollywood's] acting stars"; and, most prominently, Fredi Washington, the black actor and labor activist who played Peola (Sarah Jane) in the 1934 version of *Imitation of Life*: "The role created by Fredi Washington (Peola), sister-in-law of Congressman Adam Powell, is now trusted to a non-sepian, Susan Kohner."[39] A large, glamorous photo of Washington from the 1930s, next to a smaller, less flattering profile-image of Kohner, suggests that the memory of Washington should be the central reason to watch Kohner. This viewing strategy challenges the racist nexus of mainstream critics, the casting office, and the tragic mulatta stereotype and opens discursive and psychic space for the black audience to enjoy the melodrama. Kohner "passes" for Washington, for black talent, struggle, and dignity; the proper judge of Kohner's skill at passing is the remembering black public.[40]

In sum, *Imitation*'s melodrama can combine white female pleasure with women's struggle, and black female pleasure with black and women's struggles, in ways that may overlap but are not necessarily homologous; scholars, however, have avoided the melodrama as a potentially complex visual-rhythmic language, *especially* in the images of passing. For Dyer, race relations structure the gender narrative: "Annie . . .

is the breadwinner . . . who enables Lora to pursue her career, and she is housewife and mother to Susie. . . . In other words, *she is the reality*, the material existence, that makes Lora's appearance possible."[41] For Marianne Conroy, the narrative composes Annie as a stereotype of black servility and self-effacement: "Annie assures 'Miss' Lora that she 'like[s] takin' care of pretty things' so much that she is willing to do Lora's laundry for nothing. The vicarious pleasure that Annie takes in Lora's 'pretty things' suggests that for her, status rhetoric bespeaks an *over*identification with the tastes of those to whom she is socially and economically subordinated as a black domestic worker." Yet Conroy uses a different lens to read Lora, examining a middle-class "status panic" that exceeds strictly narrative self-evidence.[42] Although these scholars have innovative historical takes on the film's gender struggle as regards Lora and the white female viewer, they also reflect a tendency to ignore the melodramatic shaping of the passing narrative; they unknowingly follow the tack of contemporary critics who refused to see the black characters as part of the same melodrama as the white. While these critics reaffirm stereotypes, the scholars commit a different but related error—of not locating the film *within* the black freedom movement, which then remains just a historical background, and sometimes a background that foregrounds a white historical subject.

The mainstream press divided the narrative by race; by class, implicitly, separating "the race problem" (passing) from "the career-woman question" (understood to be about Lora alone); and by aesthetics, seeing the passing as realism (conveying reality) but Lora's career-rising as melodrama (conveying unreality). The critic who assails the "hideously synthetic atmosphere" and "fiercely false story" of Lora's social mobility acclaims the "intensely true" story of the tragic mulatta. The review that pans the "lachrymose floodtide" notes "a good deal of valid feeling" in the racial passing. The review that deprecates the "manufactured, or remanufactured, melodramatics" names "the stronger tragedy" as "Miss Moore's efforts to make her Susan [Kohner] accept her racial lot ('How do you explain to your child that she was born to be different?') and Susan's hysterical determination to 'pass.'"[43]

In this latter review, if "Miss Turner is quite within the frame as an actress acting an actress," Kohner also fits the frame: "Miss Kohner's role proves a showcase for her rather considerable ability. . . . [I]t is unusual today—and never easy—to attempt to play one of another race." While Turner confuses sign with signifier, as if commenting on her own acting, Kohner emanates compelling illusion. Suspiciously, Annie's line, "How do you explain to your child that she was born to be hurt?" is recalled as, "How do you explain to your child that she was born to be *different*?" Thus the realism found in Kohner's performance instantiates racial difference *as opposed to* knowledge of racial injustice, making Sarah Jane's "determination to pass" a "hysterical" refusal of "her racial lot."[44]

"As a 'woman's picture,' if there is such a thing," a *New York Herald Tribune* reviewer muses, *Imitation* "falls far short of its mark, subsiding into a sudsy formlessness." But "high above" this froth is "real drama," the racial passing: "It may not be that the acting talents of Miss Kohner and Miss Moore alone lift this part of the story so high above the rest of the picture as to leave it in a kind of shadowy, powdered vacuum. It is more probable that the *genuine drama* of their conflict stung director and screenplay writers alive." Notwithstanding his emotional involvement in "Sarah Jane's plight," he criticizes the "ugly and over-dramatized beating scene" as out-of-place.[45]

Similarly, the *Washington Post* critic believes the film "perceptively recognized" the problem of passing, yet his description of why Sarah Jane passes is implausible and evasive: "How this woman, Annie, is given shelter by the would-be actress and how Annie sticks by her through the years causes [*sic*] Annie's daughter to disown her mother." By distinguishing two opposed modalities, the critic makes racial conflict seem self-enclosed—a "Negro problem": "'Imitation of Life' is filled to its glistening hairlines with everything but life. There is, however, one interesting, life-like aspect . . . [that] recognizes the problem of a Negro who might 'pass' for white. . . . But what one has to put up with to be touched by this problem!"[46]

The confluence of the realist lens of the critics and the structural-narrative lens of the scholars is their view of the black characters as stereotypes (which the scholars attack, while the critics embrace), dispelling the urgent contradictions of the passing representations. This confluence can be explained historically. In Annie's funeral the realism appears to enter the text itself, in an image of cultural and racial difference emerging as part of a new pluralism that could check black demands for social equality. These demands, analogous to the melodramatic connections between Sarah Jane's passing and Annie's laboring, insist on social mobility and equality of education, employment, and remuneration. I now examine Elkins's *Slavery* to show that this pluralism was powerful because it offered a mode of resisting the burgeoning movement of black activism and reflected white resistance to socially reconstructive reforms.

Slavery and the Formation of White "Cultural Rights"

Elkins's ideas on race and culture developed in the 1950s as he wrote his dissertation under Richard Hofstadter.[47] *Slavery* is a curious work "initially not well received" by historians, but which "enjoyed a considerable vogue in the mid-sixties."[48] Taking my lead from Michel Foucault, who combines synchronic and diachronic approaches to history to denaturalize the unity of texts, reframing that unity in relations of power and knowledge, I explore the ideological power of the funeral scene of *Imitation* and the image of the slave as perpetual laborer in *Slavery* by examining their shared pluralist discourse and how this discourse affected the developing civil rights movement.[49]

Elkins attempts to turn history into a more natural science—explaining an *order* of historical relations—as he dresses an old representation of black labor in new clothes:

> Was ["Sambo," or the image of the slave as "the perpetual child incapable of maturity,"] real or unreal? What *order of existence*, what *rank of legitimacy*, should be accorded him? *Is there a "scientific" way to talk about this problem?* For most Southerners in 1860 it went without saying not only that Sambo was real—that he was a dominant plantation type—but also that his characteristics were the clear product of racial inheritance. That was one way to deal with Sambo, a way that persisted. . . . But in recent times, the discrediting, as unscientific, of racial explanations for any feature of plantation slavery has tended in the case of Sambo to discredit not simply the explanation itself but also the thing it was supposed to explain. . . . This modern approach to Sambo had a strong counterpart in the way Northern reformers thought about slavery in antebellum times: they thought that nothing could actually be said about *the Negro's "true" nature* because that nature was veiled by the institution of slavery. . . . In short, no *order of reality* could be given to assertions about slave character, because those assertions were illegitimately grounded on race, whereas their only basis was a corrupt and "unreal" institution.[50]

In this dense passage, "science" is a progressive force: it has apparently vanquished racial stereotypes and holds the key to unlocking the "problem" of the slave's personality. Science is also *discourse*, a mark of allegiance to reason and objectivity. Elkins discloses an "order of reality" having the power to repose the racist belief in "Sambo" according to a new "rank of legitimacy." At the same time, he corrects the "Northern" misinterpretation that the South "was a corrupt and 'unreal' institution." These projects are conceived together: *Slavery* explains the truth of the South and the truth behind a stereotype in the same instance.

In *Slavery* we see the coming together of three discourses—race, culture, and science—in such a way and at such a time (contemporaneous with black struggle for equality) that they may voice how racial and class hierarchy can maintain itself, a new knowledge that sets itself apart and disparages more complex ways of thinking. This knowledge imposes a binary made to seem legitimate by an imagined "science": we can talk about *either* social injustice *or* "about the Negro's 'true' nature," a binary formed to prescribe the latter option. I call this arrangement of discourse a new cultural pluralism.

Through a discourse of cultural difference, Elkins asserts the slave's "lack of fitness for adulthood and freedom" *and* attacks the values of the abolitionists: "'The black child,' [abolitionist James Freeman] Clarke predicted, 'will learn [after emancipation] to read and write as fast or faster than the white child, having equal advantages.' *But by focusing upon 'race' rather than culture, they could ignore a range of possibilities*: that a man's humanity, such as he has, lies not in his naked essence but in his culture—and that when a corrupt culture has corrupted his 'nature,' it is less than half a solution simply to strip away his culture and leave him *truly* naked."[51] In his reasoning, the abolitionists' disregard for the South as a hermetic and "corrupt" culture means they sought immediate emancipation and "equal advantages" *instead of* cultural reforms that would have ended slavery gradually. Such reforms were clearly preferable, Elkins believes, to the Civil War.

Among these hypothetical reforms, Elkins mentions extending rights of property, marriage, and religion to the slave.[52] However, he omits the right to vote, the enormous need for schools and teachers, and proposals to compensate freed men and women with ownership of land (what W. E. B. Du Bois called "This land hunger—this absolutely fundamental and essential thing to any real emancipation of the slaves"); in other words, he omits the ideas and history of Reconstruction.[53] In rescinding both the promise of land and eventually the project of Reconstruction, the government, in fact, *did* choose gradualism and then decided not to protect African Americans from segregation and violence. Elkins thus attacks the abolitionists, but properly speaking, his historical antagonists, those fighting gradualism, were the proponents of radical reconstruction. By writing an antebellum history, he can repose the Civil War as a preventable tragedy—to the same effect as sympathizers of segregation were portraying Reconstruction as a tragedy—while at the same time asserting his "objectivity" and implying his liberalism.

If the study of culture adopts an aura of science, then science opens to the study of culture: "role psychology" delivers "a potentially durable link between individual psychology and the study of culture." The softening of slavery as coerced labor parallels the hardening of slavery as a "closed," stable culture: "It will be assumed that there were elements in the very structure of the plantation system—its 'closed' character—that could sustain infantilism as a normal feature of behavior. These elements, *having less to do with 'cruelty' per se than simply with the sanctions of authority*, were effective and pervasive enough to require that such infantilism be characterized as something much more basic than mere 'accommodation.'"[54]

Elkins illustrates this infantilism of the slave by comparing U.S. slavery with the Nazi concentration camp, an analogy that would help popularize his book as "one of the bleakest accounts imaginable of slavery."[55] But the analogy *contrasts* as well as compares: "It is hoped that the very hideousness of a special example [the concentration camp] has not disqualified it as a test for certain features of a far milder and more benevolent form of slavery." The Nazi camps were like "a wretched childhood," contrary to the "carefree one" of the South.[56] The camps are thus a hermeneutic device to explain the effects of a closed authoritarian system and, at the same time and paradoxically, to express by subtle metaphor what the abolitionists *assumed* about slavery, not knowing that "a substantial amount of evidence" could uphold "the ideal picture of Southern life . . . of plantations teeming with faithful and happy black children young and old."[57]

Elkins's lasting contribution to racial liberalism was to merge humanist antiracism with defenses of segregation-as-culture. In 1957 Richard Russell of Georgia rose in the Senate to make a speech that led to the swift removal of provisions in the pending civil rights bill (which had already passed in the House). These provisions, attached to what would be the first civil rights act since 1875, would have enabled the federal government to protect Fourteenth Amendment rights: to prosecute lynching and to enforce school desegregation.[58] The senator painted the civil rights bill in blood-rich colors of Reconstruction's "twelve tragic years," conjuring the South as a culture in need of protection and using a tactical shift from failed attacks in the House that had baldly appealed to states' rights (i.e., that had invoked the Bill of Rights, especially the Tenth Amendment, while ignoring the Reconstruction amendments).[59] Russell spoke not of *states'* rights, not of the Constitution, but of *cultural* rights—"the social order of the South" and "the local customs, laws, or practices separating the races"; defending segregation as a culture removed a need to disown its injustice.[60] Compare Elkins's portrait of sectionalism: "In one section of the country [slavery] had existed for over two centuries, having become interwoven with the means of production, the basic social arrangements, and the very tone of Southern culture" to Russell's portrait of the South: "The social order of the South, with the separation of the races in the South, was accepted and protected by the laws of the land for nearly a hundred years."[61]

Excluding the *national* (or international) identities of abolitionists and dismissing testimonies of former slaves, Elkins represents the debate over slavery as Russell represents the stand against integration: as white regional groups fighting over a misunderstood South. Yet Elkins claims distance from sectionalism, positing a neutral description of cultural difference: "Neither antagonist [the North or the South] . . . could quite conceive of slavery as a social institution, functioning, for better or worse, by laws and logic like other institutions, mutable like others, a product of human custom, fashioned by the culture in which it flourished, and capable of infinite variation from one culture to another."[62]

Elkins sows into fertile politics ideas of race, science, and culture. This discursive combination unlocked the ideological power Russell had wielded in the Senate to refute the melting pot model for integration.[63] In *Slavery*, political reaction parallels professed concern for "the depressed state of Negro existence in this country."[64] Along this parallel we find "cultural rights," which would give the white middle class a new basis to oppose black civil and human rights—the cultural right not to integrate, by race or by class.

Imitation of Life and the New Pluralism

The most critical effect of *Slavery* was not to move white liberal guilt, as historians August Meier and Elliott Rudwick would have it, but to help remove such warranted guilt that might have aligned whites with the need to restructure society.[65] Elucidation of *Slavery*'s "extraordinary vogue" status in the midsixties begins with a text that does not cite it, but whose authors admired and gravitated to it: *Beyond the Melting Pot* by Glazer and Moynihan. This popular cityscape, which "signaled the triumph of a more pluralist view of American identity," expresses at once a clarifying sociology of ethnocultural difference—based on the premise that "the melting pot . . . did not happen"—and a mystification of race and class segregation, evoked by this same pluralism.[66] "[In both the black and Jewish enclaves of New York City] there is a distinctive and important religious and organizational life, and in time, *and indeed perhaps the time is now*, we shall have to recognize that a community that is Negro is not necessarily the outcome of discrimination, just as a Jewish community is not necessarily the product of discrimination. *In the absence of discrimination these clusters would continue to exist.*"[67]

Following the same logic as *Slavery*, Glazer and Moynihan promote cultural rather than social and legal reforms to resolve racial inequality—as if these options were mutually exclusive: "*Without a special language and culture*, and without the historical experiences that create an élan and a morale, what is there to lead [African Americans] to build their own life, to patronize their own?" But this concern, however patronizing, becomes indignation at the social demands of African Americans (*before* the Civil Rights Act of 1964): "[The black citizen] has no values and culture to protect. He insists that the white world deal with his problems because, since he is so much the product of America, they are not *his* problems, but everyone's. Once they become everyone's, perhaps he will see that they are his own too."[68] This sociology, like Elkins's historiography, examines cultural and ethnic differences to produce a new rationale for continued racial and social inequality.

Glazer wrote the introduction to *Slavery*'s 1963 reprint. His essay seamlessly merges the cultural model of *Beyond the Melting Pot* with Elkins's thesis on slave personality: "The personality of Puerto Ricans seems to be quite different and quite distinct from those of American Negroes, and this is particularly evident in New York City, where the descendants of former Southern slaves and the Puerto Ricans now form two of the largest groups in the city."[69] Following *this* pluralism—fluent in ethnocultural distinctions but inarticulate or silent around class struggle and around the persistence of race discrimination—we arrive at restrictions on civil rights policy. The controlling opinion of the Supreme Court's *University of California v. Bakke* (1978) references Glazer's attack against affirmative action to uphold affirmative action *solely* for reasons of ethnic diversity, thus "burying questions about rectifying America's racial caste system in a celebration of America's ethnic pluralism."[70]

Following Moynihan, we arrive at the influential theory that the black family is a pathological and *closed* institution, "capable of perpetuating itself without assistance from the white world."[71] To support this thesis, Moynihan quotes Glazer on *Slavery*: "Why was American slavery the most awful the world has ever known?" For Glazer, this question means that "we will have to know more about the Negro personality . . . if we are to devise effective forms of education for the 'underprivileged,' or the 'culturally deprived,' or the 'minority' child."[72] The essentialist category "Negro personality" is supported by a pluralism that frames cultural analysis as an obligatory alternative to social analysis, implying that social analysis without cultural (i.e., ethnic-personality) analysis is doomed to failure. The postponement of racial reforms and the inadequate financing of poverty relief, under such logic, are assured. Moynihan, calling the "matriarchal structure" of the black "community" a "subculture," overlooks job and housing discrimination and ignores family stress shared with the white poor.[73]

In Moynihan's report, as in Glazer's *Affirmative Discrimination*, pluralist thinking is especially powerful as a strategy for avoiding social analysis because it can seem to come from blacks. Distinguishing this moment for Moynihan is not only the black family crisis but a shift by blacks from civil rights politics to "ethnic politics," based on "the distinct persistence of ethnic and religious groups." This shift coincides with, and ironically makes suspect, black demands "not . . . for liberty alone, but also for equality."[74] Moynihan thus looks to the end of the civil rights movement, as expected from *Beyond the Melting Pot*: African Americans, with their own "values and culture," though of a pathological sort, must accept responsibility for their problems, relieving the imagined burden of whites. We can assume many whites, including President Johnson, used this report, which filtered through the media in the summer of 1965, to distance themselves from the poverty, police brutality, and the repeal of California's fair housing act that fueled the uprising in Watts that August.[75]

This sketch of the congruence between the ideas of Moynihan, Glazer, and Elkins suggests the development of a new pluralism that would insulate whites—particularly white liberals, who would need insulation if they wished to maintain their social status of whiteness—from the full meaning and measure of equality voiced in the civil rights struggle. *Slavery* and the funeral scene of *Imitation of Life* reveal this insulation being laid in 1959. In conclusion, I analyze the struggle for freedom *within* the film by contrasting the possible ideological effects of two key musical scenes.

The beating of Sarah Jane is perhaps the most radically ambiguous moment of the film, and was designed as such. She and Frankie are alone on a side street; after he strikes her, the camera pans from the violence but reframes it in a store window. She then retreats to the other side of the street, and they recede in the reflection. We cut suddenly to behind Frankie, Sarah Jane blocked by his body. He lifts and holds her; her now bloody face in the center of the screen. Frankie moves left, almost offscreen, so she receives blows as though from an overembodied source—as though from *us*, the "disembodied" spectators. Sirk describes his vision for the scene: "I had a slight feeling that the scene could be lacking in cruelty, lacking in drama. . . . Let me tell you what I told the writer. . . . I said we have to get the feeling that this is not just the boy knocking her down, but society."[76]

The music is jazz, with a quick swing; it crescendos with the violence, climaxes with Sarah Jane's collapse. We "wait" for the music to stop, then cut (no fade-out) to Lora lounging on her couch as Annie finishes massaging her feet. Lora sighs, "Mm—that felt so good!" Her pleasure refers to the massage, of course, but it can also allude to the jazz, which could serve as a bridge between Annie's labor and the violence against Sarah Jane (an emotional bridge to support the intellectual edit from one scene to the next). Lora's complacence is what we hear on the soundtrack after the jazz, and the jazz itself, in 1959, could connote a complex form to which many middle-class whites were turning to assert belief in integration while increasing their cultural capital.

In the history of mainstream uses of jazz as signifier of race, 1955 is a year when "this hitherto disreputable music—routinely associated in the mass media with drugs and crime—suddenly became America's music." The United States sponsored Dizzy Gillespie, the first "jazz ambassador," for a tour in the Middle East, and the Voice of America began airing jazz to "thirty million people in eighty countries."[77] In 1959 Willis Conover, jazz specialist for the Voice of America, explained the appeal of these broadcasts as "a sense of freedom [listeners] can detect in jazz," which leads to his second point: "Jazz corrects the fiction that America is racist. Minorities have a tough time everywhere but the acceptance and success of so many Negro musicians and singers in jazz in the United States makes it obvious that someone like Louis Armstrong, for instance, is not an exception."[78] Added to the subtext linking jazz to U.S. racial liberalism were suggestions of jazz as exotic, modern, and sophisticated—connotations we find in women's magazines, marketed to white consumers. In issues coinciding with *Imitation*'s run, *Good Housekeeping* recommends, "The best listening we know for a warm June night is old-time jazz—hectic, festive, and faintly ghostly"; among the new sounds, the "spooky and beautiful" music of Miles Davis was favored.[79] Lora, in other words, might evoke a contented white jazz listener: one who would use the cachet of jazz to support new status, her upward mobility, and who believes in racial integration also, in part, to support her status. The ambiguous use of jazz as a backdrop to racism links her taste in music to her taste for Annie's foot massages, her sensual blindness both to Sarah Jane's beating and to Annie's life outside her labor for Lora. The music and montage critique Lora's *racial* "sense of freedom" as a deeply flawed idea of integration, complicit with racial structures of social oppression.

Further, the jazz deepens our understanding of the symbolic and psychological effects of the violence. As Sarah Jane affirms to Susie, her passing would improve her life opportunities ("I want to have a chance in life"), her social status ("I don't want to have to come through back doors"), and her self-image ("or feel lower than other people"), all imperiled by a racist society. These attainments seem possible, the melodrama suggests, until the peripeteia of the beating scene. Scholars have assumed that Sarah Jane's illicit jazz dancing and singing at Harry's Club and the jazz-inflected eroticism at the Moulin Rouge express the ideological limits of the representations of passing and of women entering the public sphere. But the beating scene encodes jazz—emotionally, ambiguously— as going against her *ideals* of passing. The recurrence of jazz in her working life reminds us that we *never* see her pass in the way she wants to.

The funeral scene represents an authentic way of "being colored" (to use Lora's phrase when chastising Sarah Jane's masquerade as a slave: "You weren't being colored; you were being childish!"). It answers, *in terms of culture*, Frankie's question whether Sarah Jane is black, which she refused to confirm. In *Slavery*, we see ideas of race and culture linked to a third discourse, which I call a discourse of science, but which we can restate as an idea of self-evidence: the appearance of cultural difference possesses a constructed truth-value to make a racist stereotype seem real. In a similar way, the funeral scene imprints black culture with clarity, as if the image—in opposition to the ambiguity of the melodrama—tells us all we need to know.

Instead of "a foreshortening of lived time in favor of intensity," as when Sarah Jane is beaten, the funeral scene stretches time, with slow camera movements unfolding space in the church as Mahalia Jackson sings, and the editing that settles into shot/reaction shots of Jackson and the congregation.[80] Several other details express "realism," or self-evidence: the clumps of ice on the street, as if the temperature could be roughly measured; the depth of focus of the images; the score of Annie's unnamed friends; the lodge members and the black and white citizens outside the church—players who could all seem to be nonprofessional actors, like Mahalia Jackson, who plays "herself."

The most condensed signifier of black culture is Jackson. Lora and Susie react to her spiritual song by crying, suggesting they are more "themselves" than at any time in the narrative. But the contrast with the earlier deployment of jazz is critical to the scene's meaning: if the jazz disrupts comfortable viewing and listening positions, the "live" gospel harmonizes sound and image, stabilizing viewing relations; if the jazz makes whites complicit in racist violence and the racial divisions of labor and consumption, the staging of the gospel seems intent on white catharsis.

The ambiguity of the melodrama—most especially in the scenes of Sarah Jane's slave masquerade and her beating—give emotional truth to her ardent struggle to "pass." The funeral scene helps retract this social rebellion. We not only witness her ask for pardon, we witness integration itself, happening before our eyes, as the music brings black and white together inside and outside the church. In other words, "integration" coincides with clear delineation of racial identity along lines of cultural separations and class hierarchy.

Against this linking of gospel music with a disclosed, "true" black identity, we can set Ralph Ellison's homage to Mahalia Jackson, published a year earlier, in which he hears her music as a kind of jazz and a kind of radical melodrama: "And [her singing] is most eclectic in its use of other musical idiom; indeed, it borrows any effect which will aid in the arousing and control of emotion. Especially is it free in its use of the effects of jazz. . . . Most of all it is an art which swings."[81] For Ellison, black culture frequently resists, with canny resourcefulness, the deleterious effects of racism and social inequality. For many white viewers of this scene, participants in a new pluralism, "culture," on the contrary, might remove the urgency of struggle—and even the appearance and evidence of struggle.

NOTES

1. Thomas Elsaesser, "Tales of Sound and Fury: Observations on the Family Melodrama," in *Home Is Where the Heart Is: Studies in Melodrama and the Woman's Film*, ed. Christine Gledhill (London: BFI, 1987), 51.

2. Ibid., 55.

3. Ibid., 66.

4. See Lucy Fischer's anthology, *Imitation of Life: Douglas Sirk, Director* (New Brunswick, N.J.: Rutgers University Press, 1991), a collection of essays and source materials for scholars of the 1959 film. Jane Gaines, *"The Scar of Shame*: Skin Color and Caste in Black Silent Melodrama," *Cinema Journal* 26, no. 4 (Summer 1987): 3–21, is a seminal call for new histories of melodrama from the perspective of black cultural history. A watershed in the historical focus on context over "film text" is Barbara Klinger's *Melodrama and Meaning: History, Culture, and the Films of Douglas Sirk* (Indianapolis: Indiana University Press, 1994). Klinger examines discourse created and circulated through "institutional contexts most associated with Hollywood cinema" (xv), staking "a materialist contention . . . that the text itself has no intrinsic meaning" (xvi). My position is that to analyze the racial discourse in films we must go beyond the film-centric focus on the context that makes meaning. We must look for wider public spheres of knowledge about race, a search that ironically brings us back to the ideological importance of film-textual analysis but always in a larger investigation of social struggles.

5. On the significance of the photos of Till within the black freedom movement, see Adam Green, *Selling the Race: Culture, Community, and Black Chicago, 1940–1955* (Chicago: University of Chicago Press, 2007), 196–210.

6. Elsaesser, "Tales of Sound and Fury," 47.

7. "Harlem" is signified in Fannie Hurst's *Imitation of Life* (1932; New York: Permabooks, 1959), 263.

8. Stanley M. Elkins, *Slavery: A Problem in American Institutional and Intellectual Life* (1959; New York: Grosset and Dunlap, 1963), 128, 208.

9. Harold Cruse, *The Crisis of the Negro Intellectual* (1967; New York: Quill, 1984), 7.

10. This essay does not offer its own definition of culture, since I am referring to culture as a discourse. Another relevant context is the cold war. "Culture" in *Imitation* or in *Slavery* has the anthropological connotation of "way of life"— ways of speaking, thinking, behaving, and working, with the guiding pressures of customs, mores, laws, and particularly the media—but there is also a cold war inflection on culture that carries political overtones and that locates "culture" in stabilizing institutions.

11. Elsaesser, "Tales of Sound and Fury," 58.

12. Richard Dyer, "Four Films of Lana Turner," in Fischer, *Imitation of Life*, 204–5; Lucy Fischer, "Three-Way Mirror," in Fischer, *Imitation of Life*, 17, 28; Marina Heung, "'What's the Matter with Sarah Jane?': Daughters and Mothers

in Douglas Sirk's *Imitation of Life*," in Fischer, *Imitation of Life*, 320–21; Jackie Byars, *All That Hollywood Allows: Re-reading Gender in 1950s Melodrama* (Chapel Hill: University of North Carolina Press, 1991), 253. Yet Byars also insists, "The film's ambiguous closure may privilege dominant ideologies, but it does not obliterate alternatives" (258).

13. Fischer, "Three-Way Mirror," 17; Lauren Berlant, "National Brands/National Bodies: *Imitation of Life*," in *Comparative American Identities: Race, Sex, and Nationality in the Modern Text*, ed. Hortense Spillers (New York: Routledge, 1991), 130.

14. Heung, "What's the Matter," 304.

15. Elsaesser, "Tales of Sound and Fury," 53.

16. On Clark and *Brown v. Board of Education*, see Ben Keppel, *The Work of Democracy: Ralph Bunche, Kenneth B. Clark, and Lorraine Hansberry, and the Cultural Politics of Race* (Cambridge: Harvard University Press, 1995), ch. 4.

17. John Hope Franklin and Albert Moss, *From Slavery to Freedom: A History of African Americans* (New York: Knopf, 2003), 532.

18. Elkins, *Slavery*, 131.

19. Kenneth M. Stampp's *The Peculiar Institution: Slavery in the Antebellum South* (New York: Knopf, 1956) and C. Vann Woodward's *The Strange Career of Jim Crow* (New York: Oxford University Press, 1955) were important revisions of antebellum and postbellum southern history, respectively. In the popular press, articles such as Robert Baker's "Civil Rights Fight an Echo of 1867" analogized current racial politics to factional struggles in the past (*Washington Post*, July 5, 1959, E3). Columnist Stewart Alsop, for example, writes, "The preoccupation with the Civil War and the Reconstruction era in the South tends to astonish or amuse Northern visitors. Yet *it is an important political fact, one which must be reckoned with*" ("Faubus Plumbed a Historic Well," *Washington Post*, October 6, 1957, E5; italics added).

20. Elsaesser, "Tales of Sound and Fury," 47.

21. Nancy Fraser, "Rethinking the Public Sphere: A Contribution to the Critique of Actually Existing Democracy," *Social Text* 25/26 (1990): 68.

22. Bosley Crowther, "Sob Story Back," *New York Times*, April 18, 1959, 18; Mae Tinee, "Tears Flow at 'Imitation of Life' Film," *Chicago Daily Tribune*, March 18, 1959, B6; J. B., "Imitation of Life," *Christian Science Monitor*, March 30, 1959, 5; Richard Coe, "An 'Imitation' Despite Glitter," *Washington Post*, April 2, 1959, C22; Philip K. Scheuer, "New 'Imitation of Life' Seen as Dated in Melodramatics," *Los Angeles Times*, March 20, 1959, A9; Bosley Crowther, "Detergent Drama," *New York Times*, April 19, 1959, X1.

23. Crowther, "Detergent Drama," X1; "Wringing Wet," *Newsweek*, April 13, 1959, 118.

24. See advertisements in *Chicago Daily Tribune*, March 17, 1959, B8, and in Fischer, *Imitation of Life*, 171. Jack Smith, "Fannie Hurst's View: Women Domination of Male Debunked," *Los Angeles Times*, February 23, 1959, B1.

25. J. B., "Imitation of Life," 5.

26. Crowther, "Detergent Drama," X1.

27. "1959 Probable Domestic Take," *Variety*, January 6, 1960, 34; Murray Schumach, "Hollywood Cycle? Hit 'Imitation' Spurs 'Woman's Film' Talk," *New York Times*, May 3, 1959, X9. The most popular film at the box office in 1959, *Auntie Mame*, also featured a socially mobile female individualist.

28. Philip K. Scheuer, "Women Returning to Film Theaters," *Los Angeles Times*, April 22, 1959, A11; J. B., "Imitation of Life," 5.

29. Tinee, "Tears Flow," B6; Coe, "'Imitation' Despite Glitter," C22.

30. On acting styles in 1950s popular culture, see Marianne Conroy, "Acting Out: Method Acting, the National Culture, and the Middlebrow Disposition in Cold War America," *Criticism* 35 (Spring 1993): 239–63.

31. Mary Ann Doane, "Film and the Masquerade: Theorizing the Female Spectator," in *Femmes Fatales: Feminism, Film Theory, Psychoanalysis* (New York: Routledge, 1991), 25. See also Chris Straayer's rereading of the masquerade from a queer and class perspective, in *Deviant Eyes, Deviant Bodies: Sexual Re-orientation in Film and Video* (New York: Columbia University Press, 1996), 140–47.

32. Dyer, "Four Films of Lana Turner," 186–206.

33. Betty Friedan, *The Feminine Mystique* (New York: Norton, 1963), 19.

34. Peter Brooks, *The Melodramatic Imagination: Balzac, Henry James, Melodrama, and the Mode of Excess* (New Haven, Conn.: Yale University Press, 1976), ch. 3.

35. bell hooks, "The Oppositional Gaze: Black Female Spectators," in *Black American Cinema*, ed. Manthia Diawara (New York: Routledge, 1993), 294.

36. Izzy Rowe, "Izzy Rowe's Notebook," *Pittsburgh Courier*, March 7, 1959, 22; italics added.

37. On the score of mulatto actresses turned down by the casting office, see Fischer, *Imitation of Life*, 184.

38. My thanks to David Lugowski for this conceptual phrase, offered at the 2008 conference of the Society for Cinema and Media Studies.

39. "Freddi [*sic*] Washington as 'Peola,' Susan Kohner as 'Sarah Jane' Okayed," *Chicago Defender*, March 21, 1959, 18; "Mahalia Jackson Gives 'Imitation' New Gospel Kick," *Chicago Defender*, March 14, 1959, 19; "Pix, 'Imitation of Life,' Chicago's Latest Socko," *Chicago Defender*, March 14, 1959, 19. See also Jesse H. Walker, "Juanita's Best Role in 'Imitation of Life,'" *Amsterdam News*, May 2, 1959, 13. For another example of remembering Fredi Washington, see Jesse H. Walker, "Theatricals," *Amsterdam News*, April 18, 1959, 16.

40. On the ability of Washington's performance to invite a critical black response, see Anna Everett, *Returning the Gaze: A Genealogy of Black Film Criticism* (Durham, N.C.: Duke, 2001), 221–22, and hooks, "Oppositional Gaze," 294.

41. Dyer, "Four Films of Lana Turner," 205; italics added.

42. Marianne Conroy, "'No Sin in Lookin' Prosperous': Gender, Race, and the Class Formations of Middlebrow Taste in Douglas Sirk's *Imitation of Life*," in *The Hidden Foundation: Cinema and the Question of Class*, ed. David E. James and Rick Berg (Minneapolis: University of Minnesota Press, 1996), 131–32.

43. "Imitation of Life," *Time* 73 (May 11, 1959), in Fischer, *Imitation of Life*, 243; Coe, "'Imitation' Despite Glitter," C22; J. B., "Imitation of Life," 5; Scheuer, "New 'Imitation of Life.'"

44. Scheuer, "New 'Imitation of Life,'" A11.

45. Paul V. Beckley, "Imitation of Life," *New York Herald Tribune*, April 18, 1959, in Fischer, *Imitation of Life*, 139–40; italics added.

46. Coe, "'Imitation' Despite Glitter," C22.

47. Elkins's relation to Hofstadter, who had urged new histories of slavery "from the standpoint of the slave," is made complex by the latter's intellectual movement from a New Deal to a cold war paradigm, embracing the "vision" of "a pluralistic society defined by capitalism, guided by experts armed with social science, removed from 'the people' and a democratic tradition rooted in false consciousness." David W. Noble, "The Reconstruction of Progress: Charles Beard, Richard Hofstadter, and Postwar Historical Thought," in *Recasting America: Culture and Politics in the Age of Cold War*, ed. Lary May (Chicago: University of Chicago Press, 1989), 70.

48. August Meier and Elliott Rudwick, *Black History and the Historical Profession, 1915–1980* (Urbana: University of Illinois Press, 1986), 247.

49. Michel Foucault, *The Archeology of Knowledge and the Discourse on Language* (New York: Pantheon, 1972).

50. Elkins, *Slavery*, 82–84; italics added.

51. Ibid., 208, 170; first italics added.

52. Ibid., 194–96.

53. W. E. B. Du Bois, *Black Reconstruction in America: 1860–1880* (1935; New York: Free Press, 1998), 601.

54. Elkins, *Slavery*, 123, 86; italics added.

55. Quote is from Richard H. King, *Race, Culture, and the Intellectuals, 1940–1970* (Washington, DC: Woodrow Wilson Center Press, 2004), 158–59; see also Meier and Rudwick, *Black History*, 249–50.

56. Elkins, *Slavery*, 128.

57. Ibid., 217–18.

58. William S. White, "Russell Demands Civil Rights Issue Be Put to Nation," *New York Times*, July 3, 1957, 1; "Civil Rights Compromise?" *Newsweek*, July 8, 1957, 17; Denton L. Watson, *Lion in the Lobby: Clarence Mitchell, Jr.'s Struggle for the Passage of Civil Rights Laws* (Lanham, Md.: University Press of America, 2002), ch. 16.

59. Senator Russell of Georgia, speaking against the Eisenhower administration's civil rights bill, July 2, 1957, 85th Cong., 1st sess., *Congressional Record* 103, pt. 8:10775 (Washington, DC: Government Printing Office, 1957). The appeal to states' rights was made by Herman Talmadge and Strom Thurmond (as senators speaking in the House), in House Committee on the Judiciary, Subcommittee No. 5, 85th Cong., 1st sess., *Civil Rights Hearings: February 4, 5, 6, 7, 13, 14, 25, and 26, 1957* (Washington, DC: Government Printing Office, 1995), 1165–67, 1224–26.

60. 85th Cong., 1st sess., *Congressional Record* 103, pt. 8:10771.

61. Elkins, *Slavery*, 35; 85th Cong., 1st sess., *Congressional Record* 103, pt. 8:10775.

62. Elkins, *Slavery*, 37.

63. For example, *Brown v. Board of Education* invoked the ideology of the melting pot to argue that the embrace of citizens by the public schools constitutes not only a civil right but also the activity of assimilation. Importantly, the NAACP lawyers wanted to broaden the reasoning to include issues of class inequality. On the melting pot as a structuring myth of U.S. politics, see Werner Sollors, *Beyond Ethnicity: Consent and Descent in American Culture* (New York: Oxford University Press, 1986).

64. Elkins, *Slavery*, 92.

65. Meier and Rudwick, *Black History*, 249.

66. Philip Kasinitz, "Beyond the Melting Pot: The Contemporary Relevance of a Classic?" *International Migration Review* 31, no. 1 (Spring 2000): 250; Nathan Glazer and Daniel Patrick Moynihan, *Beyond the Melting Pot: The Negroes, Puerto Ricans, Jews, Italians, and Irish of New York City* (Cambridge: MIT Press, 1963), v.

67. Glazer and Moynihan, *Beyond the Melting Pot*, 59; italics added.

68. Ibid., 33, italics added; 53.

69. Nathan Glazer, introduction to Elkins, *Slavery*, xv.

70. Nathan Glazer, *Affirmative Discrimination* (1975; Cambridge, Mass.: Harvard University Press, 1987); quotation from Reva B. Siegel, "The Racial Rhetorics of Colorblind Constitutionalism: The Case of *Hopwood v. Texas*," in *Race and Representation: Affirmative Action*, ed. Robert Post and Michael Rogin (New York: Zone Books, 1998), 40–41.

71. Daniel Patrick Moynihan, *The Negro Family: The Case for National Action* (1965; Westport, Conn.: Greenwood, 1981), 47.

72. Moynihan, *Negro Family*, 15; Glazer, introduction to Elkins, *Slavery*, ix, xv–xvi.

73. Moynihan, *Negro Family*, 29; in graphs *charting family instability by race* (pp. 6, 7, 9, 11); class as a cross-index is missing.

74. Ibid., 3.

75. Echoing Moynihan, the state report on Watts renewed the myth of the "white man's burden": "The programs that we are recommending will be expensive and burdensome. . . . For unless the disadvantaged are resolved to help themselves, whatever else is done by others is bound to fail." The report diagnosed "the sickness in the center of our cities" as a "spiral of failure" beginning in black "home life." "McCone Report: Why Riots Struck," *Los Angeles Times*, December 7, 1965, C1. This reaction to Watts was anticipated; covering the Moynihan report a few days before the Watts headlines, an article in *Newsweek* concluded, "The disintegration of Negro families may have fallen into a self-sustaining circle" ("New Crisis: The Negro Family," August 9, 1965, 35).

Ideas in the Moynihan report circulated through a major speech drafted in part by Moynihan and delivered by Johnson in June 1965 at Howard University: "Negroes are trapped [not only] as many whites are trapped, in inherited gateless poverty," but also in "the devastating heritage of long years of slavery and a century of oppression and hatred and injustice." Thus far we might agree, but Johnson continues in a vein that shifts the need for change onto the victim— "radiating painful roots into the community and into the family and the nature of the individual." In two months, news reports on Watts would use Johnson's term "the other nation" to describe the black poor, and Johnson would urge citizens not to see legitimate protest coming from the anguished and angry Los Angeles district. "Johnson Address to Howard University Candidates," *New York Times*, June 5, 1965, 14; Tom Wicker, "The Other Nation: No Place to Hide from It," *New York Times*, August 17, 1965, 32; John Herbers, "Johnson Rebukes Rioters as Destroyers of Rights," *New York Times*, August 21, 1965, 8.

76. Douglas Sirk, quoted in James Harvey, "Sirkumstantial Evidence," in Fischer, *Imitation of Life*, 225.

77. Penny M. Von Eschen, *Satchmo Blows Up the World: Jazz Ambassadors Play the Cold War* (Cambridge: Harvard University Press, 2004), 3, 14; John S. Wilson, "Who Is Conover? Only *We* Ask," *New York Times*, September 13, 1959, SM64.

78. Wilson, "Who Is Conover?" SM64.

79. "Records," *Good Housekeeping*, March 1959, 28; "Records," *Good Housekeeping*, June 1959, 28.

80. Elsaesser, "Tales of Sound and Fury," 52.

81. Ralph Ellison, "As the Spirit Moves Mahalia," *Saturday Review*, September 27, 1958, reprinted in *The Collected Essays of Ralph Ellison* (New York: Modern Library, 2003), 252–53.

Remembering Birmingham Sunday

Spike Lee's 4 *Little Girls*

Valerie Smith

Birmingham, Alabama, especially pre-1970s Birmingham, often conjures up images of white racism at its most virulent.[1] During the period from 1947 to 1963, fifty black homes and churches were bombed. The Birmingham police department and Theophilus Eugene "Bull" Connor, commissioner of public safety, were notorious for their aggressive opposition to civil rights activism.[2] Photographs of the white military tank in which Connor patrolled black neighborhoods and footage of police officers beating, fire hosing, and setting dogs on demonstrators circulated nationally and internationally, putting a face on southern white resistance to black demands for equal rights and social justice.

After the NAACP was banned from the state of Alabama in 1956, the Alabama Christian Movement, led by the Reverend Fred Shuttlesworth, was created to fight for freedom and full citizenship rights, including the desegregation of public accommodations and schools and the integration of the police force in Birmingham. But when the city's intransigent establishment failed to respond—indeed, brutally resisted direct action—Reverend Shuttlesworth sought the support of what was by the early sixties the most prominent and nationally visible civil rights organization, the Southern Christian Leadership Conference (SCLC), headed by Rev. Dr. Martin Luther King Jr. Indeed, King himself referred to Birmingham as "probably the most thoroughly segregated city in the United States."[3]

This perception of Birmingham was only confirmed by the bombing of Birmingham's Sixteenth Street Baptist Church on September 15, 1963, just months after the Birmingham movement had won the battle over the segregation of public facilities in the city and just weeks after the march on Washington. The bombing of Sixteenth Street Church took the lives of four young African American girls—Denise McNair (age eleven) and Addie Mae Collins, Carole Robertson, and Cynthia Wesley (all age fourteen)—during Sunday School as they prepared to participate in the Youth Day worship service. Some observers saw this bombing of a movement church at a time when it was certain to be filled with young people as a deliberately calculated act of retribution because it occurred so soon after the Birmingham Children's Crusade of 1963, when hundreds of middle school, high school, and college students marched and went to jail to protest segregated public facilities. Others have seen it as an act of terrorism, an attack on a randomly selected site intended to display the perpetrators' power over black citizens and their confidence that they could operate outside of the law. Whether viewed as random, deliberately retributive, or both, this bombing is perceived as one of the key events that directed the attention of the nation, if not the world, to the savage extremes to which white supremacists, unchecked, would resort. Correspondingly, the martyred Sunday School girls have come to symbolize the innocence and moral rectitude of southern black communities under siege.[4]

The past couple of decades have seen an outpouring of literary and cinematic texts that take what is commonly known as the modern civil rights movement or the southern freedom struggle as their subject. The recent resurgence of interest in the civil rights movement among writers, musicians, performance artists, and visual artists acknowledges the transformative impact of the activism, rhetoric, theology, and iconography of the period. Not only did the civil rights movement substantially alter the social, political, and spatial configuration of relations within the United States, but it also exerted a profound influence on other movements for racial, ethnic, religious, gender, and sexual equality around the world.

Mainstream representations frequently confirm popular constructions of the movement, presented as a primarily southern phenomenon, neatly bracketed by the Montgomery Bus Boycott and the assassination of the Reverend Dr. Martin Luther King Jr. In this view, the movement is a chapter in a progressive, ameliorative vision of U.S. history where southern extremists were pitted against cross-racial coalitions led by morally courageous and spiritually inspired individuals. Through shared sacrifice and exemplary action, the movement triumphed over white supremacy and delivered the nation from its past injustices into a bright future of freedom, equality, and opportunity. This interpretation of the civil rights movement, common to Hollywood films such as Alan Parker's *Mississippi Burning* (1988), Richard Pearce's *The Long Walk Home* (1990), and Rob Reiner's *Ghosts of Mississippi* (1996) or to made-for-television films such as Robert Dornhelm's *Sins of the Father* (2002), has maintained some measure of currency because it encourages viewer—indeed national—complacency and self-satisfaction. It allows Americans to identify post-Emancipation racism with its most obvious symbols and perpetrators, confine it to the Jim Crow South, sentimentalize its spiritual discourse and sainted martyrs, and convince themselves that those days are over. It allows them to believe that with legalized segregation behind them, the doors of American opportunity are now open to all.[5]

Clearly, not all texts about the movement conform to this model. Since the 1980s, a proliferation of new scholarship, films, and literary works about the movement have expanded and complicated our vision of its goals and participants. As Charles Payne has observed, the new research challenges familiar analyses and canonical accounts in a number of ways: by highlighting the importance of local struggles and women's grassroots leadership, rather than focusing on national leaders and institutions dominated by elite men; by deemphasizing the role of moral appeals and emphasizing instead the place of public disruption and economic and political pressure; by pointing to the significance of earlier periods of struggle for understanding both the movement and the changing position of African Americans; by broadening the analysis from legislative, legal, and policy changes to encompass the movement's transformative power in the lives of individuals and in the culture; and by exploring the social and political infrastructure that sustained the movement.[6] To his list, I would add that recent scholarship has focused on specific regions of the U.S. South as well as on northern urban centers to explore the differential effects of white supremacy and the varied forms that struggles for equality and justice assumed in different places. Equally important, new research has examined the influence of international debates and conflicts on a crisis that had been regarded principally as an internal political issue. Scholars have also begun to trace the deep and mutually sustaining connections between unions and civil rights organizations, and between contemporaneous armed and nonviolent resistance movements and strategies for change.[7]

◫:

Spike Lee's 1997 HBO documentary about the Sixteenth Street Baptist Church bombing, 4 Little Girls, makes a multivalent contribution to the body of texts that revise the popular understanding of the southern freedom struggle. For those to whom the event is unfamiliar, the film presents a compelling and rich introduction. For viewers aware of its essential details, Lee complicates the story in a variety of ways. First, the film dislodges the "four little girls" from their symbolic status as a collective icon: the recollections of the young girls' friends and families disaggregate their stories, restore their individuality, and establish their identities according to many of the conventions that defined African American girlhood in the South during the mid-twentieth century. Daughters of the black middle class in at least three of the four cases—the same community that gave us both Angela Davis and Condoleezza Rice—these young women went to school, attended church, belonged to Brownie and Girl Scout troops, and loved to dance and play with their friends and siblings. Addie Mae Collins appears to have come from a less privileged background than the other three, but Denise, Carole, and Cynthia were the type of girls who took many of the kinds of lessons—piano and ballet, for example—designed to prepare them for respectable middle-class womanhood. As Julie Buckner Armstrong has written, "The film's success lies in Lee's ability to cut through the symbolic complex surrounding the bombing to reveal who these girls were and how they died."[8]

Second, the film places the murders in relation to the role of Birmingham in the movement. As editor and coproducer Sam Pollard observes, the film follows two trajectories that eventually converge: "On one track we have the girls' lives unfolding; on the other we see the movement as it moves into Birmingham, and then they collide with the bombing of the church."[9] Third, while popular accounts of the movement frequently demonize white working-class men as the perpetrators of racial violence, 4 Little Girls suggests indirectly that the more respectable white citizens enabled and provided cover for the activities of Klan members and other extremists. Fourth, through the testimony of those who knew them, the film situates the young girls in the context of black Birmingham as a vibrant microcosm that thrived even in the face of virulent racism and economic oppression. The girls appear here as active, integral members of a vital community; their premature deaths constitute a loss that can never be calculated. Yet even as the film pieces together the lives they lived and the future possibilities they might have enjoyed, they and those they left behind are portrayed as more than victims. The film manages to capture at once the depth of grief and loss as well as the community's resilience. Birmingham may have been the site of some of the most virulent acts of racial terrorism in the mid-twentieth century, but it was also a place where those who came of age in the fifties and sixties were infused with a postwar-era optimism and a sense that they would be able to move beyond the limitations of Jim Crow segregation.

Finally, like most documentaries, 4 Little Girls is also a film about time, or perhaps rather about competing temporalities. The climax of the narrative occurs at the moment at which time stopped for the four young girls, freezing them in perpetuity in early 1960s adolescence. But it is also about the passage of time, for it seeks to liberate the young girls from the moment at which they died and entered history. Although their personal stories cannot continue, the lives of those around them, the city in which they lived, and the movement that provides the context of their deaths clearly did move on. Like the omission of the details of the bombing, the girls' absence from the ongoing narrative thus speaks eloquently of the tragic implications of their deaths. By probing the effects of the passage of time on the lives of the girls' friends, neighbors, and family members, the film transforms their story from an account of victimization to one of community survival in the face of brutal oppression and profound loss.

The film opens with Joan Baez's delicate soprano singing the lyrics to her song "Birmingham Sunday."[10] This song captures the violent juxtaposition at the heart of the Sixteenth Street Church bombing. It suggests the image of children gathering around a balladeer, but the plaintive melody—a traditional English and Scottish tune performed by a poignant soprano with guitar accompaniment—conveys an account of unimaginable horror. The first three lines in most of the four-line stanzas rhyme; the final line in all but the penultimate stanza, "And the choir kept singing of freedom," suspends the predictable rhyme scheme and returns us to the haunting refrain. This line, which speaks of the unending quest for freedom, invokes an image both of the young girls' eternal status as martyrs and of the enduring struggle of those who were left behind.

Against the backdrop of these lyrics, the camera pans across the graves of Addie Mae, Denise, Carole, and Cynthia. When each girl's name is sung, the camera rests on her headstone, side by side with her photograph. As the song unfolds, archival footage and photographs from the Birmingham campaign and the bombing are interspersed with shots of the cemetery. At the conclusion of the song, we see images of the commemorative sculpture at Kelly Ingram Park, a site opposite Sixteenth Street Church that was often the scene of violent confrontations between the police and the activists. This opening sequence thus establishes the touchstones of the narrative that the film explores and connects: the sites of violent assaults and the memorial windows and statues that commemorate its victims; the childhood photos and the graves within which the victims' bodies lie; the bombing and the song that tells the story.

After the dramatic, poignant sequence with which the film opens, the narrative of 4 Little Girls takes an unexpected turn. The prologue plunges us immediately into the violence of the bombing, so we might expect the film to open with the history of segregation in Birmingham. Instead, it takes us directly into the young girls' intimate family lives, starting with the recollections of Denise McNair's parents, Chris and Maxine. In a sequence accompanied by a languorous blues riff, Denise's parents recall their first meeting at Tuskegee Institute (now University) in the 1940s and the early days of their marriage. Each appears on camera separately. They are such easy storytellers that as they speak they bring the past back to life. They slip into subtle flirtatiousness and conjure up familiar types as they reflect on their courtship in college in the 1940s: he the worldly World War II veteran, she the pretty and popular coed. After their marriage, Mrs. McNair persuades her husband that they should move back to her hometown of Birmingham, since she can't bear to be away from her family. As they describe it, with the birth of Denise, their first child, they were on track toward fulfilling their dreams of building a family together. Not surprisingly, they and their relatives and friends recall Denise in glowing terms: lovable, feisty, friendly.

Hints of the impending tragedy are evident in the McNairs' reflections, however, for Mr. McNair recalls that there were few jobs for college-educated black veterans when he moved to Birmingham. The realities of midcentury racism and segregation interfered with his dreams of economic and professional success. Following the observations of some of Denise's and Carole Robertson's relatives and friends, the focus of the film expands to provide competing interpretations of the city's history. Arthur Hanes Jr., a circuit court judge who in 1977 defended Robert Chambliss, the first man convicted of bombing the Sixteenth Street Church, opens this section of the film, providing the official Chamber of Commerce version of Birmingham, celebrating it as a booming steel town built in the late 1800s that combined human and natural resources with abundant transportation.[11] In contrast, Bill Baxley, the former lieutenant governor and former district attorney who successfully prosecuted Chambliss for the murder of Denise McNair in 1977, acknowledges that the rapid growth of the "Magic City" was partly responsible for its violent history. Howell Raines, former *New York Times* editor and another Birmingham native, offers the most elaborate analysis of the city's history, describing it as a town of union violence "condoned by the police, U.S. Steel and other big industrial companies."[12] As he goes on to say, the city possesses a "long tradition of violence flowing out of an industrial setting with the overlay of rural racism coming in from the countryside." At its conclusion, this sequence returns to Hanes, who remarks that "the fifties was a quiet time in Birmingham, a wonderful place to live and raise a family." His upbeat gloss is not consistent with the observations and recollections that preceded it, with the interspersed memories of black people, or with the archival footage and photographs of Klan marches, lynched bodies, and Jim Crow signs that accompany his, Baxley's, and Raines's reflections. Even those African Americans prosperous enough to move to Dynamite Hill lived with the daily threat of white racist violence.

The lives of the four young girls emerge out of memories and narratives interspersed throughout the larger story of the Birmingham campaign. This pattern of moving back and forth from the stories of Addie Mae, Denise, Cynthia, and Carole to the broader account of the movement restores suspense to stories whose ending we already know. The voices of luminaries (Rev. Fred Shuttlesworth, Rev. Andrew Young, Rev. James Bevel, Ossie Davis, and Diane Nash, for example) place Birmingham, as

well as the tragic loss of these lives, in the context of the southern freedom struggle. The personal recollections of those who knew the girls
restore and maintain their individuality and provide a sense of the community in the 1950s and early 1960s. Told in these different registers
rather than narrated by an authoritative voice-over, the film eschews the
illusion of an unbiased history. Instead, official history gives way to individual and collective narratives. The bombing and the events that pre-
cede and follow it are all presented through the recollections of those
whose lives were directly or indirectly affected. Thus the recurrent use
of the off-center close-up, which could be read as simply a self-conscious
gesture that calls attention to the presence of the camera, might also be
seen as a trope for the film's subjective narrative perspective.

A third of the way through the film, we are introduced to a sequence
of reflections that indirectly implicate Bull Connor and former governor
George Wallace in the bombing. The placement of Connor's and Wallace's stories suggests the interconnections among Klan violence, "law
enforcement," and elected officials and undercuts the willed ignorance
that underwrites Arthur Hanes's nostalgic view of Birmingham in the
1950s. Some of the witnesses are quick to blame Bull Connor for the violence in Birmingham. Howell Raines, for example, describes him as "the
manifestation of the perversity upon which segregation depended for its
life . . . the walking id of Birmingham, the dark spirit of Birmingham, the
hellish side of Birmingham embodied." But Chris McNair rejects that
reading, pointing instead to the systemic nature of white supremacy. As
he reflects in the film, "A Bull Connor couldn't exist without the nods
from the status quo people. . . . You know, the big boys in any town. He
may be the person who actually does the talking, but believe me, he has
the blessing of somebody else."[13]

Time figures centrally in the representations of Connor and Wallace as
much as it does of those who knew Carole, Denise, Addie, and Cynthia.
One measure of the passage of time is the fact that people who had once
been terrorized by the bombings and other modes of Klan violence are
now able to reflect calmly, even ironically, about Connor and Wallace.
Tommy Wrenn, a local activist and SCLC member, delights in recount-
ing the story of how the partially blind Connor's mistreatment of a blind
black man illustrates "just how crazy" he was. Even more powerfully,
the camera shows the toll that time has taken on the spirit, the mind, and
the body of George Wallace.

Former governor Wallace stands in for the "Big Boys" to whom Mr.
McNair refers in his observations about Birmingham's power elites, for
he is introduced in the film immediately after Mr. McNair invokes them.
Footage from several of Wallace's speeches captures his dominant role
in conservative southern politics during the first half of the 1960s. For

instance, in his January 14, 1963, inaugural address, he intoned, "In the name of the greatest people that have ever trod this earth, I draw the line in the dust and toss the gauntlet before the feet of tyranny and I say segregation today, segregation tomorrow, segregation forever." This footage is crosscut with close-ups of Wallace in the 1990s, now a feeble man seated at his desk, smoking a cigar. Subsequent archival footage shows an excerpt of a speech in which he commends the white citizens of Birmingham for their restraint and blames local violence on "lawless Negroes." The final piece of footage comes from the speech he delivered on June 11, 1963, as he blocked the entrance to the Foster Auditorium at the University of Alabama at Tuscaloosa in an attempt to prevent African American students Vivian Malone and James Hood from enrolling.[14] In 1963 he cut a charismatic figure; apparently undaunted by the federal authorities, he was the very embodiment of the doctrine of interposition and nullification.[15] Surrounded by state troopers, he stands face-to-face with Nicholas Katzenbach, the deputy attorney general whom President Kennedy had sent from Washington, D.C., and reads the oft-cited pronouncement:

NOW, THEREFORE, I George C. Wallace, as Governor of the State of Alabama, have by my action raised issues between the Central Government and the Sovereign State of Alabama, which said issues should be adjudicated in the manner prescribed by the Constitution of the United States; and now being mindful of my duties and responsibilities under the Constitution of the United States, the Constitution of the State of Alabama, and seeking to preserve and maintain the peace and dignity of this State, and the individual freedoms of the citizens thereof, do hereby denounce and forbid this illegal and unwarranted action by the Central Government.

The late 1990s image of Wallace puffing on a cigar might initially seem to be a latter-day manifestation of his earlier menace and power, but when he speaks it is clear that time and ill health have worn him down. His speech is so low and garbled that the filmmakers are forced to provide subtitles to make his words intelligible. He reads most of his remarks from a scripted text (presumably prepared by a member of his staff) and essentially disavows the positions he had taken so forcefully as a younger man. Sheepishly, he explains that when he enforced the segregation laws as governor, he was just doing what he had been taught, and he asserts that he did some good things for black children, such as providing them with free schoolbooks. One of the most striking images of this sequence, and of the film itself, occurs when he departs from the page before him to extemporize. As if to confirm his sincerity, he calls Eddie Holcey, his black "friend," into the frame and holds his hand, presumably a symbol that he has abandoned the racist attitudes he once espoused. Although Wallace repeats the assertion that Ed is his best friend and that he "wouldn't go anywhere without him," Ed does not display this same level of feeling. Perhaps he simply doesn't want to be on camera, but it seems more likely that the man is an employee, an attendant whose relationship to Wallace is only partly personal. Ed stands silently at Wallace's right whenever Wallace calls him over. (Indeed, at one point he seems to be rolling his eyes as the former governor talks about the closeness of their friendship.) His facial expression and his eyes betray his discomfort; he can't wait to step out of the frame as soon as Wallace lets go of his hand.

⬛

The film 4 *Little Girls* seeks a visual rhetoric to capture the magnitude of what was lost when Addie Mae, Carole, Denise, and Cynthia were murdered. The mere appearance of those who knew and loved them testifies to their lost potential. Not only, as Bill Cosby states late in the film, could these four young women "have gone on to become Spelman graduates, Harvard graduates, doctors, lawyers, ordinary hardworking people," but also they lost the opportunity simply to become middle-aged. The liberal use of family photographs interspersed with the interview footage emphasizes the impact of time on the bodies and faces of the witnesses. The parents, once young, vibrant, slim, have now entered their later years. Frequent off-center close-ups zoom in on the young girls' now middle-aged friends and siblings. Their crow's feet, double chins, wrinkles, and blemishes mark the passage of the decades. These are hardworking people who are fortunate to have made it to middle age. The faces and bodies of their friends and relatives thus underscore the fact that time is frozen for Addie Mae, Cynthia, Carole, and Denise, forever imprisoned in the image of their childhood and adolescent photographs.

Or rather, they would be forever imprisoned in the image of their childhood and adolescent photographs were it not for Lee's judicious insertion of the morgue photographs into the film. For just as the familiar formulation of "the four little girls" obscures the individuality of Carole, Addie Mae, Cynthia, and Denise, so too does that formulation accustom us to the image of the four familiar photographs. Although the film goes to great lengths to establish them as average black girls at midcentury, it forces us to confront as well the various levels of destruction the bomb produced. As the family members reflect on the final morning of the young girls' lives, we can imagine them asserting the pride in their appearance that they had been taught to cultivate. Mrs. Alpha Robertson, Carole's mother, remembers that her daughter was wearing her first pair of "little heels." Helen Pegues, Denise's aunt, recalls that Denise came into her Sunday School class to borrow a compact, a comb, and a quarter, before running into the bathroom and to her death. Janie Gaines recounts using her purse to play football with her sisters Addie Mae and Sarah on their way to church. As a result, Addie Mae's hair was in disarray and she and Sarah went down to the bathroom to make themselves presentable for Sunday School. And in one of the most arresting moments in the film, Shirley Wesley King reads a statement that she wrote about her mother's last words to Cynthia as she left the house. Mrs. Wesley called her back to adjust her slip, saying, "Young lady, you just don't put your clothes on any way. You're going to church. You never know how you're coming back."

These details capture the girls both as individuals and as types and encapsulate much of the information the witnesses have already provided about communal norms. They may have lived in one of the most brutally racist cities in the country. Nevertheless, it was a city in which black people—blue-collar laborers, entrepreneurs, or professionals—thrived due to their commitment, aspirations, and hard work. But in an instant, the bomb took them from their Sunday best to mutilated corpses. Although the film provides only fleeting glimpses of the morgue photographs, it offers enough visual evidence to give viewers a glimpse of the physical spectacle family members confronted that Sunday morning. It is thus little wonder that Junie Collins is traumatized not only by the bombing and by the loss of her sister but also by the experience of identifying her sister's body. As she puts it, for years afterward she was troubled by serious panic attacks that made her terrified of being "on the inside as well as the outside of anywhere." She describes these attacks as having plagued her "once upon a time," but she speaks in a monotone and her expression betrays no emotion; she appears still to be suffering from the aftermath of that traumatic experience.

Janie Gaines remembers hurrying home to play with Addie days after the bombing, only to remember after she arrived that Addie had died. She begins to weep as she explains how difficult it is to reopen these wounds. She cries not so much because the memories are painful, but because she has forgotten many of the details. As she puts it, "It's not easy. We had put so much of this behind us and we don't remember. . . . You may not remember details on what, step by step, I had to go through. But I do remember that it affected me so bad."

In contrast, when Denise's mother begins to speak about the day of the bombing, she relives her rage and despair. Just as she takes us back to her days as a college student and young wife and mother at the beginning of the film, here she makes vivid her experience of the bombing. She recalls her outrage at the way she was treated when she arrived at the hospital to find Denise. When a white hospital employee called her by her first name, even in the midst of her grief she rose up in indignation and insisted on being addressed as "Mrs. Chris McNair." The death of her daughter enabled her to demand the respect she believes she deserves as an adult married woman, and she did not on that day accede to the verbal codes that upheld the racial hierarchy.

The same hospital employee apologized and told her that she need not examine Denise's body, because her husband had already identified her. But Mrs. McNair insisted on going into the room where the bodies were being held because, as she puts it, "It was *my* privilege to identify *my* daughter's body to *me*, and I wasn't going to let anyone take that from me." Her insistence on the ocular proof recalls Mamie Till Bradley's demand that the coffin that held the body of her son, Emmett Till, be opened so she could see his body. Emmett's mother wanted the world to see what "they had done to her son." In contrast, Mrs. McNair took comfort in ensuring that her daughter could be made to look presentable in her coffin; she describes going shopping for her daughter one last time to select the outfit in which Denise would be buried and then dressing her at the mortuary.

After leaving the hospital, the McNairs went to her mother's house, where Mrs. McNair finally lost control. As she puts it, "[I] couldn't stop hollering; [I] couldn't stop screaming," and she says she wanted to rub a place she couldn't get to. As she describes "that place," she rubs her leg in a gesture that seems to transport her back to her mother's house.

⊓⋮

The testimony of the witnesses individualizes Cynthia, Carole, Addie Mae, and Denise, reintegrates them into their community, and gives voice to the suffering of those they left behind. Indeed, I would argue that the film is as much about that communal context as it is about the four young women. The community may be marked forever by this traumatic event, but it has undergone the inevitable changes that accompany the passage of time.

When 4 *Little Girls* was released in 1997, Chris McNair, Denise's father, emerged in the film as a key symbol of that resilient spirit. Indeed, in the supplementary materials that accompany the DVD, Spike Lee says he knew that he needed Mr. McNair's cooperation to get the other relatives to go along. In part, Lee's observation acknowledges McNair's public stature. His testimony at the 1977 trial of Bob Chambliss helped secure a guilty verdict against the first of the three men convicted of bombing the church. Though the film only hints at his sphere of influence (former state attorney general and former lieutenant governor Bill Baxley refers to him as a friend), McNair emerged from this tragedy into a career as a public servant and entrepreneur. He served in the Alabama House of Representatives and was for many years a Jefferson County commissioner. He also succeeded in business; in 1962, he opened Chris McNair Studios, which at the time specialized in custom photographic services but expanded to include an art gallery, custom framing, and graphic design as well as a permanent exhibit dedicated to Denise's memory. Furthermore, he and his wife Maxine went on to have two other daughters after Denise's death, of whom no mention is made in the film (except for an aunt's passing remark that "at that time Denise was an only child").

Beyond the specific details of his accomplishments, however, in the film the totality of McNair's achievements stands as an important symbol of the community's ability to heal and flourish even after traumatic loss. His prominence in the film challenges the pervasive notion of black southern communities in the Jim Crow era as vulnerable and victimized. With his deep voice, comfortable yet imposing physical presence, and understated sense of humor, he anchors the viewer with his authority and locates us in the world of postwar prosperity and optimism. Near the end of the film, Chris McNair explains his fondness for one specific picture of Denise. This photograph is not one of many in which she is dressed in her Sunday best. Rather, in this shot she wears pajamas and her hair is mussed, but she beams out at the camera, her cheek pressed against the face of her doll. He remembers this image for a couple of reasons:

> I would say it's my favorite number one because I think it's a good photograph. But I made it with her little camera, her little Brownie camera. And, she was sitting in the bed playing with her doll and said, "Make a picture of me, Daddy." And I said, "With this camera?" "Yeah, with my camera." . . . The distance that I was from her really was too close, but I made the picture because I wanted to fill the frame up pretty good.
>
> And, when the film was developed I saw that the negative was way overexposed and I never worried about it any more until after she died. And, I went back to the negatives and I reduced it and then made a print of it, and I realized what a jewel I had.

With its focus on the process by which McNair made the photograph, this moment stands out in a film in which so many of the interviews concern the bombing, the movement, or the history of Birmingham. Here, McNair positions *himself* as a documentarian, an artist who takes an image, even one that is flawed, and fashions it into both an expression of his creative talent and a piece of the historical record. This moment in the film suggests a correspondence between Lee's work as director and McNair's as photographer and points to the collaborative nature of their common enterprise. Moreover, the scene highlights McNair's status as a symbol of black agency. His pride in turning a flawed print into a "jewel" exemplifies the community's ability to transform and reconstitute itself in the aftermath of unfathomable sorrow.

Viewed from the perspective of the early twenty-first century, however, the film reads rather differently than it did when it was first released. Key figures such as Governor Wallace, Reverend Bevel, and Mrs. Robertson have passed from the scene. Moreover, Mr. McNair's authority has been compromised; in recent years he admitted to accepting bribes from U.S. Infrastructure (USI) while he was a Jefferson County commissioner. One of twenty-one defendants convicted in a sewer bribery and corruption scandal, in June 2007 he was sentenced to five years in prison but has yet to serve any time.[16]

The unfolding of the afterlife of the film thus marks it as a historical document; the passage of time shapes the meanings we attribute to it. Moreover, as Mr. McNair's political and professional successes contributed to his central role in the film, his downfall prevents us from seeing him exclusively from the perspective of his daughter's martyrdom. While he may function in the film as a corrective to the tendency within popular culture to read movement veterans as victims, his life is larger than the loss of his daughter and must be read within the full context of his humanity.

The film ends with the reflections of Mrs. Alpha Robertson, Carole's mother, who reminds us that life has continued for her beyond the traumatic loss of her daughter. This interview is one of the few in which we hear Lee's voice, as he prods her to expand on her more cryptic observations about how she has coped with her rage at the murder of her daughter. Like Maxine McNair and Junie Collins, Mrs. Robertson describes how her faith has helped her to live with her grief; she believes that prayer and spiritual self-scrutiny have allowed her to conquer her anger. Her final reflection underscores as well the fact that the redemptive power of time has given her some perspective on the loss she has sustained, for she has had other deaths to mourn as well as many reasons to celebrate. As she puts it, "I've tried to put all of that behind me and go on and live. 'Cause in addition to that, so many other things have happened, you know? My husband has gone, my three brothers, my sister, my parents. And of course, I still have my kids, my family. I have two . . . a son and a daughter, three grandchildren, and four great grandchildren. So, I have something to be thankful for after all."

NOTES

1. Numerous recent studies have analyzed the dynamic that linked the ostensibly disparate interests of Birmingham's power elites, Klan members, and municipal politicians into an alliance that was inimical to the interests of its black citizens. See, for example, J. Mills Thornton, *Dividing Lines: Municipal Politics and the Struggle for Civil Rights in Montgomery, Birmingham, and Selma*

(Tuscaloosa: University of Alabama Press, 2002); Diane McWhorter, *Carry Me Home: Birmingham, Alabama, the Climactic Battle of the Civil Rights Revolution* (New York: Simon and Schuster, 2001); and Elizabeth H. Cobbs and Petric J. Smith, *Long Time Coming: An Insider's Story of the Birmingham Church Bombing That Rocked the World* (Birmingham, Ala.: Crane Hill, 1994).

2. Connor served as commissioner of public safety from 1937 to 1953 and again from 1957 to 1963.

3. Martin Luther King Jr., "Letter from Birmingham City Jail," in *A Testament of Hope: The Essential Writings and Speeches of Martin Luther King, Jr.*, ed. James M. Washington (San Francisco, Calif.: Harper and Row, 1986), 290.

4. For a discussion of the impact of the bombing, see Howell Raines, "The Birmingham Bombing," *New York Times Magazine*, July 24, 1983, 12–13, 22–29. For an analysis of the symbolic role the four martyred girls played, see Renee C. Romano, "Narratives of Redemption: The Birmingham Church Bombing Trials and the Construction of Civil Rights Memory," in *The Civil Rights Movement in American Memory*, ed. Renee C. Romano and Leigh Raiford (Athens: University of Georgia Press, 2006), 96–133.

5. Nowhere is this sense of optimism more evident than in the rush to declare America in the age of Obama to be postracial.

6. Steven F. Lawson and Charles Payne, *Debating the Civil Rights Movement, 1945–1968* (Lanham, Md.: Rowman and Littlefield, 1998).

7. For a recent comprehensive analysis of the trajectory of civil rights movement historiography, see Jacquelyn Dowd Hall, "The Long Civil Rights Movement and the Political Uses of the Past," *Journal of American History* 91, no. 4 (March 2005): 1233–63.

8. Julie Buckner Armstrong, "Spike Lee's *4 Little Girls*: Remembering Birmingham," *The Distillery: Artistic Spirits of the South* 5, no. 2 (1998): 56.

9. "Sam Pollard," in Sheila Curran Bernard, *Documentary Storytelling for Video and Filmmakers* (Burlington, Mass.: Focal, 2003), 248.

10. The lyrics to "Birmingham Sunday" were written in 1964 by Richard Farina, the folk musician who was married to Joan Baez's sister Mimi Baez Farina. The words were set to a traditional song dating back to seventeenth-century England and Scotland titled "I Once Loved a Lass (The False Bride)." For the complete lyrics to "Birmingham Sunday," see Guy and Candie Carawan, *Songs for Freedom: The Story of the Civil Rights Movement through Its Song* (Bethlehem, Pa.: Sing Out, 1990), 121–23, or go to Lyrics Download, http://www.lyrics download.com/joan-baez-birmingham-sunday-lyrics.html (accessed April 14, 2010).

11. Hanes is the son of Art Hanes Sr., a former FBI agent, mayor of Birmingham, and close associate of Eugene "Bull" Connor. He had also won acquittals in the murder charges against the Klan members indicted in the shooting murder of Viola Liuzzo and he had briefly defended James Earl Ray, the man convicted of assassinating Martin Luther King Jr. See McWhorter, *Carry Me Home*, 574.

12. Spike Lee has said that Raines's July 24, 1983, article "Birmingham Bombing," about the bombing of the Sixteenth Street Baptist Church, inspired him to want to make *4 Little Girls*.

13. Diane McWhorter explores the multifaceted and mutually dependent relationship between the Big Mules, elected officials, and Klan members in Birmingham with extraordinary depth in *Carry Me Home*. This analysis is also central to Cobbs and Smith, *Long Time Coming*.

14. Vivian Malone and James Hood were the first two African American students to enroll at the University of Alabama.

15. According to the doctrine of interposition, states may intercede against a federal action they consider to be unconstitutional or to exceed the powers delegated to the federal government. The doctrine of nullification declares that states have the right to declare null and void any federal law they deem unconstitutional.

16. "McNair Sentenced to 5 Years in Prison," *Birmingham News*, September 20, 2007, http://blog.al.com/spotnews/2007/09/mcnair_sentenced_to_5_years _in.html (accessed April 14, 2010).

Exploitation Movies and the Freedom Struggle of the 1960s

Sharon Monteith

In the 1960s a small but significant number of pulp movies used civil rights in the South as a dramatic trigger, specifically massive resistance to the Freedom Rides in 1961 and to the voter registration drives that culminated in Freedom Summer in 1964. The movies were released in the moment in which the South became synonymous with racist mobs, burnings, and bombings in the popular imagination, and they capitalized on deleterious images of the South. The insertion of northern middle-class "foreigners"—"red diaper babies" and students from Ivy League schools—into the "savage" South was not only a media dream but a source of melodrama for filmmakers. That these films have been ignored has led to a truncated sense of the range of the civil rights movie and of the specific ways in which mass-culture forms adjusted to local circumstances to exploit dramatic, compelling, and even tragic events in the civil rights era. This gap is significant in film history because it is surprising. The movement's express intention to publicize racial violence was so effective that images of demonstrators facing down segregationists dominated television news in the first half of the 1960s. The Dixiecrats evolved their own dramatic props, including fire-and-brimstone edicts and performances such as "standing in the schoolhouse door," as well as epic scenes with state troopers and the National Guard. But the movement's expert dramatization of nonviolence—in the form of Freedom Rides, sit-ins, boycotts, marches, and demonstrations—ensured that individual stories of the freedom struggle coalesced in the kind of saga that, to borrow an aphorism, Hollywood could not have made up.

In 1962 John Steinbeck described the "strange drama" of massive resistance to civil rights initiatives as having "the same draw as a five-legged calf or a two-headed foetus at a sideshow, a distortion of normal life we have always found so interesting that we will pay to see it."[1]

However, the story of the risks civil rights volunteers took when faced with some of the most explosive and notorious episodes in U.S. history has rarely been told in cinema. Typically, civil rights workers have been caught in an epistemological drift, their stories of facing down violence overlooked as in *Mississippi Burning* (1988), dispersed through narrative subplots as in *Everybody's All-American* (1988), and located in TV movies—the dominant form through which stories of the civil rights movement have been brought to the masses—rather than big budget features. Their story began to be dramatized seriously only at the very end of the twentieth century in *Freedom Song* (1999), itself a Turner Network Television (TNT) production whose focus is the Student Nonviolent Coordinating Committee (SNCC) and its battle to register African American voters in McComb, Mississippi. It is ironic that such a vocal group as student organizers should be elided, especially when baby boomers who came of age in the 1960s have safeguarded images of the decade across the culture industries and reinvested in the moral high ground that the movement made manifest.[2] Since the 1980s there has, of course, been developing a series of films in which movement successes are celebrated, from *Crisis at Central High* (1981) to *Boycott!* (2001), honored with an NAACP Image Award, to *The Rosa Parks Story* (2002). Rather than a self-evident body of knowledge to which feature films allude, civil rights history is an arena of ideological divisions; it may serve dramatic as well as ideological ends to mythologize Rosa Parks as a tired seamstress rather than a trained activist but even the most emotionally charged movies made in recent decades overlook the civil rights delirium epitomized by the Freedom Rides and Freedom Summer and what Cornel West summarized as the "boiling sense of rage and a passionate pessimism regarding America's will to justice" that characterized the era.[3]

The reasons for this oversight are various. Nostalgic ensemble productions such as *Return of the Secaucus Seven* (1980) or *The Big Chill* (1983) tend to privilege the New Left and the antiwar movement in memory texts about a lost radicalism. The racial struggle has also been presented as the particularized cinematic province of African American directors, following controversies over British director Alan Parker's portrayal of the 1964 murders of civil rights workers in *Mississippi Burning* and as underlined by Spike Lee's reported comments that white liberal Norman Jewison, despite a long history of making sensitive movies about race relations, neither could nor should tell the story of slave insurrectionist Nat Turner.[4] A responsibility toward recent history is made even more controversial when issues of "ownership" are bound into cultural capital and directors who might otherwise have attempted to make a film about the freedom struggle feel unable to do so. The situation is compounded by the fact that remembering the movement involves focusing on events that are painful to revisit: the terrorist acts and pathological violence that characterized massive resistance against the black southern franchise and the brutality in jails that became a national scandal in the 1960s. Director Jonathan Demme, for example, having considered making a civil rights movie, confesses, "I just found that I didn't have the stomach to direct black actors and black extras to take the kind of beatings and humiliation that were visited on them in those days."[5]

As struggles over representing movement history continue, movies that preceded such debates by "wasting no time in getting in on the race problem" have been forgotten.[6] They were drive-in fare, low-budget pulp cinema, dismissed by civil rights historians as a banal or bizarre window on history and marginalized by film criticism until relatively recently.[7] They were quick to exploit and to risk offense, capitalizing as they did on tragic racist murders. However, this essay argues that the exploitation movie is a culturally suggestive product that should not be ignored for the manner in which it cannibalizes images that represent the real terror and hysteria that surrounded the freedom struggle.

The Council of Federated Organizations (COFO) was a coalition of pressure groups campaigning for voter registration, most notably the Student Nonviolent Coordinating Committee (SNCC) and the Congress for Racial Equality (CORE), that brought black and white northerners to Mississippi for Freedom Summer. The racial terrorism they endured and the conspiracies that dogged their efforts would be revealed later in the files of the Mississippi Sovereignty Commission, in interviews with civil rights workers, and from their reports, diaries, and memoirs. Norman Thomas, for example, writing to President Kennedy about Mississippi's Freedom Ballot, the mock election of 1963 that proved some eighty thousand black Mississippians wanted to use their vote, took pains to point out that the seemingly lunatic lawlessness that opposed the ballot was real: "I do not write as a sensationalist but as a veteran campaigner who has frequently covered the U.S. without finding a parallel or precedent for what I found in Mississippi."[8]

By 1963 cultural commentators had begun to talk about an "orgy of lawlessness" in Mississippi as the result of "the total breakdown of civil peace in the state."[9] Between June and September 1964 SNCC's running records of attacks by antimovement groups and harassment by officers of the law included some seventy shootings and bombings, more than a thousand arrests of civil rights workers, and around eighty beatings—of those that were reported and logged. Veterans of the movement as well as its earliest historians have described the poisonous atmosphere in which violence could be quick and its consequences final in terror-ridden towns, such as McComb, deemed "so dangerous" that the Justice Department "pleaded" with the Mississippi Project not to send volunteers there.[10] However, it was precisely the danger that the freedom struggle sought to highlight through its dramatization. For example, Mississippi Freedom Democratic Party delegates to the 1964 Democratic Convention in Atlantic City used the boardwalk to display photographs as evidence of racist atrocities and exhibited a burned-out Ford as a reminder of the vehicle from which James Chaney, Andrew Goodman, and Michael Schwerner were dragged to their deaths in Neshoba County by Klan members and police in the first week of Freedom Summer.

But instead of also dramatizing the dangers endemic in the struggle, more typically directors and screenwriters have espoused a liberal revisioning of the era with the emphasis on reconciliation and resolution. Movies about collective action, like most depictions of interracial cooperation—the battle over school integration in *Crisis at Central High* (1981) or the Montgomery Bus Boycott in *The Long Walk Home* (1994)—typically translate significant historical events into personal histories and domestic situations.[11] Identifying with a single protagonist such as conservative middle-class white teacher Elizabeth Huckaby (Joanne Woodward), whose voice-over enumerates the ways in which she is converted to the rightness of black civil rights in *Crisis at Central High*, or coed Maggie Deloach (Ally Sheady) in *Heart of Dixie* (1988), allowed the *Arkansas Gazette* to celebrate the former as "a success story for Little Rock" and the Memphis *Commercial Appeal* to describe the latter as "very sweet" and "kind of nostalgic."[12] Narratives of affirmation typically represent white moderates who come to consciousness of racism as the determining figures in a film's structures of meaning.

Hollywood's shadow cinema—or "paracinema" in Jeffrey Sconce's definition of those genres that coalesce as marginal "trash"—engaged with the weird and obscene images of racial bigotry.[13] In this way, the naked racist violence the movement sought to dramatize was, in turn, dramatized in those cultural forms that were designated popular and pulp: crime thrillers that were part of the paperback revolution of the 1950s and movies that capitalized on revisions to the Production Code, in its final throes in the 1960s, that allowed exploration of "issues" such as "miscegenation" and sexual permissiveness. While cultural commentators were analyzing what Walker Percy described in 1965 as "the collision between the civil rights movement and the racist coalition between redneck, demagogue, and small-town merchant," exploitation filmmakers sought to dramatize that very collision.[14] Larry Buchanan (*It's Alive, High Yellow, Mars Needs Women*), Jerry Gross (exploitation distributor), and Joseph P. Mawra (*Olga's House of Shame, Chained Girls*) each made movies in which the freedom struggle loomed large. Franco Moretti's thesis that narrative forms that deal with transformations in social life "have belonged to the various genres of mass literature and more broadly mass culture" has become axiomatic in studies of popular culture.[15] But it has not yet been examined in the context of the civil rights movement.

Grabbing at Headlines and Capitalizing on Tragedy

Three low-budget movies—*Free, White and 21* (written, produced, and directed by Buchanan, 1963), *Girl on a Chain Gang* (the first of only two forays into writing and directing by distributor Gross, 1964) and *Murder in Mississippi* (directed by Mawra, 1965)—exploited the civil rights movement in the early 1960s. Their setting is the small town and rural South, the movie boondocks, and their key characters are grotesque stereotypes. Righteous and naive northern students are arrayed against psychotic sheriffs, corrupt judges, rabble rousers, and racist peckerwoods. Images of marauding evil villains could be projected on to real people: segregationists battling change in evocations of the social crisis that Buchanan called "explosive," that Gross depicted as exploding, and that at the end of Mawra's film is presented as fading to a slow burn, with an aging sheriff admitting, "I'm just holding on." The films function as a melodramatic medley but also as a nightmare exposé of awful truths about the civil rights South publicized by the movement and covered by photojournalists. Many of the atrocities they depict represented prosaic realities for black southerners and civil rights workers who lived in fear for their lives yet refused to be intimidated by beatings, bombings, or shootings. However, the exploitation movie was by definition and design primarily underpinned by what W. J. Cash famously called the "romantics of the appalling"; the movies are the caricatural twin of serious studies such as George B. Tindall's "The Benighted South" (1964), which in this historical moment explored the origin of the region's derogatory image.[16] Specifically, *Free, White and 21* exploits a single news item of 1961 now long forgotten, while *Girl on a Chain Gang* and *Murder in Mississippi* sensationalize a local event of 1964 that became international news and that continues to resonate down the decades: Chaney, Goodman, and Schwerner's abduction and murder by a cabal of Klan members, including a preacher and the deputy sheriff who arrested them for a speeding violation and delivered them to the night riders.

While *Mississippi Burning* (1988), based on the FBI's investigation of the murders, has been the source of considerable controversy and some sustained film criticism, *Girl on a Chain Gang* and *Murder in Mississippi* are yet to receive critical attention, although Robert Firsching writing for *The New York Times* described the former's "oppressive air of perversity" as "hard to shake" and its exploitation of the Mississippi murders as "hard to excuse."[17]

The Freedom Summer Murders marker, Mt. Zion Church, Longdale, outside Philadelphia, Mississippi. Photo by author.

The movies exhibit the warped "justice" that allowed courts and police to punish civil rights workers for their activism. In *Free, White and 21*, a Freedom Rider is demeaned in court; voter registration volunteers are the easy prey of rabid segregationists in *Girl on a Chain Gang*, with the sole survivor exposing the heinous crimes of a sheriff and his deputies only in the final frames; three more students are murdered—shot, strangled, and castrated—in *Murder in Mississippi*. The fantasy of "race-mixing" is paramount whether conveyed in the guise of a trial movie or a horror story. *Free, White and 21* was the first film made by one of Roger Corman's protégés, Larry Buchanan. He promised "violent words and images never seen on the screen before. . . . A Motion Picture so bold it is for Adults Only," standard publicity for any "adult" film that used the challenge to censors as a means to titillate, but particularized by SNCC's radical ideas of living on "an island of integration in a sea of separation."[18]

My research seems to point to Buchanan basing his movie on a trial of December 1961 in which a British foreign student and Freedom Rider testified that an African American disc jockey had raped her in a Dallas motel room. On August 13, 1961, Freedom Riders Pauline Sims and George Raymond were jailed for their attempt to integrate Jackson's Trailways station. Subsequently, Sims left for Texas and would testify that there she met disc jockey Anthony Davis in a café and asked for his help in raising funds for CORE. Davis admitted consensual relations but denied rape and the African American man was acquitted of any crime.[19] However, if the Sims case was the nugget of news that first prompted Buchanan to make the film, one is immediately struck by wider exploitation subtexts for contemporary audiences. Buchanan changes the nationality of the foreigner, now Greta Mae Hansen (Annalena Lund), who bears an uncanny resemblance to Swedish actress May Britt. *Confidential* magazine labeled Britt's marriage to Sammy Davis Jr. in 1960 "explosive enough to make the A-bomb look like a firecracker," and a CORE field secretary remembers it being used as a pretext to provoke white prisoners to turn on blacks when he was arrested for being a Freedom Rider.[20] The extent to which the Davis/Britt relationship colored the viewing public's experience of *Free, White and 21* is unclear: few remember the film now and short reviews of a critically unpopular movie provide scant cultural context. However, what is clear is that the film recoils at the idea of "race-mixing" as much as it purports to "document" a "significant about-face in the racial climate," according to which a black man could expect to receive a fair trial in the "New South."[21]

Girl on a Chain Gang and *Murder in Mississippi* begin in exactly the same way, with student volunteers driving south to lend their support to the Freedom Summer project. In *Girl on a Chain Gang*, the students sing as they drive: "We are poor little lambs who have lost their way. Baa, baaa, baaa" and their voices also close the film in an eerie reprise. The two young men are jailed, then tricked into attempting to escape and murdered by a drunken cabal of deputies while the sheriff rapes Miss Rawlins in her cell. The only one left alive at the end is Rawlins, a Yale graduate in social sciences, described by the leering deputy who arrests the students as "free, white, and 21," as the camera slowly winds its way up from her stiletto heels and over her tightly fitted dress to her stubborn face. Only in the final frames does she become a (white) girl on a (black) chain gang, once found guilty of prostitution in a kangaroo court. In the final reel, having escaped across swampland and tied to a black convict in scenes that seem intended to recall *The Defiant Ones* (1958), Miss Rawlins literally runs into a state trooper who purports to have the cabal under surveillance: "This is the evidence we've wanted for a long time. You're the first one who's gotten out alive." He promises to arrest those of her assailants who remain alive and "put them away for quite a while." Miss Rawlins can only put her faith in this reconstructed southern official as the credits roll.

Murder in Mississippi also exploits the tragic murders of Chaney, Goodman, and Schwerner. Students drive safely through Virginia, North Carolina, Georgia, and Alabama, but as soon as they cross into Mississippi they are catapulted into the state that John Lewis called "the stronghold of the whole vicious system of segregation."[22] SNCC's attempt to "crack" Mississippi, and the individual acts of sometimes reckless heroism that the attempt involved, serves as the backdrop to exploit the image of a southern community whipped into a violent frenzy in a nightmare that was achingly topical. *Murder in Mississippi* is something of a "mash-up" of two movies, composed of long scenes, rare in a feature film, that record COFO's attempts to persuade apprehensive black southerners to register to vote and spliced with lurid and frenetically photographed scenes of rape, consensual sex between civil rights workers, and interracial prostitution. The moral vocabulary of integration is twisted into the clichés of race mixing as civil rights workers and antimovement terrorists collide. While exploitation movies do not traditionally deliver what their titles undertake to represent—the image of a girl on a chain gang in that movie's poster (p. 202) and its establishing shot is never reprised in such a lurid pose in the film—*Murder in Mississippi* depicts just what its title promises. It portrays the ease with which racist murders could be carried out and the legal conspiracies that ensured they went unpunished. That it does so in a lewd and chaotic style comments suggestively on the extremes to which massive resistance could go, especially in yoking together sex and race; the fear of race mixing was used to buttress white supremacist views and it clings pervasively to each scene of the civil rights exploitation movie.

Sexploitation, Sensationalism, and Civil Rights

Congress representative and former SNCC organizer John Lewis judges that "in the movies, directors love to toss sex and action and violence together" but argues that "in real life" they did not affect civil rights organizing: "When you're facing the razor-edge intensity of true life-and-death situations, the last thing on your mind is having sex with someone."[23] However, at the height of the civil rights crusade, censors were failing to stem the flood of risqué movies identified for popular consumption at drive-ins and small movie theaters. Movie melodrama and exploitation cinema dramatized many of the myths surrounding social "others" or "deviants" in the context of cold war–containment culture, and clashes over sex and race in Mississippi's "closed society" were prime material. Unsurprisingly, in *Murder in Mississippi* a life-and-death situation like that which Lewis describes prompts the only consensual sex in the movie. Project leader Paul Jackson (Otis Young) is depressed that his new recruits have not returned to the Freedom House. His agonized self-criticism, "I did it again. I lost three kids," summons up the real-life murders exploited in this quick-to-offend movie but leads to his sharing a marijuana cigarette with his coworker before she comforts him by making love. Much more unnerving is the scene in which

Movie poster for *Girl on a Chain Gang* (Jerry Gross Productions, 1966).

black volunteer Luther Barnes (Lew Stone), having rescued white Carol Lee Byrd (Shiellah Britton) from the shack in which she is the prisoner of her rapist, escapes with her through woods that recall the landscape of Neshoba County, the site of the real murders.[24] They collapse and hide but just as they move closer together and he gently begins to make love to her, they are ambushed by a posse that includes her rapist and which immediately drags away and castrates her defender. The films prefigure the coming together by the late 1960s of exploitation and pornography. They are infused with the conservative forces of sadistic misogyny and xenophobia, as *Girl on a Chain Gang*'s tagline makes clear: "A shocker! Any girl that's good looking just gotta be itching for action."

In each film under discussion, the audience is constructed as witnesses to scenes in which race mixing occurs and is punished, most overtly in the gimmick of an extradiegetic jury in *Free, White and 21. Girl on a Chain Gang* and *Murder in Mississippi* also include scenes where the camera looks away as a viewer might be expected to when a young woman is raped. In one film the white northern volunteer is raped by the sheriff for being a "nigger lover," and in the other southern dilettante Carol Lee Byrd is raped by poor whites conspiring with the police. In this way, the racist fantasy of the black rapist on which *Free, White and 21* pivots is twisted in *Girl on a Chain Gang* and *Murder in Mississippi*; white men use rape as a weapon in the armory of massive resistance. While Greta Mae Hansen and Jean Rawlins are beaten and bowed by the experience, Carol Lee Byrd stands up against those who would use sex to violate her civil rights as she seeks to promote the civil rights of others. She announces at the end of *Murder in Mississippi* that she will stay to fight. She admits, "When I first came down here [from Virginia], it wasn't out of real feelings or convictions" but "kicks and curiosity" and she allows that she was a bystander rather than a participant. But after witnessing the deaths of her fellow students, she is committed to the cause: "If we give up this fight, so will the government. You can't be neutral." Her words are swiftly followed by the film's closing images: news footage of another southerner, President Lyndon Johnson, similarly vowing to "overcome" bigotry and injustice.

While the formula for the exploitation movie requires a nod to a moral universe that sees the end of the rule of violence and corruption, it derives its narrative impetus from horrors that were neither imaginary nor solely psychological. Rape is the central premise on which the sexploitation narrative turns. In *Free, White and 21*, Lund's civil rights worker is represented as a naive and somewhat tawdry interloper for crossing the color line. Made to recall Sims, she is the member of CORE who tries to integrate the bus station in Jackson, Mississippi, and she too has supposedly come to Texas to collect funds from the NAACP and to liaise with "Ina" (i.e., Ella) Baker. She meets Ernie Jones, who promises her two hundred dollars for CORE if she will work for him. The premise for her charge of rape is presented as thin; the defense checks, for example, that the victim is not "weak-minded" for allowing a black businessman to take her measurements in a motel room to start her on a modeling career that will serve to raise money for CORE. But rape is a device for the outside agitator's vilification. Ernie Jones's attorney bases his defense in a rhetorical attack on the foreigner whose very presence in the South and whose behavior as "white trash" has sullied the reputation of an upstanding local black man: "Do you deny that the reason you came here was to get into the newspapers, cause racial strife in this community where there was none—and in which you don't belong? Didn't it dawn on you that something was rotten in Denmark . . . something was sour in Sweden . . . and that there was a nigger in the woodpile?" Clichés and illogicalities proliferate in the palimpsest of prejudices voiced by Ernie Jones's lawyer at every opportunity and bolstered by Jones himself. Jones tells the jury that he explained to Greta Mae that "the things CORE usually fights for we'd already attained here through negotiation and education," and his lawyer is adamant that he "wouldn't convict a yellow dog" on the testimony of "a woman like that" who understands nothing of the region because "she isn't even an American citizen." An integrated jury in Buchanan's "New South" courtroom decides in favor of Ernie Jones and as he leaves the court exonerated, white and black Texans alike congratulate him.

Buchanan cannot resist a twist in the tale. Following the formula of *Witness for the Prosecution* (1957) and *Anatomy of a Murder* (1959), a coda reveals that the jury—diegetic and nondiegetic—may have made a mistake.[25] To read the film as political critique is to allow that Buchanan conveys the idea that massive resistance to integration risks vilifying the innocent and exonerating the guilty. He closes on a pointed exchange between prosecutor and defense attorney:

> "Of course, you know she took a lie detector test and it showed she was telling the truth. How do you square that with a verdict of not guilty?"
>
> "It's a matter of definition. In her heart she thought she'd been raped. By Texas law she'd consented. . . . Is it that we love Negroes more or that we love intruders even less?"[26]

To read *Free, White and 21* as a new variation on the alien-invasion narrative of the 1950s is to see normality restored by its final image. Greta Mae Hansen leaves Texas as she arrived, alone on a Greyhound bus; having closed ranks and shrugged off the girl and her sinister activities, this fortress of a town can return to normal. The vilification and punishment of Yankees and other foreigners, outside agitators and invading "race mixers" such as Greta Mae, is a central trope of the civil rights exploitation movie as it begins to be defined by these films. Jacqueline Dowd Hall describes rumors of rape as "the folk pornography of the Bible belt," and rape became a metaphor in sensationalist anti–civil rights propaganda with one segregationist news item during Freedom Summer referring to the push for integration as "Federalized rape."[27] Rape constitutes a "joke" early in *Girl on a Chain Gang* when a barfly confides to the laughing bar owner that he enjoyed "good loving" after a fight with a sharecropper's daughter he "darned near had to rape." His reputation ensures he is enlisted by a deputy sheriff to stage the circumstances in which the student volunteers may be arrested for a second time. In this way, sex is a determining factor in differentiating hero from villain: the barfly is happy to pretend that the students have acted as pimps by offering him Jean Rawlins for money; the black student later refuses the sexual bait he is offered in jail with the haughty line "Remove your carnal offerings" before he is shot in the back. In both *Girl on a Chain Gang* and *Murder in Mississippi*, the students are threatened with prosecution under the Mann Act for having supposedly transported a female student across the state line for immoral purposes, and in *Free, White and 21*, the defense alleges that Greta Mae has been "specially trained" in France or Italy and sent as a spy "to see whether a Negro charged with rape can get a fair trial in the South." It is the question that American International Pictures (AIP) exploited in publicity materials.

Trailers and Teasers

Jerry Gross and Larry Buchanan proved adept at exploiting the drive-in movie in the moment that the target audience shifted from families to teenagers. Their chosen subject matter also reflects the locations of the most financially lucrative drive-ins in the Deep South.[28] As Thomas Cripps points out, "events provided Eisenhower with an opening to act boldly in using federal powers to hold open the schools of Little Rock, far earlier than they provided Hollywood with a crisis it could understand well enough to formulate into politically engaging or even informative movies."[29] Hollywood did indeed hold back, but independents such as Corman in *The Intruder* (1961) and Buchanan and exploitation moguls such as Gross seized the day for market forces. Their extratextual exhibition ploys forged parallels between race relations on and off the screen.

The deeply conservative moral valence bound up in even the most sensationalist pulp is made manifest in the discourse through which the films were marketed, in press books, posters, and trailers. Unlike *Girl on a Chain Gang* and *Murder in Mississippi*, thrillers whose "shock-stock" easily equipped them for the midnight horror slot, *Free, White and 21* was more equivocal in situating itself and its audience. Therefore, it is the most revealing case study with regard to promotion and reception. Its press book includes prepared stories designed to be planted to justify its subject matter and validate its relevance for multiple audiences, tie-ins to local radio and TV stations ensured that exhibitors could model the film for their particular community, and stunts such as young women parading the streets are typical of exploitation angles deployed since the 1920s. However, while genre is a key signifier for marketing most exploitation movies—as in stunts such as parking an ambulance outside a movie theater screening a horror film—the civil rights movie lacked a ready-made fan base invested in its story type. In the 1950s and the 1960s films that examined civil rights struggles in any guise at all were typically reviewed as small-town movies, melodramas, or social problem pictures. Movies about the freedom struggle also lacked a tried-and-true formula—although demonizing the white woman who is attracted to a black man was a paradigmatic formula that transcended generic categories. It was salient in promoting *Free, White and 21* not only to titillate fans of exploitation cinema but also to tempt viewers who might expect quality in terms of acting and topical interest in terms of content.

In posters, the black and white protagonists stand on either side of an unmade bed (p. 207). Frederick O'Neal, popularly known as a regular in *Car 54, Where Are You?* and an established actor who cofounded the American Negro Theater in Harlem, is the "name" star of the movie. His role as owner of the Ebony Hotel and an advertising man, as well as a disc jockey, reprises something of his best-known cameo as a hard-nosed businessperson in *Pinky* (1949). He stands on the right of the poster, a symbolic broken handcuff dangling from his wrist, as Annalena Lund stands to the left, white blouse open to reveal a black brassiere, a salacious image of a Freedom Rider. Promotion material for exploitation movies typically oversells; rarely are trailer publicity promises realized, and posters and movie titles always promise a more risqué story than the product delivers. In fact, Greta Mae remains fully clothed for most of the movie and even the bathing suit she dons in her hotel room is relatively demure.

Short publicity articles from the National Screen Service included in the press book—"New Swedish Acting Beauty Stars in *Free, White and 21*" and "Oscar Nominee Frederick O'Neal an 'Actor's Actor'"—are typical of exploitation material in that they celebrate a new female actor and use everything they can bring to bear about an established actor to sell the film to audiences. More interesting are the seat-selling slants dreamed up to ensure a "carnival ballyhoo showmanship" around the launch that exploits the idea of the civil rights rally in the popular imagination. The articles suggest that young women carry placards and handbags printed with "Free, White and 21" and theater times and that "attractive Negro women can be used in appropriate areas in the same way"—although one wonders how hard it is to sell a film with this title to an African American demographic. The press book recommends that

DAY BEFORE OPENING

Posters from the press book of *Free, White and 21* (Los Angeles: American International Pictures, 1963).

screenings be set up for the local bar association, with members' ballots forming the basis of a press release to show the unanimity or disparity of legal opinion over whether a black man may now expect a fair trial for a cross-racial sex crime. Finally, special screenings should be held for NAACP chapters, police groups, ministerial associations, and local interracial groups—including CORE, one supposes—as well as a special luncheon for magistrates and judges with the press in attendance.[30]

Free, White and 21 is a technical failure, so full of gimmicks that it collapses on itself: endless crane shots oversee the trial proceedings; rickety flashbacks tell the story from two points of view, repeating the same shots in quick and pointless succession; and there is a programmed interruption of three minutes during which time the audience/jury is left to deliberate its verdict. In this way, the film makes claims about its own reception, expecting spectators to fulfill the subject positions assigned by the subpoena they received on entering the movie theater (p. 209). But, despite the bid for audience involvement, as the clock on the screen ticks by for three long minutes, the film loses diegetic hold over the audience and the verdict of "not guilty" is less surprising than the filmmakers may have hoped. Typical of exploitation cinema, Buchanan tried to have it both ways: *Free, White and 21* is portrayed as a "legitimate" film that O'Neal praises as "done with a great deal of taste . . . nothing cheap . . . an honest and factual story," and it is also a "provocative" adult movie, its plaintiff "an irresistible tease."[31] The movie was not well-reviewed—when it received any notice at all. The *New York Times*, nevertheless, helped bolster AIP's ballyhoo when it judged the story "graphically recounted with emphasis on its most sordid aspects in language seldom heard on the screen." Allowing that "some socially conscious spectators" would find the subject matter "significant," the review struck the very balance that the film's press book sought to attain.[32]

"You in Mississippi Now"

Low-budget southern movies in any genre typically feature northerners straying South only to be harassed, tortured, and often killed: from gore-fests *Two Thousand Maniacs* (1965) and *It's Alive* (1969) to cult hit *Easy Rider* (1969) and *Macon County Line* (1974), in which the sheriff disdains "punk kids, strangers, or smart alecs from up North."

Ralph Ellison describes Tuskegee students finding themselves at the mercy of police speed traps in Phenix City, Alabama, in the 1930s in ways that prefigure tactics used to aggravate and arrest Freedom Summer volunteers: "Since Tuskegee students were regarded as on their way to becoming 'uppity educated nigras', we were especially vulnerable. The police lay in wait for us, clocked our speed by a standard known only to themselves, and used any excuse to delay and harass us." Ellison's 1985 essay cannot fail but also invoke images of the 1960s, which overlay those of the 1930s. While his highway patrol officers are "Jeeter Lester types," they also include a particularly zealous sheriff's deputy, "a big potbellied mother who chews Brown Mule Tobacco," whom readers will find reminiscent of Sheriff Lawrence Rainey in Philadelphia, Mississippi, with his penchant for Red Man tobacco.[33]

Mississippi in the mid-1960s was variously described as "The South exaggerated," a police state, and an "Orwellian nightmare."[34] Mississippi

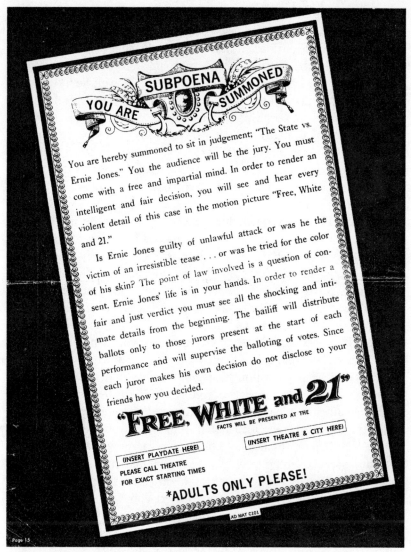

Publicity materials from the *Free, White and 21* press book (Los Angeles: American International Pictures, 1963).

law allowed police to detain suspects for up to seventy-two hours while investigating whether a crime had been committed, and its elasticity was exploited to full effect during the "invasion" of "communist" students in the summers of 1964 and 1965. SNCC organizer Ivanhoe Donaldson's account of a "routine Mississippi cop interrogation" is representative: "Nigger, where you from. . . . Boy! If you stay down here long enough, you gonna make a mistake. . . . If I had your god damned ass . . . I'd kill you."[35] Volunteers were arrested for delinquency, loitering, and vagrancy while canvassing for voter registration, and for willfully and unlawfully using the sidewalks during rallies. There are numerous examples of ludicrous policing and spurious crimes. Affidavits from locals and volunteers testify to systematic beatings in jail and out: SNCC's Silas McGee was beaten with a tire iron and on another occasion shot in the face; Jimmy Travis was shot in the neck with an automatic rifle; in Laurel, Mississippi, in August 1964 a group of fifteen white men attacked a group of COFO workers with clubs and chains. Both *Girl on a Chain Gang* and *Murder in Mississippi* begin with a gross parody of such racial rites, with fabricated reasons for arrest for driving offenses. As soon as student volunteers are arrested in *Girl on a Chain Gang*, one observes, "If they knew we were here to help with voter registration we'd disappear without a trace" (like Chaney, Goodman, and Schwerner is the unspoken addendum), and the psychotic sheriff is reminded by his murderous deputies that he probably should not keep boasting that he has killed a man with his bare hands because "they'll be an investigation after a while" (a sly allusion to Sheriff Rainey's having killed two black men for supposedly resisting arrest). One volunteer is expected to sign a blank confession and the sheriff's financial tally for their fictive crimes totals $150: "Seven crimes at $7 each times three plus $3 for collecting the fee."

The civil rights volunteers are presented more ambiguously than their enemies; as new exploitation protagonists, they run the gamut from shockingly naive to recklessly courageous. In *Girl on a Chain Gang* they never even attempt to register a voter. Arrested on entering fictional Carson's Landing they are immediately out of their depth, tricked because they lack the caution that would have been carefully taught at COFO's orientation sessions in Oxford, Ohio. They are unaccompanied by an experienced civil rights worker and foolishly treat southern law officers as stage villains whose lack of education they openly disdain. The students are beleaguered innocents and once the male volunteers are dispatched, the film focuses on the sexploitation of the lone girl so that the "invader" is herself sexually invaded, first by the sheriff who rapes her and latterly by the town "doctor" who performs a gynecological examination that will convict her.

Like the spurious crimes with which the students are charged, the kangaroo court was a renowned modus operandi, both at state and local levels. In Alabama, George Wallace paroled a Klan member who had been convicted of castrating a black man. Nine white men convicted of bombing black homes in McComb were let off with probation because Judge W. H. Watkins ruled them "unduly provoked" by civil rights workers "of low morality and hygiene."[36] In *Girl on a Chain Gang*, after the doctor's expert "evidence" that he has found "black" as well as "white" sperm in her vagina, Jean Rawlins is convicted of soliciting by a jury of a single stooge. Nor is her sentence of ninety days on a chain gang as sensationalist as it might appear, considering that a number of activists, including SNCC's Charles Sherrod and Charles Jones, were consigned to a chain gang as punishment for taking part in sit-ins and that Bayard Rustin served three weeks on a chain gang for taking part in the first Freedom Rides of 1947. In *Murder in Mississippi*, the federal judge laughs at the U.S. attorney presenting the case brought by Carol Lee Byrd. The judge accuses her of "testifying" instead of giving evidence and is disdainful of "hearsay" about "theoretical state crimes." As the camera pans around the accused men, they laugh openly as she declares herself unable to find "a statute for castration" that will allow her to charge the men for the murder of Luther Barnes. When she quickly dismisses the case, the scene recalls Esther Carter, U.S. commissioner of the Southern District of Mississippi, who in December 1964 dropped all charges against the twenty-nine Klan members arraigned for violating the civil rights of Chaney, Goodman, and Schwerner, at their preliminary hearing—on the basis of hearsay.

In these exploitation movies, the civil rights movement is both the source of the originating news to be exploited and the pretext for melodrama. Villains are depicted with the simplistic clarity typical of grindhouse and drive-in cultures, yet the films also manage to make political comment on the tension manipulated by segregationists between states' rights and federal laws, for example. One of the first things the sheriff in *Girl on a Chain Gang* says to the students his deputies have apprehended is, "We don't cotton to no Feds in local matters," and in *Murder in Mississippi* the refrain is, "We ain't gonna let communist Yankees run our town for us."

◼

The largely forgotten pulp movies unearthed for discussion in this essay were part of the "new" generation of films of the early 1960s that pushed the boundaries of "bad taste." Although it does not refer to any of these movies, by 1965 the industry's magazine *Variety* had recognized a burgeoning genre it called the "racism-sex-violence genre of civil-wrongs films." However, *Free, White and 21*, *Girl on a Chain Gang*, and *Murder in Mississippi* also contributed to making manifest legalized racial terror and making visible what black southerners and those campaigning alongside risked. Whatever the motives of their producers may have been, exploitation movies about the civil rights movement should not be summarily dismissed as *only* a debased form of entertainment and a low form of diversion and escapism. Certainly, the films are irreverent but the tragic murders used and abused in *Girl on a Chain Gang* and *Murder in Mississippi* were already notorious for the very violence and cruelty that the films depict in lewd and grotesque imagery. In *Girl on a Chain Gang*, for example, the bodies of dead students covered with bloody sheets litter the sheriff's office and in *Murder in Mississippi* the scene in which a civil rights worker is castrated is a chilling reminder that such racist rites were a very relevant and contemporary nightmare image. Read in this way, the films are more open cultural texts than their "tasteless" excess, unrefined cinematography, stripped-down mise-en-scène, and wooden acting make them appear. They are demotic movies that release multiple cultural meanings contemporary to their moment of production. They pinion the grotesque at the heart of the southern civil rights story in an apocalyptic pantomime of social breakdown.

The tragic murders that inaugurated Freedom Summer were still raw when these films were made and they are unmediated either by hindsight or restraint. Events are treated with irreverent haste as well as vulgar excess—*Girl on a Chain Gang* was released within weeks after the bodies of Chaney, Goodman, and Schwerner were discovered. Exploitation movies, like mass cultural productions more generally, open up a space that other films carefully avoid. In each film there is a strong sense of marauding evil and while it may be inexpertly navigated so that characters topple over into caricature, it is uncannily close to that which civil rights workers remember. But films made over subsequent decades have lost sight of the racial terrorism that the freedom struggle sought to end. They screen it behind narratives that, while affirming civil rights successes, ignore the grassroots battles that brought them into being. The risk is nostalgic complacency. James Baldwin warned, "To overhaul a history or to attempt to redeem it . . . is not at all the same thing as the descent one must make in order to excavate a history."[37] Excavating 1960s film history, one rediscovers the civil rights exploitation story that has been subsumed.

Acknowledging exploitation movies forms part of an ongoing discursive struggle to recover the diverse popular forms in which recent historical events have been dramatized and disseminated. At the end of the twentieth century in *Black and White Strangers*, Kenneth Warren argued that the construction of racial relations in the United States has been "so central to our political, imaginative, and economic practices that it ought to be possible to trace the process of this construction in a variety of cultural places, many of them unexpected and not yet adequately examined."[38] Civil rights pulp from the 1960s is a neglected corner in a storehouse of the different cultural forms in which the freedom struggle has been represented. The movies are degenerate and cliché ridden, but at the height of the freedom struggle Robert Penn Warren wondered whether clichés may "give us, after all, the fresh, appalling vision of truth."[39] Indeed, a volunteer in a letter home during his orientation in the days preceding Freedom Summer described watching "Mississippi and the Fifteenth Amendment" on *CBS Reports* with veteran organizers: "Some of the film was absolutely ridiculous and ludicrous—a big, fat, really fat and ugly white county registrar prevents Negroes from voting; the stupid really, really completely irrational and dishonest views of some white southerners and so on. Six of the staff members got up and walked out of the movie because it was so real to them while we laughed because it was so completely foreign to us."[40] The clichés that new volunteers find ludicrous are as real and offensive to the COFO organizers as the laughter of the new recruits. The exploitation movie captured what was ugly and irrational about segregationist rites of racial self-preservation, and it emphasized the dreadful immorality behind massive resistance that movement strategies such as the Freedom Rides and Freedom Summer had both dramatized and exposed. In later decades civil rights stories would be domesticated, but in the 1960s they were not only the stuff of aberrant sex and violence in an exaggerated South but also, even despite themselves, a subversive and critical commentary on the racial atrocities perpetrated in a period of menacing antimovement activity.

NOTES

1. John Steinbeck, *Travels with Charley: In Search of America* (New York: Penguin, 1980), 256.

2. See, for example, Sharon Monteith, *American Culture in the 1960s* (Edinburgh: Edinburgh University Press, 2008), 69–71, 173, 186–203.

3. Cornel West, *Race Matters* (Boston: Beacon, 1993), 18.

4. The controversy is discussed by Tony Horowitz in "Untrue Confessions," *New Yorker*, December 13, 1999, 80–89.

5. Ann Hornaday, "Waiting for 'Action!'" interview with Jonathan Demme, *Washington Post*, July 10, 2007, 11. Demme's comment is interesting considering that he was willing to direct black actors to endure beatings and humiliations meted out during slavery in *Beloved* (1998) but not portray racial violence in recent history.

6. Margaret Harford, "*Free, White and 21* Screening City-Wide," *Los Angeles Times*, December 12, 1964, C8.

7. For example, in special issues of *Velvet Light Trap* and *Film History* on exploitation movies and in Eric Schaeffer's epic study *Bold! Daring! Shocking! True! A History of Exploitation Films 1919–1959* (Durham, N.C.: Duke University Press, 1999) the southern exploitation movie has only just begun to receive attention. See Riché Richardson's discussion of *The Klansman aka The Burning Cross* in *Black Masculinity and the U.S. South: From Uncle Tom to Gangsta* (Athens: University of Georgia Press, 2007), 40–72, and Sharon Monteith, "Movies, Exploitation," in *The Encyclopedia of Southern Culture: Media*, ed. Allison Graham and Sharon Monteith (Chapel Hill: University of North Carolina Press, forthcoming).

8. Norman Thomas, quoted in Jeannine Heron, "Underground Election," *Nation*, December 7, 1963, 23.

9. Ira Harkey, *The Smell of Burning Crosses* (1967; New York: XLibris, 2006), 210.

10. Howard Zinn, *SNCC: The New Abolitionists* (1964; Cambridge, Mass: South End, 2002), 250.

11. See Sharon Monteith, "The Movie-Made Movement: Civil Rites of Passage," in *Memory and Popular Film*, ed. Paul Grainge (Manchester: Manchester University Press, 2003), 120–43, which includes a discussion of *The Long Walk Home, Crisis at Central High*, and *Mississippi Burning*.

12. Martha Douglas, "Central High Crisis Dramatized," *Arkansas Gazette*, February 4, 1981, 5B; "Oxford Turns Out for Dixie," *Commercial (Tenn.) Appeal*, August 25, 1989, B3.

13. Jeffrey Sconce, "'Trashing' the Academy: Taste, Excess, and an Emerging Politics of Cinematic Style," *Screen* 36, no. 4 (Winter 1995): 371–93.

14. Walker Percy, "Mississippi: The Fallen Paradise," *Harpers Magazine*, April 1965, 168.

15. Franco Moretti, "The Spell of Indecision," *Marxism and the Interpretation of Culture*, ed. Cary Nelson and Lawrence Grossberg (London: Macmillan, 1988), 344.

16. George B. Tindall, "The Benighted South: Origins of a Modern Image," *Virginia Quarterly Review* 40 (Spring 1964): 281–94.

17. Robert Firsching, review summary of *Girl on a Chain Gang*, *New York Times*, 1966, http://movies.nytimes.com/movie/19832/Girl-on-a-Chain-Gang/overview (accessed March 3, 2009).

18. Robert Moses, quoted in *Voices of Freedom*, ed. Henry Hampton and Steve Fayer (New York: Vintage, 1995), 183.

19. Ray Arsenault provides these details of the trial and of the attempt to integrate the Jackson Trailways terminal in *Freedom Riders: 1961 and the Struggle for Racial Justice* (New York: Oxford University Press, 2006), 579, 389.

20. Hy Steirman, "Will Hollywood Blackball Sammy Davis and May Britt?" *Confidential*, January 1961, reprinted in *The Sammy Davis Jr. Reader*, ed. Gerald Early (New York: Farrar, Strauss, and Giroux), 259; Thomas Gaither, quoted in James Peck, *Freedom Ride* (New York: Grove, 1962), 80–81. After seeing May Britt in *The Blue Angel* (1959), Davis pursued her and they were married the day after Kennedy's election in 1960. Controversy dogged them, with Davis alleging the wedding was postponed at the incoming president's request and that he was excised from the election campaign rostrum because his relationship with May would damage the Democrats' hold over the southern bloc.

21. Larry Buchanan, "*Free, White and 21*: Explosive Tale of Racial About-Face," press book for *Free, White and 21* (Los Angeles: American International Pictures, 1963), 4.

22. John Lewis, quoted in James Atwater, "If We Can Crack Mississippi," *Saturday Evening Post*, July 25, 1964, 19.

23. John Lewis, *Walking with the Wind: A Memoir of the Movement* (New York: Simon and Schuster, 1998), 265.

24. Britton established her niche in erotic movies from *Blonde and Brutal* (1962) and *Warm Nights and Hot Pleasures* (1964) to *Pleasures of the Plantation* (1970).

25. In many ways the film is a cheap rehash of Otto Preminger's *Anatomy of a Murder*. Hugely controversial, largely for having defense attorney James Stewart utter the words "panties" and "spermatogenesis" and for showing the jury Lee Remick's torn underwear as evidence of rape, it was also critically acclaimed for demystifying sexual taboos and for subverting both the Production Code near its end and the Legion of Decency (a Catholic organization formed in 1933 that rated films according to its code of moral decency). Preminger, as a pioneering independent, had already succeeded in undoing both with *The Moon Is Blue* (1953) and *The Man with a Golden Arm* (1955).

26. Mamie Garvin Fields's memoir *Lemon Swamp* (1983) provides another example of the southern justice system siding with a black southerner over an outsider. When she is involved in a car crash, she is supported by the police as a black southern woman over the white northern man whose car she crashed into.

27. Jacqueline Dowd Hall, "The Mind That Burns in Each Body: Women, Rape, and Racial Violence," in *Powers of Desire: The Politics of Sexuality*, ed. Ann Snitow, Christine Stansell, and Sharon Thompson (New York: Monthly Review, 1983), 335; James Ward of the *Jackson Daily News*, quoted in Susan Weil, *In a Madhouse's Din: Civil Rights Coverage by Mississippi Daily Press, 1948–1968* (Westport, Conn.: Praeger, 2002), 141.

28. See, for example, Bruce A. Austin, "The Development and Decline of the Drive-in Movie Theater," in *Current Research in Film: Audiences, Economics and the Law*, ed. Bruce A. Austin (Norwood, N.J.: Ablex, 1985), especially pp. 67–79.

29. Thomas Cripps, *Making Movies Black: The Hollywood Message Movie from World War II to the Civil Rights Era* (New York: Oxford University Press, 1993), 285–86.

30. Buchanan, *"Free, White and 21,"* 13.

31. "Frederick O'Neal Praises Film, Asks 'Balanced' Negro Roles," press book, 4; "Teasers: Seven to Twenty-one Days in Advance," press book, 7.

32. Eugene Archer, "Free, White, and 21: A Court Drama Based on Freedom Rides," *New York Times*, June 25, 1963, 29.

33. Ralph Ellison, "An Extravagance of Laughter," in *Going to the Territory* (New York: Vintage, 1986), 167–69.

34. James W. Silver, *Mississippi: The Closed Society* (New York: Harcourt and Brace, 1964); review of *Mississippi: The Closed Society*, *Journal of Higher Education* 35, no. 7 (1964): 409–10.

35. Ivanhoe Donaldson, "Southern Diaries," *Freedomways* (New York: Southern Negro Youth Congress, 1964), excerpted in *Mississippi Freedom Summer*, ed. John F. McClymer (Belmont, Calif.: Wadsworth, 2004), 90.

36. "Text of Judge's Sentence for Bombers," *Enterprise (Miss.) Journal*, October 28, 1964, 5; Sherrill, *Gothic Politics in the Deep South* (New York: Ballantine, 1969), 316, 199. Governor Barnett suggested the civil rights workers

would benefit from "a couple of cases of Mister Clean," as quoted in the Jackson *Clarion-Ledger*, July 6, 1964, 3.

37. James Baldwin, *Just above My Head* (London: Michael Joseph, 1979), 478.

38. Kenneth Warren, *Black and White Strangers: Race and American Literary Realism* (Chicago: University of Chicago Press, 1993), 139.

39. Robert Penn Warren, *Who Speaks for the Negro?* (New York: Random House, 1965), 108.

40. Elizabeth Sutherland Martinez, ed. *Letters from Mississippi* (Brookline, Mass.: Zephyr, 2007), 7.

 PART THREE

Crossing Borders

Mapping out a Postsouthern Cinema

Three Contemporary Films

Jay Watson

In *Inventing Southern Literature*, critic Michael Kreyling credits his pre-decessor Lewis P. Simpson with coining the concept of the "postsouth-ern."[1] Simpson unveils the term in an essay from his 1980 collection, *The Brazen Face of History*, that traces a crucial shift in regional literary sen-sibility from the so-called Southern Renascence of the 1930s and 1940s—whose modernist quest for "a vision of social order at once strongly sac-ramental and sternly moralistic" was, according to Simpson, complicated and ironized by the contingencies, displacements, and "mystery" of the southern past—to a postwar stance marked by increasing skepticism toward the legitimacy of such grand, stabilizing concepts as myth, com-munity, nature, and history.[2] "The Southern Renascence will not come again," Simpson proclaims, because southern artists could no longer bal-ance regional myth against regional history in credible, mutually illu-minating ways.[3] Translating Simpson's argument into the language of a contemporary, theory-influenced generation of literary critics, Kreyling cites the work of Umberto Eco, Linda Hutcheon, and Fredric Jameson to suggest that a postsouthern intellectual landscape is one that has come "to question the natural authority of the foundation term: *Southern*," a term that "has been used so much, been invested with so much meaning, that we can no longer distinguish between what if anything is inherent" in regional identity or culture "and what other interests have attached over time."[4] A postsouthern South is thus one that appears to rest on no "real" or reliable foundation of cultural, social, political, economic, or historical distinctiveness, only on an ever-proliferating series of rep-resentations and commodifications of "southernness." So "multivalent" has that term become, writes Kreyling, that it may seem to have "no core."[5] More recently, Scott Romine has embraced this position in his study *The Real South*, which locates southernness in the ongoing process of constructing and negotiating a regional imaginary rather than in the specific contents or referents of any particular instance of that process.[6]

In this way the postsouthern is gaining a foothold in southern literary studies, and it is crossing over into other disciplines as well.[7] But the concept has been slow to make its way into the burgeoning field of southern film studies. I want to begin to remedy that deficiency here by examining a pair of 1991 films that are set in the contemporary South: *Slacker*, directed by Richard Linklater and shot in and around Austin, Texas, and *Mississippi Masala*, directed by Mira Nair and shot primarily in and around Greenwood, Mississippi. Though these films have attracted a significant amount of scholarly attention, virtually none of that scholarship draws on southern problems and paradigms, let alone postsouthern ones, as the basis of analysis or critique.[8] Nair's film, for instance, is at the center of a contentious debate about the nature and authenticity of South Asian identity and agency in a diasporic context, while *Slacker* is most often discussed as a portrait of disaffected American youth in an era whose spiraling consumerism is complicated by downward mobility among the middle and working classes.[9] As I hope to demonstrate here, however, the two films also offer provocative deconstructions and reconfigurations of regional identities, themes, and signifiers, reworkings that it is appropriate and productive to view as postsouthern. They do this, moreover, in significantly different ways. *Slacker* gets at the postsouthern by way of the postmodern, drawing on a range of effects and motifs now closely associated with what Jameson has christened the "cultural logic of late capitalism," but also taking these techniques and themes South to a new place, as it were.[10] *Mississippi Masala*, on the other hand, gets at the postsouthern by way of the postcolonial, and in doing so, Nair's ambitious film takes Simpson's and Kreyling's concept in new directions that neither critic seems to have anticipated.

Before turning to these works, however, I want to open with a brief look at a third film, which on its release in 1981 stirred my first vague (and decidedly nonscholarly) inklings of something like a postsouthern sensibility or ambience at work in the South of my youth. That film, which hints at the postsouthern without embracing it, is *Sharky's Machine*, directed by and starring Burt Reynolds.

"You're from out of state": *Sharky's Machine*

Sharky's Machine (1981) is no cinematic masterpiece, but it is fair to call the film a competent, enjoyable crime drama with noirish elements. Reynolds, an actor perhaps best known in 1981 for a series of southern roles, including Lewis Medlock in John Boorman's adaptation of *Deliverance* and a string of good old boys with a wild streak in comedies such as

Gator, W. W. and the Dixie Dance Kings, and the *Smokey and the Bandit* films, plays a vice squad cop whose investigation of a ring of high-end prostitutes leads him into the highest circles of organized crime in Atlanta. Alongside Reynolds, the film's other major icon is not an actor but a building, the recently completed Westin Peachtree Plaza, Atlanta's first true skyscraper, a 722-foot, 73-story cylinder lined with the gleaming panels of green reflective glass that had emerged by the late 1970s and early 1980s as a leading architectural symbol of corporate power.[11] On its completion in 1976, John Portman's elegant tower (he designed and developed it) was the tallest hotel building in the world and the tallest building of any kind in the southeastern United States. It was one of the first and most visible signs of a coming internationalism, or perhaps multinationalism, that would transform Atlanta into a world metropolis by the 1990s: site of the 1996 Olympic games, corporate headquarters for IBM, Coca-Cola, and other mega conglomerates, and seat of Ted Turner's global media empire.[12]

The Peachtree Plaza is a signature element in Reynolds's film. Both the opening and closing credits roll against helicopter-tracking shots that pick out the tower as the dominant feature of the city's skyline, then zero in to linger on its cool, crystalline, almost iridescent exterior. Throughout the narrative, brief establishing shots capture the tower in a variety of aspects—by night and at dawn, from ground level and from high in the air—giving the structure almost the roundness and range of a character in its own right. It hovers in the background of scene after scene, only to emerge as foreground at film's end, site of a climactic chase and shoot-out between Sharky and a drugged-out assassin for the syndicate.

Many of these undercurrents, of course, were completely lost on me at the time of the film's release. In 1981, I was a nineteen-year-old undergraduate at the University of Georgia in nearby Athens, and as naive about the semiotics of film as I was about the question of my own southernness. Still, unequipped as I was to decipher the film's subtler nuances, I did register its obsessive attention to that beautiful yet inscrutable tower. In the South yet somehow not of it—as if plucked from the skyline of Tokyo or Los Angeles—it seemed silently to announce that Atlanta had changed, that the South was changing. It had a new look that signified a new order, a new arrangement of power, lying just over the horizon.

In the film, these new arrangements also govern the action on the mean streets below.[13] The film opens with a drug bust gone bad, followed by Sharky's messy takedown of the dealer on a city bus, a lapse of judgment that gets a civilian killed and Sharky demoted from narcotics to vice. The bad guy is black, stylish, and, despite his violence, urbane in his own way—which is to say that in the context of 1981 he evokes an old-school Atlanta, whether of enterprising black elites that rose to economic and political prominence during the civil rights years or of urban refugees displaced during that same era by the huge development projects of the city's new downtown.[14] Either way, though, he and Sharky represent the film's first ground-level images of the local, locked in a familiar southern dynamic of black-white antagonism.

As the plot unfolds, however, we learn that the dealer's local black underworld (there is an interrogation scene set in a blues club) is actually a front for a much more sophisticated and ruthless crime ring that the film presents, in very pointed terms, as multinational. The ringleader, Victor Scorelli, is Italian, with requisite Mafia overtones. So is the assassin, Victor's brother, also known as Billy Score. The Italians, however, also employ a pair of Chinese strongmen who eliminate a police informant with nunchucks and kung-fu moves; later they torture Sharky by cutting off two of his fingers. What is more, the syndicate's ensemble of thousand-dollar-a-night prostitutes, bought as children on the international sex market and personally instructed in the erotic arts by Victor himself, is a multiethnic group that includes Asian, Australian, and African American (or possibly African) women. The only southerners to be found in the cartel are underlings: a corrupt narcotics officer, a gubernatorial candidate who, the film makes clear, is simply Victor's political puppet, and the black drug peddlers on the streets. Sharky underscores the foreignness and invasiveness of the city's new regime of crime in the film's snappiest bit of tough-guy dialogue: "I'm gonna pull the chain on you, pal," he tells Victor. "And you wanna know why? 'Cause you're fucking up my city. You're walking over people like you own 'em. And you wanna know the worst part? You're from out of state!" Out of state: not so unlike the corporate power and capital—itself increasingly multinational—filtering into cities like Atlanta at sites like Portman's tower. As Martyn Bone explains, Atlanta was aggressively marketed during the 1960s and 1970s "as a prime investment site in the European business press, and boosters embarked on trade junkets to the commercial capitals of Europe and Asia." As a result of "[s]uch promotional maneuvers," he continues, the city's downtown development projects "were often financed by transnational capital."[15] In *Sharky's Machine* this international cast of corporate investors and absentee owners remains invisible; instead, the film displaces it downward into Victor's rainbow coalition of the criminal minded.

In the film, this is not simply a loose connection, since Victor in fact makes his home at—where else?—the Peachtree Plaza, in a luxurious condominium on one of the building's upper floors. His lordly height over the city signals his mastery of the urban territory below, the extension of his influence through its major corridors of power. In this way the full panoptical function of the Plaza becomes clear. As a centralized, circular tower presiding over an unruly space subjected to emergent configurations of power, it is not simply a place to *see* at all times but a place to see *from* as well. (Thanks to its reflective facade, it is also consistent with Foucault's panoptical observation posts in being difficult to see *into*, rebuffing the attempt of the observed to direct a reciprocal gaze at their overseers.) In the anxious logic of *Sharky's Machine*, then, the contemporary skyscraper becomes the incongruous site and symbol where the alien forces of corporate capital and organized crime converge (from out of state) to invade and menace the regional community.

Sharky does his best to stand up to these monolithic structures of power on behalf of his local world. As the film rushes toward conclusion, he and his men pursue Billy Score through the upper reaches of the tower: the roof, a fire escape stairwell, a suite of unoccupied corporate offices, a veritable labyrinth of capitalist infrastructure.[16] He finally corners Billy in what looks like an empty boardroom, where the wounded fugitive perches in front of an enormous sun-filled window panel, ready to take his own life. Sharky, however, denies him the satisfaction, emptying an entire clip into his foe. The force of the rounds shatters the glass behind Billy and sends him hurtling through the gaping hole in the building's polished exoskeleton to plunge hundreds of feet to his death. (The stunt was perhaps the most heavily publicized feature of the film.)

With the same shots, then—and in the same cinematic "shot"—Sharky leaves his mark on the monstrous representative of the criminal underworld and on the corrupt edifice of corporate power. The latter demon, however, is not so easily slain. For as it turns out, not all of the chase scene's unoccupied offices are going unused. A few of them are full of large storage boxes, and it seems unlikely that in a building this new there would be corporate tenants moving out already. On the contrary— the owners of these boxes are almost certainly moving *in*, which would mean that even the capable Sharky cannot turn back the inexorable tide of capital as it bears down, like a latter-day version of Sherman's march, on his hometown. The new conquerors have already arrived.

My brief discussion of *Sharky's Machine* has come close to suggesting that the Peachtree Plaza serves the film as Atlanta's version of another late-century marvel of mirrored glass and steel, the Bonaventure Hotel of Los Angeles. Designed by none other than John Portman, the Bonaventure has been canonized, in an analysis by Jameson that became an instant classic of cultural criticism, as one of the definitive expressions of U.S. postmodernism.[17] Jameson points out how the "glass skin" of the Bonaventure not only reflects but actively "repels" its urban surroundings, "achiev[ing] a peculiar and placeless dissociation . . . from its neighborhood."[18] He describes the structure's disorienting symmetry, the baffling inconspicuousness of its entranceways and exits, and the strange combination of "busyness" and "emptiness" that produces "milling confusion" in the visitor.[19] In an interpretive tour de force, he reads the general sense of "disjunction" and "bewilderment" produced by the building "as the symbol and analogon of that even sharper dilemma which is the incapacity of our minds, at least at present, to map the great global multinational and decentered communicational network in which we find ourselves caught as individual subjects," the network of late capital.[20] As such, the "mutation in built space" simultaneously referenced and effected by buildings like the Bonaventure (and, one might add, its Atlanta cousin) amounts to a provocation and an injunction, "something like an imperative to grow new organs, to expand our sensorium and our body to some new, yet unimaginable, perhaps ultimately impossible, dimensions," the dimensions of what Jameson calls "the new hyperspace" of multinational capitalism.[21] When I wrote earlier of "register[ing]" the fascination of *Sharky's Machine* with the singularity of the Peachtree Plaza, the building's sheer mesmerizing incongruity with its surroundings, it was this same inarticulable imperative I was attempting to evoke: the film's subtle injunction to evolve new receptors capable of recognizing, and responding to, the postsouthern (rather than strictly regional) elements of its changing cityscape.

"You should never name things in order": *Slacker*

Slacker, on the other hand, wears its postmodernism on its sleeve. The 1991 film, Linklater's first full-length work, is perhaps best known for its unusual narrative technique. *Slacker* consists of more than thirty short narrative segments linked only by brief moments of physical contiguity between the characters during a single day in Austin, Texas. Beginning with its opening scene, in which a young man (played by Linklater himself) arrives at a local bus station and takes a cab into town, the camera simply follows a character or small group of characters as he/she/they pass through the nondescript urban space of various streets, businesses, or neighborhoods. The focal figure or group now and then intersects with other characters on their own local missions or following their own urban muses. "Encounter" is probably too strong a word to describe these brief convergences; there may or may not be any significant interaction or even any mutual acknowledgment. Often the characters simply pass each other on the street. Eventually, however, the camera breaks away from the initial focal figure(s) at one of these intersection points to follow a new character or group on his/her/its path through the city, and a new narrative thread begins. Moreover, once this restless, impulsive camera eye leaves a character behind, that character never, as far as I have been able to tell, reappears in the film.[22]

The impact of this technique on the traditional narrative categories that have dominated the film medium from early in its history is drastic, and consistent with Jameson's influential account of postmodern representation.[23] The film's style obviously works to prevent the emergence and development of a central story line. Nor do the individual micronarratives really develop; they don't have time to. (Some, in fact, last only a few seconds.) The result is a loose, yet also somehow crowded, sense of actions reminiscent in its own way of the packed, busy emptiness Jameson ascribes to the lobby of the Bonaventure, actions arranged sequentially (there appear to be no flashbacks, flash forwards, or other deviations from strictly linear chronology in the film) and intermittently sharing space with each other but otherwise uncoordinated and seemingly plotless. Even the odd hint of a deeper narrative continuity, or the rare opportunity for narrative development, is allowed (in what I am convinced is a deliberate strategy) to fall flat. At an early scene in a coffeehouse, for example, a young man asks his buddies, "Have you seen Gary around? Is he still living in the same place?" No one knows, so the man sets off to look for his missing friend. Perhaps, then, Linklater is spicing up his thin, decentered plotline with a dash of suspense—with that vertical-depth dimension that, according to Roland Barthes, the "hermeneutic function" brings to narrative?[24] Well, no, since only a few minutes later, just as the friend arrives at the door of Gary's house and marches in, the camera decides to turn away and follow a young couple as they stroll down the street to a different house and into a different plot thread. We never learn how the search for Gary turns out—in fact we never meet Gary in the film, nor see his friend again.

If it seems counterintuitive that a character we never see receives a proper name while his on-screen friend and pursuer remains nameless, the paradox takes us deeper into the postmodern logic of character in *Slacker*. The same narrative technique that prevents plot from developing has a similar effect on the film's characters, none of whom remains on camera long enough, or is discussed by other characters in sufficient detail, to achieve the depth or roundness that we expect from at least some of the human figures we encounter in a film. Instead, *Slacker* is, in characterological terms, absolutely nonhierarchical: all of the roles are equally major (which is to say, equally minor) and equally round (which is to say, equally flat).[25] Jameson has described the postmodern turn away from modernist models of subjectivity based on depth psychology toward a new understanding of the subject as an effect of signification, a depthless yet self-reflexive figure without ground or even much affect.[26]

Slacker's participation in this general turn can be seen in the credits, which identify its huge cast of characters by means of short descriptions rather than names. Only four of these figures (out of a hundred!) receive proper names in the closing credits. Two of them are police officers whose names are not actually revealed in the film proper; a third, "Stephanie from Dallas," has just returned to Austin from a stint in rehab or possibly in a mental institution; and the fourth, "S-T-E-V-E with a van," believes (incorrectly) that he is on the guest list at a punk club. The far more common use of descriptions to designate the film's characters underscores their postmodern status as products rather than sources of signification. Some are identified in terms of the books they have read (or misread), like "Dostoevsky wannabe." Others are named for the pop culture signifiers they eagerly embrace, explicate, or expound: "Scooby doo philosopher," "Papa Smurf," "Koo koo for cocoa puffs," and so on. Indeed, so generally beleaguered and attenuated is the naming function in the film that one character, a customer in a diner who obviously suffers from some sort of pathology that causes her utterances to skip like a broken record, attaches Post-It labels to the objects around her to identify them: KETCHUP, CUP, KEYS. ("You should never name things in order," she warns.)

A similar sense of evacuation hangs over the film's setting. Like *Sharky's Machine*, *Slacker* takes place in a specific local world, the capital city of one of the former Confederate states. All of the characters circulate within this urban space, and it provides the points of contact linking the nearly three dozen micronarratives that compose the action. If any feature of the film were capable of unifying it, of offering a coherent framework for its other principal elements, that feature should be the Austin locale. Nevertheless, the film's presentation of its urban setting remains disorienting.

Unlike *Sharky's Machine*, *Slacker* does not contain aerial shots of the cityscape that would afford viewers some rudimentary sense of how different features of the urban grid are interrelated. Only two scenes in the entire film make any use of a vertically elevated perspective: one is very near the beginning, a crane shot from above an intersection where a hit-and-run accident has just occurred, while the other is the very last segment of the narrative, shot from atop one of Austin's nearby hills but mainly unengaged with urban space. The rest of the film is shot more or less at eye level, largely depriving spectators of the deep backgrounds or panoramic perspectives that would allow nonnatives to locate themselves, at least approximately, in the landscape.[27] Nor for the most part does the film refer visually to architectural or other public landmarks that might be recognizable to an uninitiated viewer—with one important exception that I return to later. Finally, the fragmentary quality of each of the film's narrative threads ensures that we never follow the peregrinations of any individual or group from beginning to end. Instead, over and over we are plunged, in medias res, into journeys and lives very much in process, neither backtracking nor lingering long enough to obtain a wider view of the characters or the urban landscape they traverse. The film is thus as much a crazy quilt of microenvironments as it is a pastiche of micronarratives.

What do such thoroughly postmodern credentials have to do with the "southern" versus "postsouthern" inflection of *Slacker*? At first glance, the film does not seem heavily invested in the idea of regional identity or community. No one in the film talks about the South per se—and these people talk incessantly, about seemingly anything and everything—nor do any of the characters identify themselves as southern, though several of the actors speak with noticeably southern accents (including Linklater, whose voice may remind some viewers of his fellow Texan Owen Wilson). Still, the film carries on a kind of running flirtation with a set of core motifs that have long dominated discussions of southern literature and culture. These motifs appear in *Slacker* in attenuated or distorted forms, as parody, pastiche, or grotesque. The film often irreverently treats these traditionally "southern" themes—family, storytelling, community, history, and place—recognizing the necessarily partial and provisional nature of such a discussion.

Many students of southern literature and culture have claimed that the South places a higher valuation on family—and in particular on the vertical, generational dimension of family—than does the highly individualized society of mainstream America. Despite its emphasis on the experiences (and nonexperiences) of a postundergraduate and largely unmarried cohort, *Slacker* does not disavow the southern theme of family so much as defamiliarize it into fractured or otherwise disconcerting forms. There are four sets of family connections depicted or alluded to in the film, all of them generational relationships between parents and children. When "Stephanie from Dallas" confides to a friend that she has recently been institutionalized, the friend is sympathetic. "Parents, probably?" he asks. "Yeah, you could say they put me there." Later, a hitchhiker on his way into town reveals that he has just been to his stepfather's funeral. But when his fellow travelers express condolences, he confesses to being "glad the son of a bitch is dead. . . . I couldn't wait for the bastard to die." Nor, it seems, is he particularly fond of his mother. After hamming it up for a pair of videographers—"I may live badly, but at least I don't have to work to do it!"—he is asked about his relationship with her. "End of interview!" he bellows. Soon afterward, though, we learn that the whole twisted family saga may be nothing but a fabrication, that the hitchhiker is actually returning from a prison term rather than from a funeral.

This fellow, however, has nothing on the driver involved in the hit-and-run accident mentioned earlier. It soon emerges that the accident victim was the driver's own mother. As the cops lead him away from his apartment in handcuffs, an old Super-8 movie projector plays an endless loop of what appears to be a scene from the killer's childhood, in which he sits behind the wheel of a miniature automobile scooted along the driveway by his mom. This, the film's only on-screen mother-son pair, finds what another Texan might call a kinder, gentler complement in a single father-daughter relationship. The man is a widower and self-described anarchist whose daughter takes him grocery shopping and affectionately indulges his habit of lying about his past. Even their amicable relationship, then, is based on falsehoods and illusions. All in all, *Slacker* denatures and parodies the southern cult of family by presenting generational relationships as fragmented, violent, mendacious, and grounded in oppressive, perhaps even maddening, structures of authority.

Scholars often point to the centrality of an oral storytelling tradition as another definitive feature of southern culture. *Slacker* can certainly boast its fair share of fervent, even fixated storytellers, but their intense, idiosyncratic tales are a far cry from the front-porch, kitchen-counter, or campfire varieties favored by traditional critics who preach regional distinctiveness. Many of the film's embedded narratives resist easy comprehension, block more meaningful communication between speaker and listener, or invite self-reflexive musings on the fictionality and artifice of character, experience, and identity. The first segment, for instance, depicts Linklater's character as he unwinds for his cabdriver an epic account of a dream that he had on the bus. Whereas on an older, depth-based Freudian model we might expect the dream narrative to be—in its peculiar, displaced-and-condensed way—revelatory of personality, here the dream offers little insight into the dreamer, since instead of the bizarre events that usually transpire in dreams, there was by the dreamer's own admission nothing going on at all. What is more, the cabbie isn't even listening. Not once does he interrupt his passenger to push the long monologue toward something more interactive.

Another character treats a stranger to an obsessive (though still somehow amiable) rant that manages to cobble together every conceivable motif from Cold War–era conspiracy theory into a tour de force of late-eighties paranoia: NASA and the moon walk (closely monitored by extraterrestrials from "giant spacecraft"), antigravity technology stolen from the Nazis, "zombies" created by psychosurgery to colonize the moon and Mars, ecological chaos, kidnapped scientists, the Colombian drug wars, 350,000 missing children, a "secret group in charge of the government," and an experimental drug harvested by the CIA from the rainforests of Guatemala.[28] A rare named figure, Paul—who may be the same Paul caught later in the film in the act of burgling the anarchist's house—moves out on his roommates but leaves behind a stack of numbered, cryptically worded postcards, which, arranged in sequence, form a micronarrative within a micronarrative, a "little story or something," whose belabored absurdity and Barthelme-like language games are only intensified by the kitschy images on the cards themselves: Uncle Fester from *The Addams Family* TV series, a Fourth of July firecracker, a long row of palm trees, a racist caricature of Sambo, an old photo of soldiers in drill formation.

Still another of Linklater's cracked narrators, a video junkie who wears a television on his back, delivers what sounds at first like a conventional account of southern honky-tonk violence, only to plunge into postmodern ironies that reveal how fully he has rejected an orally mediated reality for an electronically mediated one: "I was walking down the street, and this guy that came barreling out of a bar fell right in front of me, and he had a knife in his back. . . . I can't refer back to it. I can't press rewind; I can't put it on pause; I can't put it on slow-mo and see all the little details. And the blood, it was all wrong; it didn't look like blood. The hue was off—and I couldn't adjust the hue. I was seeing it for real but it just wasn't right." The man's story thus participates in his technologically induced alienation from his own experience.

Finally there is the old anarchist, the closest thing to a traditional raconteur that *Slacker* has to offer, and nearly the only figure in the film to acknowledge, and freely share, a personal history that reaches deep into the past. Like many of the storytellers of classic southern literature, he unwinds a Civil War narrative, but it is doubtless a symptom of Linklater's iconoclastic postsouthern wit that the conflict in question is not the U.S. Civil War but the Spanish one, where the old man claims to have fought alongside Orwell in Catalonia. His daughter, however, soon sets the record straight for a guest: "He tells everybody he fought in the Lincoln Brigade in Barcelona, in Spain. Him and my mom went to Spain in, I guess, '55. Little late. The Lincoln Brigade," she sighs, adding a wry chuckle. "More like the Hemingway Brigade." In this way the one character who dares to articulate a thick individual history turns out to be perhaps the most thoroughly textualized, derivative identity in the film: a postmodern impostor who merely mimics a past expropriated from books. The pastiche job itself mirrors the way Linklater has in turn lifted signature moves and defining elements of southern storytelling as conceived by earlier generations of regional artists and critics and run them through his postsouthern culture-mulcher.

Indeed, inasmuch as anything like a group history or sense of community emerges among the film's characters, it is rooted not in shared stories of a traditional regional past but in the shared experience of consuming the mass media spectacles of a much more recent and broadly disseminated past, one that dates roughly from the end of the Eisenhower era.[29]

In a film where, as one critic has put it, characters have been "atomized . . . into subcultures of which they are the only member," this is the one language that everybody seems to speak, the one form of cultural literacy they possess in common.[30] It encompasses phenomena as diverse as Saturday morning cartoons, the JFK assassination, tabloid journalism, serial killers and mass murderers (the 1966 sniper attacks by Charles Whitman on the University of Texas campus are referred to by the old anarchist as "this town's finest hour"), popular sitcoms, breakfast cereals, international pop stars, lurid accounts of road rage, the space race, lunar landings, the 1986 Challenger explosion, hostage situations, Elvis Presley, the Medellín drug cartel, and on and on. These are the stories and signifiers that create and perpetuate a group identity for Linklater's slackers, in a McLuhanesque conflation of the global and with the local.[31]

More than anything, it is this media-molded collective consciousness that shapes a postsouthern experience of locale in the film and distinguishes that experience from the much-ballyhooed "sense of place" that is probably invoked more than any other single quality by critics seeking to define and valorize a southern regional sensibility.[32] To get a feel for how this new coding of space operates in *Slacker*, it is enough simply to reflect on how the film assigns semantic content to the Texas cities that figure most prominently in its script. As home to NASA, for example, Houston becomes, in the paranoid imagination of the conspiracy theorist, "the main headquarters" of the invisible empire he fears and craves: a postsouthern locale envisioned neither as marginal nor, in the more recent formulation of Jon Smith and Deborah Cohn, as "liminal," but as absolutely central, the heart of a vast global cabal.[33] Dallas, of course, signifies neither as the home of Southfork Ranch and Ewing Industries nor as the host city for the region's most successful professional football franchise but as the site of Dealey Plaza and the Texas Book Depository. San Antonio vomits up a freeway madman who drives all the way to Austin, guns blazing, before finally "off[ing] himself" in the median (or as our informant puts it, "the grassy knoll").[34] And Austin itself is most vividly summed up in the pair of landmarks that the anarchist points out in the film's most panoramic shot: at one visual extreme, the dome of the state capitol building, which the old man dreams of bringing down "like Guy Fawkes" someday, and at the other extreme, the Texas Tower from which Charles Whitman picked off his victims one by one. Where *Sharky's Machine* presents the southern skyscraper as quietly infiltrated by organized capital and crime, *Slacker*'s version of the urban tower functions as a platform for the violent rogue elements that captivate a society of the spectacle. In the end, the film seems to say, if Texas is responsible for any distinctive gift to a postmodern, postsouthern awareness, that legacy consists in the state's contributions to a global archive of mediatized madness.

All this brings us back to the perambulations of Linklater's characters through the decentered neighborhood landscape of Austin. Borrowing from contemporary architectural theory the insight that "our physical trajectories" through space can be thought of "as virtual narratives or stories, as dynamic paths and narrative paradigms which we . . . fulfill and . . . complete with our own bodies and movements," Jameson characterizes the postmodern city as an alienating urban space that threatens the ability of these narratives to cohere.[35] The answer to this predicament lies in what Jameson, following the urban geographer Kevin Lynch, calls "an aesthetic of cognitive mapping." "Disalienation," he writes, "involves the practical reconquest of a sense of place and the construction or reconstruction of an articulated ensemble which can be retained in memory and which the individual subject can map and remap along the moments of mobile, alternative trajectories." As Jameson elaborates, cognitive mapping is neither a mimetic nor, strictly speaking, a cartographic operation but a "precartographic" one, a matter of "itineraries rather than . . . maps: diagrams organized around the still subject-centered or existential journey of the traveler, along which various significant key features are marked." Cognitive mapping thus allows the inhabitant and consumer of the postmodern city to develop "a situational representation" of "that vaster and properly unrepresentable totality" that is the contemporary urban grid.[36]

The spatial or geographic alienation Jameson describes resembles that of the viewer of *Slacker*, or at least any viewer not already on intimate terms with Austin and its environs. The scene in which the camera follows the anarchist's pointing finger from capitol dome to campus tower is the exception that proves this general rule, perhaps the only moment in the entire film when an uninitiated viewer could actually locate the characters' position on a map of Austin. The rest of the time, we remain lost in the nondescript local immediacies of an urban world that will not quite cohere for us. But this is precisely what differentiates the viewer's situation from that of the characters themselves. They, after all, are engaged throughout the film in just those "mobile, alternative trajectories" that Jameson describes, going out to meet their urban world head-on, to occupy, traverse, use, and claim its spaces, in *Slacker*'s own version of cognitive mapping.[37] Whether cutting through alleys or across vacant lots, winding around street corners, or navigating the dark interior of a nightclub, the characters, as opposed to the viewer, know where they are, carry a viable map of their postmodern locale in their heads. Their itineraries are what give the film its energy, movement, and structure. Linklater's title, and the media attention it generated, ironically work to obscure how competent and kinetic most of these people actually are. They do an extraordinary amount of walking, for instance, over the course of a ninety-seven-minute film.[38] And, of course, an extraordinary amount of talking.[39] Both endeavors contribute to the project of cognitive mapping.[40]

Jameson's ultimate goal is to "extrapolate" from "the mental map of city space explored by Lynch" to the "mental map[s] of the social and global totality we all carry around in our heads in variously garbled forms"; by "totality" he means the huge multinational web of late capitalism.[41] My goal here is to extrapolate from the city space of *Slacker* to the somewhat more modest totality of region, to suggest—cautiously—that in their individual and collective, kinetic and verbal acts of cognitively mapping Austin, Linklater's characters are also performing a preliminary, provisional mapping of the contemporary post-South. They are figuring out—to some extent even making up—the contours of this emergent world as they go along. Moreover, if Jameson is right to temper the force of the "post-" in his postmodernism, to suggest that it signals not the *end* of something—modernism, capitalism—but rather "a transitional period between two stages . . . in which the earlier forms . . . are in the process of being restructured," then perhaps we should approach the category of the postsouthern in similar terms.[42]

Seen this way, the postsouthern would not denote an end of the South so much as a transition between Souths, in which "earlier forms" of regional consciousness, affiliation, and discourse are "restructured" into new regional identities and stories, new ways (a new "stage") of being southern.[43] To those viewers who would see Linklater's film as "not southern at all" (much as my Mississippi students sometimes protest that *Texas* is not southern at all), I would respond that it is differently southern and that the words and movements of its characters represent an incipient if still inchoate attempt to map the South's complex new spaces and tell its strange new stories. They aren't slackers, really—they are the new cartographers of the postsouthern era, and if the maps they sketch seem weird and random to us, this is precisely because they have not yet achieved the consensus and comfortable familiarity that governs (but also limits) existing guides to the region. Or as Linklater himself has put it in an interview, his characters are seekers.[44] Their southernness has not vanished into the abyss of the "post-" but is being renegotiated and tentatively rearticulated, and if they are quick to reach for media culture to clarify or illustrate their thoughts about their brave new world, it is because they recognize its potential, wide accessibility, and critical power as a source of tools to map with.[45]

The closing segment of the film, in which a carload of young people leave Austin for a day in the surrounding hills, filming their own antics along the way on a pair of Super 8 movie cameras, lends an expansive, exuberant energy to this mapping process. Whereas Kellner reads this ending as advancing the "nihilistic" contention "that nothing really matters in a totally absurd world," I see it as Linklater's charge—not just to filmgoers or filmmakers caught up in the conspicuous self-reflexiveness of the scene's movie paraphernalia, but to all actual or potential cartographers of the postmodern and postsouthern—to go forth from urban enclaves like Austin and carry that mapping process to other regional spaces (and beyond), including the rural and natural landscapes that have for so long been considered strongholds of the traditionally southern.[46] Those spaces, too, await their postsouthern stories, stories reshaped by the regional, national, and global exigencies of the contemporary scene.

"We never been there before either": *Mississippi Masala*

Mississippi Masala (1991) begins with a similar movement away from a capital city, but the prevailing mood associated with this movement is not expansive and outward looking as in *Slacker* but mournful and diasporic. The city is Kampala, capital of Uganda, where, in the autumn of 1972, Idi Amin has ordered the expulsion of all "Asians" from the country. Amin voices his resentment against these "Asians," the lion's share of whom are the descendants of Indians brought in by the British at the turn of the century to build railways in East Africa, as shown in a scene from later in the film: "Asians have milked the cow but not fed it. Africans are poor; Asians are rich. The Asians are sabotaging the economy of Uganda. They have refused to allow their daughters to marry Africans. They have been here for seventy years but they live in their own world." With the British gone, Amin seems to be reaching for an ethnic scapegoat that can evoke both racial difference and the scars of colonial occupation and rule.[47]

Hit hard by Amin's edict is the Loha family: Jay, a lawyer who has made a name for himself first by defending the rights of blacks under British rule and then by criticizing the new Amin regime on the BBC; Kinnu, his wife; and their six-year-old daughter, Mina. They are Ugandan nationals but ethnic South Asians (Gujarati), so they must go.[48] Particularly devastating for Jay is the deterioration of his relationship with Okelo, his best friend since childhood, who although sharing his view that Amin is mad, still embraces aspects of his nationalism. In an early key scene, Okelo quietly but firmly quashes his friend's assertion that "Uganda is my home": "Not anymore, Jay. Africa is for Africans. Black Africans." Jay hears this expression of black pride only as a personal betrayal; he refuses to shake Okelo's hand or tell him good-bye as the family prepares to leave for the airport.[49] We begin to sense the simmering ethnic rivalries and tensions that, here as elsewhere throughout the postcolonial world, begin to bubble toward the political and social surface with the departure of a common colonial oppressor.

Even before the Lohas step onto the London-bound plane to become diasporic subjects, the film hints at the multiple cultural and national inflections of their identity. In Uganda the family seems to be quite wealthy, and the cosmopolitanism of their consumption patterns can be inferred from one verse of a tape recording that is clearly meaningful enough to the family to be carried along in Kinnu's luggage. The subtitles of the film translate the song's Hindi lyrics as follows: "My shoes are Japanese / My pants are English / My red hat is Russian / But my heart, it's all Indian."[50] Adding to this hybridity is the family's facility with languages. Kinnu speaks English, Swahili, and Urdu; young Mina is at the very least bilingual, since she converses with others in English and Swahili. Jay is seen wearing traditional African clothing and, in a photograph, sporting the black robe and white wig of an English barrister. These plural identities are further complicated affectively, by swirling emotions of love, anger, and grief. Tears and good-byes hang heavily over the film's early scenes: one little boy says "Bye" nine times as he waves to Mina's departing car. So does the bittersweet resonance of the word "home." Nair has described herself to an interviewer as "drawn to the stories of people who live on the margins of society—on the edge, or outside, always dealing with the question of what and where is home."[51] The Lohas are no exception. "Where's Okelo?" Mina asks her father at one point, and his reply, "Gone home, I suppose," carries the clear subtext that the black Ugandan, unlike the brown ones, still has a home to go to. Indeed, the Lohas are about to become doubly diasporic, having now been dispossessed of a national homeland as well as an ethnic one. "Emigrants twice displaced," Binita Mehta calls them in a 1996 essay.

With the Lohas' departure from Uganda, *Mississippi Masala* begins to do its cognitive mapping out in the open. From the airport, the camera cuts away to a map, in a close-up of East Africa that centers on Kampala and Lake Victoria. The shot then tracks northward across the Mediterranean to linger briefly on the British Isles, following the family's path to England, where, we later learn, they live for the next fifteen years. But the shot tracks on, moving westward until, right over the middle of the Atlantic Ocean, the soundtrack shifts abruptly from Indian tabla music to a raucous electric blues.[52] The camera then continues down the eastern seaboard of North America before dipping inland to arrive at the Mississippi Delta town of Greenwood. If the characters of *Slacker* could be considered "global" in their voracious appetite for, and encyclopedic command of, the mass culture that now saturates the planetary media village, the transnational itinerary so plainly mapped here reveals the Lohas to be global subjects in a much more literal and immediately physical sense. Indeed, Mina will sleep with a globe beside her bed in Mississippi. The continent of North America, her new home, faces her pillow; Africa and India face away from her and directly toward the camera. So radically transnational a character is she, then, that even her globe will not allow her to visualize or otherwise encompass the many roots of her identity in a single glance.

Interestingly, Greenwood is designated on Nair's map with a circle and star, like the nearby state capitals of Jackson and Nashville, and unlike the major metropolitan center of Memphis to the north. Nair additionally reserves a larger typeface for the word "Greenwood" on the map than for the much larger cities around it, the same size typeface, in fact, that the national capital of Kampala receives in the close-up of Africa. This is the film's way of presenting Greenwood as the symbolic center and seat of what Demetrius, an enterprising young African American, calls "the new Mississippi," a phrase that designates much the same conceptual territory as the postsouthern: not a state so much as a sensibility, a contemporary country of the mind that more than anything else seems to represent equal economic opportunity to the young entrepreneur who describes it ("[If] you got a good business, there's no reason to leave"). If the old Mississippi was associated with poverty, this new one seems to be associated with abundance: in the opening Greenwood scene, set in 1990, Mina, now twenty-four, wheels a shopping cart completely filled with gallon jugs of milk toward the checkout line at a grocery store, past enormous pyramids of Coke cans. Still, as the film develops, we learn that the family is just scraping by: Mina works as a maid in one of the Delta's numerous Indian-owned motels; Kinnu, thanks to a stake from Anil, a local businessperson and fellow Indian, owns a small liquor store; and Jay squanders his legal skills on a fanciful lawsuit against the Ugandan government to recover the property he has lost there.[53] By 1990 the suit has already dragged on for five long years, with no resolution in sight.

Some of the complexities of the new Mississippi become evident when Mina heads home in Anil's car with her groceries. Driving too fast, she rear-ends a carpet-cleaning van, which in turn smashes into a pickup truck that has stalled out in the middle of the street. As the drivers emerge and begin to argue, we are introduced to a contemporary South in miniature, one that is conspicuously multiethnic rather than, as in traditional conceptions of the region, biracial; Purnima Bose and Linta Varghese describe the moment as a literal collision of cultures.[54] Mina and her passenger, an older woman, are Indian. Demetrius, the driver of the van (and co-owner of the cleaning business), is African American. And the guy in the pickup is not just white but coded redneck by his thick accent,

scraggly facial hair, and tacky T-shirt and baseball cap. Mina and Demetrius exchange insurance information, and—this being a movie—a romantic spark is kindled. Mina's postcolonial presence on the scene thus
brings to the new Mississippi a supplementary element that portends
a new dimension, a broader conceptual reach, for the postsouthern; if
Bone is right to observe that the "postsouthern 'international city'" can
be "defined by its multicultural population" and not just by the "globalization" of its "capital flows," then Greenwood, despite its modest size,
fits the bill.[55] Nevertheless, older accents can still be heard there. The
redneck calls Demetrius "boy" as the argument escalates, and he scuffles
with a black policeman as well, clearly confident in the privileges his
whiteness buys him. This Mississippi is not so new after all. Despite its
intimations of postsouthernness, it is also all too southern.

Indeed, *Mississippi Masala* does not for a moment attempt to down-
play, conceal, fracture, or distort its southern elements, as *Slacker* does.
Rather, Nair's film works overtly with these elements to recontextualize
them in wider global and postcolonial frameworks. The accident, for example, occurs just in front of a railroad crossing, which, as the scene's
racial tensions emerge, begins to seem less incidental as an element of
setting. Those railroad tracks, after all, are perhaps the classic material
symbol of the residential segregation found in the cities and small towns
of the old Mississippi during the Jim Crow years. Demetrius in particular
knows what it's like to come from the wrong side of those tracks. But the
image also evokes the railways of East Africa that provided the occasion
and fulcrum for the colonial displacement and exploitation of Mina's
ancestors in Uganda. As a historical symbol, then, the railroad links the
pasts of Demetrius and Mina while placing a specifically southern geography of injustice within the larger context of white colonial power. An
earlier scene works the same way, only in reverse. On their way to the
Kampala airport, the Lohas, and Kinnu in particular, are harassed by
a pair of black soldiers. The scene takes place on a crowded bus, a site
that, as students of the U.S. civil rights movement would instantly recognize, had been made archetypal by Rosa Parks in 1955 as a symbol of the
struggle against segregation—though in Montgomery, of course, the harassed woman was black and the oppressive authorities were white.[56]

The skill with which Nair develops "repeated structural parallels"
between Mississippi and Uganda, and between black and brown histories
of oppression and diaspora, is one of the film's true pleasures and challenges.[57] Even as the deepening romance between Mina and Demetrius
brings out tensions between and within the Indian and African American
communities, it also draws members of these communities together for
glimpses of common ground. When Demetrius invites Mina to a family
picnic, his brother Dexter is surprised to learn that Mina, though Indian,

has never been to India. "You just like us," he decides. "We from Africa but we never been there before either." When Dexter learns how Mina's ancestors came to be there, he supplies the appropriate analogy himself: "Like slaves." He remembers, in other words, that the same British who ruled Uganda used African chattel to build their North American plantations. For Mina, dispossessed of nearly everything but her mother and father, the multigenerational picnic is a revelation. "Your family's great," she tells Demetrius. "There's a real feeling of home there." But beneath Dexter's words, there is a similar diasporic yearning for a lost homeland, the same African homeland, in fact, that Mina has left behind.[58] In the new Mississippi, it seems, everyone is some sort of migrant; everyone is an ocean away from home. Even the redneck in the pickup has probably never seen his ethnic homeland in Britain or on the European continent. And the original residents of the area, the American Indians for whom Mina and her folk are sometimes mistaken ("Send them back to the reservation!" gripes an old white man before his buddy reminds him that "they're not *that* kind of Indian!"), have been shuttled down the Trail of Tears by the redneck's ancestors—another colonial dispossession that Nair subtly underscores with a pair of children who run around playing cowboys and Indians at Anil's otherwise traditional wedding.

Unfortunately, this sense of solidarity and shared history slips in and out of focus for Greenwood's communities of color. Even before Mina and Demetrius become an item, there is concern among the Indian immigrants that Demetrius may be a litigious American who will slap a lawsuit on them for wrecking his van. An older Indian, Napkin, who already employs Demetrius to clean his carpets, goes to sound out the young man's intentions. "Black, brown, yellow, Mexican, Puerto Rican, all the same," Napkin diplomatically (and hopefully) observes. "As long as you're not white, it means you are colored. . . . All of us people of color must stick together!" This remark prompts a wry "Power to the People!" from Demetrius's partner, Tyrone—a slogan that Napkin, missing the irony, is delighted to adopt as his own.

The problem is that the Indians are sporadically but acutely color-conscious themselves. They are intensely attuned, for instance, to gradations of color within their own community. As the child of a light-skinned mother and a darker father, Mina is caught in this pinch, which hurts her chances with Harry Patel, the community's most eligible bachelor: as a local gossip puts it at Anil's wedding, "You can be dark and have money, or you can be fair and have no money. But you can't be dark and have no money and expect to get Harry Patel."[59] These words of wisdom are borne out in the next scene, when Harry takes Mina to the Leopard Lounge, a local juke joint. Everyone else in the club is black.

Mina is unfazed—she catches up with a friend, Tadice, whom she knows from their days cleaning motel rooms together, and she runs into Demetrius, who asks her to dance. At this point Harry leaves, clearly uncomfortable with the situation. The implication seems to be that Mina's easygoing interaction with African Americans makes her black by association—blacker by the minute, in fact—for Harry. Mina is philosophical about all this. "Face it, Ma," she tells Kinnu at one point, "you've got a darkie daughter." If Mina's specific word choice here, "darkie," may be a reminder that the African American community that is the more usual object of the slur also suffers from its own issues of intraracial color-consciousness, this is not a point that Nair works hard for in her film.

When Mina sneaks off to Biloxi for a romantic tryst with Demetrius and is caught in his motel room by the vacationing Anil, Napkin, and a third Indian named Pontiac, the tensions between brown and black tilt over into outright racism. "Listen, you leave our women alone!" bellows Anil, suddenly sounding with that possessive pronoun "our" a lot like the endogamous "Asians" that were the subjects of Amin's racial vitriol in Uganda. After Anil and Demetrius come to blows, a pair of white cops is only too happy to haul in brown and black alike for fighting and "whoring." The scandal triggers a crisis in the African American and Indian communities back in Greenwood, each of which circles its wagons in a nasty display of infighting and backbiting that Nair stages as a rapid-fire series of gossipy phone calls.

Demetrius's ex-girlfriend, the haughty Alicia, gives him hell for dating outside the race and "letting down" his people. Local whites, now questioning the character of Demetrius, talk to his loan officer, who calls in the mortgage on the van. Having lost so many clients as a result of the scandal (including all the Indian motel owners), Demetrius can't pay, so he hires a lawyer to sue Mina and Anil over the accident after all.[60] The same Indian rumormongers we heard from at the wedding continue to titter into their phones about Mina's indiscretions, and both of the lovers are scolded for shaming their tradition-minded parents.[61] Meanwhile, a white racist chortles into his phone, "You all having nigger trouble?" Even Tyrone, at first completely charmed by Mina, turns on her. On one hand, he marginalizes her as an alien, a "fucking foreigner" who "ain't nothing but trouble."[62] On the other hand, he aligns her and her people with the white oppressors who once lynched African American men for sexual transgressions against the color line: "If you fall in bed with one of their daughters, your ass gonna swing." The second accusation is not entirely unfounded. What Tyrone realizes is that the Indian community faces the same predicament as every other nonblack immigrant group in America, the same pressure to distance itself from African Americans to assimilate into the mainstream and claim the privileges that

U.S. society assigns to and associates with whiteness. As such, his words reveal what Susan Stanford Friedman calls "the anger of African Americans who have been embittered by the Americanization of successive immigrant groups, a process that Toni Morrison describes as learning to say 'nigger'—learning, in other words, to raise their own status by seeing African Americans at the bottom of a system of racial stratification."[63]

What Tyrone seems less aware or at least appreciative of, however, is the impossible position in which this state of affairs places Mina, as a dark-skinned member of an upwardly aspiring and partially white-identifying ethnic group. Earlier in the film, she has described herself to Demetrius as a "mixed Masala," which she explains is "a bunch of hot spices."[64] In Biloxi, Demetrius extends the culinary metaphor: "Well, Miss Masala, racism, or as they say nowadays, 'tradition,' gets passed down like recipes. Now the trick is, you got to know what to eat and what to leave on your plate." As African American and Indian "traditions" flirt with their own forms of racism, Mina, an exotic in all three of Greenwood's racial communities—black, white, and brown—finds herself alternately nibbled at and left on the table.

A related problem is that the African American community is plagued by its own internal jealousies and contradictions that lead it to follow other local groups in devaluing blackness. Dexter's friends rib him by deriding Demetrius for thinking "he large" because "he got himself a white chick" (by which they mean Mina). Another wag taunts Demetrius at the barbershop about his cleaning business, implying that the work is servile. This may sound like black pride talking, but the barber knows better. "You know, we're just as bad as everybody else," he tells Demetrius. "Black folk don't like to see other black folk do good. . . . They just sit back on their butts and wait to see if you fall on your face," like Booker T. Washington's proverbial crabs in a basket. Demetrius's Aunt Rose says something along the same lines to his father, Willie Ben: "All you and the rest of them want is that he should know his place and stay in it." Willie Ben works as a waiter at a white-owned restaurant whose customer base also appears to be all-white: a de facto Jim Crow establishment persisting into postsouthern times. As Rose recognizes, he is concerned primarily with how his son's deviations from southern racial etiquette will affect his own job security. In this way *Mississippi Masala* attests to the persistence, even into the postsouthern era, of older structures of consciousness, rooted in slavery and segregation, which work within the black community to keep black people down. Demetrius is treated as ambivalently by his own people as Mina is treated by hers. In this way the film charts what Friedman describes as shifting and interdependent conditions of "privilege and alterity" between and within the black and brown communities.[65]

So crucial to the film is Jay's response to his daughter's relationship with Demetrius that it deserves its own separate analysis. Demetrius thinks that the father's opposition is due to racism, pure and simple. "You and your folks can come down here from God knows where and be about as black as the ace of spades," he tells Jay, "and as soon as you get here you start acting white and treating us like we your doormats." Touching his own black face, he continues, "I know that you and your daughter ain't but a few shades from this right here." But the next scene, a flashback in which Jay remembers sharing a crowded prison cell with dozens of black Ugandans after giving his inflammatory anti-Amin interview to British broadcasting, reveals Demetrius's accusation to be simplistic: Jay is only too aware of his kinship with "this right here." In fact, he understands *himself* to be the victim of racism. "Once I was like both of you," he tells Demetrius. "I thought I could change the world, be different. But the world is not so quick to change." Of his expulsion from Uganda, he tells Mina that "[a]fter thirty-four years that's all it came down to: the color of my skin." His opposition to the romance, then, is on practical grounds, stemming from his own bitter firsthand knowledge that "[p]eople stick to their own kind." He doesn't want the young lovers to get hurt.

Still, the real hurt at work here is Jay's own. What he sees in—projects onto—Mina's love for Demetrius is his own deep affection for a black man, Okelo, a love that he believes was betrayed, much like his love for Uganda itself.[66] In the figure of Demetrius, then, are condensed a number of powerful images from and of Africa: Okelo the grown man with a mind of his own; Okelo the boy with whom a young Jay runs alongside a rushing river (Mina and Demetrius share their first kiss as they walk along a bayou); Mina's childhood playmate of the nine good-byes; and, most problematically, the Idi Amin who "articulates a critique of South Asian racism" with his "charge that . . . Indian immigrants 'act white.'"[67] Jay cannot yet affirm these figures, in their own right or in the person of Demetrius. When he finally meets Mina's sweetheart face to face, he refuses to shake hands, just as—or to put it more strongly, *because*—he could not bring himself to shake Okelo's hand before leaving Kampala in 1972. The ghosts of the African past haunt the Mississippi present and threaten the future.[68]

Jay's chance to put those ghosts to rest, and seemingly the film's only chance to break the gridlock of misunderstanding and recrimination and move forward again, finally comes when his lawsuit reaches the Ugandan courts and he is summoned to a hearing in Kampala. By this point, Mina and Demetrius, convinced that Greenwood holds nothing for them ("All those years of building up my business are gone," says the onetime promoter of the new Mississippi), are making plans to try their luck elsewhere running a cleaning business together.[69] Faced with the loss of his daughter and adamant that the family is "not wanted here," Jay decides to return to Africa for the hearing: "I don't want to die in some stranger's country," he tells Kinnu. What she tells him just as firmly is that he is going back alone. "I can't go to Uganda. What could I do there?" As perhaps the wiser and truer diasporic subject of the two, she knows that the lost homeland can no longer be her home—that you can't go home again, as a fellow southerner and exile once put it.[70]

Jay, however, must learn this for himself. Back in Uganda, he is greeted by a black cab driver with a hearty but unintentionally ironic "Welcome back, *bwana*," the Swahili term of respect once used to address the British colonizers. Jay then searches for Okelo, only to find that his friend died back "in Amin's time," apparently a victim of political violence and very likely persecuted for his efforts to help his Asian friend. Then, as Jay wanders the ruins of the old family home, now home only to livestock, we hear a blues harp playing on the soundtrack, as the worlds of Uganda and Mississippi once again converge. The moment seems to trigger, or at least to signal, an interior transformation in Jay. Overcome by grief and regret—for his dead friend and for his own stubborn, self-defeating pride—he decides to give up the lawsuit and return to America, just as, back in Mississippi, Demetrius, in yet another parallel, drops *his* suit against Anil.

In a letter to Kinnu, Jay at last acknowledges that "[h]ome is where the heart is. And my heart is with you." If this sounds sentimental, the sentiment has been hard enough won to ring true. Jay's letter traces an important shift in the orientation of the heart from the Lohas' Hindi theme song: from a heart that's "all Indian," affiliated with a nation or ethnic population, to a heart that's "with you," drawn into relationship with a specific loved one. Mina, of course, has traced a similar path in choosing Demetrius over homeland, folk, or even family. Now the father has learned the daughter's lesson, and his conversion works to purge the element of nostalgia, so crippling and toxic in earlier scenes involving Jay, from the film's diasporic sensibility.[71]

Perhaps for this reason, Nair rewards Jay with a beautiful and moving scene of closure. In the final scene of the film proper, Jay stands amid a throng of black Ugandans in one of the public squares of Kampala. Music is playing, and a young woman is dancing, first shyly, then with increasing exuberance. Standing beside Jay to watch the dancing is a man holding a young boy. Caught up in the joy of the moment, Jay holds out his arms, takes the child, and hugs him, long, close, and tight. The boy is clearly a stand-in for the cherished Okelo—and also, we somehow sense, for Demetrius. Here at last is the good-bye Jay never got to utter, the love and warmth of which he felt robbed, the affirmation of blackness and Africa he never allowed himself to give.

Only now, after the credits, with their African graphic design elements, have already begun to roll, can the camera rejoin Mina and Demetrius in Mississippi. When last we saw them they were about to leave the state for good, but here they are, dancing and cuddling out in a cotton field, having traded in their blue jeans (Mina) and work uniform (Demetrius) for traditional Indian and African garments, as the tune from Kampala continues to play. Bose and Varghese suggest that "the couple's positioning" here "is anything but arbitrary or ridiculous. Given the role of cotton in the plantation economy of slavery and in the colonial economy of British India, Nair visually reinscribes Mina and Demetrius within the historical contexts that produced them by placing them in this setting."[72] More than that—the scene begins to look an awful lot like what Jameson might call the "practical reconquest" of a formerly unaccommodating place, a cognitive *re*mapping of Greenwood and the Delta as newly viable parts of an itinerary for living—and moreover a remapping and reconquest with the specifically transnational dimension that Bone calls for in the epilogue to his study of postsouthern space.[73] The film thus concludes by honoring all three of the homelands that give Mina's identity its postcolonial flavor and Nair's South its multiethnic depth and spice. Rather unlike Linklater's postsouthern Texas, Nair's postsouthern Mississippi is itself a mixed masala. As Nair herself has commented, citing Nehru, "you have to be terribly local to be global."[74] The Mississippi of Mina and Demetrius bears her out. It has become one of the "transnational diasporic spaces" in and across which change occurs and agency emerges in Nair's world.[75]

Toward a Postsouthern Cinema

In *Reconstructing Dixie*, Tara McPherson makes an eloquent case for Ross McElwee's 1986 film, *Sherman's March*, as a paradigmatic example of a postsouthern cinema. In her words, *Sherman's March* "enacts a mobility of landscapes that resists the too easy privileging of place that is central to many regional and national myths." The film thus "allows one to deal with a region that has accumulated a multiplicity of frozen, staid images of the past without resorting to nostalgia." McElwee's postsouthern South is thus less "a site of stultifying authenticity" than "a contested terrain mobilized for alternative histories," "a site of possibilities both emergent and sometimes foreclosed."[76]

A similar case can be made for *Slacker* and *Mississippi Masala*, if not necessarily for *Sharky's Machine*, as vital texts in a postsouthern film canon.[77] As we have seen, the two films retain elements that could be considered traditionally southern only to subject these elements to clever reworkings, recodings, and recontextualizations that evoke a range of new trajectories, affiliations, and perspectives to characterize contemporary life in the region. *Slacker* explores these new regional possibilities and configurations in a spirit of parody and play that recalls the ludic literary postmodernism of Barry Hannah, Donald Barthelme, Randall Kenan, and, in some of his zanier moments, Walker Percy. *Mississippi Masala*, on the other hand, presents its South in a very different emotional key. Nair's film is suffused with a longing and loss, an anger and grief, that more nearly resembles the Linda Hogan of *Power*, the Toni Morrison of *Beloved*, or the Toni Cade Bambara of *Those Bones Are Not My Child* than the writers just cited. Even *Mississippi Masala*'s final movement outward from the ambivalent atmosphere of Greenwood to the surrounding cotton fields where Mina and Demetrius can embrace, kiss, twirl, and reinvest their small-town world with possibility, is still a far cry from the near-giddiness of *Slacker*'s closing trek from Austin into the hills. Even when Nair finds a sense of hope in the postsouthern landscape, that hope is much more embattled and dearly bought than anything in Linklater's more emotionally noncommittal film. Taken together, however, the two films hint at the affective range, the wide variety of tonalities and moods, available to the postsouthern filmmaker.

Moreover, both *Slacker* and *Mississippi Masala* are simultaneously representations and products of what is coming to be known in the new southern studies as a global South, no longer defined solely in terms of its relationships with "the U.S. North" but also in terms of its deep historical and economic ties with other regions of the developing world. If what makes *Slacker* global is its immersion in the mass cultural signifiers exported to all points of the international compass by the U.S. news media and entertainment industry, what makes *Mississippi Masala* global is, first, its account of the South's long, and continuing, history as a world *import* center, into and through which centuries of exiles, diaspora victims, and other migrant subjects have passed on their transnational itineraries, and, second, its deep recognition that "when people move, identities, perspectives, and definitions change."[78] Collectively, then, the two films trace a larger rhythm of cultural systole and diastole, a two-way ebb and flow of people and representations that is not just the soundtrack but the very heartbeat of a postsouthern temper.[79]

NOTES

1. Michael Kreyling, *Inventing Southern Literature* (Jackson: University Press of Mississippi, 1998), 153–54.

2. Lewis P. Simpson, *The Brazen Face of History: Studies in the Literary Consciousness in America* (Baton Rouge: Louisiana State University Press, 1980), 255, 269.

3. Ibid., 269.

4. Kreyling, *Inventing Southern Literature*, 155.

5. Ibid., 154.

6. It should be noted that Romine largely refrains from using the term "post-southern" in *The Real South*. But his witty and nuanced account of what he likes to call the "late South" covers similar conceptual territory: "I refer to the contemporary South as the 'late South,' a term that references simultaneously the condition of intensified continuity (as in 'late modernity' and 'late capitalism') and the condition of recent termination (as in 'the late C. Vann Woodward')." *The Real South: Southern Narrative in the Age of Cultural Reproduction* (Baton Rouge: Louisiana State University Press, 2008), 2; see also 9–17, 229–36.

7. Stephen Flinn Young's 1989 essay, "Post-southernism: The Southern Sensibility in Postmodern Sculpture," in fact, predates Kreyling's musings on the post-southern turn in literary representation by several years. *Southern Quarterly* 27, no. 1 (Fall 1989): 41–60.

8. The sole exception my research has uncovered is Mark A. Reid, "Rebirth of a Nation," *Southern Exposure* 20, no. 4 (Winter 1992): 26–28. Reid discusses *Mississippi Masala* alongside *Fried Green Tomatoes* and *Daughters of the Dust* as efforts to expand the conceptual range and vocabulary of southern film in the 1990s. It is much more typical of scholarship on Nair's film to situate it in the context of South Asian and/or feminist cultural production.

9. Detractors of *Mississippi Masala* have accused Nair of inauthentic and oversimplified depictions of ethnic culture, of commodifying South Asian femininity for western masculine visual consumption and pleasure, and of subtle and not-so-subtle forms of complicity with the colonialist discourses that the film outwardly appears to challenge and question. These critics include Prateeti Punja Ballal, "Illiberal Masala: The Diasporic Distortions of Mira Nair and Dinesh D'Souza," *Weber Studies* 15, no. 1 (Winter 1998): 98–104; bell hooks and Anuradha Dingwaney, "Mississippi Masala," *Z Magazine* 5 (July–August 1992): 41–43; R. Radhakrishnan, "Is the Ethnic 'Authentic' in the Diaspora?" in *The State of Asian America: Activism and Resistance in the 1990s*, ed. Karin Anguilar–San Juan (Boston: South End, 1994), 219–33; and Sonia Shah, "'Presenting the Blue Goddess': Toward a National Pan-Asian Feminist Agenda," in Anguilar–San Juan, *State of Asian America*, 147–58. Some of their criticisms have been addressed by advocates of the film such as Kum-Kum Bhavnani, "Organic Hybridity or Commodification of Hybridity? Comments on *Mississippi Masala*," *Meridians: Feminism, Race, Transnationalism* 1, no. 1 (Autumn 2000): 187–203; Lan Dong, "Diverse Identities in Interracial Relationships: A Multiethnic Interpretation of *Mississippi Masala* and *The Wedding Banquet*," *Xchanges* 4, no. 1 (September 2004): n.p.; Susan Stanford Friedman, "Beyond White and Other: Relationality and Narratives of Race in Feminist Discourse," *Signs* 21, no. 1 (Autumn 1995): 1–49; Binita Mehta, "Emigrants Twice Displaced: Race, Color, and Identity in Mira Nair's *Mississippi Masala*," in *Between the Lines: South Asians and Postcoloniality*, ed. Deepika Bahri and Mary Vasudevav (Philadelphia: Temple University Press, 1996), 185–203; Alpana Sharma, "Body Matters: The Politics of Provocation in Mira Nair's Films," *Quarterly Review of Film and Video* 18, no. 1 (January

2001): 91–103; and Jaspal Kaur Singh, "Globalization, Transnationalism, and Identity Politics in South Asian Women's Texts," *Michigan Academician* 35, no. 2 (Summer 2003): 171–88. For less partisan attempts at analysis, see Dharina Rasiah, "*Mississippi Masala* and *Khush*: Redefining Community," in *Our Feet Walk the Sky: Women of the South Asian Diaspora*, ed. Women of South Asian Descent Collective (San Francisco: Aunt Lute Books, 1993), 267–73; and Purnima Bose and Linta Varghese, "*Mississippi Masala*, South Asian Activism, and Agency," in *Haunting Violations: Feminist Criticism and the Crisis of the "Real*," ed. Wendy S. Hesford and Wendy Kozol (Urbana: University of Illinois Press, 2001), 137–68.

On the economic and class subtexts of *Slacker*, see Julian Crockford, "'It's All about Bucks, Kid. The Rest Is Conversation': Framing the Economic Narrative from *Wall Street* to *Reality Bites*," *Post Script* 19, no. 2 (Winter–Spring 2000): 29–33; Ryan Moore, "'. . . And Tomorrow Is Just Another Crazy Scam': Postmodernity, Youth, and the Downward Mobility of the Middle Class," in *Generations of Youth: Youth Cultures and History in Twentieth-Century America*, ed. Joe Austin and Michael Nevin Williard (New York: New York University Press, 1998), 253, 259; Jon Radwan, "Generation X and Postmodern Culture: *Slacker*," *Post Script* 19, no. 2 (Winter–Spring 2000): 42–43; and Susan Willis, "Teens at Work: Negotiating the Jobless Future," in Austin and Williard, *Generations of Youth*, 349–51.

10. Fredric Jameson, *Postmodernism, or the Cultural Logic of Late Capitalism* (Durham, N.C.: Duke University Press, 1991).

11. See "Westin Peachtree Plaza," Answers.com, http://www.answers.com/topic/westin-peachtree-plaza (accessed August 4, 2006).

12. Portman is an important figure in Martyn Bone's excellent case study of Atlanta as a "postsouthern 'international city,'" a "metropolis of transnational capital and mixed-use developments constructed between the 1960s and the 1980s." Bone, *The Postsouthern Sense of Place in Contemporary Fiction* (Baton Rouge: Louisiana State University Press, 2005), 171, and see 139–241 for the case study. For more on Portman specifically, see 109–10, 162–64, 167, 195, 239.

13. In its attention to both domains, and to the way in which vertical space figures social and class relations in the contemporary metropolis, the film anticipates such later classics of Atlanta literature as Tom Wolfe's *A Man in Full* (1998) and Toni Cade Bambara's *Those Bones Are Not My Child* (1999). On the strategic use of vertical elevation in the two novels, see Bone, *Postsouthern Sense of Place*, 195–212, 227–31, and 239–40.

14. See Bone, *Postsouthern Sense of Place*, 178.

15. Ibid., 159–60. Indeed, writes Bone, Portman's Peachtree Center, the mammoth mixed-use development that includes the Plaza, went on to become "a telling example of the transition of Downtown Atlanta's development and ownership from the local to the global. Having been funded initially by the likes of Atlanta developer Ben Massell and the Texas real estate magnate Trammel Crow, Peachtree Center passed to lenders from New York and Japan when Portman went bankrupt in 1990" (*Postsouthern Sense of Place*, 162).

16. Fredric Jameson has described how the "spectralities" of contemporary finance capital, flows of money seemingly unconnected to material commodities

or to the human labor that produces them, underwrite "postmodern ghost stories" (quoted in Bone, *Postsouthern Sense of Place*, 67). As Billy Score drifts through the upper floors of the Peachtree Plaza, trailing blood from multiple gunshots that wound him without ever bringing him down, *Sharky's Machine* flirts with its own version of Jameson's postmodern gothic. "He ain't real," whispers one of Sharky's partners, himself badly wounded in an exchange of gunfire with Billy, who nonetheless manages to vanish again. "He's a ghost." Billy, of course, is no finance capitalist, but the close associations throughout *Sharky's Machine* between invading capital and the mob allow him to play the ghost in the Plaza's corporate machinery.

17. Jameson, *Postmodernism*, 38–44.

18. Ibid., 42.

19. Ibid., 43–44, 39, 43.

20. Ibid., 44.

21. Ibid., 38, 39, 38.

22. Douglas Kellner also notes the "aleatory itinerary" of the film, while Willis calls it a "consummate example of narrative parataxis." See Kellner, *Media Culture: Cultural Studies, Identity and Politics between the Modern and the Postmodern* (New York: Routledge, 1995), 140, and Willis, "Teens at Work," 348. Radwan, who offers the most exhaustive analysis of Linklater's camera work in *Slacker*, notes intriguingly that the film's technique "evokes a documentary tone, like a nature photographer exploring the slack habitat" ("Generation X and Postmodern Culture," 35).

23. On the film's explicit challenge to the basic conventions of narrative cinema, see also Kellner, *Media Culture*, 141; Radwan, "Generation X and Postmodern Culture," 35, 37, 38, 40–41; and Willis, "Teens at Work," 348.

24. "Under the hermeneutic code, we list the various (formal) terms by which an enigma can be distinguished, suggested, formulated, held in suspense, and finally disclosed." Roland Barthes, *S/Z*, trans. Richard Miller (1970; New York: Hill and Wang, 1974), 19.

25. This leads Crockford to characterize the narrative as "democratized" ("It's All about Bucks, Kid," 26) and Radwan to describe Linklater's technique as "egalitarian" ("Generation X and Postmodern Culture," 40; see also 37). Moore offers a dissenting view: "The way in which the camera quickly pans from one person to the next leaves us with only a rubble of depthless caricatures" ("And Tomorrow," 255). The effect is compounded by the absence of recognizable stars; casting his friends and other local oddballs helped Linklater ensure that audiences would not assign added value or depth to characters on the basis of the perceived value or reputation of the actors.

26. See Jameson, *Postmodernism*, 10–16, 26–28; cf. Moore, "And Tomorrow," 253–54. Moore additionally suggests that the film's narrative strategy of fragmentation actively undercuts a sense of history and narrativity as depth-based models of temporality (261).

27. "Most movement in *Slacker*," writes Radwan, "occurs on the X and to a lesser extent Z (usually away from the camera) axes. The camera never rises (or even tilts), and characters rarely go up or down." For Radwan, the

"predominance of lateral movement" in the film "expresses ... postmodern depthlessness" ("Generation X and Postmodern Culture," 39). These shots also contribute to a sense of postmodern disorientation and restless spatial dislocation; however, lateral movement can also work to alleviate such disorientation.

28. "Generation X's appreciation for conspiracy theories," suggests Radwan, "may rise from the widespread replacement of youthful idealism with a heartfelt cynicism, especially with regard to institutions and power. . . . Raised in a media saturated society, slackers are both aware of vast social machinations and their individual inability to affect much beyond themselves" ("Generation X and Postmodern Culture," 44–45).

29. Kellner notes optimistically that "as the characters in the film wander from one scene to another, and as some characters leave the frame, while others enter, one gets a sense of something of a Slacker community in which the Slackers are connected to each other, even if temporarily or minimally" (*Media Culture*, 141). The basis of this community is to be found "in the products of media culture" (140). On how consumerism works to efface, replace, and produce a sense of history, see Moore, "And Tomorrow," 262.

30. Chris Walters, "Freedom's Just Another Word for Nothing to Do," in booklet accompanying *Slacker*, DVD, directed by Richard Linklater (New York: Criterion Collection, 2004).

31. Kellner is quick to point out that "[t]he slackers are not passive products of media effects, but active participants in a media culture who use media to produce meaning, pleasure, and identity in their lives." They "appropriate media culture for their own ends," often turning it "into material for radical social and political critique" (*Media Culture*, 140).

32. Bone traces the term to a 1933 essay by Donald Davidson, "Sectionalism in the United States," and acknowledges the role of Eudora Welty's 1956 essay, "Place in Fiction," in canonizing the concept for southern literary critics (see Bone, *Postsouthern Sense of Place*, 28–29, 38). Revisionist approaches to the concept, including a full-blown deconstruction or two, can be found in Barbara Ladd, "Dismantling the Monolith: Southern Places—Past, Present, and Future," in *South to a New Place*, ed. Suzanne W. Jones and Sharon Monteith (Baton Rouge: Louisiana State University Press, 2002), especially 48–51, 55–57; Scott Romine, "Where Is Southern Literature? The Practice of Place in a Postsouthern Age," Jones and Monteith, *South to a New Place*, especially 23–24, 35–36, 41–42; Patricia Yaeger, *Dirt and Desire: Reconstructing Southern Women's Writing, 1930–1990* (Chicago: University of Chicago Press, 2000), 13–24; and, of course, Bone himself (*Postsouthern Sense of Place*, see especially 45–52).

33. Jon Smith and Deborah Cohn, "Introduction: Uncanny Hybridities," in *Look Away! The U.S. South in New World Studies*, ed. Smith and Cohn (Durham, N.C.: Duke University Press, 2004), 13.

34. Radwan also catches the "grassy knoll" reference ("Generation X and Postmodern Culture," 44).

35. Jameson, *Postmodernism*, 42.

36. Ibid., 51–52.

37. If the connection with Jameson seems forced, it's not exactly unmotivated. In one early scene in *Slacker*, a copy of *The Anti-aesthetic*, a 1983 collection of essays on postmodern art and aesthetics edited by Hal Foster, can be seen lying on a table at an espresso bar. Jameson was one of the contributors to *The Anti-aesthetic*; his essay is in some ways a trial run for the more comprehensive and definitive 1984 statement, "Postmodernism: The Cultural Logic of Late Capitalism," reprinted as the first chapter of the 1991 book *Postmodernism*. See Jameson, "Postmodernism and Consumer Society," in *The Anti-aesthetic: Essays on Postmodern Culture*, ed. Hal Foster (Port Townsend, Wash.: Bay, 1983), 111–25. Significantly, however, one topic Jameson does *not* yet write about in "Postmodernism and Consumer Society" is the potential of cognitive mapping as a postmodern coping strategy, an insight that emerges in the longer 1984 essay.

Kellner, the only other critic to have noticed and commented on the presence of Foster's collection in Linklater's film, adds that in the same scene, "a copy of Marshall Berman's book on modernity and modernist culture, *All That Is Solid Melts Into Air* (1982), is visible on a table." Since "[t]he two books articulate opposing contradictory aesthetic evaluations," Kellner reads their joint presence in the scene as Linklater's way of acknowledging the influence of both "modernist and postmodernist aesthetic strategies" on his film. Kellner thus concludes by positioning *Slacker* "between the modern and the postmodern" (*Media Culture*, 142). Perhaps this is so, but not midway between; the film's debts to postmodernism far outweigh its modernist lineage or credentials. For a comprehensive inventory, see Radwan, "Generation X and Postmodern Culture."

38. Radwan sees all this walking in terms of "freedom of movement," "a central metaphor for slacker culture as a whole" ("Generation X and Postmodern Culture," 38). In my view, however, it represents a much more specific tactical response to the historical and cultural exigencies of the film's postmodern moment and milieu than Radwan's all-purpose notion of personal autonomy can hope to capture.

39. Several critics have noted this thematic emphasis on speech. According to Crockford, having posited an "incompatibility between cash and conversation, and having rejected the previous generation's material greed, Generation X culture is forced to found itself instead on verbal achievements. Its core values are expressed in a respect for the erudite and the articulate" ("It's All about Bucks, Kid," 32). Willis also links the film's fetish for the spoken word with its general critique of consumerism: "Because nothing is produced in *Slacker* . . . social exchange is most often based on the interchange of words in conversation or the exchange of goods and services" ("Teens at Work," 349). Radwan cleverly describes the experience of viewing the film as being "guided 'laterally' through a talkative ocean of possibilities" ("Generation X and Postmodern Culture," 47).

40. Moreover, the aleatory dimension of the urban itinerary, to which *Slacker* attests again and again, helps create the idiosyncratic moments and experiences that become purchase points for cognitive mapping. Radwan finds a similar valorization of the aleatory in the "Oblique Strategies" cards created by a woman in the film as part of a performance art exhibition. Plucked face down from her

deck, the cards offer cryptic proverbs and riddles for slackers, like fortune cook-
ies for Generation X: "Withdrawing in disgust is not the same thing as apathy";
"Look closely at the most embarrassing detail and amplify it"; "Repetition is a
form of change." This generation, explains Radwan, "requires strategies that are
oblique because direct approaches do not work when you have no power. These
are coping strategies or maxims to live by in the post-industrial world. Appropriately, they are not provided by established value systems, they come at random"
("Generation X and Postmodern Culture," 47). As such, they offer another set of
possible reference points for cognitive mapping.

41. Jameson, *Postmodernism* 415.

42. Ibid., 417.

43. Indeed, one reason why Bone prefers "postsouthern" to other labels for
the contemporary moment in the region like "Sun Belt" or "New South" is the
way the term follows the example of "postmodern" in etymologically retaining
the concept it appears to signal a break from (the modern, the southern), leaving
open the possibility of "historical-geographical continuities" between the new
category and existing ideas about the region (Bone, *Postsouthern Sense of Place*,
50–51, 168–69).

44. "President Clinton . . . did this graduate address at UCLA and he was saying, 'I don't think you're a generation of slackers. I think you're a generation of
seekers,' but to me that's what slackers *were*: seekers." See Ben Thompson, "The
First Kiss Takes So Long," *Sight and Sound* 5, no. 5 (May 1995): 21.

45. "[I]n the present world-system," Jameson argues, "a media term is always
present to function as an *analogon* or material interpretant for this or that more
directly representational social model. Something thereby emerges which looks
like a new postmodern version of the base-and-superstructure formula, in which
a representation of social relations as such now demands the mediation of this
or that interposed communicational structure, from which it must be read off directly" (*Postmodernism*, 416). He's not saying anything that Linklater's slackers
don't already intuitively know.

46. Kellner, *Media Culture*, 142.

47. For a fuller account of this historical context, see Mehta, "Emigrants Twice
Displaced," 186–87. Bose and Varghese argue that "Idi Amin's background as
one of only two native officers in Uganda's military forces during the colonial
period points to his status as a native collaborator" cynically manipulating nationalist rhetoric for his own gain "rather than an ardent nationalist engaged in
the anticolonial struggle against the British" ("*Mississippi Masala*," 144).

48. See Ballal, "Illiberal Masala," 95, and Bhavnani, "Organic Hybridity," 196.

49. Bhavnani, however, suggests that Okelo's nationalist position is a strategic
stance he adopts to persuade his friend to leave Uganda before he is killed ("Organic Hybridity," 200).

50. Ballal describes the song as a metonymic evocation of the Lohas' diasporic
condition ("Illiberal Masala," 96). Bhavnani points out that the lyric's emphasis
on how difficult it is to dislodge Indian ethnic and cultural identity from the heart
works to undercut the Lohas' claims to be Ugandan first and foremost ("Organic
Hybridity," 202n6).

51. Quoted in John Lahr, "Whirlwind: How the Filmmaker Mira Nair Makes People See the World Her Way," *New Yorker*, December 9, 2002, 101.

52. According to Singh, "the sound track—Indian music, Delta blues, and African drums—suggests that in diasporic spaces in the West identities are being reconstructed and are evolving into a new hybrid reality for the new immigrants" ("Globalization, Transnationalism, and Identity Politics").

53. Rasiah notes that by "solidif[ying] the fact that there is a working-class South Asian experience," the character of Mina represents an important contribution to the cinema of the South Asian diaspora (*"Mississippi Masala* and *Khush,"* 269). Mainstream films typically present South Asians as upwardly aspiring, upwardly mobile, and middle class. Nair's presentation of the Lohas productively complicates that view.

54. Bose and Varghese, *"Mississippi Masala,"* 140.

55. Bone, *Postsouthern Sense of Place*, 210.

56. Indeed, Greenwood, Mississippi, became an archetypal civil rights epicenter in its own right, as the site of Stokely Carmichael's famous "Black Power!" speech in 1966.

57. Friedman, "Beyond White and Other," 32.

58. "The attempt to establish historical links between enslavement and indentured labor, despite the different consequences of these forms of domination, could be seen as an overly simplistic way by which to move from historical particularities to cultural commonalities," notes Bhavnani ("Organic Hybridity," 197). "However, given the apparent cultural and class differences between the two families, such a move is not simplistic, but, rather, is a way of negotiating cultural differences into mutually comprehensible experiences and representations." In the picnic scene, Bhavnani notes, "there is no suggestion of either group's cultural specificity being appropriated by the other. Rather, the exchange is an attempt to show how such negotiations are desired and, therefore, made possible," in "an active and enthusiastic engagement with difference" that "shows that asking for information about cultural differences need not always be racist" (198).

59. Friedman ("Beyond White and Other," 29–30) and Mehta ("Emigrants Twice Displaced," 193) also discuss the intraethnic color consciousness among the film's South Asians.

60. "[B]y portraying the Indian community's calculated devastation of Demetrius's business as a collective response to his relationship with Mina," Bose and Varghese argue, *"Mississippi Masala* raises questions about the nature of community, such as the grounds on which it claims a representative status, the relationship between those claims and the constitution of its membership, and the extent to which it is a stable formation" (*"Mississippi Masala,"* 153).

61. On the South Asian cultural institution of *sharam* (loosely translated as shame) and its gender politics, see Bose and Varghese, *"Mississippi Masala,"* 160–61. Singh's account of the gendering of Indian cultural nationalism helps make it clear how much family and communal identity, cohesiveness, and honor hinges on the conduct of women, especially daughters.

62. Incongruously but also suggestively, just barely audible on the van's radio during this scene is the Hindustani ditty we heard back in Africa: "My shoes are

Japanese / My pants are English / My red hat is Russian / But my heart, it's all Indian." The song works here to undercut Tyrone's xenophobia by defusing the menace of the foreignness he is trashing.

63. Friedman, "Beyond White and Other," 31; also see Mehta, "Emigrants Twice Displaced," 192–93.

64. The term *masala*, however, also denotes a popular Indian film genre, "generally produced in Bombay" and mixing "romantic comedy, melodrama, and action sequences" (Bose and Varghese, "*Mississippi Masala*," 154–55). For a detailed discussion of masala genre conventions and the often irreverent or revisionary uses to which Nair puts them in *Mississippi Masala*, see Bose and Varghese, "*Mississippi Masala*," 154–62.

65. Friedman, "Beyond White and Other," 32.

66. Bhavnani is one of the only critics to discuss the relationship between Jay and Okelo specifically in terms of love ("Organic Hybridity," 200). Bose and Varghese note how this relationship, like the one between Mina and Demetrius, "become[s] overdetermined with questions of individual and national identity" ("*Mississippi Masala*," 155).

67. Bose and Varghese, "*Mississippi Masala*," 157.

68. Friedman points out how Nair's flashback technique throughout the film underscores "how what happened in 1972 shapes the events in 1990" ("Beyond White and Other," 30).

69. Bose and Varghese remind us of just how unorthodox Mina's plan is in cultural terms: "The business of manually cleaning other peoples' homes and businesses violates Hindu notions of caste and class, purity and pollution" ("*Mississippi Masala*," 159).

70. And more than one postcolonial scholar shares this sentiment as well: Mehta cites Stuart Hall, who "speaks about the notion of *migranthood* and the attitudes of migrants who know deep down that they are not going home, because 'migration is a one way trip. There is no "home" to go back to. There never was.' Ashis Nandy observes that South Asians in the diaspora 'cling to the memories of [a] South Asia which no longer exists and to a myth of return to the homeland which is no longer shared by their children or grandchildren'" (Mehta, "Emigrants Twice Displaced," 199).

71. "Jay's resolve," adds Mehta, "signals an important moment of commitment, to his wife and, by extension, to the 'home' he must build with her in their new domicile, thereby recalling [Ashis] Nandy's suggestion that 'the diaspora must work towards dismantling links with the mother-country and entering the political realm of the new country'" ("Emigrants Twice Displaced," 199).

72. Bose and Varghese, "*Mississippi Masala*," 159.

73. See Bone, *Postsouthern Sense of Place*, 250–52.

74. Quoted in Andrea Stuart, "Mira Nair: A New Hybrid Cinema," in *Women and Film: A Sight and Sound Reader*, ed. Pam Cook and Phillip Dodd (Philadelphia: Temple University Press, 1993), 214.

75. Singh, "Globalization, Transnationalism, and Identity Politics." As such, the film arguably represents an innovation in migration narrative, as Stuart explains, "The experience of migration has been a dominant cultural concern for

most of this century. But . . . the migrant is usually depicted as a victim and his [*sic*] contribution is all too often seen as negative by the community he enters; a source of anxiety rather than positive renewal. Increasingly, this is a position that feels outmoded, particularly for migrants themselves." In Nair's film, by contrast, "the victim has turned protagonist. Instead of anguish, Nair revels in the mélange migration creates; instead of sinking into nostalgia, her characters move forward to embrace their hard-won new place" ("Mira Nair," 212).

76. See Tara McPherson, *Reconstructing Dixie: Race, Gender, and Nostalgia in the Imagined South* (Durham, N.C.: Duke University Press, 2003), 129–30, 141. McPherson also discusses McElwee's running obsession with Burt Reynolds in the film (131–32), as if to help bring my essay full circle.

77. Romine's recent analysis of Julie Dash's *Daughters of the Dust* suggests that the canon I am sketching here should be widened to include that film as well. See *Real South*, 122–30.

78. Radhakrishnan, "Is the Ethnic 'Authentic,'" 224.

79. I allude here, with an eye toward updating it, to Robert Heilman's influential essay, "The Southern Temper," an important text of the "old" southern studies. "Southern Temper," in *Southern Renascence: The Literature of the Modern South*, ed. Louis D. Rubin Jr. and Robert D. Jacobs (Baltimore: Johns Hopkins University Press, 1953), 1–13.

The Native Screen

American Indians in Contemporary Southern Film

Melanie R. Benson

> To understand the various ways Americans have
> contested and constructed national identities, we
> must constantly return to the original mysteries
> of Indianness.
> —Philip J. Deloria, *Playing Indian*

> To understand the South and southerners, we need to
> understand southern representations of Indians.
> —Joel Martin, "My Grandmother Was a
> Cherokee Princess"

One of the greatest literary hoaxes of all time occurred when Forrest Carter successfully passed off as autobiography his charming little book *The Education of Little Tree* (1976).[1] The purported memoir tells the story of a young boy orphaned at the age of five and sent to live with his grandparents in the Smokey Mountains of Tennessee. His grandmother is Cherokee and his grandfather, while white, is well tutored in the "Native Way." Young Forrest is thus introduced to his heritage, aided by a shamanlike Cherokee called John Willow. Heartwarming episodes ensue. The novel enjoyed modest but steady success until, in 1991, it gained the top spot on the *New York Times* bestseller list and won the American Booksellers Book of the Year award. That's when the quiet rumblings, stifled since 1976, erupted and scandal hit the airwaves: Carter was not a Cherokee orphan but an alcoholic Klan member from Alabama whom Dan T. Carter (no relation) describes as "a kind of psychopath" with no trace of Cherokee ancestry in his family tree.[2] Born Asa Earl, Carter changed his first name to Forrest in honor of the Confederate general Nathan Bedford Forrest. Although he later denied it, as "Asa," Carter had served as a speechwriter for Alabama's prosegregationist governor

George Wallace, penning some of the most indelible racist rhetoric in U.S. memory.[3] He cofounded the *Southerner*, a white supremacist rag; formed a White Citizens Council but disbanded it to avoid communing with Jews, even segregationist ones; started his own "new and improved" branch of the KKK when he decided the original organization had grown "soft"; and had a cohort who was linked in 1957 to the brutal mutilation of an African American maintenance worker who had reportedly talked too cavalierly about the prospect of integration.[4] How, many wondered, could this endearing, sympathetic portrait of Native American culture emerge from a man with such brutish, intolerant views?[5] Many dismissed the incongruity as irrelevant; certainly, the controversy did not block subsequent republications of the book (stripped of its autobiographical label), which continues to be taught routinely in grade school classrooms across the United States. Even Henry Louis Gates Jr. defended *Little Tree*'s literary merits as separable from the author's less than savory biography.[6] Objections from actual Indians such as Sherman Alexie (Spokane/Coeur d'Alene) went virtually unheard: "*Little Tree* is a lovely little book," he commented, "and I sometimes wonder if it is an act of romantic atonement by a guilt-ridden white supremacist, but ultimately I think it is the racial hypocrisy of a white supremacist."[7]

Alexie's view was not shared by most of mainstream America, for whom *Little Tree* represented an act of spiritual "redemption" rather than a racist outrage on par with his past offenses.[8] This outlook became even more obvious when in 1997 director Richard Friedenberg adapted the book for the big screen, creating a sentimental smash hit that was nominated the next year for the prestigious Humanitas Prize—an award recognizing "stories that affirm the human person, probe the meaning of life, and enlighten the use of human freedom. The stories reveal common humanity, so that love may come to permeate the human family and help liberate, enrich, and unify society."[9] While Friedenberg's film did not take home the top honor (losing out to *Good Will Hunting*), his was one of only three features nominated, and the glowing recognition of the Humanitas Foundation coincided with the overwhelmingly positive reception of the moviegoing public. Viewers easily detached the film version of *Little Tree* from the controversial book; even though the adaptation was largely faithful, most urged that the film be "taken on its own terms."[10] Consequently, the U.S. public indulged guiltlessly in a sentimental, stereotypical tale of wise, mystical, resilient Indians and Appalachians coexisting harmoniously in the southern hills, where "Indians are no longer the continent's indigenous people, they are . . . just like the rest of us. They like to hunt, make moonshine, gather wild herbs in season, and have a close relationship with the earth. In short, they are a lot like the hill people in the Tennessee mountains, with Indian stuff added to their lives as a kind of cultural spice."[11] Yet, given the ease with which Indian identity is so hungrily subsumed in the United States, and in particular the South, such "humanitarian" depictions are in fact disturbingly consonant with white racism and nativism. Suppressing Carter's destructive past is essential if we are to continue cloaking the sinister underbelly of contemporary white liberalism.

When Friedenberg adapted Carter's specifically southern nativist project for the screen, he transposed it into a readily recognizable and lucrative genre: the New Age quest for redemption in the wild, narratives that often employ indigenous figures as sources of spiritual wisdom and primal intimacy with the natural world. Friedenberg's prior directorial and screenplay credits include *The Life and Times of Grizzly Adams* (1974), *The Adventures of Frontier Fremont* (1976)—with the tagline: "The true story of one man's struggle to make the wilderness his home and the animals his friends"—and the made-for-TV version of James Fenimore Cooper's *The Deerslayer* (1978). No stranger to epic wilderness sagas, he had most recently written the Oscar-nominated screenplay for *A River Runs Through It* (1992), an adaptation of Norman Maclean's quasi memoir about fly-fishing and male-bonding in rural Montana. Robert Redford—himself a visible activist and ally of the Native and natural worlds—directed the film. With *Little Tree*, Friedenberg works again in comfortable, universal terrain and thus manages to jettison both Carter's (and the unreconstructed South's) racist baggage, achieving instead a more encompassing American story about survival, tradition, and nature that functions as a spiritual salve. One critic, drawing on a Lummi woman's similar reaction to *Dances with Wolves*, categorizes such representations as "instant pudding": a soft, uncomplicated, generic version of indigenous identity easily digested by the American viewer.[12] And as Bill Cosby confirms, Americans do love pudding: Andrew L. Urban, and critics like him, praises the film as a "journey into the healing power of mother nature, complete with its lessons of growth and survival" and declares it "balm to the burnt out film critic's soul."[13]

Non-Indians who hang dream catchers from their rearview mirrors do so out of a well-intentioned desire to play Indian, and in the process achieve a state of spiritual enlightenment and natural wonder. As Philip Deloria documents in *Playing Indian* (1998), innumerable white and black Americans since the nation's birth have slipped on Native disguises to perform pageants of cultural authenticity; the Boston Tea Party, enacted by British American colonists wielding tomahawks and war paint, is a particularly iconic example. For African Americans in New Orleans, the Mardi Gras Indian krewes are borrowings of a more ostensibly beneficent yet equally self-serving kind.[14] Safely disposed in a hidden corner of history, the Native story becomes a veritable Halloween costume available for adoption by various groups wishing to inhabit nobility, resistance, and New Age spirituality; in the process, real Indians have virtually disappeared from mainstream view.

One of the most striking paradoxes in Southern culture is that while resident Native Americans are apparently extinct, every third or fourth southerner asserts some degree of Cherokee heritage; Theda Perdue and Michael Green report that in 1996, 40 percent of southerners claimed Native ancestry (usually in the form of a "Cherokee grandmother"), which is "considerably more than the 22 percent who claim descent from a Confederate soldier" or the mere 2 percent who can officially declare themselves "Indian."[15] This phenomenon reveals more about white southern nativism than it does about rampant Indian promiscuity. As Joel W. Martin avers, "to understand the South and southerners, we need to understand southern representations of Indians."[16] As with any colonizing project, the original inhabitants of Native American territory or culture must be imaginatively erased or refigured to make the settler culture appear autochthonous.[17] Such invisibility is particularly obvious in the U.S. South, where entire nations were relocated north and west of the Mississippi by President Andrew Jackson's removal policies of the 1830s; the Trail of Tears ended in Oklahoma, and the South's plantation economy flourished on land effectively cleared of its Native obstacles.

In the post-Reconstruction decades that taxed their economic, social, and cultural integrity, southerners began to appropriate Native experience in particularly potent ways, usurping an identity assumed to be obsolete to contain and express their own perceived victimization and dispossession and to tacitly validate their own residency in a critical time of regional rehabilitation. Most prominently, the Nashville Agrarians, who together penned the conservative manifesto *I'll Take My Stand*, famously allied the white South with the hardy, resistant, and sadly obsolete Natives who had been similarly crushed by inimical federal policies and colonial-capitalist invasions.[18] In a more recent example, Barry Hannah's protagonist in *Geronimo Rex* uses the violent Apache figure as a conduit for his own repressed desires and rage: "What I especially liked about Geronimo," Harry enumerates, "was that he had cheated, lied, stolen, mutinied, usurped, killed, burned, raped, pillaged, razed, trapped, ripped, mashed, bowshot, stomped, herded, exploded, cut, stoned, revenged, prevenged, avenged." As a southerner with a score to settle, Harry finds Geronimo's reckless retribution against invading forces appealing. Yet like so many such maneuvers, the Indian ally must be both kindred and strange, too savage to remain in civilized society but a convenient proxy for one's secret, uncensored desires for vengeance.[19] Indian identity, like the area's Natives themselves, was effectively absorbed into a dominant biracial order.

However, we know that many southern Indians successfully resisted removal by hiding in the woods, mountains, and less desirable lands, or by choosing to assimilate into white and black societies; yet the South's strictly biracial identity and narratives have been uniquely persistent.[20] Even though Little Tree's grandmother and her people are clearly part of this resistance, the film suggests that such groups have blended into white Appalachian society; they marry, work, and interact fluidly with the other white southerners around them. In the film, Granma (Tantoo Cardinal) wears heavy, country dresses and head scarves that temper her obvious indigenousness with the trappings of her Appalachian hill life. Similarly, the elder Cherokee John Willow (played by the ubiquitous Oneida actor Graham Greene) has long hair and mystical ways but otherwise dresses in flannel shirts and country hats much like Little Tree's white grandfather. Even Little Tree's mixed heritage invites viewers to identify their own secret desire to reunite with a long-lost Cherokee grandmother. The boy who plays Little Tree, Joseph Ashton—with his cherubic upturned nose, wide brown eyes, and syrupy charm—appears only vaguely Indian (his parents reportedly have some Cherokee ancestry). Such choices make the Indian characters seem as if they could be anyone among the white populace and yet also, when appropriate, founts of spiritual wisdom. Their Native legacy lives on primarily in the virtues of "The Way," an indigenous code as old as the land and endorsed emphatically by natural law, with tenets regarding moderation, sustainability, and the survival of the fittest—a philosophy that can also be likened to the beaten South's conviction that it "will rise again," if only it can restore reverence for the land and dominance of lesser species.[21] Such sinister undertones and oversimplifications of Native creeds have been repeatedly pointed out by Cherokee individuals themselves, who balk at the inaccurate and crude renditions of their culture. Actual cruelty toward Native Americans is figured briefly in the film when Little Tree's grandparents are caught moonshining, and Little Tree is summarily sent away to a boarding school. Historically, such institutions attempted to Americanize Native youth, ensuring a new generation of "civilized," docile citizens—"killing the Indian to save the man," as the creed went. Of course, when Granpa comes to rescue Little Tree they defy the complete horror suffered by so many historical Indians. In Little Tree's world, family, tradition, and cultural defiance routinely triumph over government intervention in ways that have been impossible for real Indians. It becomes easy to see why such renditions of Native American experience held such appeal for a southern segregationist like Carter and why it would serve as a balm for white America's inherited guilt.

Such fantasies are no less disturbing because they are explicable. When film intervenes in the cultural blank space of Native identity, particularly that of the South, where we lack enduring visual representations of events such as the Trail of Tears, the genre powerfully reenvisions Native identity for popular, national needs. Given the particular insistence on racial and ethnic ocularity in the United States, and particularly for Native Americans expected to continue wearing feathers and animal skins while hunting buffalo along the interstate or lunching at McDonald's, film provides one of the most potent and corrosive media for posing and perpetuating such anachronistic images.[22] In a panoply of popular Westerns from the beginnings of cinema, we have watched endless permutations of the stock "Indian" character (nation usually unknown or irrelevant), occasionally dangerous and sneaky, sometimes noble and loyal, and invariably different and distinct from white, Euro-American culture.[23] As Beverly R. Singer notes, these depictions have fixed in the American mind a generic "Indian" whose culture is ineluctably supplanted by a more "normative" and valuable western one. According to Jacquelyn Kilpatrick, as a spectacle of colonial anxiety, the challenge posed by the "savages" enables "a confirmation of the dominant value structure." Film plots tend to get away with more blatant stereotyping and symbolism as long as there is a beneficent message or empowering narrative at stake. Westerns in particular, as Kevin Brownlow reminds us, "were not made for educational purposes, but simply to make money."[24] Put another way, the popular viewing community pays to see their national fantasies—not their repressed colonial nightmares—writ large on the big screen.[25]

Deepening the ideological impact of these representations is the fact that, in early Westerns, Native characters were usually played by a white actor with "ethnic" features, such as Jeff Chandler in his Academy Award–winning turn as Cochise in Delmer Daves's 1950 *Broken Arrow*. As Marxist screen theory and cultural studies suggest, we exist in a mutually reinforcing and sustaining relationship to the images we both watch and purvey. Nothing could more accurately describe the way Indian stereotypes have become permanently impressed on our national consciousness in the twenty-first century, inhibiting us still further from recognizing what real Indians look and act like—even for Natives themselves. As Alexie recalls, "I loved all movies about Indians, loved them beyond all reasoning and saw no fault with any of them"; and like most viewers he often sided with John Wayne rather than the "savage" Indians. Ironically, the only character he truly disliked was Tonto—one of the few on-screen Indians played by an actual Native. "I watched the movies and saw what kind of Indian I was supposed to be," Alexie says, and "hated Tonto because Tonto was the only cinematic Indian who looked like me."[26]

If white America needs Indian ancestors and allies to staunch a gaping spiritual wound, then African American artists have gravitated toward indigenous allies for more well-intentioned yet no less self-serving needs. Historically, Native and African Americans in the South mingled—as slaves, as conspirators and allies helping one another to escape, and often as lovers and spouses.[27] After emancipation, numerous nations accepted into their families the ex-slaves known as "freedmen." Several nations, such as the Lumbees of North Carolina and the Seminoles of Oklahoma, have become so heavily intermixed with African Americans that their federal status as Indian nations has been questioned or denied. A distinct folk literature borne of contact between the two cultures sprang up.[28] Yet relations between the two minority groups have not always been harmonious: there was such a thing as slaveholding Indians in the antebellum South, which naturally bred antagonism rather than solidarity; and more recently, in March 2007, the Cherokee Nation of Oklahoma ignited a racial firestorm when the tribe voted overwhelmingly to deny citizenship to more than two thousand descendants of former slaves on their rolls. Still, no two cultures in the South had more opportunity to commune and bond over their shared exploitation and dispossession. It is in this vein of kinship that Julie Dash, an African American director from New York, creates her own Cherokee warrior in a remote southern landscape. Yet, like Carter's vision, Dash's owes more to her own cultural perceptions and needs than to those of actual, surviving Native Americans.

Dash's avant-garde film *Daughters of the Dust* (1991) portrays a Gullah family in the secluded Sea Islands of South Carolina. The year is 1902, and the Peazant family is readying to leave the island community where they have lived since arriving from West Africa as slaves; now they are seeking a better life and the opportunities of the industrialized North. That's where "plot" as such ends. To convey the immense cultural change about to occur, Dash relies on images dense with symbolism, surreal and poetic movements, and a magical-realist collision of fantasy and reality that disturbs any conventional sense of narrative or plot development. Moreover, her characters speak in their heavy Gullah dialect, which makes the dialogue at times extremely difficult to follow. The effect of all this is a representation as stubbornly close to the beauty of lived experience and cultural specificity as she can get. As one reviewer puts it, "I'd wager that the portrait of turn-of-the-century African American women you get in *Daughters of the Dust* is like nothing you've ever seen before."[29] Despite its gaps in linearity and clarity, the film is so visually and lyrically affecting that, as Roger Ebert puts it, "we relax like children at a family picnic, not understanding everything, but feeling at home with the expression of it."[30] Much of the film does center on a family picnic of sorts—a going-away feast on the shore that draws the entire extended family, with most of the women dressed in ethereal white gowns and holding parasols. This need to recapture and expose an utterly alien, forgotten world is what seems to drive Dash's vision. As Ed Guerrero avers, Dash's film "pointedly sets out to reconstruct, to recover a sense of black women's history, and to affirm their cultural and political space in the expanding arena of black cinematic production."[31] In this way, her film resonates with Native American efforts to depict a culture and community irretrievably altered and lost to history and to present it in tones of magical realism that more accurately reflect the stories and wisdom of the past rather than the narrow linearity of the present.

Among the Peazant family, attitudes toward the migration differ widely and a general tension between modernity and primitivism runs throughout; the matriarch of the family, Nana, has emphatically resolved to stay behind. By the end of the film, she convinces a few other family members to remain on the island as well. Refusing to go forward into the corrupt, commercial U.S. society of the twentieth century signifies a potent, profound measure of resistance not normally available to the marginalized. While the Peazants have suffered irremediably under slavery, they have also enjoyed the relative luxury of seclusion, isolation, and cultural preservation. They remain intact as a veritable "tribe" with living connections to their West African heritage and folkways, and many of the family members know that dispersing from the island will disrupt those ties permanently and irrevocably. As Dash has noted, the Sea Islands were "the region with the strongest retention of African culture"; leaving that oasis effectively meant losing any remaining links to histories long erased from the lives of most American blacks.[32] Nana knows this, and that is why she stays.

However, one of the younger women, Iona ("I Own Her"), must be convinced. When the rest of the clan tearfully boards the rowboats that will take them to the mainland, Iona is suddenly swept off her feet and spirited away on horseback by her Cherokee lover. The young warrior instantly confirms our most basic stereotypes of the lusty Indian on horseback—and he ostensibly provides for Iona and the others a living symbol of the noble primitivism and fragile cultural tradition that the Gullah family fosters and protects. "For Dash," Scott MacDonald concludes, "and for the characters in *Daughters of the Dust*, the idea of a natural Eden remains a crucial element in any recovery from the racial horrors that brought Africans to America and kept them in chains to develop the land."[33] When the Cherokee invites Iona back to the greener pastures of this natural Eden, Dash draws on the well-rehearsed correlation between Indians and the natural world; more than that, however, by making him an ambassador from Eden, she denies him and his people the reality of their own colonial past and "racial horrors." He is there simply to serve Iona. His only other appearance in the film occurs earlier, when he delivers a letter imploring Iona to remain on the island with him. The letter translates effortlessly into Iona's own highly specific Gullah dialect; as such, we understand that his voice and language are irrelevant and that this message of cultural continuity is intended only for the Gullah people.

Where is his family, his people? We know that Native Americans inhabited parts of the Sea Islands before they were settled by white planters and African slaves; it is widely believed that the Gullah people themselves got their name from a Spanish rendition of a Native tribal name, and that the Gullah nickname "Geechee" derives from a Creek word.[34] Yet the frozen, anachronistic, solo Cherokee warrior is, like these bits of language, the residue of a past that functions merely as parable. Dash's aim is not to prioritize one group's suffering over another or even to establish priority in a landscape that is obviously not home; yet the effect of her symbology is to obliterate the Native inhabitants from the landscape and resurrect one, alone, as a moving prop who speaks in the voice and tones that the Gullah need to hear, inviting them to stay and be healed in his everlasting Eden that has space and salve for everyone but the Indians themselves.

Following the Red Road Home: Randy Redroad's *The Doe Boy* (2001) and Native Southern Diaspora

Given these bleak contexts, where does the Native begin the formidable project of self-representation? And how does one achieve even modest visibility in a genre driven largely by nationalist fantasies and market demands? The lack of a mainstream audience (desiring to see *real* Indians) results in a lack of funding, opportunity, support, and attention—an equation that Cherokee writer-director Randy Redroad calls "the cold mathematical reality of genocide." "For us to even choose filmmaking is a huge thing," Redroad knows. "We have no Indian celebrities. We don't represent a market. . . . We have no voice. If you live in Hollywood and hope to make movies for Indians, it isn't going to happen. It's that simple."[35] And yet a crucial step in the decolonizing process has involved moving behind the camera and revising the images that have long dominated the American screen. Indians harnessed the genre as early as the 1970s to produce short, independent films and documentaries that served as both historical correctives and political activism.[36] Yet it was not until 1998's *Smoke Signals*—the screen adaptation of several of Sherman Alexie's short stories—that a Cheyenne-Arapaho filmmaker (Chris Eyre) became the first Native American to direct a major feature film. *Smoke Signals* won the Filmmaker's Trophy and the Audience Award at Sundance that year, making it clear to more than specialized, academic, or ethnic audiences that "American Indians can make a good commercial project while telling a good story with Indians as the central characters."[37] No feature film by a Native filmmaker has received such acclaim since.

The extraordinary task and tension of telling, selling, and *becoming* a "good story" is at the heart of Randy Redroad's autobiographical feature *The Doe Boy* (2001). Shot in just twenty-four days and on a meager indie budget, the slender, eighty-five-minute film manages largely to avoid the stereotypes and sentimentality that plague white, black, and even Natives' own representations of the American Indian. As one reviewer rejoices, "This ain't no *Dances with Wolves*, and for that we should be very grateful." More seriously, the critic notes that Redroad's effort "just may serve to re-define what a 'Native American Movie' should be"— primarily because it takes place in the "bleak real-world" of Tahlequah, Oklahoma, circa 1984 rather than in a remote, anachronistic realm of mythology, spiritualism, and "noble red men."[38] Indeed, Redroad's script seems in large part an attempt to negotiate his own experience as a mixed-blood from west Texas, part Cherokee (on his mother's side) and part white (on his father's): "Consider the psychology of that for a moment," he says, "and you'll have a new understanding of the term 'at war with one's self.'" Add to that an alcoholic father who declared himself to be "the last of the cowboys" and was "prone to poetic, yet hateful tirades that . . . made for stressful bedtime stories."[39] Redroad's anger takes aim partly at his father and partly at the white world, and in his work the two often seem interchangeable. Film allowed him a conduit for his "pride and anger and all those things that we go through when we're young and we realize that things aren't right or whatever. I was such a very angry early-twenty-year-old Native person" and "[film] was a perfect way to speak about these things and forcefully."[40] After completing a short workshop at New York City's Third World Newsreel, Redroad cobbled together enough in the way of skills and equipment to shoot his first short, *Cowtipping: The Militant Indian Waiter* (1992), which stunned him by garnering an award at a local film festival. That spurred his confidence to make more professional-quality shorts, documentaries, and full-length features such as *Haircuts Hurt* (1992), *High Horse* (1994), *Moccasin Flats* (2003), and *133 Skyway* (2006).

But by far his most acclaimed effort to date has been *The Doe Boy*, which swept nearly all of the major categories at the annual American Indian Film Festival in 2001. The title refers to a pivotal episode in both the film and Redroad's own childhood: the autobiographical protagonist, part-Cherokee Hunter Kirk (young Hunter played by Andrew J. Ferchland; teenage Hunter by James Duval), is on his first hunting excursion with his Anglo father, Hank (Kevin Johnson). While Hank falls asleep in wait against a tree, young Hunter spots a deer and eagerly shoots it. Too late, Hunter and his father discover the boy's error: instead of a buck, he has shot a doe. As happens at key moments throughout the film, Hunter's full-blood grandfather, Marvin (Gordon Tootoosis), interprets the event in a sage voice-over delivered in unmistakably Indian-flavored English: "There was a boy who shot a woman while his father slept," Marvin intones, "a boy with bullets in his eyes and arrows in his chest." The closest thing to an Indian elder in the film, Marvin reminds us that the deer and the man are intimately bound. But this is more than Native mysticism; we understand that Hunter's fatal hunting error has much more to do with the human world than the animal kingdom and that Hunter himself embodies a kind of weapon—an aptly named "Hunter"—searching for masculinity and spirituality in a world engineered against Indian victory, with no help from his father.

Hank "sleeps" through these trials, it seems, because he lacks both indigenousness and machismo: he is a working-class white man whose greatest disappointment was failing to fly and fight in Vietnam. Hank is further distressed by his son's congenital frailty—the boy suffers from hemophilia. Hunter's mother Maggie (Jeri Arredondo), an overprotective nurse, makes him wear football shoulder pads to accompany his father into the woods; the pads mock his inability not just to hunt but to play football like the other boys. His Indian friend, Junior, points this out to him rudely, cloaked imperiously in his own sporting gear: "You don't play football," he sneers. Junior and his apparently full-blood father, Manny, have just returned from hunting as well. As a father-son hunting duo, Junior and Manny are the exact inverse of Hank and Hunter: Manny's very name implies masculinity, and unlike Hank, Manny not only served in Vietnam but learned to hunt there, peppering the field with shots and hoping he'd hit something. "Junior" literally heralds a continuation of that line; after high school, he and another friend, Cheekie, head off for basic training while delicate Hunter stays behind. As robust, virile Indians, Manny and Junior enjoy the blood purity, strength, and virility that Hank and Hunter lack.

Yet Redroad's parable is not quite so simple or reactionary; being full-blood in a white world does not ward off contamination either. Hunter's hemophilia provides Redroad the perfect symbology to critique the excessive importance placed on blood quanta by both Natives and whites: "everyone wants to know how much blood runs through an Indian," Granpa Marvin observes in the opening frames of the film, which shift rapidly from images of a running deer to three young Indian boys (Hunter, Junior, and Cheekie) racing through the woods. Hunter speeds out of the frame, while Cheekie pauses midforest to bend and puff on his asthma inhaler.[41] The moment abruptly undercuts our expectations: this will not be a film about communing with the deer in an anachronistic, indigenous landscape or about magical warriors who tear bare-chested through the trees. Instead, Redroad shows how, like it or not, Native and white blood and culture have been irretrievably mixed and that the collision has left a biological mark; the introduction of white diseases into indigenous societies is a sober historical fact. Redroad conjures such historical knowledge at the same time that he converts biological fact into a metaphor for acute cultural crisis. Indian cultures simply could not remain healthy and unadulterated in the face of colonial invasion. Everywhere in this Oklahoma town, whites and Natives meet, mingle, and coexist. None too subtle, Redroad's central metaphor for this cultural cross-pollination and weakening is Hunter's hemophilia. In an environment slowly erasing the Indian out of existence, this uncontrollable blood loss becomes an urgent, evocative sign of both biological and cultural erasure. Hunter likens himself to the Scarecrow in *The Wizard of Oz*: "every time I bleed," he says, "it's like 'there goes some of me again.'" The image reminds us that the Indian's very identity, like the Scarecrow, is composed by white hands for white needs; he will be "stuffed" back up with infusions from multiple, anonymous sources, a world of alien blood running through his veins. Importantly, he chooses to describe this condition borrowing from a celluloid text, an American cinematic fantasy about realizing that there is "no place like home"—but only after yearning for greener pastures "over the rainbow" that do not exist. Hunter's dreamland resides in a mistaken belief that being a full-blood will restore his health and happiness. "Your blood ruined me," he accuses his father in a fit of rage, with that "white disease."

What Hunter must eventually learn, though, is that there truly is "no place like home" for Indians in the world, in the most literal sense of the phrase, and that full-bloodedness offers no protection from contamination by the modern white world. Granpa Marvin downplays the advantage of blood purity: "sometimes I feel like a tick that ate too much . . . like I might blow up." In white America, being full-blood amounts to overabundance of an obsolete commodity, a fullness of identity that has cultural significance but little use value. By contrast, Marvin deems Hunter "lucky" to be part-white in a white world; he even chooses Hunter over all his full-blood children and grandchildren to pass down his flute and his woodworking skills to, knowing that Hunter will eventually pass them on. Hunter is less certain. Masochistically, he tempts fate—instigating barroom fights ("Limp on over here, you gimpy redneck," he taunts a drunk white man) and, in a still more explosive scene, taunts his own father until Hank slaps him roughly in the face. The blow draws blood, and in that moment the camera focuses in on Hunter's stunned but satisfied face while Hank's visage fades in the background—emphasizing that he is the biological agent but not the true cause of

Hunter's existential pain. Being mixed-blood amplifies his condition, but an Indian need not be hybrid to experience the slow extinction of cultural vitality and sovereignty. The fact that his mother is a nurse, taking care of him and supplying his medicine and infusions, deepens our recognition that the white world of modernity, science, and "progress" is always already an ambivalent fact of contemporary Indian life, regardless of blood purity. Simply existing in white, "postcolonial" America accomplishes this.

Seen through this lens, Hunter and his father suffer similarly—simply from their inability to enact their greatest dreams and desires in a world that routinely frustrates these efforts. Hank drinks beer after beer while watching fighter planes on television, loudly asserting his wasted prowess as a fighter pilot and berating those who had the chance he missed. As he sneers at invisible enemies on the screen, Maggie silently mouths each word along with him, suggesting that she has heard this tirade repeated enough to have memorized it. Like Hunter's renegade blood, an integral part of Hank has leached out, and no amount of courage-inducing alcohol can replace it. A visual parallel later in the film confirms their shared plight: when Hunter goes to the hospital for an HIV test for AIDS, which he may have contracted from a tainted blood supply, the camera lingers over a large bottle labeled "ALCOHOL" in the foreground. Clearly, it is a bottle of isopropyl alcohol to sterilize the skin before the needle is inserted, but the reality of the HIV test makes such measures belated and futile. Hank's drinking seems similarly ineffectual; it also provides another bridge between the film's white and Native communities, given the harsh fact of alcohol abuse among contemporary Natives. What both father and son suffer from, it seems, is not simply the "white disease" but the American one, and there is no cure in sight.

It is the United States' voracious appetite for space, power, and wealth that has instigated and justified its most brutal crimes against entire cultures and races. Early in the film, Marvin's voice-over informs us that "a strong buck won't hesitate to attack a weaker one and run him out of his territory." Marvin's pronouncement implies an anxiety about changing traditions in the contemporary, assimilated world, and it prompts the question: who, now, is the stronger buck? U.S. hegemony gives the edge to those perceived to dominate by class, race, and gender, who exploit others to maintain a competitive advantage and fatten their own egos and pockets. Yet, as Redroad's hunting metaphor suggests, such notions are antithetical to indigenous tradition. A "real hunter" has respect and reverence for the animal he stalks; he plays fair and assumes his opponent is worthy and strong. A "real hunter," Marvin advises, is "no weekend warrior like your daddy"—emphasizing, again, that Hank is neither an Indian nor a proper U.S. soldier. A "real hunter" is, instead, someone like Tommy Deer in the Water, who always hunts alone and takes only one arrow. "I heard he got so close to one [buck] once," Marvin relates, "he hung some beads around his neck." Hunter, amazed, asks, "Is that true?" Marvin shrugs almost imperceptibly. The story may be entirely apocryphal, but Marvin insists on the lesson: "a good hunter always gives the deer a chance." This becomes one of the rare elements in the film where Redroad resorts to an element of Native mysticism, to the transcendent authority of fables. And yet Tommy Deer in the Water is not a mythological hero but an actual resident in the town, sitting at an adjacent picnic table at the Magik Burger drive-in when Marvin tells Hunter the story. Later, Hunter plays pool with Tommy at the bar. Redroad emphasizes the new realm in which magic and myth operate, one kept alive by traditional Indians like Marvin and Tommy in the midst of a new order. Hank repeatedly blames Marvin for filling the boy's head with nonsense: "there's no magic around here," he objects, "just real life." The distinction, we come to understand, is not so simple.

What rules instead is a persistent divide not between cultures so much as between the powerful and the powerless, a demarcation that still adheres to cultural and racial difference but in much messier ways. In an exchange between Manny and Hank at the start of the film, Hank comments, "damn deer are about to run us out of the state." Manny responds mirthfully, "they ain't exactly endangered, are they?" A thinly veiled metaphor for the eviction of Native Americans from their ancestral homelands, this utterly unironic exchange makes it unclear just which community is being threatened in this new, mixed landscape. Hank's weakness derives from his failure to fulfill the American cultural expectations of honor, service, bravery, and virility. Because Manny did serve in Vietnam, he is ostensibly the stronger buck; but Redroad makes clear just what this power amounts to: he is hopelessly inaccurate with a gun, unable ever to hit his mark. "You couldn't hit water if you fell out of a canoe," his friend teases. It is profoundly significant, then, when Manny finally does hit something: he fires wantonly into the woods and one bullet fatally wounds not a buck but Hank, sleeping in wait, as usual, against a tree. For both the Indian and the white man, methods of hunting are entangled with U.S. militarism: Hank is "dressed like a tree" in camouflage, while Manny shoots blindly into the woods the way he learned to do in war. In a sense, Hank's accidental death is a sober commentary on the United States' constant state of warfare, literal and intercultural, and the alternate blind fury or somatic repression with which it is carried out. The accidental Indian-white duel, then, also exemplifies the "war" within Hunter's own body; the symbology reflects Redroad's acute sense of his mixed heritage as "a new understanding of the term 'at war with one's self.'"[42] Hunter's battle is filtered through the deer, the reification of his hunted self.

In the scene's very opening frames, Marvin's sage voice predicts that this will be a story about a boy who "followed in the deer's footsteps instead of his father's." As the film progresses, Hunter's movements are routinely depicted alongside those of the deer. A montage repeated throughout the film at key moments goes as follows: Hunter races off angrily in his car, speeding into the dark, a close-up on his fuming face from the passenger's seat; quick cuts to a deer running through the forest, and at times we inhabit the buck's point of view as we crash through the darkened woods. Back in the car, we see yellow deer-crossing signs steadily come into view through the windshield, and as we close in on them, we (and Hunter) invariably see that they have been altered, presumably by local kids, to include red blood droplets, or a red cowboy boot, and in the last instance, what appear to be red wings. These sequences repeatedly ally Hunter with the deer he hunts, eliding the tenuous boundary between hunter and hunted. Both are perpetually in flight, running away from something or someone over and over again, and never finding true escape. And yet, the deer signs that mark these circular travels remind us that the deer itself is simply a sign, a signifier. As poststructural theory tells us, the sign has no inherent, immutable relationship to the thing itself; the frequent modifications to the standard deer image indicate the mass-produced symbol's inability to reproduce the reality of the deer. More to the point, these doctored images signify what the deer hunters need and want the deer to be, signifying their control over its image and interpretation and, ideally, its very existence. As an Indian, Hunter's kinship to the deer is always already assumed; he, too, is a fixed stereotype, as superficially rendered and just as vulnerable to misinterpretation, and perpetually under assault and running.

And yet, because it is simply a sign, the deer offers Hunter the perfect screen. In a voice-over late in the movie, Marvin says, "A deer is a perfect hiding machine. It can disappear in any terrain in any season." Hunter learns to disappear too, running away from whatever he cannot handle. Unable to tell Geri about his tainted blood, he flees her bedroom; as she calls out, "Don't run away," the scene cuts quickly to a deer running through the woods. In the next moment, we see Hunter eating a sandwich at the Magik Burger; then, abruptly, we cut back to the racing deer again. Both the deer and Hunter seem to be on an endlessly recoiling loop, through the same woods, down the same roads, back to the same spots in this white, modern world. The Magik Burger, a rural McDonald's of sorts and a quite literal specimen of U.S. consumer culture, retains the word "magik"—misspelled for apparent marketing effect—as if to taunt the Native culture for all it has lost. The deer and Indian are a part of that bastardized, mechanical world that hides the residues of lost "magic" behind its doctored signs. These hiding machines make indigenousness effectively invisible, unseen by a viewing public that cannot bear to view the damage they have wrought.

In what seems at first a disappointingly stereotypical, mystical resolution, Hunter goes on one last epic hunt, equipped with a bow and arrow he and Marvin handcrafted, and with a black mask painted around his eyes and eagle feathers in his long hair. Coming face-to-face with the mythical deer that still wears Tommy Deer in the Water's legendary bead necklace, Hunter is unable to shoot, as if this hunter knows how much he needs the hunted, knows that they are one and the same, and that killing the deer would be like committing suicide. The deer races off, hidden again. Wounded in the pursuit, Hunter pauses to rinse his profusely bleeding hand in a stream where, magically, he finds the deer's beads; he wraps them about his injured hand as if they have the power to stem the dangerous flow of blood. The scene ends, and we have no idea if the magic works. Probably, it doesn't. The next and final scene in the movie opens on a shot of Hunter's hand wrapped not in red beads but a white gauze bandage, knocking on Geri's door. She asks if he is okay, and he cannot answer her through his sudden sobbing. Rather than end the film in such an aching silence, Redroad cuts one last time to an image of a young Hunter in camouflage and shoulder pads, lifting his bow in the air triumphantly.

Shuttling back and forth between magic and Magik, Redroad doesn't allow us to get comfortable in either realm for long. That is Hunter's essential plight, and that of the Native artist generally. When basic visibility and viability are embattled privileges, deer and magic screens are both a necessity and a pitfall; they are a starting point and a roadblock. To establish voice, credibility, and distinctiveness, a certain amount of deer screening must take place; feathers and powwows must appear; authenticity must be displayed satisfactorily in the most essential and rudimentary ways. The problem, ultimately, is that while such narratives imply control and voice beyond what Indians have traditionally enjoyed, at the same time, they force artists to depend above all else on rote stories and symbols that provide temporary balms but not permanent solutions to the global, genocidal casualties wrought by the intrusion and infections of colonization. The Native screen is not just an artistic ploy but a sober postcolonial fact. Perhaps the most dangerous and distasteful implication of such depictions is that they may fulfill white expectations and stereotypes more than defy them, that perhaps after a sustained era of cultural genocide, that is all that is left.[43] As a character in Louis Owens's (Choctaw/Cherokee) Mississippi novel *The Sharpest Sight* admits, "I don't understand how to be Indian anymore. . . . I've been reading books and imagining how it was back then and trying to figure out how to think and act."[44] The incredible difficulty of resituating real Natives in the landscapes that underlie and undermine them is a sober demonstration of the power of narrative to efface even as it manifests.

Add to this the fact that American art, to gain visibility in cultural as well as aesthetic terms, must negotiate the politics of market demand. "Instant pudding" hits like *Dances with Wolves* and *Little Tree* satisfy the public hunger for romanticized, one-dimensional archetypes to warm our hearts and deepen our spiritual reservoirs from a safe, celluloid distance. *The Doe Boy* gives us Magik Burgers that are harder to swallow. For art to be tangled with finances at all signifies a terrible, postcolonial compromise for Indian people. Redroad makes this clear in an early scene that begins with a close-up of Marvin playing a melancholy tune on his handcrafted wooden flute; as the camera pans out slowly, we see Hunter seated beside Marvin on a park bench in town and behind them cars parked along storefronts in the town square. A small red can sits at Marvin's feet; a passerby crosses the screen and bends to place money in the cup before continuing on. This carefully framed scene of commerce cuts quickly to the parking lot of the Magik Burger, where Hunter and Marvin sit in the bed of their truck eating french fries. Marvin wags a fry at Hunter and admits, "your great granddaddy would have disowned me if he saw me playing the flute for a hamburger." *The Doe Boy*, it seems, is Redroad's own Magik Burger, and the past both owns and disowns us no matter what we do.

The lesson of the deer is a difficult one. The Indian hides behind and within it because he has no choice. "Nobody cares how much blood runs through a deer, but everyone wants to know how much blood runs through an Indian," Marvin observes. "It's kinda hard to tell unless you cut one of us open and watch all the stories pour out." It is unclear whether "one of us" includes the deer or simply the Indian community, but Redroad seems to intend such slippages throughout the film. All have stories, and the stories are what constitute Native tradition. These are not stories we listen to, though, but ones we "watch" pour out like blood. As Dean Rader notes, while the power of language and story has always held transformative appeal for Indian cultures, "the site of cultural colonialism and erasure has shifted . . . to the empty expanses of television and movies screens"; so too, I would add, have the most potent and promising methods of resistance.[45] Yet given the totality of colonialism's erasures, such counterefforts have practical limitations. In the space of such expansive silence, Redroad's Indian slips behind the deer screen and refuses to relinquish the little magic and voice he has left after so much has been taken. Even place here represents a loss: Redroad chose to set the film based on his southern boyhood not in the South but in the place where many of the region's evicted Cherokees settled. While the town is officially called Tahlequah, it is known colloquially as "Upper Shit's Creek"—an appropriately generic designation for the "Indian Territory" that received the South's removed tribes after they were driven north and west of the Mississippi River. "Place" as such is decentered from the lives and experiences of these characters for whom "home" has historically been unstable. There is, very literally, no place like home for the Indian in contemporary America.

In the blank spaces of removal and history, artists have the opportunity to rebuild through story: "Not everyone will succeed as a filmmaker, but we all have stories," Redroad declares. "We need to make our own legacy. We're mythmakers. We need to know it could be us—it should be us."[46] As viewers, we watch the stories pour out, and we—like Hunter and the Scarecrow and Redroad himself—must pay no attention to the man behind the curtain. What hides behind the deer screen is yet another casualty of U.S. colonialism—and maybe some magic, too.

NOTES

1. Forrest Carter, *The Education of Little Tree* (1976; Albuquerque: University of New Mexico Press, 2001).

2. Dan T. Carter, *George Wallace: Settin' the Woods on Fire*, directed by Daniel McCabe and Paul Stekler (Arlington, Va.: PBS, 2000). Quote from "Asa Carter," American Experience, PBS, 2000, http://www.pbs.org/wgbh/amex/wallace/peopleevents/pandeo1.html (accessed June 18, 2008). Whether or not Carter had any distant Native ancestry in his family tree has been disputed, but it is at least certain that he was not raised in the culture. For more on Carter's biography, see Dan T. Carter, *The Politics of Rage* (New York: Simon and Schuster, 1995), and "Southern History, American Fiction," in *Rewriting the South: History and Fiction*, ed. Lothar Honnighausen and Valeria Gennaro Lerda, Transatlantic Perspectives 3 (Tubingen: Francke, 1993); Diane McWhorter, *Carry Me Home* (New York: Simon and Schuster, 2001); Calvin Reid, "Widow of 'Little Tree' Author Admits He Changed Identity," *Publisher's Weekly*, October 25, 1991, 16; and Allen Barra, "The Education of Little Fraud," *Salon.com Books*, December 20, 2001, http://www.salon.com/books/feature/2001/12/20/carter (accessed April 1, 2010).

3. In *Politics of Rage*, Wallace biographer Dan T. Carter credits Asa Carter with penning the indelible lines, "Segregation now! Segregation tomorrow! Segregation forever!" in Wallace's 1963 inaugural speech.

4. Barra, "Education of Little Fraud."

5. In addition to *Little Tree*, Carter also wrote a number of popular Westerns, including a "biography" of the Apache Geronimo called *Watch for Me on the Mountain* (New York: Delacorte, 1978). Perhaps his most well-known Western was *The Rebel Outlaw: Josey Wales* (Frankfort, Ky.: Whippoorwill,

1973), with Clint Eastwood playing (in the 1976 film adaptation) the protagonist Josey Wales, whose ecological sagacity includes statements such as "don't piss down my back and tell me it's raining."

6. A handful of critics have uncovered and discussed the novel's underlying racism and white supremacist messages; see especially Eileen Elizabeth O'Connor Antalek, "Deforrestation Begins with a Little Tree: Uncovering the Polemic of Asa Carter in His Novels as Forrest Carter" (master's thesis, Clark University, 1994) and Shari M. Huhndorf, *Going Native: Indians in the American Cultural Imagination* (Ithaca: Cornell University Press, 2001). When Oprah learned the truth about Carter's biography, she stated, "I no longer—even though I had been moved by the story—felt the same about this book. . . . There's a part of me that said, 'Well, OK, if a person has two sides of them and can write this wonderful story and also write the segregation forever speech, maybe that's OK.' But I couldn't—I couldn't live with that." Yet the book remained on her virtual bookshelf of recommended reads (apparently due to an archival error) until late 2007 and even then remained a "wonderful story" in her memory. See Hillel Italie, "The Education of Oprah Winfrey," *Reznet: Reporting from Native America*, University of Montana School of Journalism, 2008, http://www.reznetnews.org/article/ap/education-oprah-winfrey (accessed July 6, 2008).

7. Italie, "Education of Oprah Winfrey."

8. Roger Ebert, for example, suggests that Carter's apparent empathy for the Native American experience might constitute his "redemption" for his prior bigotry. See review of *The Education of Little Tree*, *Rogerebert.com*, January 20, 1998, http://rogerebert.suntimes.com/apps/pbcs.dll/article?aid=/19980120/reviews/801200301/1023 (accessed July 5, 2008). For a Native American response more in tune with Alexie's, see Daniel Heath Justice, "A Lingering Miseducation: Confronting the Legacy of *Little Tree*," *Studies in American Indian Literature* 12, no. 1 (2000): 20–36.

9. JumpStart Media Group, LLC, "Humanitas Prize," *Humanitasprize.org*, 2007, http://www.humanitasprize.org/About_Mission.html (accessed November 24, 2008).

10. Elisabeth Keating, editorial review of *The Education of Little Tree*, *Amazon.com*, http://www.amazon.com/Education-Little-Tree-James-Cromwell (accessed July 6, 2008)

11. Michael Marker, "*The Education of Little Tree*: What It Really Reveals about Public Schools," *Phi Delta Kappan* 74, no. 3 (November 1992): 226.

12. Ibid.

13. Andrew L. Urban, "Education of Little Tree," *Urban Cinefile*, http://www.urbancinefile.com.au/home/view.asp?a=1564&s=Video_files (accessed November 23, 2008).

14. Mardi Gras Indian krewes comprise mainly African American groups from inner-city New Orleans neighborhoods who name their krewes after imaginary nations. The tradition began as a way for blacks to participate as a group in the historically white Mardi Gras festivities in a way that strengthened their cultural ties and solidarity. The official Mardi Gras Indians' Web site explains that the use of Native guises constitutes a gesture of "respect for their assistance in escaping

the tyranny of slavery." Unfortunately, the history of the Mardi Gras Indians has been troubled by "intertribal" competition, antagonism, and violence. For more, see Rick Bragg's editorial on the subject, "Another Battle of New Orleans: Mardi Gras," *New York Times*, February 19, 1995, and the full-length study by Michael P. Smith and Alan B. Govenar, *Mardi Gras Indians* (Gretna, La.: Pelican Books, 1994).

15. Theda Perdue and Michael Green, *The Columbia Guide to American Indians of the Southeast* (New York: Columbia University Press, 2001), 147.

16. Joel W. Martin, "'My Grandmother Was a Cherokee Princess': Representations of Indians in Southern History," in *Dressing in Feathers: The Construction of the Indian in American Popular Culture*, ed. S. Elizabeth Bird (Boulder, Colo.: Westview, 1996), 129.

17. See, for instance, Robert F. Berkhofer, *The White Man's Indian: Images of the American Indian from Columbus to the Present* (New York: Vintage, 1979). According to Homi Bhabha, such stereotypes function within colonial societies as a primary means of control and suppression, a way of identifying the Others and keeping them in their purported place; see "The Other Question," in *The Location of Culture* (New York: Routledge, 1994), 66–84, especially 75–84.

18. Nashville Agrarians, *I'll Take My Stand* (1930; Baton Rouge: Louisiana State University Press, 1978); see, for instance, a number of the contributors' implicit and explicit references to Native Americans as kindred to southerners in their harmonious relationship with nature (John Crowe Ransom, "Reconstructed but Unregenerate," 20; John Gould Fletcher, "Education, Past, and Present," 99–100; Herman Clarence Nixon, "Whither Southern Economy?" 183). The Agrarians also glorify and sanitize the mythology of hardy U.S. settlement (Ransom, "Reconstructed but Unregenerate," 8; Frank Lawrence Owsley, "The Irrepressible Conflict," 71) and refer to themselves (without irony) as "natives" and to northern carpetbaggers as "invaders" (see, for example, Ransom, "Reconstructed but Unregenerate," 23; Nixon, "Whither Southern Economy?" 193). Nixon's nonchalant reference to the time before "Indians departed" (183) strengthens the fiction that the South's succession was natural and ordained. Others have made similar observations about the South's pervasive use of Indian figures and histories, most recently and thoroughly Annette Trefzer in *Disturbing Indians* (Tuscaloosa: University of Alabama Press, 2006).

19. Barry Hannah, *Geronimo Rex* (New York: Penguin, 1972), 231. Displacing such fantasies onto a western rather than a southern context further aids writers such as Hannah (who wrote numerous quasi Westerns) and Forrest Carter (particularly in his ex-Confederate cowboy sensation, *Rebel Outlaw*) in the effort to "affix the romance of the 'frontier' to their region's narrative" and to participate symbolically in a "wild past" (Martin, "My Grandmother," 140).

20. Dominated by the histories and legacies of slavery, Jim Crow, and civil rights, the South and its complicated and conflicting colonial histories do not easily admit Indians into their pages; it is simpler and more common to cast the indigenous story as a national one, with the southern chapter merely underwritten by *federal* removal policies. But this narrative tells only part of the story of

Native American dispossession, and it effectively effaces both the southern colonial prologue and the survival coda. By focusing on the Trail of Tears and removal as the defining tragedy of southeastern Indian experience, and by perpetuating it as a narrative of total erasure, the South obscures the original European exploration and settlement of the region that decimated thousands of individuals by disease and slaughter in the sixteenth century. The South also ignores the subsequent, slow spread of the lucrative plantation economy that converted the economies and the cultures of the remaining Natives and eventuated in the official federal removal of them from the most fertile territories. Thomas Jefferson and Andrew Jackson were the Washington masterminds of these policies, and they were first and foremost southerners and wealthy landowners.

21. In one explicitly symbolic scene, Granpa and Forrest watch as a slow quail is killed by a fierce hawk, which prompts Granpa to counsel: "'Don't feel sad, Little Tree. It is The Way. Tal-con caught the slow and so the slow will raise no children who are also slow. . . . It is The Way. . . . When ye take the deer, do not take the best. Take the smaller and the slower and then the deer will grow stronger and always give you meat" (9). Granpa's Darwinian vision escalates quickly into a rant against greed that begins to sound transparently political: "Only Ti-bi, the bee, stores more than he can use . . . and so he is robbed by the bear, and the 'coon . . . and the Cherokee. It is so with people who store and fat themselves with more than their share. They will have it taken from them. And there will be wars over it . . . and they will make long talks, trying to hold more than their share. They will say a flag stands for their right to do this . . . and men will die because of the words and the flag . . . but they will not change the rules of The Way" (10). Cloaked in stereotypical Indian mysticism, Carter inserts his own fanatical (some might say fascist) tenets of social conservatism. These "wise" revelations in fact come to sound much more like the vengeful philosophies of Josey Wales, Carter's ex-Confederate hero who also happens to be part-Cherokee, determined to find the Union soldiers who killed his family and shattered his quiet farm life in the name of the "flag."

22. As Wilcomb Washburn writes in the foreword to Peter C. Rollins and John E. O'Connor's *Hollywood's Indian* (Lexington: University Press of Kentucky, 1998), "The image of the American Indian, more than that of any other ethnic group, has been shaped by films. Why? Because the characteristics that define the American Indian are dramatically conveyed by this powerful twentieth-century medium . . . no other provides the opportunity to convey that image in a narrative form in terms of rapid physical movement, exotic appearance, violent confrontation, and a spirituality rooted in the natural environment" (ix). Because of its inherent power, Washburn also sees film as instrumental in the "recovery" and "renaissance" of the Indian in the early and mid-twentieth century (ix–x).

23. The evolution of the Indian stereotype in American cinema throughout the twentieth century has been explored in a number of full-length works: Gretchen Bataille and Charles Silet, *The Pretend Indians* (Ames: Iowa State University Press, 1980); Michael Hilger, *From Savage to Nobleman* (Lanham, Md.: Scarecrow, 1995); Rollins and O'Connor, *Hollywood's Indian*; Jacquelyn Kilpat-

rick, *Celluloid Indians* (Lincoln: University of Nebraska Press, 1999); Armando Jose Prats, *Invisible Natives* (Ithaca, N.Y.: Cornell University Press, 2002); and most recently, Angela Aleiss, *Making the White Man's Indian* (Westport, Conn.: Praeger, 2005).

24. Beverly R. Singer, "Native Americans and Cinema: Native Americans in the Movies," *Film Reference*, 2007, http://www.filmreference.com/encyclopedia/Independent-Film-Road-Movies/Native-Americans-and-Cinema-Native-Americans-in-Movies.html (accessed June 30, 2008); Kilpatrick, *Celluloid Indians*, xvii; Brownlow quoted in Aleiss, *Making the White Man's Indian*, xi.

25. Such narratives reinforce the long U.S. tradition of downplaying its colonial past as an exceptional exercise in freedom and democracy. In a 2005 Sunday editorial commemorating the bicentennial of the Lewis and Clark expedition, William T. Vollman suggests that the expedition typified the uniquely American "hunt for happiness" and the unbridled joy of being "free—yes, free!—to rove a rolling land of uncounted possibilities." Vollman brushes off the disturbing implications of this exploration and freedom with a rhetorical shrug of impatience: "Yes," he admits, "we had slavery; we massacred Indians; women lacked the vote; and yes, today our government supports torture . . . but I remain proud of our hopes for ourselves." "Lewis and Clark on the Edge," *New York Times*, November 20, 2005, http://query.nytimes.com/gst/fullpage.html?res=9C06E5D81E3EF933A15752C1A9639C8B63 (accessed April 1, 2010). Vollman's blithe optimism echoes a persistent assumption among Americans that the nation's beneficent ends have ultimately justified its otherwise indefensible means and occasional myopia. What such logic obscures, however, is the fact that while crimes like slavery, removal, and genocide may have finite historical narratives, their epilogues continue to haunt our contemporary lives and plague our brightest hopes.

26. Sherman Alexie, "I Hated Tonto (Still Do)," *Los Angeles Times*, June 28, 1998, http://www.fallsapart.com/tonto.html (accessed April 7, 2009).

27. See Jack D. Forbes, *Africans and Native Americans: The Language of Race and the Evolution of Red-Black Peoples* (Urbana: University of Illinois Press, 1993), and Theda Perdue, *"Mixed Blood" Indians: Racial Construction in the Early South* (Athens: University of Georgia Press, 2005).

28. See Jonathan Bradford Brennan, *When Brer Rabbit Meets Coyote: African–Native American Literature* (Chicago: University of Illinois Press, 2003).

29. Marjorie Baumgarten, "Daughters of the Dust," *Austin Chronicle*, February 14, 1992, http://www.austinchronicle.com/gyrobase/Calendar/Film?Film=oid%3A139192 (accessed November 23, 2008).

30. Ebert, review of *Daughters of the Dust*, *Rogerebert.com*, March 13, 1992, http://rogerebert.suntimes.com/apps/pbcs.dll/article?aid=/19920313/reviews/203130303/1023 (accessed November 23, 2008).

31. Ed Guerrero, *Framing Blackness: The African American Image in Film* (Philadelphia: Temple University Press, 1993), 175.

32. Dash, quoted in Scott MacDonald, *The Garden in the Machine: A Field Guide to Independent Films about Place* (Berkeley: University of California Press, 2001), 302.

33. Ibid.

34. Dash even named her production company "Geechee Girls."

35. Jackie Bissley, "Randy Redroad Takes Indie Route to Success with 'The Doe Boy,'" *Indian Country Today*, February 7, 2002, http://indiancountry.com/content.cfm?id=1013095548 (accessed July 12, 2008).

36. For a comprehensive look at the rise of Native American filmmaking since the 1970s, see Beverly R. Singer's pivotal study of Native American filmmaking, *Wiping the War Paint Off the Lens* (Minneapolis: University of Minnesota Press, 2001); special issue on film and video, *Wicazo Sa Review: Journal of Native American Studies* 16, no. 2; and Sol Worth, *Through Navajo Eyes* (Albuquerque: University of New Mexico Press, 1997).

37. Singer, *Wiping the War Paint*, 61.

38. Jon Bastian, "The Doe Boy," *FilmMonthly.com*, May 30, 2001, http://www.filmmonthly.com/indie/the_doe_boy.html (accessed November 22, 2008).

39. Randy Redroad-Snapp, "Through a Mythic Lens," in *Screenwriting for a Global Market*, ed. Andrew Horton (Berkeley: University of California Press, 2004), 113, 114.

40. Michelle Svenson, "Randy Redroad Interview," *Native Networks, Smithsonian National Museum of the American Indian*, April 2001, http://www.nativenetworks.si.edu/eng/rose/redroad_r_interview.htm#top (accessed July 5, 2008).

41. The condition is also tacitly autobiographical, as Redroad himself suffers from acute asthma.

42. This way of framing hybridity is not new—perhaps most famously, W. E. B. Du Bois in *The Souls of Black Folk* described the plight of the African American in the twentieth century as a kind of vexed "two-ness": "an American, a Negro . . . two warring ideals in one dark body, whose dogged strength alone keeps it from being torn asunder" (New York: Library of America, 1986), 364–65.

43. Native critics are only beginning to acknowledge and explore the paradox of what happens when American Indians, confronted by the demands and desires of white society, are left to "play Indian" themselves. Sherman Alexie illustrates this phenomenon brilliantly in his own 1998 film *Smoke Signals*, adapted from stories he published earlier in *The Lone Ranger and Tonto Fistfight in Heaven* (New York: Atlantic Monthly Press, 1994). On a bus trip to Arizona to retrieve the ashes of his dead father, Alexie's protagonist Victor Joseph tries to teach his quirky, storytelling friend Thomas how to be a "real Indian": his advice consists of a litany of stereotypes gleaned from pop-cultural images of the indigenous warrior, with long, loose hair and a dangerous reticence. "You gotta get stoic," he warns Thomas, or risk being taken advantage of. Such portrayals offer bitter commentaries on the paltry options left for Native Americans whose defense mechanisms consist largely in turning these stereotypes to their own use; as Homi Bhabha has suggested, there *is* space for subversion within the realm of stereotype. See, for example, Bhabha, "The Other Question: Stereotype, Discrimination and the Discourse of Colonialism," in *The Location of Culture* (New York: Routledge, 1994). See also Fergus M. Bordewich, *Killing the White Man's Indian: Reinventing Native Americans at the End of the Twentieth Century* (New York: Anchor Books, 1997).

44. Louis Owens, *The Sharpest Sight* (Norman: University of Oklahoma Press, 1992), 56.

45. Dean Rader, "Word as Weapon: Visual Culture and Contemporary American Indian Poetry," *MELUS: Journal for the Study of the Multi-ethnic Literature of the United States* 27, no. 3 (Autumn 2002), 149.

46. Bissley, "Randy Redroad Takes Indie Route."

The City That *Déjà Vu* Forgot

Memory, Mapping, and the Americanization of New Orleans

Briallen Hopper

In the first Hollywood movie made and set in post-Katrina New Orleans, the Jerry Bruckheimer–Tony Scott action thriller *Déjà Vu* (2006), a spectacular disaster hits the Crescent City. Hundreds of men, women, and children die horribly in the water; corpses float to the surface; and body bags line the streets. Doug Carlin, a New Orleanian federal agent played by Denzel Washington, is angered by the devastation and haunted by the needless death. He risks his life to go back in time and prevent an American tragedy.

Viewers may have the feeling that they've been here before. But the tragedy in *Déjà Vu* isn't a flood. It's a bomb. *Déjà Vu* can't help but dredge up memories of Katrina, but from the beginning, the film works hard to displace Katrina with terrorism—and specifically to displace it with 9/11, the Oklahoma City bombing, and the War on Terror. In the opening scene, a ferryboat full of navy sailors and their families explodes in the Mississippi, thus moving the violent deaths of military personnel from Baghdad to New Orleans. In slow-motion shots echoing the iconic photographs of 9/11, men jump from the upper deck against a backdrop of fire and smoke. Images of the Navy families' blonde children, also killed in the blast, recall the young victims in Oklahoma City, and this allusion is reinforced later when we learn that the explosion's investigators are veterans of the Oklahoma City investigation. The scene's overwriting of Katrina with terrorism is made explicit as a banner on the boat declaring "Katrina Only Made Us Stronger" goes up in flames: the past and present devastation of the flood is first denied with words and then completely consumed by the overwhelming present catastrophe of terrorist violence. As a film about terrorism and time travel that concludes with a dedication to "the strength and enduring spirit of the people of New Orleans," *Déjà Vu* causes us to consider again the vexed relations between national and international memory and geography in the wake of Katrina. What are we to make of *Déjà Vu*'s replacement of Katrina with terrorism? What are the politics of layering Oklahoma City and Baghdad on New Orleans, of superimposing 2001 and 1995 on 2005 and 2006?

Most reviewers of the film answered these questions by saying that there are no answers. They characterize *Déjà Vu*'s attempted engagement with Katrina and terrorism as incoherent and gratuitous: "senseless exploitation," according to David Denby in the *New Yorker*; "grandiloquent pornography," writes Desson Thompson in the *Washington Post*; "a cheap exploitation of current fears," from Pam Grady on *Reel .com*; "a silly, shallow project garbed in pretensions of importance," proclaims Peter Suderman in the *National Review*.[1] The consensus, articulated most scathingly by Nathan Lee in the *Village Voice*, is that the political content of *Déjà Vu* is both superficial and simplistic: "[Director Tony] Scott wouldn't know subtext if it rose out of the bayou and ripped off his arm, but that doesn't stop him from sprinkling on references to Katrina . . . domestic terrorism, and Iraq."[2] Though most reviewers are troubled by *Déjà Vu*'s political allusions, Manohla Dargis claims the film reaches such an extreme of gratuitous exploitation that it becomes harmless and inoffensive. As she writes in the *New York Times*: "'Déjà Vu' is more removed from reality than most of [Bruckheimer and Scott's] collaborations, which makes their exploitation of Sept. 11, Katrina, and Oklahoma City . . . less offensive than it might in a film that bore some relation to the real world. . . . 'Déjà Vu' is so wildly divorced from the here and the now of contemporary politics, policy and people that it's impossible to get worked up by its invocation of these three calamities."[3] Echoing Dargis, Kenneth Turan observes in the *Los Angeles Times*, "What is interesting is not how little sense *Déjà Vu* makes, but how little that matters"; it's a film "that nobody should be thinking about too hard."[4]

The critics are partly right. *Déjà Vu* is a problematic movie that attempts (sometimes unsuccessfully) to invest its enormous explosions with equally immense emotional and political meaning. But unlike Dargis, I believe that *Déjà Vu*'s politics bear a striking and worrying relation to "the here and the now of contemporary politics, policy and people," and thus, unlike Turan, I believe *Déjà Vu* is worth thinking about quite hard. Katrina and the War on Terror remain ongoing crises with a disputed yet high-stakes relation to each other, and popular articulations of their relationships matter. As 9/11 and Katrina continue to vie for status as "defining national tragedy" in the U.S. political imaginary, a battle for meaning is being waged on many cultural fronts, notably film. Spike Lee's 2006 masterpiece *When the Levees Broke* suggests a zero-sum relationship between the rebuilding of New Orleans and the waging of the War on Terror, as the U.S. government resources that by rights should rebuild the U.S. Gulf Coast are invested in a Gulf War instead. Carl Deal and Tia Lessin's award-winning 2008 documentary *Trouble the Water* takes this logic to its inexorable life-and-death conclusion; in a memorable scene, a woman who survived Katrina sternly admonishes her son: "You're not going to fight for a country that does not give a damn about you."[5] But these acclaimed premium cable and art-house documentaries compete for interpretive authority with popular fictional filmic representations such as Fox's 2007 series *K-Ville*, in which a New Orleanian criminal is able to escape from prison during Katrina's chaos and subsequently finds redemption as a soldier in Afghanistan. In *K-Ville*, both Katrina and the War on Terror become occasions for the liberation of individual U.S. citizens. On a grander scale than *K-Ville*, *Déjà Vu* works to forge a naturalized, positive, and coherent connection between Katrina and the War on Terror, using New Orleans as a place to reimagine and defend the U.S. domestic and foreign policy of the Bush era to a mass audience.

In making New Orleans the place to think about the relationship of the United States to the rest of the world, *Déjà Vu* both perpetuates and departs from long-standing Hollywood tradition. *Jezebel* (1938) draws frightening parallels between antebellum New Orleans and the "antebellum" political geography of pre–World War II Europe. *Suddenly, Last Summer* (1959) makes New Orleans the setting for a parable about how the American desire for eternal innocence and stasis is predicated on the victimization and consumption of international others (a vision of the city that is evoked less critically in the 1994 film *Interview with the Vampire*). In *Easy Rider* (1969), New Orleans enables a cosmopolitan and carnivalesque critique of the violent Vietnam-era patriotism that the film locates in the rural South. Making imaginative use of the mixed resonances of the city—described by Kristen Silva Gruesz as "contamination, backwardness, and danger on the negative spectrum; romance, exoticism, and sensual pleasure on the positive"—these films ground their critical international perspective with their insistence on New Orleans's foreignness: its unique status as a microcosm within U.S. borders.[6]

In contrast, *Déjà Vu* represents an unambiguously "American" New Orleans, avoiding both ends of the spectrum that Gruesz describes. Geographically, in a kind of paradoxical hyperdomestication, *Déjà Vu* remaps New Orleans both locally and internationally, redrawing the city's borders to keep out the Ninth Ward and the "Third World," and then locating New York, Oklahoma City, and an Americanized international War on Terror within these new city limits. Temporally, through the metaphors of time travel and (naturally) déjà vu, the film articulates a mode and politics of remembering Katrina in relation to other events in national time. Just as it replaces Katrina with 9/11, *Déjà Vu* replaces nostalgia with déjà vu as the defining structure of memory in a time-travel film, advocating a mode of remembering that effaces rather than emphasizes temporal and geographic difference. Partly imposing its ideology on the city, partly relying on and shaped by the city's unique identity and history for its authority and affect, *Déjà Vu* remaps, remembers, and Americanizes New Orleans.

The Americanization of New Orleans

Déjà Vu is an American story set in New Orleans for reasons having everything and nothing to do with the city itself. The film was initially conceived in the early 2000s as a star vehicle for Denzel Washington, and the plot was established long before its setting was decided. Washington would play Doug Carlin, a federal investigator working on a major case of domestic terrorism. Falling in love with the beautiful corpse of one of the victims, he would be inspired to use government-funded satellite surveillance technology to see, and ultimately to change, the past. He would travel back in time to fight terrorism and to save the life of the woman whose corpse he had come to love.

The search for a setting for *Déjà Vu* began long before Katrina, and it did not begin in New Orleans. Director Tony Scott, aesthetically averse to computer-generated special effects, was always committed to blowing up a real ferry with hundreds of barrels of gasoline in a real port, and New York—his overdetermined first choice of a setting for domestic terrorism—refused to risk the environmental and safety hazard posed by the explosion. Other cities were uncooperative as well. In the end, only New Orleans felt the money the film would bring in was worth the havoc it might cause. *Déjà Vu* was still in the preproduction stage when Katrina hit, and after the storm the filmmakers decided to keep the story and the filming in New Orleans and to rewrite the plot to accommodate the city's recent history. The decision to stay in New Orleans was a matter of pride for many involved with the film, although when production began there was some concern that the ferry explosion might cause the Mississippi to breach its banks once again. The city government gave Scott the go-ahead anyway.[7]

From its inception, then, *Déjà Vu* was intended to be a story about terrorism in the United States, with New Orleans as its accidental yet inevitable location. Chosen by reason of its poverty and its government's consequently lax attention to its inhabitants' safety, New Orleans was the only place this narrative of American terror could be set in 2005. Thus, the exceptionalism of New Orleans and the prehistory of Katrina were implicit in the film's setting from the beginning. But to remain a film primarily about the unique and unparalleled nature of the threat of terrorism on U.S. soil, this local specificity had to remain implicit. *Déjà Vu* needed to create a sense of New Orleans as quintessentially American—as a site of national rather than local color. It had to represent its imagined post-Katrina, pre-terrorist-attack New Orleans as a familiar, antediluvian, even prelapsarian place.

When *Déjà Vu* was released, New Orleanians struggled to recognize the city it represented as their own. "The chief disappointment is how little the flavor of New Orleans permeates the film. Despite the shots of the ferry landings, the French Quarter, the streetcars and other local touchstones, 'Déjà vu' feels as if it could have been shot anywhere," mourned Michael H. Kleinschrodt in the *New Orleans Times-Picayune*.[8] This "anywhere" accurately describes the uncanny unplaceability of the New Orleans in the film—an unplaceability expressed not just in the absence of any sense of complexity or flux in the depiction of the city's life but also in the deracinated quality of the tourist touchstones that are pointedly included. There are many such "Old New Orleans" cameos. Satchmo, ferries, a brass band playing "When the Saints Go Marching In," streetcars, Mardi Gras, and jazz funerals are all referenced in the film. *Déjà Vu* has everything but chicory coffee. But each of these gestures at city-by-synecdoche is perfunctory and static, emptied of movement or function. We see Louis Armstrong as a statue frozen in time on the Algiers dock and as a mural on a wall, but never hear his music. The ferry never reaches its destination, and New Orleanian native Doug Carlin rides the streetcar merely to pass the time, not to get anywhere. We see the trash sitting in the streets after the first post-Katrina Mardi Gras, but not the anger and vitality of the celebration itself, which was unforgettably documented by Spike Lee. We are told that Claire Kuchever (Paula Patton), the dead woman Carlin loves, enjoyed jazz funerals, but her own funeral is a quiet gathering by the graveside, according to usual Hollywood convention. The faint sound of the New Orleans brass band at the beginning of the film is drowned almost immediately by the film's doom-laden, preexplosion soundtrack.

These immediately emptied gestures at a universally familiar, static New Orleans are best exemplified by the film's empty yet emphatic insistence on Doug Carlin's status as a New Orleanian native son. Early in the investigation, FBI agent Paul Pryzwarra (Val Kilmer) explains to Carlin why it is crucial that he be assigned to the investigation: "You're local; you know the people; you know the area." But unlike one of Denzel's earlier detectives, Ezekiel "Easy" Rawlins in *Devil in a Blue Dress* (1995), whose skill as a crime solver is an expression of his embeddedness in a richly represented black Los Angeles, Carlin is a character without a neighborhood, a family, a history, or any world outside of his work. His supposed familiarity with the people and the area is never referred to or relevant again, and the only sign of his connection to New Orleans is his Dillard baseball cap.

By making reference to New Orleans icons every American tourist is familiar with while failing to represent any aspect of the city that would be foreign to a general American audience—even something as simple and quotidian as using a streetcar as public transportation—*Déjà Vu* represents New Orleans as a comfortably and recognizably U.S. city far removed from pre- or post-Katrina reality. This representation has profound political implications. *Déjà Vu*'s domesticated version of the city can be read as symptomatic of the much broader cultural move to Americanize (or re-Americanize) New Orleans in the wake of the storm. The widespread post-Katrina effort to characterize the city as unambiguously and even quintessentially American, and specifically the highly charged insistence that victims and survivors of the storm were "citizens" rather than "refugees," was a well-intentioned but troubling choice that made unlikely bedfellows of Spike Lee and George W. Bush.

The ambivalence implicit in this hypernationalist terminology can be read in David Dante Troutt's *After the Storm: Black Intellectuals Explore the Meaning of Hurricane Katrina* (2006), which begins with a powerful epigraph from an interview with New Orleanian Sharon White, speaking from a shelter in Baton Rouge: "I am not a 'refugee.' I wasn't shipped here. . . . We are not refugees. You hold your head up. We are United States citizens, and you be proud of that. A lot of us are taxpaying, honest, hardworking people. I'm like, when did I come from another country? That's what they used to call people that was in the boats, and that was sneaking over here."[9] The binary that White sets up, in which residents of New Orleans must claim attention and respect at the expense of un-American others, is undermined later in the book in an essay by Adrien Katherine Wing, who argues that people like Sharon White might have been better served if they had been refugees under the jurisdiction of the International Convention on Civil and Political Rights or the International Convention on the Elimination of Race Discrimination rather than U.S. citizens under the jurisdiction of the Constitution.[10] Wai Chee Dimock and Anna Brickhouse demonstrate how the Americanization of post-Katrina New Orleans obfuscated the Caribbean, trans-American, and global connections the storm uncovered and suppressed the insights that the early recourse to the terms "refugees" and "Third World" had consciously or unconsciously expressed.[11]

Richard Iton eloquently and economically expresses the cost of this Americanization and suggests better alternatives: "After some public debate, it would be decided that 'refugees' was not the correct term but rather 'displaced persons.' But by that time it did not matter, as the positions had been staked out. Who are they, where do they belong, where did they come from, on one side. From here, and only here, on the other. Not a thickly cosmopolitan 'we are from here *and* there' or an existentialist 'from nowhere *just like you*' but 'from here and only here.'"[12] Iton's "here *and* there" and "from nowhere *just like you*" gesture at the missed utopian possibilities ("utopian," literally "no place") in post-Katrina geographic rhetoric—the transnational connections that were glimpsed only to be immediately dismissed. *Déjà Vu*'s "here and only here" version of New Orleans demonstrates as much as any post-Katrina text the losses inherent in claiming an unequivocal Americanness for the city, however politically necessary this move might seem. Though Spike Lee and Sharon White characterized New Orleans as unexceptionally "American" to gain sympathy and justice for the survivors of the storm, *Déjà Vu* shows how an insistence on the Americanness (or lack of foreignness) of New Orleans also serves to erase the dramatic "Third World" inequality and cultural difference that Katrina revealed. Ultimately, the Americanization of New Orleans in *Déjà Vu* allows the film to erase and radically rewrite the story of the storm.

Remapping and Remembering Katrina

In *Déjà Vu*, New Orleans is not a drowned city evoking Caribbean hurricanes and Asian tsunamis, but the wounded national site of terrorism with which all Americans can easily identify ("We are all New Orleanians"). But in the process of this Americanization, as Iton suggests, the city Katrina revealed must be forgotten, its geography remapped. For New Orleans to achieve national status, Katrina must be recapitulated, rewritten.

Déjà Vu effaces Katrina most obviously by representing New Orleans as much smaller than it actually is (or was). The New Orleans of *Déjà Vu* consists almost entirely of the French Quarter and Uptown, locally and colloquially known as "the Sliver by the River" and "the Isle of Denial"—and denial is a key term here. These are the parts of the city that were not as deeply affected by Katrina, and the film's focus allows viewers to avoid the sight of storm damage. More metaphorically, the elaborate surveillance and time-travel system at the center of the film's plot "sees" only the center of the city and not the outer wards. Much of the film takes place in a control room, in which Doug Carlin, Paul Pryzwarra, and other investigators navigate giant screens displaying images of the city. Through science-fiction satellite technology, they are able to see crystalline digital footage of the city from four and a half days before. Using joysticks, they can quickly pan out for an overview, then zoom in on a house or phone booth that might be important to the crime, seeing through walls and even getting close enough to read Claire's diary. But the investigators' incredible powers of surveillance fail as soon as the person they are watching leaves the French Quarter: the screen goes black and an error message informs them that the subject is "out of range." The newly constricted borders of New Orleans are thus doubly demarcated both by what the film shows and what the surveillance technology knows (and does not know). In this remapping and shrinking of the city, the film refuses to see the parts of the city devastated by the storm.

Déjà Vu resolutely denies the extent of the damage in other important ways as well, even within the narrow city limits it sets. This denial was a conscious decision on the part of the filmmakers. In the DVD extras, producer Bruckheimer comments, "It's kinda sad that the media's kinda playing up the destruction," and insists that the only inconvenience he encountered in post-Katrina New Orleans was the scarcity of readily available dry-cleaning services. In contrast to "the media," *Déjà Vu* downplays the destruction. The filmmakers even invisibly towed a nonfunctioning streetcar to make it look as if the streetcars were running.[13] As Kleinschrodt writes, "Scott . . . missed a great opportunity to use the realities of post-Katrina life to heighten the tension of his story. The characters never have trouble finding a working telephone or getting a cell phone signal. The electricity never cuts off at an inopportune time. No vital street signs are missing. All businesses are open."[14] But *Déjà Vu*'s most egregious erasure of Katrina's effects is the absence of any human beings affected by the storm. Viewers never once see a survivor of Katrina, or hear about one. A brief helicopter-view shot of the ruins of the Ninth Ward recapitulates George W. Bush's flight over the devastation, but in human terms it is as if Katrina never happened.

The human story of Katrina is further obfuscated by *Déjà Vu*'s revisionist narratives of class and race. New Orleans is one of the nation's poorest cities, but there are no poor people in the film, with the exception of the terrorist. New Orleans is also one of America's blackest and most segregated cities, but the film racially recasts (and recastes) its story to undo the connections between racism and poverty that many observed in Katrina's aftermath. This recasting begins with the character of Claire, whose corpse is found in the river after the explosion at the beginning of the film. Claire both evokes and replaces the archetypal black female Katrina victim who has come to stand in for both the city and the storm. Judith Jackson Fossett describes this figure as follows: "Her evolution . . . finds its most potent embodiment in the contemporary welfare mother, filling the city's derelict public-housing projects with illegitimate children. During the storm, she clung helplessly to nearly submerged rooftops or yelled loudly from the chaos of the convention center. The storm had become a racialized and feminized anthropomorphism, serving up its own black female population as fuel for civic degradation."[15] In contrast to these ubiquitous media images of poor, dark-skinned black women, Claire, the black female victim in *Déjà Vu*—a victim of terrorism, not Katrina—is a middle-class, light-skinned, and racially indeterminate (though presumably Creole) woman who lives in the French Quarter. A quintessentially beautiful corpse who neither clings nor yells, Claire rewrites Katrina's connections between victimhood, class, and color.

The film's racial and class recasting extends to both villains and heroes as well: the terrorist, who lives in the Ninth Ward, is white, while Denzel, the representative of the federal government, is a dark-skinned black man. But racial terms and even racial awareness are strenuously and carefully avoided in *Déjà Vu* even when they would typically come up in real life: for example, when the police are describing a dead black body or when a white man is answering a question about what a black man looks like. Both Claire and Doug have white best friends, and this is again taken for granted. There is no race consciousness or residential or social segregation in this post-Katrina New Orleans. The film's recasting and remapping allows viewers to revise the racial and economic story of Katrina and even, by extension, of the South: Claire's Creole father lives uptown in a large white house with columns, while the white terrorist lives in a trailer in the Ninth Ward, and a dark black New Orleanian is the face of the federal government.

The casting of Denzel Washington as a federal agent has political resonance beyond race. A warm and serious screen presence, Denzel as Doug rewrites the federal government's response to Katrina, turning the government into something to be trusted and even loved, and thus providing it with a measure of emotional redemption. Doug's intense and intimate concern for Claire—we see him talking with her family, hearing her life story, carrying her photograph, reading her diary, attending her funeral, and risking his life for her, all in his role as a caring representative of the federal government—makes the government seem self-sacrificially obsessed with the well-being of the disaster victims. As Claire's father says when he hands Doug a photograph of his daughter, "I want her to matter to you." Kanye West, angered by the federal response to Katrina, said that George Bush didn't care about black people. Doug Carlin portrays the government as an embodiment of care.

Déjà Vu's emotionally redemptive revision of the federal response to the suffering of black New Orleanians complements its representation of the government as reliable and heroic at every level. In contrast to the real-life government response to Katrina, the government response to the fictional ferry explosion is instant, efficient, and effective. Federal, state, and local agencies appear on the scene immediately, and billions of dollars are instantly invested in addressing the crisis. The Bureau of Alcohol, Tobacco, and Firearms; Emergency Medical Services; the New Orleans

Police Department; the Coast Guard; the Federal Bureau of Investigation; the National Transportation Safety Board: all make a prompt appearance. Many real government workers were cast as extras to "play themselves" in the film—real responders to a fake disaster, when many of these agencies did not respond adequately to the real disaster. The lavish and competent government response to the disaster in the film rewrites the government's response to Katrina to an overcompensatory degree.

The Americanization of the War on Terror

Déjà Vu's revisionary history of the Bush administration extends beyond Katrina and its aftermath to reenvision the War on Terror. This is true at the most fundamental level of plot. Structurally, *Déjà Vu* is like *Rambo*: a film about a lone government representative who single-handedly saves Americans in distress to symbolically and retroactively win a lost war. Just as Rambo symbolically wins the Vietnam War by rescuing American POW's, Doug Carlin symbolically wins the War on Terror by rescuing Claire and preventing a 9/11-style attack. But *Déjà Vu* engages with the War on Terror in more local ways as well: it domesticates the War on Terror, as it does for post-Katrina New Orleans, by setting it entirely within the small borders of this newly Americanized New Orleans, and hence within a knowable and controllable place. This domestication is a geographic fiction that makes manageable the real out-of-control proliferation of war fronts in Iraq, Afghanistan, Pakistan, and elsewhere.

Déjà Vu also Americanizes the war ideologically. The terrorist is not a foreigner but an U.S. citizen, an athletic, handsome, patriotic, white Christian who blows up the ferry as an act of revenge against the military because he kept trying to enlist and was turned down on the grounds of psychological instability. (It is hard to believe that today's all-volunteer army would turn him away.) Making the terrorist a white Christian may avoid racist clichés about Arabs and Muslims, but it also has the effect of saying that there is no ideology outside U.S. patriotism and its variants. And the fact that the terrorist is an insane person acting alone portrays anti-American sentiment as an individual aberration rather than an expression of a worldview supported by millions of people. *Déjà Vu* thus reduces the present realities of global terrorism to an isolated individual story reminiscent of Theodore Kaczynski or Timothy McVeigh. This Americanization of the War on Terror makes it seem containable, comprehensible, and winnable.

But perhaps the most immediate and dangerous way *Déjà Vu* engages with the War on Terror is by justifying government surveillance on private citizens. At the center of its plot is the surveillance machine turned time machine. The investigators in the film routinely spy and eavesdrop on U.S. citizens who are not criminals or suspected of any crime. The sole woman on the investigative team objects when her male colleagues watch Claire take a shower, but no one objects when they read her diaries or listen in on her phone calls. There is never any sense that government agents need permission to look at anything or that they are violating civil liberties. As *Déjà Vu*'s screenwriter Bill Marsilii explains in the DVD extras, "All these things that would normally be considered incredible invasions of privacy are actually necessary."[16] Total surveillance on ordinary U.S. citizens in their homes is represented as both glamorous and effective, a thrillingly high-tech practice guaranteed to catch terrorists and prevent terrorism. Its morality and legality are taken for granted.

Déjà Vu's defense of surveillance-based national security was ominously prescient. Less than a year after *Déjà Vu* was released, the *New York Times* reported that a satellite surveillance system like the one in the film had been proposed by the Department of Homeland Security: "Congress already has had to head off the homeland department's plan to create its own spy satellite program for tracking threats from nature, terrorists, and illegal intruders. Lawmakers were rightly wary that it was yet another way for this administration to invade citizens' privacy and mangle civil liberties."[17] Like *Déjà Vu*, the Bush-era Department of Homeland Security sought to create a connection between natural disasters, terrorism, and border crossings. And like *Déjà Vu*, it characterized legalized surveillance as the universal response to this triple threat.

Do You Know What It Means to Miss Nostalgia? *Déjà Vu* and Time Travel

The Bush administration's fantasy of using surveillance technology to control the future seems only marginally less fantastic than Doug Carlin's desire to use surveillance technology to change the past. Carlin's heroism lies in his refusal to accept the reality of the terrible event that has happened. Lesser men might mourn or reflect, but Carlin turns confidently to technology, and it does not disappoint him. Technology allows him to attack terrorists before they attack him. The time machine is preemptive warfare. It is Bush Doctrine in a box.

In fact, *Déjà Vu*'s internal logic requires that the surveillance machine turn into a time machine, because there is no other way to resolve the film's politics of violence. *Déjà Vu* wants to insist on the shocking reality of death and destruction (the ferryboat is really on fire, and the stunt performers jumping from its deck are really on fire as well; those burning bodies are not computer generated) while utterly undermining its finality and denying the possibility of real loss. The only heroic and virtuous response to violence in *Déjà Vu* is to insist, against all evidence, that everything will eventually be okay. In the DVD commentary on the ferry explosion scene, screenwriter Marsilii defends the troubling proliferation of violent images with time-travel logic: "I don't think I could ever open a movie this way if I didn't know that somehow we were gonna save everybody at the end."[18] Marsilii's insistence on happy endings no matter what echoes George W. Bush's steadfastly sunny statement in Mobile, Alabama, on September 2, 2005: "The good news is—and it's hard for some to see it now—that out of this chaos is going to come a fantastic Gulf Coast, like it was before."[19] Both Marsilii and Bush subscribe to the philosophy contained in the Beach Boys song that plays during the final scenes of *Déjà Vu*: "Don't worry, baby, everything will turn out all right."

Déjà Vu dramatizes the political philosophy and praxis of the Bush administration, which demanded a kind of public memory that functioned like time travel. As Charles Tryon argues, "for the time traveler, *no event is final until we get it right*. In other words, through the logic of time travel, traumatic events can be rewritten in order to produce a de-traumatized historical narrative."[20] International critics were more attuned than U.S. critics to *Déjà Vu*'s posttraumatic revisioning of national disaster. The British critic Peter Bradshaw named 9/11 as "the major trauma that this movie is, in its way, clearly trying to heal"; more tartly, his colleague Philip French observed, "A pity the Pentagon and State Department can't use this machine to revisit 2003 and remedy their disastrous errors."[21]

The government may not have had a time machine, but it was able to use the machinery of the media to achieve similar ends. Like *Déjà Vu*, the closing months of the Bush administration became a time to both rewrite and deny historical trauma through technology. When the levees were breached in 2005, President Bush was at John McCain's birthday party eating cake, but the fortuitous timing of Hurricane Gustav during the 2008 Republican National Convention allowed for this history to be overwritten on national TV. "It just wouldn't be appropriate to have a festive occasion while a near tragedy or a terrible challenge is presented in the form of a natural disaster," McCain told the press in August 2008, explaining why the Republican Party had decided to cancel many convention events.[22] Like the ferry explosion in the film, the real-world déjà vu experience of yet more hurricanes in the Gulf states gave the Republican establishment a second chance to prove itself to be spectacularly sensitive and humane in response to disaster.

If the Republican reaction to Gustav sought to overwrite the shameful aspects of the Katrina narrative, Bush's exit interviews in January 2008 simply denied them. In a press conference a week before leaving office, Bush explained why if he had to do it all over again he would do exactly the same thing:

> I thought long and hard about Katrina. You know, could I have done something differently, like land Air Force One either in New Orleans or Baton Rouge? . . . The problem with that and—is that law enforcement would have been pulled away from the mission, and then your questions, I suspect, would have been, "How could you possibly have flown Air Force One into Baton Rouge, and police officers that were needed to expedite traffic out of New Orleans were taken off the task to look after you?" . . . People said, "Well, the federal response was slow." Don't tell me the federal response was slow when there was 30,000 people pulled off roofs right after the storm passed.[23]

In his widely broadcast revisionist narrative of the government's response to Katrina, Bush seemingly took the uncanny repetitiveness of the experience of déjà vu as his model for public memory. When asked to acknowledge his own responsibility and to demonstrate change over time, Bush told a story in which there was no other option except to repeat what he had already done. If given the chance to travel back in time now, he would fly over the devastation once again. He would insist, once again, that the federal government was doing a "heckuva job." In his last days as president, Bush misleadingly mapped his own need for a blameless present onto a detraumatized past.

Bush's exit interviews illuminate the political significance of the filmmakers' surprising choice of déjà vu rather than nostalgia as the defining trope in their time-travel film. Time-travel narratives are almost always by definition nostalgic; most time-travel films express a desire for a lost world that existed in the past. No place has generated more nostalgia than New Orleans, and one would expect a time-travel film made in New Orleans in 2006 to be overwhelmingly nostalgic. But by representing post-Katrina New Orleans as exactly the same as pre-Katrina New Orleans, *Déjà Vu* performs a trick of false memory. By equating the present with the past, the film denies, as Bush did in 2005 and 2008, any history of shame, any possibility of irrevocable loss.

Déjà Vu's refusal of nostalgia is thus an expression of its refusal to acknowledge the past. Nostalgia has been famously criticized by Frederic Jameson for its conservative tendencies, and fictions of the U.S. South have supplied some of the most troubling examples of imperialist nostalgia. But even in its most imperialist forms, nostalgia always offers an implicit critique of the status quo. For better and worse, as Tryon argues, "nostalgia must be understood as a profound dissatisfaction with the present." Tara McPherson's work on the South in cultural memory shows how nostalgia "can function as a wedge to introduce a critical distance into cultural practices and cultural theory"—how it can enable "mobility or revisioning" as well as "reaction and stasis." But unlike nostalgia, which can be a conscious critical practice and an escape from critique, déjà vu is an involuntary and false memory that effaces temporal and spatial difference.[24]

"Katrina brain" and "Katrina time" entered the language in 2005. "Katrina brain" means a momentary lapse of memory, and the term and the phenomenon were ubiquitous in the city in the months after Katrina.[25] New Orleanians were forgetting common words, forgetting to pick their kids up after school, forgetting how to get home. "Katrina time" refers to the long delays prisoners had waiting for trial as the justice system slowed to a standstill. In the midst of all the other loss, there was lost time as well, and lost memory, forgetting and being forgotten. Déjà vu as a model of memory is symptomatic of posttraumatic New Orleans. Like Katrina brain, déjà vu is an involuntary slip of memory. Like Katrina time, it is the experience of the passage of time without narrative development or change. It is the perfect mapping of present and past in one static repeated event. *Déjà Vu* puts its own lapsed and lost memory in the service of a revisionist national narrative.

NOTES

1. David Denby, "Déjà Vu," *New Yorker*, December 18, 2006, http://www.newyorker.com/arts/reviews/film/deja_vu_scott (accessed February 12, 2009); Desson Thompson, "Déjà Vu," *Washington Post*, June 10, 2008, http://www.washingtonpost.com/gog/movies/deja-vu,1123978.html (accessed February 12, 2009); Pam Grady, "Déjà Vu," *Reel.com*, June 3, 2008, http://www.reel.com/movie.asp?mid=142826&buy=closed&Tab=reviews&cid=13 (accessed February 12, 2009); Peter Suderman, "Doin' the Time Warp Again: *Déjà Vu* and *The Fountain* go back and forth," *National Review Online*, November 22, 2006, http://article.nationalreview.com/?q=ZjkyNmE4OTZhMGZlMzFhNWNlNWFi MjNiZmUwYjU3OWY= (accessed February 12, 2009).

2. Nathan Lee, "Tony Scott, Trailblazer: Despite the Title and Familiar Genre, Mr. Explosion Says Something New," *Village Voice*, November 14, 2006, http://www.villagevoice.com/2006-11-14/film/tony-scott-trailblazer/ (accessed February 12, 2009).

3. Manohla Dargis, "After a Big Bad Boom, Clues Lead Anywhere, Even Back in Time," *New York Times*, November 22, 2006, http://movies.nytimes.com/2006/11/22/movies/22deja.html (accessed February 12, 2009).

4. Kenneth Turan, "'Déjà Vu': Beneath the Average Potboiler Façade of 'Déjà Vu' Lies Classic Noir," *Los Angeles Times*, November 22, 2006, http://www.calendarlive.com/printedition/calendar/cletdejavu22nov22,0,4649918.story (accessed February 12, 2009).

5. Judith Orr, "Trouble the Water," *Socialist Review*, December 2008, http://www.socialistreview.org.uk/article.php?articlenumber=10648 (accessed February 12, 2009).

6. Kristen Silva Gruesz, "The Gulf of Mexico System and the 'Latinness' of New Orleans," *American Literary History* 18, no. 3 (2006): 468.

7. Bruckheimer, Jerry, Tony Scott, and Bill Marsilii, "Audio Commentary Track," *Déjà Vu*, DVD, directed by Tony Scott (Burbank, Calif.: Touchstone Pictures, 2006).

8. Michael H. Kleinschrodt, "Entertaining 'Déjà Vu,' Filmed in New Orleans, Tops the List of Six Thanksgiving Movies Opening Today," *New Orleans Times-Picayune*, November 22, 2006, Louisiana Film and Television, http://www.lafilm.org/media/index.cfm?id=862 (accessed February 12, 2009).

9. David Dante Troutt, ed. *After the Storm: Black Intellectuals Explore the Meaning of Hurricane Katrina* (New York: New Press, 2006), book epigraph.

10. Adrien Katherine Wing, "From Wrongs to Rights: Hurricane Katrina from a Global Perspective," in Troutt, *After the Storm*, 133.

11. Wai Chee Dimock, afterword to *ESQ: A Journal of the American Renaissance* 50 (February 2006): 226; Anna Brickhouse, "'L'Ouragan de Flammes' ('The Hurricane of Flames'): New Orleans and Transamerican Catastrophe, 1866/2005," *American Quarterly* 59, no. 4 (2007): 1097–1127.

12. Richard Iton, *In Search of the Black Fantastic: Politics and Popular Culture in the Post–Civil Rights Era* (New York: Oxford University Press, 2008), 285.

13. Bruckheimer, Scott, and Marsilii, "Audio Commentary Track."

14. Kleinschrodt, "Entertaining 'Déjà Vu.'"

15. Judith Jackson Fossett, "Sold Down the River," *PMLA* 122, no. 1 (2007): 328.

16. Bruckheimer, Scott, and Marsilii, "Audio Commentary Track."

17. "Homeland Bunkers and Alien Litterbugs," editorial, *New York Times*, October 13, 2007, http://www.nytimes.com/2007/10/13/opinion/13sat3.html (accessed February 12, 2009).

18. Bruckheimer, Scott, and Marsilii, "Audio Commentary Track."

19. Office of the White House Press Secretary, "President Arrives in Alabama, Briefed on Hurricane Katrina," September 2, 2005, http://www.tornadochaser.net/president_02.html (accessed March 31, 2010).

20. Charles Tryon, "Time Lapse: The Politics of Time-Travel Cinema," (PhD diss., Purdue University, 2002), 6.

21. Peter Bradshaw, "Déjà vu," *Guardian*, December 15, 2006. http://www.guardian.co.uk/film/2006/dec/15/denzelwashington.actionandadventure (accessed March 31, 2010); Philip French, "Déjà Vu," *Guardian*, December 17, 2006, http://www.guardian.co.uk/film/2006/dec/17/thriller.sciencefictionandfantasy (accessed March 31, 2010).

22. Ewen MacAskill, "Hurricane Gustav: Republican Convention Thrown into Crisis," *Guardian*, September 1, 2008.

23. "ABC, CBS Report Bush's Defense of Katrina Response without Noting Congressional Criticism," *Media Matters for America*, January 13, 2009, http://mediamatters.org/research/200901130019 (accessed March 10, 2010).

24. Frederic Jameson, *Postmodernism, or the Cultural Logic of Late Capitalism* (Durham, N.C.: Duke University Press, 1991); Tryon, "Time Lapse," 5; Tara McPherson, *Reconstructing Dixie: Race, Gender, and Nostalgia in the Imagined South* (Durham, N.C.: Duke University Press, 2003), 9–10.

25. Tony Freemantle, "New Orleans Struggles to Its Feet," *Houston Chronicle*, August 27, 2006, http://www.chron.com/disp/story.mpl/front/4142554.html (accessed February 12, 2009).

Humid Time

Independent Film, Gay Sexualities, and Southernscapes

R. Bruce Brasell

Independent feature-length fictional filmmaking is a relatively recent phenomenon in the southeastern United States, one that opens an avenue of self-representation different from Hollywood. In the 1980s Ross McElwee and Victor Nuñez were hailed as regional southern voices, McElwee in the area of documentary film and Nuñez in fiction film. Nuñez's position as the premier southern audiovisual fictional storyteller solidified in the 1990s with the release of *Ruby in Paradise* (1993) and *Ulee's Gold* (1997).[1] Nuñez, however, was considered an anomaly until the beginning of the twenty-first century, when David Gordon Green arrived on the scene with *George Washington* (2000). Both of Nuñez's 1980s films were screened at the Sundance Film Festival, the premier independent film festival in the United States. The festival, however, rejected Green's first feature film, the one that put his name on the national independent filmmaking map. In contrast, his second feature-length film, *All the Real Girls* (2003), was accepted by Sundance.

With the 2005 Sundance Film Festival, southeastern independent filmmaking burst full force on the national scene when four of the sixteen feature-length dramatic films at the festival were made in the South, about the South, by southerners (although most of them no longer lived in the region). The 2005 films were *Loggerheads* (Tim Kirkman), *Junebug* (Phil Morrison), *Forty Shades of Blue* (Ira Sachs), and *Hustle and Flow* (Craig Brewer). One need only add to this list David Gordon Green and Victor Nuñez to arrive at a roster of southern independent fictional filmmakers who are nationally recognized. Kirkman's and Morrison's films were shot in North Carolina, and Sachs's and Brewer's in Memphis, the areas in which the filmmakers grew up. The local alternative presses touted with pride the regional connection. The 2005 Sundance even included the panel "Southern Exposure" as a result of the films. In a local interview the week his movie opened in Memphis, Morrison noted about the Sundance panel experience: "We all struggled to say we're not trying to define the South with our movies. You can tie your brain in knots trying to talk about that."[2] Although these four filmmakers may not have set out to "define the South," three of the four made a special trip back to the southeast specifically to shoot their film; choosing this region was not a matter of convenience.

As filmmakers and film critics are quick to point out, this occurrence at Sundance did not represent a film movement, consciously or unconsciously. An element of randomness and coincidence permeates them as a group of filmmakers. But this does not negate their being part of a regional zeitgeist or, to borrow a phrase from Raymond Williams, a regional "structure of feelings," one that leaves traces in their films.[3] Journalists and film reviewers did grapple with the issue of southern film. Godfrey Cheshire, the moderator of the 2005 Sundance Southern Exposure panel, recounts that he tried to approach the event through the question: "Why not a Southern cinema, in the same way that there's Southern literature?"[4] Using genre theory and Mikhail Bakhtin's concept of chronotype, I provide a new category for understanding a dominant trend in films set in the South: "Humid Time," a key ingredient of which is oppression, resulting from not only the insufferable heat but also society. Historically, the social oppression featured in southern films has been strongly linked to race. To demonstrate Humid Time, I turn to a different form of oppression, but one that does not preclude racial issues. I focus on four dramatic (as opposed to comedic) independent gay feature-length films set in the U.S. South, which all overtly rather than covertly (as in earlier allusions to homosexuality in Hollywood cinema) display the features I associate with Humid Time.[5]

Southern Cinema and Genre Theory

A number of academic attempts have been made to define regional film. When these attempts move beyond the general definition of a film that is "not simply *about*, but comes *from* the region," they privilege accuracy in the filmic representations as a constitutional component of the definition. For example, Brooke Jacobson claims that the regional film "is distinguished from a wider range of independent film by the degree to which it portrays actual conditions of life as experienced by a specific segment of the population in a particular locale."[6] Accuracy, like authenticity, is a politically loaded concept and quickly becomes an intellectual quagmire. The issue arises when discussing stereotypes, whether national, economical, racial, sexual, or in this case, regional. The now cliché position is that mainstream filmic representations contain negative stereotypes and are bemoaned as inaccurate, lacking authenticity. Stephen Neale notes that the issue of stereotypes typically focuses on characters rather than form, comparing a character to either a reality or an ideal. Neale claims that such comparisons are based on a naive understanding of reality, one that results in comparisons not to the real but to "other discourses *about* the real."[7] In other words, comparisons are dialogic in the Bakhtinian sense that all utterances are expressions of social relations and interact with other discourses.

While some southeastern independent filmmakers do appeal to the notion of authenticity, others—in particular Craig Brewer and Phil Morrison—freely acknowledge that their films play with regional stereotypes rather than challenge them through the substitution of idealized images. For example, when discussing his use of character types in *Junebug*, Morrison notes, "I knew that what that meant was that some people would just see the caricature. I had to accept the possibility of people seeing this movie and just seeing 'quirk.'"[8] Similarly, when discussing writing *Black Snake Moan*, Brewer muses, "I thought that it would be this mixture of everything I love about Southern mythology and exploitation, drive-in, Daisy Duke–wearing type of narrative."[9]

How does one answer the question, "What is southern cinema?" without relying on claims of accuracy and authenticity? While the call for southern cinema is much broader than that for a film genre of Southern comparable to the Western in that it implies issues of production infrastructures and not just on-screen filmic representations, the latter typically dominates the discussion.[10] To classify a group of films based on some characteristic, in this case southern, is the terrain of film genre theory.[11] The authors of *Hollywood's Image of the South*, Larry Langman and David Ebner, "seek to establish the 'southern' as a legitimate film genre." Their book, however, is primarily an annotated filmography of movies *about* the South, categorized under such topics as "Slaves and Slavery," "Political Conditions," "Family Survival," and "Economics in the New South." Their idea of the Southern is juxtaposed to the already established film genre of the Western. They acknowledge that while the Western is "instantly recognizable," the Southern is "a bit subtler."[12]

Although early film genre theory drew from work on literary genres, since the 1980s film genre theory has come into its own through the writings of such theorists as Thomas Schatz, Stephen Neale, and Rick Altman.[13] In a landmark essay in the 1980s, Altman proposes a semantic/syntactic approach to film genre, which his book revises to a semantic/syntactic/pragmatic approach. His earlier formulation considers how genres are typically defined based on either their semantic or syntactic elements, in other words, iconic codes or narrative construction, respectively. He argues that engagements with film genre tend to privilege one over the other and counters that these two approaches should not be seen as an either/or proposition but should be engaged simultaneously. He defines the semantic as the building blocks used to construct the genre and the syntactic as how these building blocks are put together. The semantic approach results in a large body of films within the rubric of the particular film genre yet provides little explanatory power, while the syntactic approach results in the opposite effect: an increase in explanatory power but a very narrow canon of films.

A classic example often used in film genre theory is the Western, which directly relates to Langman and Ebner's attempt to equate their genre of the Southern with the Western. The semantic approach focuses on common characteristics of films such as characters and locations, while the syntactic approach considers the structural relationship of various components of the text. In the Western, for example, semantic elements would be the location of the U.S. West, characters such as sheriffs and Indians, and the horse and train as modes of transportation. In contrast, a syntactic element for the Western is the struggle between wilderness and civilization. An alternative syntactic clash occurs between the individual and community, in which the protagonist often saves the community but is unable to integrate into it. Langman and Ebner's definition of the Southern relies on a very simple semantic component. They classify a film as a Southern if it meets their "Confederate test," by which they mean, "The action takes place *at any time* in one of the states that composed the Confederacy or else it takes place during the Civil War in some other state but southern troops are involved."[14] Although simple, such a definition avoids engaging with the difficult foundational conceptualizations of both the U.S. South and film genre. They ignore the common practice of including Kentucky and Maryland as southern states that did not secede from the Union, but more importantly their approach eliminates theory from the equation. Although they offer the one-dimensional semantic element of geography, they offer no particular syntactic approach for their Southern genre. Their definition is so inclusive that from a genre perspective it becomes useless in providing any explanatory power about how films on the South operate within society.

The problem is further complicated when Altman's revised theory is considered. Although he labels his revised approach as semantic/syntactic/pragmatic, it is really a critique of text-based approaches that rely on semantic and syntactic elements to define a film genre and ignore how genres have been constructed by users, both historically as well as in the present. After investigating how film genres are formed, Altman comes to the realization that genres are not stable over time, nor are the borders among them fixed. In fact, he believes that many different configurations of film genres exist simultaneously, depending on the user's "reading position." This means studio executives, theater exhibitors, film critics, audiences, and academic scholars can all simultaneously view films through different genre lenses. A particular film may be perceived as belonging to a number of different genres, depending on the reading positions created by the critical discourse surrounding the film text.

Although a number of writers have expressed desire for a meta-Southern genre, the scrutiny of historical records does not uphold that such a genre existed in the past.[15] But this does not prohibit the reconfiguration of these films into one today. Langman and Ebner's Southern would be a retroactively constructed genre since one does not currently exist. If one is using reception as a basis for genre construction, then various film audiences exist across time and the reception of a film in the year of its release can change a quarter of a century later. While the text may be the same, its meaning and generic classification can be very different. When I screened the Rock Hudson/Doris Day romantic comedy *Pillow Talk* (Michael Gordon, 1959) for one of my Language of Film classes, the students were amazed by the numerous gay jokes about Rock Hudson, especially given their perception of the 1950s as the squeaky clean and innocent decade before the wild and outlandish 1960s. The contemporary audience receives the film very differently from its initial historical audience now that Hudson's gayness is common knowledge. Many older films have been reappropriated by contemporary audiences, forming what Patricia White calls "retro-spectatorship."[16] Clare Whatling explores how lesbians have reclaimed such films as *The Killing of Sister George* (Robert Aldrich, 1968) and the southern gothic classic *Walk on the Wild Side* (Edward Dmytryk, 1962) and grapples with this contemporary nostalgia for abjection in lesbian spectatorship.[17] One of the most intriguing reappropriations emerging today is *Cruising* (William Friedkin, 1980). During production in Greenwich Village, gay and lesbian activists disrupted the filming and sponsored a nationwide boycott of the film because of its depiction of a gay serial killer. Today, some younger gay men are embracing the film, forming a very different reception for it, one that also exists in a very different historical context, both in terms of the social acceptance of gays and lesbians and the media representation of them.

The desire for a Southern genre, especially one read retroactively, raises a number of questions: Where does this desire spring from? Why is it perceived as a desirable goal? Why do we need one today? This desire for such a genre relates directly to Altman's proposition that genres change over time. Academic and cultural critics as users can form new genres out of older films, but Langman and Ebner propose no syntactic components, no pragmatic basis to justify such a genre (although groundwork is being laid by the call itself), and the only semantic element identified is that of state geography. Although the films they discuss were not marketed or reviewed as Southerns, they were often promoted and/or reviewed as being *about* the South and received by audiences and critics as representations of the South. The South, however, was typically framed in relationship to other elements, such as the plantation, the gothic, or the road. A number of genre configurations (or, if preferred, cycles) do exist in which the South has played a significant role and would hold up under interrogation by Altman's semantic/syntactic/pragmatic approach. When looking at Hollywood films, four potential candidates immediately come to mind: the plantation, civil rights, "hick flick" (or, in its retrogenre form, hixploitation), and southern gothic.[18] And, of course, not every film about the South fits into one of these categories, nor are these categories mutually exclusive. For example, while *To Kill a Mockingbird* (Robert Mulligan, 1962) is typically referenced as a civil rights film, it contains elements associated with southern gothic, in particular the character Boo Radley and the house where he lives. My goal is not to offer a semantic/syntactic/pragmatic justification for the Southern as a film genre or to define southern cinema but rather to raise some of the issues surrounding these topics to inform my narrower concern of exploring the intersection of independent film, gay sexualities, and the U.S. South.

Gay Independent Film and Southernscapes

A common way of approaching the U.S. South is through the concept of place and much is touted about the southern "sense of place." Like reliance on authenticity, I believe the appeal to place likewise leads to a theoretical quagmire. But place in its most literal sense is a spatial concept. Michel de Certeau claims that "space is a practiced place."[19] Although the phrase "sense of place" directly references space, it is not only a spatial framework but also a temporal one, because it also invokes time, typically soaked with past nostalgia and/or historicity. So while I make no claims about the South per se, the filmic images of the region do offer spatial and temporal representations of it. Framing these southern representations through the basic concepts of space and time will hopefully avoid the pitfalls that result from the preconceived (and often unspoken) notions about the South attached to the concept of sense of place.

Bakhtin holds that in textual representations space and time are interconnected, inseparable. He developed the concept of the chronotope (which literally means "time space") to fuse spatial and temporal indicators "into one carefully thought-out, concrete whole." The chronotope turns space and time into a "formally constitutive category" where "neither category is privileged; they are utterly interdependent."[20] According to Bakhtin, chronotopes are not immutable but rather each chronotope "can include within it an unlimited number of minor chronotopes." They "are mutually inclusive, they co-exist, they may be interwoven with, replace or oppose one another, contradict one another or find themselves in ever more complex interrelationships."[21] Bakhtin views chronotopes as "the organizing centers for the fundamental narrative events of the novel." In other words, "the knots of narrative are tied and untied" through chronotopes and "to them belongs the meaning that shapes narrative."[22] Besides welding narrative to the chronotope, Bakhtin also weds character to it as well, claiming the "chronotope as a formally constitutive category determines to a significant degree the image of man [sic] in literature." In other words, the "image of man [sic] is always intrinsically chronotopic."[23] Although conceived for analyzing literature, the concept is applicable to any narrative-driven medium, and film scholars such as Robert Stam, Michael V. Montgomery, Vivian Sobchack, and Paula J. Massood have successfully adopted it to the audiovisual medium of film.[24] Because the chronotope shapes both narrative and character the spatiotemporal system of the chronotope generates film genres; the chronotope is a textual-based approach to film genre. As Massood notes, "Places as disparate as roads, castles, salons, thresholds, and trains function as 'materialized history,' where temporal relationships are literalized by the objects, spaces, or persons with which they intersect."[25] What does such a concept mean for the study of the U.S. South in American film? Film can be approached for its southernscape, a spatiotemporal configuration that informs both its narrative development and character construction. Of course, many types of southernscapes exist and an individual film can contain more than just one.

Although independent filmmaking is as old as the institution of cinema itself, the contemporary strain is historically traced back to the 1970s, with *Shadows* (John Cassavetes, 1959) an early forerunner.[26] Independent film provides a space not only for racial and sexual minority filmmakers but also regionalist ones, as indicated by such highly praised 1970s independent films as *Heartland* (Richard Pearce, 1979), *Northern Lights* (John Hansen and Rob Nilsson, 1979), and *Gal Young 'Un* (Victor Nuñez, 1979).[27] In the past decade, a number of fictional feature-length independent films have been made that combine minority sexualities and regionalism, in this particular case gay men in the U.S. South. These films include *The Delta* (Ira Sachs, 1997), *Red Dirt* (Tag Purvis, 2000), *Strange Fruit* (Kyle Schickner, 2004), and *Loggerheads* (Tim Kirkman, 2005).[28] Although some of these films were released theatrically, all of them were screened at film festivals (both gay and nongay, both in and outside of the southeastern United States) and circulated in mainstream video rental stores such as Blockbuster.

One of the numerous degeneracies aligned with the U.S. South through southern gothic literature in the 1940s and transferred to the screen through its filmic adaptations in the 1950s was homosexuality. Sebastian, the southern homosexual character of Tennessee Williams's *Suddenly Last Summer* (Joseph L. Mankiewicz, 1959), is canonical in contemporary gay and lesbian studies. During most of the classical Hollywood studio period the filmic representation of gay and lesbian characters was created through innuendo and inference. While today they are overt, such characters are typically restricted to supporting roles as best friends and that includes those set in the South, such as *Sling Blade* (Billy Bob Thornton, 1995), *Midnight in the Garden of Good and Evil* (Clint Eastwood, 1997), and *Sweet Home Alabama* (Andy Tennant, 2002).[29] One must turn to independent films to find southern gay characters as leads.[30]

The four films under consideration are a diverse lot and on first glimpse appear to be a collection of isolated occurrences with no aesthetic commonality. They do, however, share a number of similarities. The driving force behind their narratives is a gay man on a search in the South. Although this gay man is a southerner, in the particular context of the film he is perceived as an outsider. In *The Delta*, late at night, Lincoln abandons his girlfriend and seeks out sex in the gay cruising areas and porn parlors of Memphis, Tennessee, where he encounters Minh Nguyen, an Amerasian immigrant from Vietnam whose father was an African American GI. The two men embark on an overnight excursion down the Mississippi River in Lincoln's family boat, returning the next morning to their separate worlds. In *Red Dirt*, Lee, a restless drifter, arrives in Pine Apple, Mississippi, and rents a cottage from Griffith, who before Lee's arrival passed time having sex with his cousin Emily. Lee feels constrained by Pine Apple and desires to escape and then finds himself sexually attracted to the outsider with whom he makes plans to leave town. In *Strange Fruit*, Billie returns to his hometown of Bordock, Louisiana, to investigate the rape and lynching of his cousin and close friend Kelvin. Although black, Kelvin was murdered because he was gay, the hanging occurring outside the local gay bar. In *Loggerheads*, a forlorn drifter named Mark, who has been rejected by his adopted parents because he is gay, arrives at Kure Beach, North Carolina, where he meets a local motel owner, George, who takes him in and nurses him as he dies of AIDS. (Mark refuses to take any medicine to prolong his life.)

Besides providing narrative motivation, the longing of these characters contains a negative existentialist component that endows them with a feeling of melancholy. While Lincoln, Lee, Billie, and Mark may be gay outsiders restlessly searching for something not always verbally or consciously expressed, this longing does not accrue to just the outsider; it also applies to those narratively connected to that character: Minh,

Griffith, Billie's straight school buddy Deputy Matthew Mathers, and Mark's birth mother Grace and adopted mother Elizabeth. While for a few characters the desire for change assumes that of physical space, for all of them it pertains to the nature of life itself, of life in the South. The gay outsider is not always the main or sole focalizing force in the film. While Billie is the main force in *Strange Fruit*, the nonoutsider Griffith is for *Red Dirt*. And in *The Delta* and *Loggerheads* the focalization is shared by two and three characters, respectively.

Media Reception

Although all four films can be considered "gay," as attested by their screening at gay and lesbian film festivals, a survey of media reception demonstrates the diversity of genre classifications within which review-ers positioned these films. Today film reviews, unlike those of the past written by critics such as James Agee and Pauline Kael, are written to assist consumers in choosing which film to attend.[31] Viewers typically make that choice through a combination of genre classification and lead-ing stars, often the two reenforcing each other, for example, a roman-tic comedy with Sandra Bullock and an action adventure with Arnold Schwarzenegger. Two of the gay independent films mentioned earlier were routinely placed in easily identifiable Hollywood genres, while the other two were received as art films, a classification presumed to stand outside those of the Hollywood genre system. Of course, many of the major Hollywood studios have had at one time or another a specialty di-vision to distribute selected U.S. independent and foreign art films even if they did not produce and finance them.

Red Dirt is referred to explicitly as southern gothic and *Strange Fruit* as a civil rights thriller. For example, when *Red Dirt* was shown at the Eighth Annual Michigan Lesbian and Gay Film Festival, the reviewer for *Detroit Free Press* advised, "Think Tennessee Williams meets Eudora Welty, with a touch of *God's Little Acre* tossed in for spice." And, when *Strange Fruit* screened at the Eleventh Philadelphia International Gay and Lesbian Film Festival, the reviewer for *Philadelphia Weekly* referred to the film as a "gay *In the Heat of the Night* knock-off."[32] The lead character in the film, Billie, self-consciously references the film's generic status in his dialogue. At one point he quips, "What is this? A Grisham novel?" and at another he tells the local sheriff to "call me Mr. Boyals," referencing Sidney Poitier's line, "They call me 'Mr. Tibbs'" from *In the Heat of the Night* (Norman Jewison, 1967). A number of reviewers cite the film's own genre self-classification.

Of course, numerous art films play with Hollywood genres. One has to only think of Todd Haynes, whose films consistently engage with the issue of genre, the most overt *Far from Heaven* (2002) that references Douglas Sirk's 1950s melodramas and in particular *All That Heaven Allows* (Douglas Sirk, 1955). Although *Red Dirt* is beautifully shot, a matter routinely mentioned by reviewers, rather than an art film that critically interrogates genre or even offers a revisionist take, the film mimics the older genre. During the classical Hollywood studio era, the Production Code explicitly prohibited reference to homosexuality, so connotative rather than denotative means had to be used to represent it. In an age of overt sexual representations, *Red Dirt* continues this older tradition with one difference: the two gay characters are allowed a kiss before they go their separate ways, a nice change from the classical period's narrative conclusions of heterosexual conversion, murder, or suicide. While the kiss adds the twist of spiritualizing same-sex love, it still remains the love that dare not speak its name as the gay body is metaphorically erased through its denial of sexual expression. At least Billy Joe McAllister was allowed a night of blissful man-sex in *Ode to Billy Joe* (Max Baer Jr., 1976) before he jumped off the Tallahatchie Bridge out of guilt and shame.

Rather than frame the films through Hollywood genres, reviewers position the other two films—*The Delta* and *Loggerheads*—as art films, either directly or indirectly. When discussing *The Delta*, they sometimes invoke the art cinema of American independents, other times European. One of the aesthetic features that differentiates art cinema from Hollywood films is narrative construction. Although flashbacks are a staple of Hollywood films and the industry has made films that play with temporal resequencing such as *Citizen Kane* (Orson Welles, 1941), temporal disjunctions, radical ellipses, and open-ended narratives are typically the terrain associated with art cinema, not Hollywood. The popular success of *Pulp Fiction* (Quentin Tarantino, 1994) introduced such narrative constructions to a wider contemporary audience. *The Delta* was shot in sixteen-millimeter film and reviewers routinely refer to it as a low-budget film in a quasi-documentary style, assuming the two matters are connected. The film's use of mostly nonprofessional actors harkens back to Italian neorealism. While the use of nonprofessionals is typically mentioned, which invokes art cinema, the direct correlation to neorealism is not. In contrast to *The Delta*, reviewers rarely compare *Loggerheads* to European filmmakers, while American independent film is routinely invoked. When describing the film, reviewers always mention its temporally disjunctive structure, which indirectly signals to readers its art-cinema status.[33] Both *The Delta* and *Loggerheads* were released by Strand Releasing, a distribution company that specializes in art cinema—both American indie and world cinema—and known for its large selection of gay and lesbian films, another signifier of the films' art cinema status for a discerning viewer. The use of Strand Releasing also means that after appearing on the festival circuit the films received a limited theatrical release.

In the case of all four films, "Southern" was not a genre classification for reviewers comparable to that of "gay," although they always position the films as transpiring in the region, sometimes with further elaboration, other times without. When approached from the perspective of the films' representation of the American South, reviewers and audiences alike invoke the concept of authenticity as a criterion for evaluation, often explicitly expressed. For example, after the films were theatrically released, the reviewer for the *Atlanta Journal and Constitution* maintained that *The Delta*'s "Southernness is admirably authentic," while the reviewer for the *New York Times* declared that *Loggerheads* exhibits "a pungent authenticity."[34] Reliance on authenticity as a criterion for evaluating a film's representation of the region, however, is not limited to gay independent films set in the region; it is routinely applied to southern independent films in general. When David Gordon Green's *All the Real Girls* appeared at Sundance, *indieWIRE* praised the film as "effortlessly authentic to the humidity and timelessness of the American South."[35] Some film reviewers, exemplified by this one, conflate a southern chronotope that they have discursively encountered with being the "real" South, fulfilling Neale's claim that comparisons of film texts to the real are to other discursive constructions of the real, not the real itself. Because the South is a discursive formation, a film's representation will *always* be a discursive one.[36] The issues of humidity and timelessness raised by the *indieWIRE* critic provide linchpins for considering in more detail the use of space and time in these films and in the question of whether they share a common southernscape.

Space and Time

Appeals to the American South as either unknowable or as timeless are clichés that have outlived their usefulness. But, is one of the chronotopes related to the South that of a timeless space? Bakhtin's idyllic chronotope is a "little spatial world . . . limited and sufficient unto itself, not linked in any intrinsic way with other places, with the rest of the world."[37] The "unity of place" created by this self-containment and segregated space blurs temporal boundaries. Massood applies Bakhtin's idyllic chronotope to the all-black musicals produced in Hollywood between 1929 and 1943 that are set in a pastoral southern setting, a chronotope she calls "antebellum idyll." Massood notes, "Without explicitly identifying the time frame, the image identifies the narrative in a specific historical moment by referencing forms of preindustrial, and antebellum, labor, thereby erasing the distinctions between historical moments: it could be the early nineteenth century or it could be the early twentieth century."[38] While Massood identifies the idyllic chronotope as applying to these black films set in the rural South, the question arises: Does the idyllic chronotope apply to films about the rural South that do not include an all-black cast? In other words, is Massood's antebellum idyll a subset of a larger southern idyll?

Of the four gay independent films under analysis, two—*Red Dirt* and *Strange Fruit*—are set in the rural South, a matter film reviewers routinely note. Does their rural South partake of a regional idyllic chronotope? Although both films transpire in the present, they are generically stuck in a bygone era, *Red Dirt* in that of a 1950s and 1960s southern gothic film genre and *Strange Fruit* in that of a civil rights film from the same era. This borrowing of past genre configurations lends an air of timelessness to the South in these two films, as they create a rural world unaffected by outside influences and the passing of time. In other words, the blurring of temporal distinctions that occurs here frames the rural South as timeless. Civil rights films typically reference historical events, even if obliquely, such as *To Kill a Mockingbird* (Robert Mulligan, 1962) to the Scottsboro Boys trial. In *Strange Fruit* this connection is severed as other civil rights films become the point of reference. In addition to Billie's comments mentioned earlier, another indicator of this filmic referentiality is the white sheriff who is a clichéd character right off the screen of the 1950s, except now he also openly expresses hatred of gays as well as blacks. While the world is changing, the South, as signified by the continuation of such stock characters from the past, is not; it is a world unto itself. Although transpiring in rural spaces, the timelessness of these films emerges not from their ruralness but from their recycling of older generic forms, genres in which the main characters encounter a hostile world.

A key ingredient of the rural idyllic is the pastoral, where nature is idealized or romanticized as constantly renewing itself. Such is not the case in these films where the environment is experienced by the gay characters (and some straight ones) as draining and constrictive, not regenerative. While a southern idyll chronotype may exist, neither of these two films uses it. *The Delta*, however, does contain a short rural sequence that is idyllic. In other words, the southern idyll is a minor chronotope in the film, making a brief appearance but not descriptive of the film overall.

Unlike *Red Dirt* and *Strange Fruit* that use retrogenre timelessness, temporally *The Delta* and *Loggerheads* are not outside of time although their narratives are elliptical. Historical references occur through a number of means. During a dinner conversation in *The Delta*, fleeting reference is made to a local congressional representative's lawsuit against an airline and, because Minh is an Amerasian immigrant from Vietnam, the historical legacy of the Vietnam War saturates portions of the film. In *Loggerheads*, speeches by Bill Clinton and George W. Bush air on the radio, grounding the film to concrete historical time. The first time a town or city appears on-screen, a title appears over the scenery announcing not only the place but the year—"Kure Beach, North Carolina 1999," "Eden, North Carolina 2000," and "Asheville, North Carolina 2001." Because the film crosscuts between the various stories, time becomes elliptical. Although the film informs viewers up front that these stories are occurring in different time periods as well as locations, watching the film one quickly forgets, because as good viewers we have been trained to read crosscutting as temporal simultaneity.

Temporally, these films cluster around two configurations, those of retrogenre timelessness and elliptical historicalness. When approached spatially, the question arises: should space be conceptualized through the framework of rural versus urban or public versus private? While the rural locations of *Red Dirt* and *Strange Fruit* are fictional (although they were shot around Meridian, Mississippi, and Lake Arthur, Louisiana, respectively), the cities and towns in *The Delta* and *Loggerheads* actually exist. When discussing *The Delta*, film reviewers constantly reference the cityscape of Memphis. Audiences were already familiar with a cinematic version of the city as a result of the filmic adaptations of John Grisham's novels *The Firm* (Sydney Pollack, 1993) and *The Client* (Joel Schumacher, 1994). The Memphis on display in *The Delta*, however, is not the popular one known through Grisham thrillers and tourism (Graceland, Sun Studio, and Beale Street). As a result of this shift in geographic and sociocultural focus, the film, as one reviewer expresses, "strips the city of all its Southern charm and pretension."[39] And what do we get instead? A version of the city that is "seedy" and "cheap" with routine references thrown in about the "hot," "humid," "muggy" weather. Since *The Delta*, Brewer's 2005 film *Hustle and Flow* has navigated a similar version of the city, one centered on pimps and sex workers rather than sexually active gay men. In contrast, reviewers mention the cities and towns of *Loggerheads* only in passing. In an interview with *Gay and Lesbian Review*, Kirkman confessed, "I put them [Asheville, Eden, and Kure Beach] in there because I wanted to make North Carolina a character in the film."[40] Kirkman located the three stories in the three different landscapes of North Carolina: the mountains of the western portion of the state, the piedmont of the middle section, and the coastline of the eastern part. Although reviewers routinely mention the specific cities and towns, they focus on how the temporal disjunctions related to the locations affect the characters, ignoring the spatial correlation of topography to them. In other words, reviewers emphasize time over space when considering the characters even though the film is constructed to privilege neither.

Approaching space from the perspective of rural versus nonrural, these films align along lines similar to their constructions of time. As noted earlier, chronotopes intertwine and rural timelessness forms a minor chronotope in some of these films, just not their main one. The specific spaces shown in all four of these films—whether rural or urban—are typically unknown except to local audiences. For example, when *The Delta* screened at the Memphis College of Art, the reviewer for the local daily newspaper specifically named the park—Overton Park—where the outdoor cruising scene occurs.[41] Rather than iconic natural or architectural sites that nonlocal viewers would immediately recognize (i.e., the historical landmarks and tourist attractions), these films rely on everyday spaces. The term *urban* invokes the space of the large city, with dense populations and a high skyline. The small city and town, in contrast, is horizontal in nature and, although distinguishable from the rural, elements of the rural bleed into it. For example, the outdoor noise of chirping insects often used to aurally signify ruralness also applies to urban areas in the southeast as well, thereby minimizing their distinction. Although *The Delta* and *Loggerheads* are not rural, because of the visual nature of small cities and towns combined with the use of locations not readily recognizable by nonlocals, these films are not identifiably urban in the way the term is typically employed. While these two films are nonrural, they do not partake of the visual language that dominates the media representations of urban and suburban terrain. As a result, their use of space should be handled not through the differentiation between rural versus urban but rather through that of public versus private.

When space is viewed from the perspective of public versus private, the films align along different axes than those which result from a consideration of their use of time. The narrative thrust of *Red Dirt* and *Loggerheads* centers primarily on the private space of the home, while for *The Delta* and *Strange Fruit* that node is the public one of parks, bars, and other such locations. In *Loggerheads* the open beach where we first observe Mark is not public as it might first appear because it is a protected nature sanctuary for the loggerhead turtles, in other words, a home, where the female turtles lay their eggs and depart, leaving the hatchlings to fend for themselves. The loggerheads function as a metaphor for Mark's own family situation of being abandoned by both his birth and adopted parents, a metaphor a few reviewers found a little too heavy handed, though I did not.[42] Similarly, George's hotel is presented as a personal home rather than a public place. If the automobile is a signifier of mobility and movement outside of the home, then the pickup trucks in *Red Dirt* and *Loggerheads* are telling. In *Red Dirt*, Lee returns in his truck to take Griffith away from Pine Apple, but Griffith declines his offer of a ride, choosing to remain at Aunt Summer's house. Along similar lines but in reverse, at the end of *Loggerheads* Mark leaves George's hotel to continue wandering, but George finds him walking down the street and offers him a lift back. Mark accepts. Although the truck offers escape from home in one film and return to it in the other, the decision of whether to hop in depends on its direction in relationship to the private space of home.

In contrast to *Red Dirt* and *Loggerheads*, the narrative impetus of *The Delta* and *Strange Fruit* centers around public spaces and as a result the closet occupies a more prominent position, although all four films invoke the closet in one form or another. While a few scenes do occur in the homes of the main characters, the private space of the home is typically navigated through the perspective of a guest, whether there to visit, party, or sleep. Because the films focus on racial and sexual minorities, the action routinely occurs in not only general public spaces but also subcultural ones. The narrative trajectory of *The Delta* traverses a black bar, a Vietnamese bar, and a gay bar, allowing viewers to observe Minh's ability to negotiate all of them comfortably even though he is not fully accepted by any. The black gay bar in *Strange Fruit* is the site of the lynching that provides the impetus for the story—that of Billie's investigation—and the black straight bar we learn about at the end of the film is where the individual that organized that act of violence holds court. In both films the automobile is not just an instrument for moving bodies from one location to another but also an avenue to homoerotic possibilities. While vehicles in *Red Dirt* and *Loggerheads* are framed as private means to travel across space, in *The Delta* and *Strange Fruit* they are instruments of public participation as they drive through gay cruising areas performing a sexual mating ritual with men walking on foot.

These four films align along different axes depending on whether spatial or temporal coordinates are emphasized. In terms of time, *Red Dirt* and *Strange Fruit* use retrogenre timelessness while *The Delta* and *Loggerheads* use elliptical historicalness. In contrast, from the perspective of space, *Red Dirt* and *Loggerheads* negotiate predominately the private space of the home, while *The Delta* and *Strange Fruit* occupy the public space of heteronormativity and the subcultural space of same-sex desire. None of these films share an identical combination of spatial and temporal characteristics when these two factors are approached individually, but when space and time are considered as one unit, these four feature-length dramatic independent films about gay men in the U.S. South do share a mutual southernscape, what I call Humid Time.[43]

Humid Time Southernscape

In 1929 Ulrich Bonnell Phillips pronounced, "Let us begin by discussing the weather, for that has been the chief agency in making the South distinctive."[44] Attributing certain behaviors of southeastern residents to the hot and humid climate (be it slow speech, laziness, or violence) began long before Phillips's now famous and often quoted remark. Whether documentary or fictional, literature and film as discursive enunciations form the South, although they are just two avenues among many oral and mass communication means that contribute to its formation. Any distinctiveness claimed on behalf of the South is always mediated. As a consequence, multiple Souths exist simultaneously, although certain ones dominate at particular historical moments and new ones periodically emerge.

Just as many southern historians once assumed a literal cause-and-effect relationship between the weather and human behavior, many southern literary scholars also offered literary analysis that assumed texts represented this particular condition. Although the impetus for this essentialist perspective sprang from a belief in its actual existence, regardless of its scientific verifiability, its presence contributed to the discursive formation of the South and was incorporated into the dominant construction of the region at that time. While today most academics—be they liberal arts scholars or scientists—do not hold a deterministic relationship between weather and human behavior, residual traces of this discursive manifestation remain, especially in popular cultural forms.[45] The Humid Time chronotope is not dependent on a literal cause-and-effect relationship between the two factors because it does not reference a physical condition but a discursive practice, as any statement referencing an entity called the South does.

Reviewers of the four films constantly associate the South with humid and torrid weather, sometimes as represented in the particular film under review, other times as a general statement about the region itself. Humid Time, however, traverses the terrain of the human landscape as well as the natural one. In other words, the intolerability of the environment includes the social climate as well as the weather. Weather and society share a symbiotic relationship in this southernscape, both affecting characters similarly. Just as the weather is represented as oppressive—hot and muggy—making the characters physically uncomfortable, similarly the society is suffocating; only some characters bear the burden of it more directly than others—in these particular films people of color, gays and lesbians, and unmotherly women. Just as the sweltering weather makes one physically tired, the stifling society does the same to one's human spirit. In other words, just as the southern weather is burdensome to one's body, affecting one's energy level, southern society is burdensome to one's selfhood, affecting one's emotional well-being. This association often occurs through framing the South as backward, an easily available means for such representation because of its long association with the South in popular culture. But the defining characteristic of Humid Time is not backwardness per se but rather a socially oppressive society, which can be represented through means other than just backwardness.

The social stifling in these four films is not limited to the gay characters; however, when nongay ones experience it, a gay character provides the motivational jolt that causes it. For example, in *Red Dirt* the suffering of Aunt Summer derives from a love affair she had with her brother-in-law, which produced Griffith. She allowed her sister and brother-in-law to raise Griffith as their own child, resulting in his perceiving her only as an aunt and not a mother, a burden she eventually unloads in the film. In *Loggerheads* Grace and Elizabeth both suffer because of their relationship to Mark: Grace because she abandoned him at birth and Elizabeth, his adopted mother, because she abandoned him as a teenager. The South becomes a space where a socially hostile heteronormativity reigns supreme and requires cautious navigation by sexual minorities and their parents.

The spatial construction of Humid Time is not that of the more common chronotopes such as the road, the shopping mall, and the lounge, where space is defined by what can be seen. Rather than define space through created structures and natural landscapes that one sees, here space is based on what is felt, the air on one's skin: space is defined tactilely, not visually. As a result, Humid Time crosses not only the traditional division of space between rural and urban but also that of public and private. Defining space tactilely creates a representational problem for the medium of film, which communicates through the senses of sound and vision and not touch (nor smell or taste). This means the tactile sensation of being touched by air must be translated into an audiovisual correlate through sight and sound. Such visualizations often approach cliché—perspiration on the face (often mopped up by a handkerchief), wet spots on clothing (such as around the back, chest, and underarms), the waving of a hand in front of the face (typically with a fan), shadows flickering across the room (from a fan, often mounted on the ceiling), water flowing over the body to cool off (the most cliché using a garden hose), buzzing flies, and a hazy atmosphere caused by heat rising from the ground. Aurally, the sound of chirping insects invokes summer heat. In terms of temporality, Humid Time is sticky, its flow clammy, whether time passes with hermetic circularity or elliptical linearity. In other words, it also crosses the division of time between timelessness and historicalness. This southernscape accentuates the stickiness of time similarly to the mugginess of its social and physical space.

Because chronotopes share similar textual terrain to that of genre, Humid Time is a retroactively constructed framework for approaching the representation of the U.S. South in audiovisual media. Although historically references to humid weather—through words such as "hot" and "muggy"—routinely appeared in reviews of films set in the South, the references were not meant as genre classifications. Many films during the 1950s and 1960s based on adaptations of southern gothic literature or dealing with race relations utilized the Humid Time chronotope. The title of one popular Hollywood civil rights film from the era alludes to it: *In the Heat of the Night* (Norman Jewison, 1967). Because the classical Hollywood imperative of narrative closure and a happy ending was not seriously challenged until the mid-1960s, Hollywood films prior to that time rarely violated these conventions. Although traces of a negative existentialism may appear, the film ending ultimately provides a happy resolution, which was often defined as punishing characters who "sin" if they do not repent. One of the many problems the producers of Tennessee Williams's *A Streetcar Named Desire* (Elia Kazan, 1951) encountered with the Production Code Administration was this very issue related to its ending, which had to be changed from the play. During the 1960s Hollywood was in turmoil as it struggled at the beginning of the decade to adapt to the new production system of freelance deals and during the later half of the decade to cater to new corporate owners as well as to an audience that not only continued to shrink but whose demographics changed significantly. As a result, in the mid-1960s a temporary lacuna opened in which deviations from the formulas of the classical period could be openly challenged in Hollywood films through such characters as the antihero. In terms of the Humid Time chronotope, this fissure meant that Hollywood films were no longer bound to a resolution of hope but could now assume a fatalistic stance toward social oppressions. The Paul Newman vehicle *Cool Hand Luke* (Stuart Rosenberg, 1967) is just such a film, one where the site of oppression is white working-class men and the region's prison system. The ending of the film offers no hope of change, neither for Luke, who is dead, nor for the prison system and the society that created it. Societal upheaval and industry turbulence created a condition that enabled a strong form of Humid Time to surface in mainstream American cinema. By the end of the 1970s, however, this lacuna had closed but the strong version of Humid Time continued in independent film. In other words, Humid Time comes in two forms: a weak version, which maintains that justice will eventually prevail, and a strong one, which assumes a fatalistic stance toward societal oppression.

While the strong version of Humid Time is not a new phenomenon, today it saturates gay independent films set in the U.S. South as exhibited by the fatalistic narratives and angst-filled characters of these four films. In *The Delta*, although Minh drifts effortlessly between the gay, Vietnamese, and black communities of Memphis, he is ultimately not accepted by any. The film ends with Minh picking up a black man in a gay bar—a substitute for his deserted African American GI father—and killing him. In *Red Dirt*, Griffith decides not to leave Pine Apple with Lee, choosing to stay with his Aunt Summer, whom he recently learned is his birth mother, and settling for the experience of kissing Lee and the memory of an unconsummated love. Rather than distinguish between sexual acts and sexual identity, the film places the emphasis on sexual acts versus sexual desire. Griffith's acknowledgment of his same-sex desire but self-denial of acting on it conforms to the homophobic demand many Protestant Christian denominations place on individuals with homosexual tendencies who desire to be ordained as pastors, that of agreeing not to act on their sexual desires. In other words, they must accept a life of celibacy, a sexual renunciation not required of heterosexuals who desire to be ministers. Unlike its treatment of heterosexual desire, the film denies physical expression to same-sex desire. Griffith can have sex with his cousin Emily but not with Lee. As a result, unfulfilled desire becomes situated as more honorable than physical expression for gay men, a rather bleak proposal. In *Strange Fruit*, although the racist and homophobic sheriff is killed and Billie is rescued at the last minute from being lynched, the leader of the lynch mob escapes and the one member of his crew who repents commits suicide out of remorse. The big surprise in the film is that the homophobic lynch mob is black, not white. Given the cultural resonance of lynching, explicitly with racism toward blacks, the idea of blacks appropriating this instrument and applying it to sexual minorities in homophobic rage is fatalistic in that the lessons of history are meaningless to our lives. In *Loggerheads*, after a failed suicide attempt, Grace hires a detective to find her son, given up for adoption when she was a teenager, only to learn he recently died of AIDS. Mark died thinking his birth mother did not care about him when in fact abandoning him emotionally destroyed her life. (Reviewers routinely note that the film is based on a true story. The true story is even more fatalistic than the film, in that the adopted mother never reconciled with her son before he died nor would she meet with his birth mother.)

Rather than fatalism, a more appropriate term to describe the sense of hopelessness and/or meaninglessness that engulfs the narratives and characters in these films is nihilism. Cornel West, in a now famous article, argues that nihilism is the most basic issue threatening the existence of black people today. West conceives of nihilism "not as a philosophical doctrine that there are no rational grounds for legitimate standards or authority; it is far more, the lived experience of coping with a life of horrifying meaninglessness, hopelessness, and (most importantly) lovelessness." As he notes, "This usually results in a numbing detachment from others and a self-destructive disposition toward the world."[46] West attributes black nihilism to consumerism and the loss of community. While I make no claim of a gay nihilism or a southern one comparable to West's black nihilism, the southernscape of these films contains a nihilistic component as a result of the existential angst expressed by the main characters and the fatalistic narrative conclusions. The association of the South with social oppression is an integral component of Humid Time and the southernscape formed by dramatic feature-length independent films in which gay men occupy the central narrative thrust partake of the strong version of this chronotope by framing their experience in the region nihilistically.[47] As more and more gays, lesbians, and transgender people live openly in the southeastern United States and change its social habitat, the question remains whether the strong version of the Humid Time chronotope will continue to dominate the southernscape of films about them.

NOTES

1. Nuñez's other films include *Gal Young 'Un* (1979), *A Flash of Green* (1984), and *Coastlines* (2002). McElwee made his national reputation with *Sherman's March* (1986).

2. Chris Herrington, "Of Ozu and Opie," *Memphis Flyer*, September 14, 2005, 52.

3. Raymond Williams, *Marxism and Literature* (New York: Oxford University Press, 1977), 132.

4. Godfrey Cheshire, "A Southern Sundance," *Raleigh-Durham–Chapel Hill (N.C.) Independent Weekly*, February 9, 2005, 22.

5. I use the word *gay* with "independent film" hesitantly and only as a convenient label for discussion purposes. Though these filmmakers may be gay (or bisexual), my inclination is that they would resist limiting themselves artistically by placing the word as an adjective before "filmmaker." While such labels can function as a market segmentation tool to find an audience, they also typically serve to limit and restrict, or even ghettoize, the work of such artists.

6. Brooke Jacobson, "Regional Film: A Strategic Discourse in the Global Marketplace," *Journal of Film and Video* 43, no. 4 (Winter 1991): 20.

7. Stephen Neale, "The Same Old Story: Stereotypes and Difference," in *The Screen Education Reader: Cinema, Television, Culture*, ed. Manuel Alvarado,

Edward Buscombe, and Richard Collins (New York: Columbia University Press, 1993), 43.

8. Jeannette Catsoulis, "The Insider Outsider: An Interview with Phil Morrison, about His New Film *Junebug*," *Reverse Shot*, no. 13 (Summer 2005), www .reverseshot.com/legacy/dogdayso5/morrison.html (accessed April 19, 2010).

9. John Beifuss, "Where Do Craig Brewer's Ideas Come From?" *Bloodshot Eye*, March 16, 2007, http://blogs.commercialappeal.com/the_bloodshot_eye/ 2007/03/where-do-craig-brewers-ideas_come_from.html (accessed April 19, 2010).

10. I use a capital "S" to differentiate between "southern" as a reference to the region and "Southern" as a reference to a filmic genre category.

11. Other alternative approaches would be to engage southern cinema through the framework of film movement or national cinema. When considering the issue of southern cinema one must differentiate between being prescriptive and descriptive. The former focuses on what a southern cinema should be while the later describes what exists. Of course, from a Foucauldian perspective, the very act of description is inherently also analysis because words are not neutral instruments; the very act of word choice always results in an interpretation even when one strives for impartiality. The goal here is not to be prescriptive but to explore the theoretical issues surrounding the notion of southern cinema by using film genre theory.

12. Larry Langman and David Ebner, *Hollywood's Image of the South: A Century of Southern Films* (Westport, Conn.: Greenwood, 2001), ix.

13. See Thomas Schatz, *Hollywood Genres: Formulas, Filmmaking, and the Studio System* (New York: Random House, 1981); Stephen Neale, *Genre and Hollywood* (New York: Routledge, 2000); and Rick Altman, *Film/Genre* (London: BFI, 1999).

14. Langman and Ebner, *Hollywood's Image of the South*, ix.

15. An earlier call for a Southern film genre appeared in Warren French's "'The Southern': Another Lost Cause?" in *The South and Film*, ed. Warren French (Jackson: University Press of Mississippi, 1981), 3–13.

16. See Patricia White, *Uninvited: Classical Cinema and Lesbian Representability* (Bloomington: Indiana University Press, 1999).

17. See Clare Whatling, *Screen Dreams: Fantasising Lesbians in Film* (Manchester: Manchester University Press, 1997).

18. Edward D. C. Campbell Jr. makes a convincing argument in support of the plantation as a genre cycle in his *The Celluloid South: Hollywood and the Southern Myth* (Knoxville: University of Tennessee Press, 1981). Although not books about genre per se, Allison Graham's *Framing the South: Hollywood, Television, and Race during the Civil Rights Struggle* (Baltimore: Johns Hopkins University Press, 2001) provides support for a civil rights cycle and J. W. Williamson's *Hillbillyland: What the Movies Did to the Mountains and What the Mountains Did to the Movies* (Chapel Hill: University of North Carolina Press, 1995) similarly does so for a hick flick one.

19. Michel de Certeau, *The Practice of Everyday Life*, trans. Steve Rendall (Berkeley: University of California Press, 1984), 117.

20. Mikhail Bakhtin, *The Dialogic Imagination: Four Essays*, trans. Caryl Emerson and Michael Holquist (Austin: University of Texas Press, 1981), 84, 425.

21. Ibid., 252.

22. Ibid., 250.

23. Ibid., 85.

24. See Robert Stam, *Subversive Pleasure: Bakhtin, Cultural Criticism, and Film* (Baltimore: Johns Hopkins University Press, 1989); Michael V. Montgomery, *Carnivals and Commonplaces: Bakhtin's Chronotope, Cultural Studies, and Film* (New York: Lang, 1993); Vivian Sobchack, "Lounge Time: Post-War Crises and the Chronotope of Film Noir," in *Refiguring American Film Genres: History and Theory*, ed. Nick Browne (Berkeley: University of California Press, 1998), 129–70; and Paula J. Massood, *Black City Cinema: African American Urban Experience in Film* (Philadelphia: Temple University Press, 2003).

25. Massood, *Black City Cinema*, 4.

26. On American independent film, see Emanuel Levy, *Cinema of Outsiders: The Rise of American Independent Film* (New York: New York University Press, 1999); Geoff King, *American Independent Cinema* (Bloomington: Indiana University Press, 2005); and Yannis Tzioumakis, *American Independent Cinema: An Introduction* (New Brunswick, N.J.: Rutgers University Press, 2006).

27. I use the term *sexual* to include both sex and sexuality, thereby encompassing both women as a minority based on sex, and lesbian, gay, bisexual, and transgender people as one based on sexuality.

28. An interesting film released around the same time as these is Milford Thomas's *Claire* (2001). I have excluded the film because it is not feature length; its running time is less than one hour. The film uses the style of 1920s silent cinema, even including a live orchestra during its screenings on the festival circuit. I have also excluded the early precursor *Ode to Billy Joe* (1976). The director, Max Baer Jr., played Jethro on the television show *The Beverly Hillbillies*. The film is a screen adaptation of the Bobby Gentry song of the same title and answers the question: why did Billy Joe McAllister throw himself off the Tallahatchie Bridge? The answer is because he had sex with a man and enjoyed it. Is my melancholic nostalgia for the film a gay male form of Whatling's lesbian nostalgia for abjection mentioned earlier?

29. A few exceptions do exist where a gay character is the lead in a Hollywood film, for example, *Making Love* (Arthur Hiller, 1982) and *The Birdcage* (Mike Nichols, 1996), a Hollywood remake of the French film *La Cage Aux Folles* (Edouard Molinaro, 1978). While Tom Hanks's gay character may be one of the two leads in *Philadelphia* (Jonathan Demme, 1993), the film's focalization privileges the straight character played by Denzel Washington. *Making Love* is often touted as Hollywood's first "positive" gay-themed film. Some film scholars hold that the financial failure and sociopolitical fallout of *Making Love* frightened Hollywood from any sustained engagement with gay-themed films.

30. Indicative of the continued disparity between the sexes, to date I have encountered only one feature-length fictional film set in the southeast with a lesbian main character, *Monster* (Patty Jenkins, 2003). If others exist, they have received

very limited circulation, which is just another indicator of the sex disparity. Although the lead actress of *Monster* won an Independent Spirit Award, the film's approximately eight million dollar budget places it significantly beyond the production context of these four films, which were all low budget.

31. I ran across two exceptions worth noting of a sustained critical analysis of the film and its southern component that went beyond a typical film review. For *The Delta*, see David Ansen, "Delta Skin," *Film Comment* 33, no. 5 (September/October 1997): 6–8, and for *Loggerheads*, see Godfrey Cheshire, "Riders to the Sea," *Raleigh-Durham–Chapel Hill (N.C.) Independent Weekly*, October 19, 2005, 65. Cheshire has written a number of pieces for *Independent Weekly* exploring independent film and the South.

32. John Monaghan, "17 Films Screen at Gay-Themed Film Fest," *Detroit Free Press*, January 26, 2001; Leo Charney, Dan Buskirk, Matt Prigge, Emily Brochin, and J. Cooper Robb, "Screen and Heard: The 11th Philadelphia International Gay and Lesbian Film Festival Is the Biggest Yet," *Philadelphia Weekly*, July 12, 2005, 37.

33. For example, the film is described as having "temporal disjuncture" and a "fractured timeline" and as being "elliptical" by, respectively, Godfrey Cheshire, "A Southern Sundance," *Raleigh-Durham (N.C.) Independent Weekly*, February 9, 2005, 22; Ken Hanke, "*Loggerheads*," *Asheville (N.C.) Mountain Express*, December 28, 2005, 48; and Kevin Thomas, "The Consequences of Hard-Shelled Beliefs: Tim Kirkman's *Loggerheads* Effectively Shows How Irrevocable Life's Choices Can Be," *Los Angeles Times*, October 14, 2005, E10.

34. Eleanor Ringel, "*The Delta*," *Atlanta Journal and Constitution*, January 30, 1998, 11P; Stephen Holden, "An Adopted Gay Son Set Adrift Makes Spiritual Connections," *New York Times*, October 14, 2005, E17.

35. Ray Pride, "David Gordon Green's *All the Real Girls*: The Magic and Madness of Young Lovers," *indieWIRE*, January 2003, http://www.indiewire .com/article/david_gordon_greens_all_the_real_girls_the_magic_and_madness _of_young_lover (accessed April 19, 2010).

36. See my manuscript, *Mediated Distinctiveness: The American South, Race, and Documentary Film*, working paper, 2010.

37. Bakhtin, *Dialogic Imagination*, 225.

38. Massood, *Black City Cinema*, 15.

39. Renee Graham, "Mesmerizing Performance Keeps *The Delta* on Track," *Boston Globe*, March 13, 1998, D7.

40. John Esther, "Tim Kirkman: Storyteller of Human Complexity," *Gay and Lesbian Review* 13, no. 1 (January–February 2006): 45.

41. John Beifuss, "Gay, Asian Cultures Meet in Mid-South-Based *Delta*," *Memphis Commercial Appeal*, April 26, 1997, C3, and John Beifuss, "Little-Known Worlds of Memphis Open Up in *The Delta*," *Memphis Commercial Appeal*, April 26, 1997, C1.

42. See, for example, Walter Addiego, "*Loggerheads*," *San Francisco Chronicle*, October 21, 2005, E5; Marjorie Baumgarten, "*Loggerheads*," *Austin Chronicle*, January 13, 2006, http://www.austinchronicle.com/gyrobase/Calendar/

Film?Film=oid:323187 (accessed April 19, 2010); and Stephen Holden, "An Adopted Gay Son Set Adrift Makes Spiritual Connections," *New York Times*, October 14, 2005, E17.

43. Although the earlier *Ode to Billy Joe* is not included in this analysis, it conforms to the strong version of Humid Time found in these four films.

44. Ulrich Bonnell Phillips, *Life and Labor in the Old South* (Boston: Little, Brown, 1929), 3.

45. On the issue of climate and human behavior related to the American South, see A. Cash Koeniger, "Climate and Southern Distinctiveness," *Journal of Southern History* 54, no. 1 (February 1988): 21–44; Mark A. Stewart, "Southern Environmental History," *A Companion to the American South*, ed. John B. Boles (Malden, Mass.: Blackwell, 2002), 409–23; and William R. Baron, "Climate and Weather," *The New Encyclopedia of Southern Culture*, vol. 8, *Environment*, ed. Martin Melosi (Chapel Hill: University of North Carolina, 2007), 39–43.

46. Cornel West, "Nihilism in Black America: A Danger That Corrodes from Within," *Dissent* 38, no. 2 (Spring 1991): 222–23.

47. Independent films set in the South with a straight African American in the lead(s)—such as *Daughters of the Dust* (Julie Dash, 1992), *Eve's Bayou* (Kasi Lemmons, 1997), and *Constellation* (Jordan Walker-Pearlman, 2005)—do not partake of the Humid Time chronotope as I have defined it, while the much earlier *Nothing But a Man* (Michael Roemer, 1964) does. So, although the chronotope is not limited to gay independent films, that site is where its strongest expression is currently found. One factor contributing to the appearance of nihilism in gay independent films about the South is the legacy of new queer cinema from the early 1990s, which broke the hold of "positive images" over gay and lesbian films.

Papa Legba and the Liminal Spaces of the Blues

Roots Music in Deep South Film

Christopher J. Smith

This essay is about an *idea* of the blues: as it has been perceived, appropriated, framed, selected, and reflected in the medium of four films set in the U.S. South. It is about the blues as they were, and are, *imagined* to be in the world of Hollywood fiction, the flickering chiaroscuro of the narrative cinema. I analyze liminality—the use of ritual to create social states permitting the transformation of identity or behavior—as representation in filmic blues experience. Just as Delta blues virtuosity existed in the liminal "space in-between," filmic fiction has sought to portray and evoke that liminality—with often only marginal success. Walter Hill's *Crossroads* (1986), Ruben Santiago-Hudson's *Lackawanna Blues* (2005), Craig Brewer's *Black Snake Moan* (2006), and the Coen Brothers' *O Brother, Where Art Thou?* (2000) all employ the blues (as well as other southern rural idioms) as central, multisemiotic metaphors; all four films likewise invoke—and struggle with—the blues' capacities for representation of community, alienation, and integration.

As with other media of southern artistic expression, the blues serve as a tool for embodying, facing, and resolving alienation. By employing the intentional binarism of African American culture, and the blues' ability to evoke liminal spaces and communitas, these four films have sought, more or less successfully, to depict, if not evoke, the blues' ability to reconcile and integrate Southern black experience.

African American Music and Hollywood Film

Though African American music has been employed in a wide range of Hollywood films since before the age of sound, there is relatively little scholarly analysis of its function as part of fictional narratives. In part this gap is due to the comparative neglect of black experience by film historians, but it is also a product of music's slippery semiotic connotations and its resistance to conventional narrative or literary-critical analytic tools. This slippery trait is especially true in the case of African American performance idioms, which have typically operated at multiple layers of paradox, irony, and "signifyin(g)," a term coined by Henry Louis Gates Jr. to describe a conscious, intentional, and manipulated multireferentiality.[1] The conscious creation by musicians of performances that permit multiple, even paradoxical, interpretations, is a product of very old African American and African cultural strategies, particularly as translated in the complex and fraught social circumstances of the Jim Crow South. Signifying music such as the blues, then, played differently to white audiences than black ones and likewise played differently in its original southern contexts versus those of fictional film. Though Michele Faith Wallace suggests that "the techniques of feature film inscribe and underwrite dominant racial paradigms," in some cases, representations of black music have resisted these paradigms.[2]

Music in film typically is employed to enable multisemiotic interpretations by different audiences: what David Brackett has called "a field of relationships and oppositions that are then associated with characters, places, personal qualities, objects, and events."[3] In his examination of the allusive power of the W. C. Handy song "St. Louis Blues" in film noir, Peter Stanfield has similarly described "the mobilization of songs [in order] to code race, class, and gender," but his study focuses on the transgressive associations of the Handy song with the Caucasian "urban primitive." While Stanfield's "transgressive" associations are intended in some filmic depictions of the blues, in other cases the music's intensity, attributed authenticity, or "double-consciousness" is the focus.[4]

African and African American spiritual, sociological, and musical traditions have historically displayed a predilection toward binarism: encompassing dualities not in opposition to but rather in balance with one another. Ideas (beliefs, communities, identities, artworks) are not fixed except in terms of their symbiosis with others. In such a cosmology, joy and sorrow, phonemic language, polyrhythm, twinned gods, all become part of a cultural call-and-response, whose dynamic tension makes the negotiation of existential contradictions possible: Paul Oliver, for example, quotes the Igbirra proverb "God made all things double."[5] Such a "disposition towards binary classifications" is likewise an essential part of the Delta blues experience, inscribed on every waking moment: roots versus wanderings, saints versus sinners, the country church and the juke joint, the cash for drinks on Saturday night and the tithes for church on Sunday morning. All reflect and require one another:

The binary character of blues was not one of conflict, of opposites that could not be reconciled. On the contrary . . . parallelisms . . . were all brought together. Blues as song is the combination of numerous pairings, creatively reconstructed and reshaped. . . . It is this resolution of oppositions and tensions, this coordinating of apparently contrary elements, which gives it the peculiar force that has made it so important in black secular life. . . . [F]or the blues singer[s] . . . the idiom provided a matrix in which could be worked out, in innumerable ways, the conflicts and problems that assailed them.[6]

Similarly, Bernt Ostendorf has described a "binary compulsion in the hermeneutics of black culture" and the centrality of "signifying inversions" in black popular culture. Such intentional binarism has not typically translated to the narrative cinema: more often, inclusion of African American musical performances has served as a simplistic marker of "authenticity," "the primitive," or the underclass: that is, to serve Stansfield's "transgressive" functions.[7]

Something different is intended in each of the four films this essay discusses; these filmmakers attempt, with variant success, to employ the blues to signify union, integration, and *communitas*. Cultural anthropologist Victor Turner calls "communitas" an "underlying bedrock . . . a generic human relationship undivided by status-roles or structural oppositions, which is also vouched for by myths and histories stressing the unity and continuity of the widest group to which all belong by birth and tradition."[8]

In such a construction, performance-ritual becomes a cultural tool, which can serve to elicit such an experience of communitas.[9] Bobby C. Alexander and Samuel A. Floyd Jr. have applied Turner's model to various African American cultural expressions, including music. Alexander has studied the African American musical idiom of the Pentecostal church and suggests, "Pentecostal possession offers concrete opposition to social structure by suspending some of the requirements of everyday social norms when it removes participants from social structure by way of ritual liminality; it also creates structural ambiguity as well as direct and egalitarian social arrangements in ritual communities. Ritual possession poses its greatest opposition to the dominant social structure by introducing into everyday life the alternative, communitarian relations that are generated in ritual liminality."[10] Floyd has located this appreciation for uncertainty's expressive and social power in the most ancient of African musical imports to the Americas, the ring shout. Describing the ring as "a dance in which the sacred and secular were conflated," he cites "the similar conflation—indeed, near-inseparability—of Afro-American music and dance in black culture, both in the ring and outside it."[11] Floyd further connects the symbiotic dualism of music and dance both to Gates's contemporary semiotics of the "Signifyin[g] Monkey" and to ancient Esu-Elegbara-Legba, a member of the Yoruba sacred pantheon. Floyd calls Legba the "guardian of the crossroads and grantor of interpretive skills;" he is therefore the ancient archetype of the devil to whom Mississippi blues player Robert Johnson was claimed to have sold his soul in return for musical skill, and who appears as a character in Hill's *Crossroads*.[12]

Nick Bromell has likewise argued for the blues' essential social-psychological work in balancing the brutal contradictions of southern black life, commenting that the music's binarisms "seem continually to mediate between two traditions and two worlds, and to meditate on the relationship between an abstracted whiteness and an intonated coloring."[13] Cynthia Mahabir has located parallel identities and behaviors in the personae and social roles of the Trinidadian calypso singer and the Delta blues player. She makes the useful observation that, though on the surface "blues . . . tell of despair and suffering and calypsos are statements of mockery," both blues and calypso are multisemiotic and employ sardonic humor as a way to "encode messages." Finally, she suggests that "in both [these] popular musics there is a common quest on the part of the performers for a collective . . . experience with audiences" (that is, the creation of communitas).[14]

But the analysis of black music in these films adds another wrinkle: while communitas can be identified in the blues' original performance contexts, its presence or availability shifts in the distanced medium of film. As opposed to the dynamic of communal performances, film necessitates a representational rather than participatory interaction between audience and art-object. The four films under discussion, dating between 1986 and 2006, all treat African American music in general, and the blues in particular, as essential parts of their stories and provide the opportunity for useful comparisons of Hollywood's approaches to southern black music and its conception of the blues' artistry and community.

Crossroads (1986)

Walter Hill's 1986 film *Crossroads*, which paired the callow heartthrob Ralph Macchio (ex–*Karate Kid* and *The Outsiders*) and the veteran musician and character actor Joe Seneca, was roundly panned by blues aficionados, if not by film critics.[15] Though riddled with stereotypical blues clichés, the film nevertheless contains a powerful opening sequence, replicating Robert Johnson's first 1936 recording session, performed on the soundtrack by guitarist, music director, and longtime Walter Hill collaborator, Ry Cooder.[16]

Less widely remarked on but equally effective is a later scene in which Seneca's superannuated blues player returns to the Delta crossroads, where decades before, in exchange for musical mastery, he had sold his soul to the devil's sidekick—unnamed in the film, but whose oldest archetypal roots are in the West African orisha Eshu, a trickster god. Though a hackneyed blues fiction, this bargain and Hill's particular American personification of "Papa Legba" nevertheless capture the seductive power of the liminal "space in-between"—the dichotomy between Jesus and the devil, between Sunday morning and Saturday night, between sanctity and sin—which, as Bromell shows, the blues both ritualized and resolved.

The sepia-tinged opening sequence, which prefaces the main narrative, grounds the story in both the mythic and the historical biographies of Robert Johnson, the would-be blues player (Tim Russ) who is depicted awaiting the bargain at a crossroads, a West African and African American place of liminality, uncertainty, and, potentially, of power. But the scene cuts off before the devil keeps the rendezvous; this deferred confrontation, which tropes the popular legend of a blues player trading his soul in return for musical talent, builds tension and anticipation for a narrative arc that bends toward an inevitable return.[17]

The opening sequence then shifts to Johnson's timid entry into a hotel in San Antonio, where he made his first historical recording sessions in November 1936.[18] It is a reasonably accurate and sympathetic portrait of both Johnson and of Ernie Oertle, the technician who, recognizing the newcomer's naïveté, instructs him despite Johnson's seemingly arbitrary insistence, recounted by H. C. Speir, of turning his face to the wall before playing. While this back-turned posture became powerfully iconographic of Johnson's alienation, solitude, and emotional fragility, being employed in several variants on 1970s LP covers—not least because the back-turned anonymous portraiture was convenient in the days prior to discovery of two authenticated photographs of Johnson—it also, according to Ry Cooder, served a practical purpose: acoustical "corner-loading," which would reinforce the bass register and focus the overall sound.[19] Historical fact and acoustical practicality thus fed the myth, and the myth in turn became a powerful construct of the historical imagination—certainly 1960s and 1970s blues fandom believed the back-turned posture was emblematic of Johnson's Satan-tortured, doom-ridden soul. In addition, the image recalls the archetypal blues couplet "I turned around and I slowly walked away" but also reaches back through African American iconography to Ibo cults of West Africa, in which the back is turned as a grave is closed and the door to the next world is sealed.[20]

The film's climax comes when Macchio's young would-be blues player "Lightnin'" is portrayed as "cutting heads"—that is, trading guitar fireworks—with the devil's own sidekick (guitarist Steve Vai) in a battle for Seneca's soul. After the long-dreaded confrontation at the crossroads, when the devil finally comes to collect his due, the scene shifts through a hallucinatory dissolve to a kind of Baptist version of the inverted liturgy: framed in a church interior and featuring black-clad parishioners, a Satan figure nicely dressed in preacher's garb, and a hellish gospel chorus. The setting thus is a trope of damnation, which, in the African American South, was conventionally understood to be the eventual end of any blues player devoted to the "devil's music."

But Hill—and Cooder, who recruited the musical talent for the soundtrack and supplied the screaming slide guitar licks that form Macchio's part of the duel—also portray the reckless joy that the film seeks to find in the blues experience: music, dance, and a kind of gloomy celebration as the obverse of popular history's sense of the Delta's grinding daytime oppression. Certainly one can imagine a slick con artist like Mississippi's Charlie Patton (1891–1934), one of Johnson's principal inspirations, playing here, spinning his guitar, cadging drinks, fobbing off the most onerous playing duties on his second guitarist (or on the band, here that of the great Clarksdale harp player Frank Frost), and then, next day, blithely delivering the hellfire-and-brimstone sermonizing that he recorded on *The Prayer of Death* (1929) and attributed pseudonymously to Elder J Hadley.

One can likewise imagine Clarksdale blues player Son House (who reappears in *Black Snake Moan*) drinking and playing here—but, in contrast to Patton, paying a much greater price: torturing himself the next morning in church with the certainty of damnation and yet doing it again next Saturday night. And indeed it is not necessary to "imagine" House doing this: his vacillations about the moral implications of his blues lifestyle are well documented. The literal and psychological dichotomies that many blues players experienced were very real and echo throughout the music's history: Little Richard, hearing of Sputnik's launch, experiencing an apocalyptic crisis of conscience at performing rock 'n' roll, the devil's music, and flinging his jewelry into Sydney Harbor; or Al Green, assaulted with hot grits by a jealous woman, spurning the secular physicality of rhythm and blues and going back to the gospel church.

The inverted liturgy scene in *Crossroads* thus seeks to portray the "Saturday night/Sunday morning" binarism to which both the blues players and their original audiences subscribed: that Jesus and Satan, the Church and the juke joint, were locked in close, even intimate combat on the common battleground of the individual's soul. The measure of blues virtuosity thus became the trickster's ability to balance these dichotomies' connotations of salvation versus damnation, in such a way as to create liminality, an experiential "place-in-between," and thus the opportunity to construct new identities and communal realities. Filmed performances of the blues can never function with the moment-by-moment two-way interactivity of the original blues contexts, performers, and audiences—but in *Crossroads*, it seems clear that Hill and Cooder grasp and seek to represent that immediacy, if they cannot fully recreate it.

It is unfortunate then, that the slide guitar and blues-rock fireworks of the duel (rendered on the soundtrack, respectively by Cooder and by Steve Vai himself), should finally be decided only when Macchio's callow Long Island blues player reverts to his own classical-music "roots"—playing a flashed-up guitar transcription of violinist Niccolò Paganini's *Fifth Caprice* in A minor (Op. 1, 1819) and thereby defeating his opponent. It's in fact quite peculiar that classical music, from whose performance and aesthetics Macchio's Lightnin' has fled throughout the film, should provide the deus ex machina that saves Seneca's soul. In another screenplay, perhaps the Paganini could represent Lightnin's reintegration of both sides of his musical identity; here, however, classical music disappears in the wake of his victory. In nineteenth-century Paris, the *Fifth Caprice* might have conveyed some of the sense of Dionysian liminality that the blues creates and the film seeks to replicate—but in *Crossroads* it simply reinscribes clichéd high culture/low culture hierarchies attached to European American versus African American music.

Hence, despite the climactic duel's iconic status among Steve Vai fans (more than 2.6 million viewings of various versions on YouTube as of April 4, 2010), it is not the most effective evocation in *Crossroads* of the blues' semiotic power.[21] That scene comes earlier and directly employs Legba and the *Crossroads* to specifically evoke, even for the audience, the "in-between-ness" of the blues experience. In overalls and cloth cap, brogans, and steel-rimmed spectacles, Seneca's Willie Brown stands in sepia flashback at the crossroads, when up pulls a shiny new T-Model Ford. In seersucker suit and straw boater, the driver (Joe Morton), not named but certainly implicating elements of both Legba and Satan, with "uptown's" friendly contempt for "country," says, "What you want, blind boy?" Brown replies with a request to trade his soul for musical talent, and the hellish contract is negotiated and signed.

Much later in the film, after many misadventures, Brown and Lightnin' find themselves back at that same dusty place. At Willie's insistence, Lightnin' begins to play, and through the heat haze, we again see a distant vehicle approaching. Yet this time it is no Model T that pulls to a stop, but a coal-black, late-model Chevy Camaro. A window hums down, and we see Joe Morton, aged not at all since the prior encounter, dressed in the height of 1980s Italian couture, saying, "Y'all need a ride?" In its uptown flash, in the way that Satan's offer is made materially, sardonically, sartorially—and concretely—appealing, we see the seductive legendary escape that the devil, the juke joint, and the blues offer. And in this moment at the crossroads, the moment in the story when Willie Brown and Lightnin' are poised between going forward toward an unpredictable potential or fleeing back to the painful but knowable past, they, and we, are in that liminal space-in-between that both the physical symbol of the crossroads, the cognitive space of the blues, and the personification of Papa Legba were all employed to create.

It is out of this narrative moment, and the knowledge that he risks his eternal soul, that Seneca's elderly blues player, stooped and spectacled, responds with calm, venomous contempt to the driver's challenge: "Ain't riding with the likes of you, smart-ass. Or your bitch neither." Willie Brown recognizes the essential choice that Legba the trickster symbolizes. It is only in the salvation-or-damnation of the liminal moment that the transformation of experience and identity becomes possible. An ability to negotiate the binarism of southern black existence is integral to African American survival in the Deep South. And it is in this moment, as no other in *Crossroads*, that the blues' *meaning* is thus most powerfully invoked.

Lackawanna Blues (2005)

Lackawanna Blues, a 2005 HBO film, was based on Ruben Santiago-Hudson's one-person theatrical show, which was in turn based on his experience growing up as a child of mixed parentage in a multiracial immigrant community outside Buffalo. In *Lackawanna*, though set in the semiurban North, the period, culture groups, and music depicted are all rooted in the rural South, and the blues serve as a marker of Ostendorf's "authenticity." Santiago-Hudson, a musician himself who had previously starred on Broadway in *Jelly's Last Jam* and *Seven Guitars*, and whose own acting career replicated the "in-between-ness" of racial identity (he was denied roles in Puerto Rican theater because of his mixed ethnicity, and in African American companies precisely because of his Spanish patrimony), creates a script that gives central importance to music's meanings within his natal community.

The film opens with a Friday night fish fry, which Alessandra Stanley in the *New York Times* aptly describes as being "so inviting that viewers wish they could leap into the frame and join the madness."[22] That bravura opening is matched in the second act by an equally effective nightclub sequence in which Mos Def, playing a Cab Calloway–style zoot-suited bandleader, tears down the house with a version of Louis Jordan's "Caldonia." Interpolated within these scenes, each time musically effective but narratively rather implausible, are performances by acoustic guitarist Robert Bradley, playing the recently emigrated Otis McLanahan, of the deepest, most Southern, most "country" of blues. Bradley, though a powerful screen presence (blind, white-haired, missing teeth) and a fine singer, is used as an icon, not a character: a kind of Greek chorister whose acoustic blues signify roots, naked emotion, and catharsis. He serves as young Ruben's sounding board, as commentary, but no more. His blues is thus a symbol of these expatriate communities' authenticity and stands as an intentional, ameliorating counter to the "primitive" or "transgressive" associations that Stansfield locates in white filmmakers' uses of related music. But the blues communitas, which Turner identifies in ritual and Floyd in the ring shout, which Walter Hill and Ry Cooder depict in the liminal spaces of the crossroads, is only cursorily referenced in *Lackawanna*'s use of Otis McLanahan. During the second-act forties night club sequence, a marvel of physical and cinematic choreography, the action is abruptly halted so that Otis can sing the slow blues "Something inside Me." While it is possible to imagine that these club goers might, at another time in the week or in the privacy of their own homes, appreciate what would have been a rather country entertainment, the slow blues feels incongruous here, in the context of a 1950s nightclub celebration. It is unlikely that the Dionysian celebration helmed by Mos Def would be abruptly interrupted by such an intimate, inward performance as that of "Something inside Me"; rather, its presence at this particular point in the narrative is to enable editorial crosscuts with an intimate monologue, in which Jeffrey Hudson's Mr. Paul provides his own backstory of adultery and murder—the blues, then, providing a marker for a particular type of tragic *individual* experience. The musical interludes that feature his blues function primarily to "hammer home," as Stanley says, certain "treacly" plot points, in its story of survival and redemption.

Though far less exploitative, and far more celebratory, than *Black Snake Moan*, and while sharing with that film great respect for and top-notch execution of black music, *Lackawanna* is still overly romantic. Both voyeurism (*Black Snake*) and hagiography (*Lackawanna*) are essentially passive: they facilitate the gaze but restrict the ability of the viewer to *share* the music's capacity to create the transformation of personal experience. The treacly nostalgia—the golden-hued, soft-edged distance with which producer Halle Berry and her cast of Hollywood stars treat Hudson's childhood experience—is equally present in the film's treatment of the blues. Far more vital, and central to the tale, are the rhythm and blues chestnuts that drive both the opening fish fry and the second-act nightclub scene; in Mos' Def's rubbery-voiced homage to Louis Jordan and Cab Calloway, we find a much more convincing evocation of Legba's empowering "in-between-ness." By comparison, in *Lackawanna*, the blues itself is a kind of afterthought—or artifact. Sadly, particularly in light of Santiago-Hudson's own obvious roots in and love for the music, the film version of *Lackawanna Blues* fails to recognize either the *risk* or the *hope*—that is, the liminal *possibility*—that the Deep South blues brought into its communities' being.

Black Snake Moan (2006)

Like Joel and Ethan Coen for their earlier (2000) *O Brother, Where Art Thou?* writer/director Craig Brewer seems to have known that he wanted to use southern deep blues for 2006's *Black Snake Moan*, just as he seems to have visualized the promotional materials (a takeoff of mass-market paperback art, featuring Samuel L. Jackson in wife-beater T-shirt looming over a chained, minimally clad, kneeling Christina Ricci)—before he knew what the story was to be.

And the music he chose is unquestionably marvelous: wonderful greasy blues, credibly sung by leading man Samuel L. Jackson, expertly accompanied by musicians out of the Fat Possum Records stable, who appear both on the soundtrack and in the juke-joint sequences at the film's Bucket of Blood nightclub, and featuring updated versions of songs ("Stack-O-Lee," "Catfish Blues," and "Black Snake Moan") that are iconic in the blues tradition. The music is excellent, the cast is strong, and, in the intensity and charisma of their performances, both Jackson and leading woman Cristina Ricci are well matched and deeply invested in the material.

But in *Black Snake Moan*, unlike *O Brother* (or for that matter *Crossroads*), the blues are employed not as a symbol of community but of Stansfield's "transgressive." Perhaps it is Brewer's adoption of the visually sexual tropes of pulp novels and exploitation films: chains, sweat, half-clad women, and so forth; perhaps the difference is that the Coen Brothers, seeking a structural model on which to hang their shaggy-dog story of adventure, travail, and redemption, opted for one of the oldest examples of picaresque epic in Western literature, that of *The Odyssey*. In contrast, Brewer's film plays like a mash-up of *The Defiant Ones* (1958) and *Cleopatra Jones* (1973).[23] Like Quentin Tarantino, Brewer intentionally and very effectively invokes, exploits, and subverts audience responses to controversial black-versus-white iconography—but his film, gleefully voyeuristic in conception and execution, reduces the blues to another transgressive manifestation of African American "primitivism."

There is a profound disingenuousness in the film's relationship to its music: the creative team claims that *Black Snake Moan* is about their great respect for the blues, but their visual and narrative rendering of the blues' meanings, associations, and communities is a caricature of race and class. Endemic throughout the film is the use of specific musical idioms—like specific accents—to signal not only characters' backgrounds but also their moral or social values: Ricci's Rae, in the grip of sexual hysteria after her fiancé Ronnie's (Justin Timberlake) departure, visits a massive booze and drugs party to a hard rock soundtrack; Michael Raymond-James's Gill, who after the party rapes and beats Rae, leaving her for dead, meets a returning Ronnie in a loud country-music bar; Jackson's Lazarus, picking Rae up and attempting to soothe her hysteria, croons gospel to her; and at Rae's moment of psychological redemption, Lazarus accompanies her singing of Harry Dixon Loes's 1920 "This Little Light of Mine." Each of these usages—hard rock, country music, gospel—inscribes, just as clearly as some of the exaggerated accents (with Raymond-James again being the most notable culprit) and salacious visual images, stereotypical tropes about race, class, and music.

In both print interviews and in several of the DVD's included special features, writer/director Brewer, music director Scott Bomar, and producers Stephanie Allain and John Singleton heap encomia on the musicians.[24] The music and the musicians featured on the soundtrack are a virtual dream team of Memphis and Mississippi artists, including the Sound of Memphis gospel choir, the remarkable multiple generations of keyboardist Jim Dickinson and his sons Cody and Luther, guitarists Jason Freeman and Kenny Brown, members of the extended family of Hill Country fife-and-drum patriarch Otha Turner, and drummer Cedric Burnside (grandson of R. L. Burnside, to whom the film is dedicated), as well as the Chicago harmonica player Charlie Musselwhite. The music on the soundtrack, which is the creation of a quite multiracial and multigenerational cast of players, defies any easy generalizations about who plays the blues; yet on-screen the blues is nearly exclusively identified with black musicians and the black community: of the white players, only Fat Possum guitarist Kenny Brown has screen time. Moreover, at no place in *any* of the DVD's special interviews is there any address of the disconnect between the "reverence" with which the production speaks of the music and the cartoonish exploitation inherent in the scenario, dialogue, and visual imagery.

Black Snake Moan, as planned, shot, and marketed, is a very different film than the creative team *claims* to have been making. The film is blatantly sensational: from the posters that displayed undershirted Samuel L. Jackson and chained, half-naked Christina Ricci; to the camera's lingering, extended shots of Ricci's pantied buttocks and pudendum; even to the heavy chain she wears around her waist through the first act (even the menu icons on the DVD release are chains). Producer John Singleton describes his initial response to Brewer's submitted treatment: "Man, you are a sick fuck."[25] And this salacious stance extends to the central scene of apotheosis: after the chain has come off Rae, Lazarus in turn metaphorically rises from the dead by returning to sit in with blues musicians Cedric Burnside and Kenny Brown at the juke joint. There, he rocks the house with an updated, profane version of "Staggerlee" as Rae drinks and dances orgiastically: the scene is shot in slow motion, with a beautiful, rich color palette and camera work, lingering on sweaty, grinding hips, buttocks, and breasts, and in which Rae is virtually the only white person (dailies excerpted in the Special Features confirm that the crowd of extras in the juke joint was of diverse ethnicity, but the film cut almost completely omits whites from the scene).

The result is that the blues, in *Black Snake Moan*, are employed as markers, not of communitas or personal transformation, but once more— at least as flagrantly as in earlier uses of Handy's "St. Louis Blues"—as the object of the white gaze. Here, the blues itself functions in the same objectified fashion as does Jackson's own character: that is, as A. O. Scott put it, "a tried-and-true Hollywood stock figure: the selfless, spiritually minded African American who seems to have been put on the earth to help white people work out their self-esteem issues" (it may be no coincidence that Jackson's hair-style—mutton-chop sideburns and white receding hair—evokes both Memphis patriarch Rufus Thomas and even, arguably, stage portrayals of Harriet Beecher Stowe's Uncle Tom).[26]

It is possible Brewer intuited that simple voyeurism, Hollywood's stereotyping "white gaze," could not evoke blues communitas. So he punts, or tropes, adopting a shortcut to "authenticity," by including in *Black Snake Moan* interpolated archival footage of Son House, whose own life story reveals the tortured oscillation between Satan and Jesus that *Black Snake Moan* seeks to capture, and whose quiet, courteous ferocity makes even Samuel L. Jackson's pale by comparison. As Scott puts it, "Two short archival clips of the great Son House, explicating the place of sexual jealousy in his music, contain more pain, humor and wisdom than the entirety of Mr. Brewer's overloaded, overheated script."[27]

There is a quality of minstrelsy, even of blackface, in *Black Snake Moan*, of reducing the complexity of southern African American blues experience to the cardboard stereotypes accessible to white fantasy. Samuel L. Jackson has made a career out of over-the-top (and often brilliant) performances of "blackness" written by white directors, his scripture-howling assassin Jules in *Pulp Fiction* (1994) being the archetype. In *Black Snake Moan*, his ex-blues player, now preacher, Lazarus functions like Morgan Freeman's Hoke from 1989's *Driving Miss Daisy*, only with a guitar and a heavy chain instead of a chauffeur's cap and a Buick. The juke-joint scenes in which Lazarus-as-blues-player "rises from the dead" recall the carnivalesque dance parties that open *Lackawanna Blues* and close *Crossroads*, but they are, like those earlier sequences, essentially voyeuristic: in all three sequences, which honestly seek to celebrate the power of black music, that music is submitted to Hollywood reductionism to suit it for an outsider's middle-class gaze.

In his *Village Voice* review Rob Nelson sought to exculpate Brewer, commenting approvingly that "ex- and blax-formulas are merely the short cuts that underprivileged properties take to *getting themselves funded and promoted and seen.*"[28] But this is misdirection if not disingenuous. As with the sheet music of minstrelsy, film "properties" do not "get themselves funded"—the treatments and screenplays are not sentient agents, pitching and producing themselves—but are rather the outgrowth of canny and typically referential, ironic, and opportunistic choices made by human agents targeting a human (mainstream, middle-class, white-tinged, voyeuristic) market and medium.[29]

Black Snake Moan's producers bear responsibility, regardless of what they *claim* for the portraits they draw. And those pictures, like the pulp-magazine trope of the poster's iconography, while massively titillating, say more about the white privileged gaze than about the culture and community that are the subjects of that gaze. As Scott says, there is more "pain, humor and wisdom"—more truth about the blues, if much less transparency to the voyeuristic gaze—in two minutes of Son House's trancelike "John the Revelator" or, I would argue, in Blind Lemon Jefferson's original 78-rpm record of "Black Snake Moan #1" in 1927, than in all the 116 minutes of Brewer's cockeyed Hollywood minstrelsy.

O Brother, Where Art Thou? (2000)

A gleefully magic-realist fable of the world of the musical South and an episodic transmogrification of Preston Sturges, *The Wizard of Oz*, Homer, Deep South fables and shaggy-dog stories, tales of heroes, travel, adventure, and "strange lands," Joel and Ethan Coen's epic *O Brother, Where Art Thou?* (2000) creates a visionary rapprochement based on the *idea* of southern music. Probably the best known of these four films, with the widest impact on contemporaneous mass culture's musical tastes, *O Brother* and its concert-based companion *Down from the Mountain* (also 2000) sparked a brief "old-timey" music revival in the pop press. The Coen Brothers themselves freely admitted the limits of their own southern-music knowledge prior to beginning the film. However, as a writing-and-production team, they have been sensitive to the expressive and affective qualities of music in all their films (from the pot-aroma'd eighties pop of *Big Lebowski* and the haunted, spooky Hardanger fiddle of *Fargo* to the twenties jazz and sentimental Irish 78-rpms of *Miller's Crossing* and the whooping hillbilly songs of *Raising Arizona*), and in *O Brother* they are no less sensitive to the semiotic—and sociological—possibilities implicit in the South's music.[30]

O Brother depicts an endlessly and ubiquitously musical society, peopled with outsized, mythologized giants, sirens, gargoyles, and clowns, which certainly never existed in reality, but which *does* legitimately reflect what Peter Guralnick calls the "Southern Dream of Freedom"—that is, the possibilities for transformation and liberation in the boundary-crossing, genre-melding worlds of southern music.[31] The world depicted in *O Brother* wasn't real on the ground, and in the day-to-day experience, of pre–World War II Jim Crow. But in the semiotic universe of southern music and in the history of American culture that imagined world exerts a powerful reality—because it represents another world, one less alienated, more egalitarian, and more fully integrated (in every sense of the word).

In *O Brother*, the blues are explicitly concretized in the persona of Chris Thomas King's Tommy Johnson, the name of a real blues player (1896–1956), whose self-generated creation myth was later attached to the same Robert Johnson referenced in *Crossroads*.[32] Like Willie Brown in that earlier film, here Tommy, encountered by the Clooney/Nelson/Turturro slapstick trio of fugitives from a chain gang as they drive a stolen Model T into the center of a crossroads, has made the iconic pact with the devil. *O Brother* layers additional tropes on its version of Satan, conflating him with the brutish, backward rednecks Brackett identifies in earlier films as representing the South.[33] Tommy Johnson says, "He's white, as white as you folks, with empty eyes and a big hollow voice. He likes to travel around with a mean old hound" (an allusion to the sunglassed superhuman officer who tracks the fugitives throughout the film). In contrast to *Crossroads*'s hierarchies of authenticity, *Black Snake Moan*'s blackface titillation, or *Lackawanna*'s sepia-toned hagiography, but much more true to the carnivalesque sardonic humor of the blues, *O Brother* signifies on the devilish bargain, playing it initially for laughs (Delmar: "O son, not your ever-living soul?"; Tommy: "Well, I wasn't *usin'* it"; after a flaming-hot guitar performance of "Man of Constant Sorrow," Everett exclaims, "Hot damn, son, I believe you *did* sell your soul to the devil!").

Later, in the most harrowing yet black-humored (or perhaps, "blues-humored") sequence, Tommy has been kidnapped by Klan members who intend to lynch him. The Coens well understand the cinematic history of such depictions, reaching all the way back to *The Birth of a Nation* (1915). As Roger Ebert notes, the nightmarish, red-lit Busby-Berkeleyan choreography of the Coens' version, which mocks the Klan's dim-witted solemnity by resembling a mash-up of *Triumph of the Will* and *The Wizard of Oz*, is simultaneously deadly serious: dragged toward the Fiery Cross, Tommy gasps, "I don't believe anything can save me now. The devil's come to collect his due."[34]

But *O Brother* intentionally abandons the historical "reality" of southern black-white/rich-poor dichotomies in favor of a fable of social rapprochement achieved through music. The film understands, and seeks to evoke for its audience, the communitas that the blues also understood: that we have to laugh to keep from crying and that laughter (direct or indirect, overt or covert) could be a form of resistance. *O Brother* thus provides an apt and apposite representation of the magic, the humor—the "mojo"—that the blues originally made possible.

The bargain at the crossroads was the concretization of personal, conscious choice: in that magical liminal space, when Legba offers the deal, the musician can opt to move forward toward transformation or to retreat into the brutal mundanity of Delta life. Once made, the contractual exchange is guaranteed and unbreakable. In *Crossroads*, the contract for Willie Brown's soul cannot be broken or renegotiated, but another person can freely choose to assume the same terms—and thus, through this shared risk, drive a new bargain.

In *O Brother*, the trickster role is abrogated by the supposed victims themselves—black blues players and oafish fugitives—and the devil, represented by inhuman officers and racist demagogues, is outwitted by the power of comradeship, musical community, and the shared assumption of cosmic risk. When Tommy's companions rescue him, they defy the reality of southern racial life and escape the penalty by themselves taking on the role and attributes (including masking, dance, and music) of Legba the trickster. It's no accident that, in the climactic confrontation at the political rally (another liminal space, created by display, music, dance, heightened speech, costume, and so on), Everett, Pete, Delmar, and Tommy *together* reclaim power and personal agency by making music. Their second, string-band version of "Man of Constant Sorrow," which parallels their earlier, driving blues version, is masked as hillbilly, not blackface, minstrelsy. But it's still dancing to Legba's liminal, comical, risky, transformative, empowering tune.

⌐⌐

The point—that *O Brother* captured, that *Lackawanna Blues* lost in a garbled "authenticity," that Craig Brewer in *Black Snake Moan* recognized in Son House but could not match himself, that *Crossroads* abandoned through the reinscription of high-art versus low-art hierarchies—is the reality that the blues and the blues players understood and made the very stuff of their day-to-day, hand-to-mouth existence. That is, music truly is magic: a set of cognitive tools that can transform consciousness, can create the only sacred space out of which new possibilities, for individuals and communities, became reality. In Deep South culture, Legba was not the demonic villain depicted in Hollywood films about the South, any more than the blues were simply markers of "authenticity" or "transgression." For southern musicians, and blues players in particular, the blues was rather the bridge to new possibilities, balancing Legba's clients on the knife-edge between forward or back, endlessly mutable and enticing: the door to new possibilities, the energy for self-transformation, and the place where the "Southern crosses the Dog."[35]

The crossroads.

NOTES

1. For the original articles laying out the approach, see Henry Louis Gates Jr., "The 'Blackness of Blackness': A Critique of the Sign and the Signifying Monkey," *Critical Inquiry* 9, no. 4 (June 1983): 685–723, and Gates, "Talkin' That Talk," *Critical Inquiry* 13, no. 1 (Autumn 1986): 203–10; for demonstrations of the technique's applicability to questions of allusion in African American music, see Robert Walser, "Out of Notes: Signification, Interpretation, and the Problem of Miles Davis," *Musical Quarterly* 77, no. 2 (Summer 1993): 343–65, and Gary Tomlinson, "Cultural Dialogics and Jazz: A White Historian Signifies," *Black Music Research Journal* 11, no. 2 (Autumn 1991): 229–64; for application in film, see Krin Gabbard, "Signifyin(g) the Phallus: *Mo' Better Blues* and Representations of the Jazz Trumpet," *Cinema Journal* 32, no. 1 (Autumn 1992): 43–62.

2. Michele Faith Wallace, "The Good Lynching and *The Birth of a Nation*: Discourses and Aesthetics of Jim Crow," *Cinema Journal* 43, no. 1 (Autumn 2003): 101. In his 1978 article, Charles Merrell Berg provides a reasonably comprehensive survey of the use (to that date) of black music in Hollywood productions, including *Pete Kelly's Blues* (1955), *Paris Blues* (1961), *The Connection* (1961), *Too Late Blues* (1962), *The Man with the Golden Arm* (1955), and *Anatomy of a Murder* (1959); see "Cinema Sings the Blues," *Cinema Journal* 17, no. 2 (Spring 1978): 1–12. However, Berg's text, like that of Daniel J. Leab, is flawed by inadequate critical or analytical perspective; see *From Sambo to Superspade: The Black Experience in Motion Pictures* (Boston: Houghton Mifflin, 1975). Albert Johnson's magisterial two-part survey of African Americans in feature films is comprehensive to 1990, but its treatment is essentially critical, not analytical; see "Moods Indigo: A Long View," *Film Quarterly* 44, no. 2 (Winter 1990–91): 13–27, and 44, no. 3 (Spring 1991): 15–29.

3. See David Brackett, "Banjos, Biopics, and Compilation Scores: The Movies Go Country," *American Music* 19, no. 3 (Autumn 2001): 249.

4. See Peter Stanfield, "An Excursion into the Lower Depths: Hollywood, Urban Primitivism, and 'St. Louis Blues,' 1929–1937," *Cinema Journal* 41, no. 2 (2002): 84. For a good filmic depiction of black music's "transgressive" nature, see also Spike Lee's *Bamboozled* (2000), which, though ridden with Lee's usual directorial flaws (didacticism, pedantry, and a tendency to default to the tritest Hollywood narrative clichés), captures the liminality, performative risk, and semiotic genius of archetypal blackface minstrelsy.

5. Paul Oliver, "'Twixt Midnight and Day: Binarism, Blues and Black Culture," *Popular Music*, vol. 2, *Theory and Method* (Cambridge University Press, 1982), 192.

6. Ibid., 181.

7. Berndt Ostendorf, "Celebration or Pathology? Commodity or Art? The Dilemma of African-American Expressive Culture," *Black Music Research Journal* 20, no. 2, "European Perspectives on Black Music" (Autumn 2000): 224. For analysis of music's filmic "authenticity" in a parallel genre, see Brackett, "Banjos, Biopics, and Compilation Scores," 249, 262–63, 274, and 279–80; for the blues' similar signification (but outside the realm of film), see Marybeth Hamilton's useful analysis of the "romantic" view of blues authenticity in "The Blues, the Folk, and African-American History," *Transactions of the Royal Historical Society*, 6th ser., 11 (London: Royal Historical Society, 2001): 20–22. See also Stanfield, "Excursion into the Lower Depths"; Bruce Tucker, "'Tell Tchaikovsky the News': Postmodernism, Popular Culture, and the Emergence of Rock 'n' Roll," *Black Music Research Journal* 22, Suppl. *Best of BMRJ* (2002): 23–47.

8. Victor Turner, "Images of Anti-temporality: An Essay in the Anthropology of Experience," *Harvard Theological Review* 75, no. 2 (April 1982): 250.

9. As Turner states, "The primary motivation behind ritual is the desire to break free temporarily of social structure in order to transcend its existential limitations and reconfigure it along communitarian lines." Quoted in Bobby C. Alexander, "Correcting Misinterpretations of Turner's Theory: An African-American Pentecostal Illustration," *Journal for the Scientific Study of Religion* 30, no. 1 (March 1991): 27.

10. Ibid., 35.

11. Samuel A. Floyd Jr., "Ring Shout! Literary Studies, Historical Studies, and Black Music Inquiry," *Black Music Research Journal* 11, no. 2 (Autumn 1991): 198.

12. Floyd goes crucially wrong, however, when he claims that Legba the trickster "is embodied most obviously in the gladiatorial improviser of the jazz tradition," for, as the reference to Roman combat makes clear, the heroic figure of the virtuosic jazz player is far closer to the classical European tradition than is the down-and-dirty, mojo-handed, juke-joint-jumping, liminality-bearing, communitas-building figure of the trickster blues player. Ibid., 268–69.

13. Bromell describes the blues lick itself—the melodic/rhythmic figure which could be originated, lifted, quoted, or modified—as a kind of Gatesian "Signifyin[g]," where ability to employ such material to improvise semiotic commentary in performance is a litmus test of cultural expertise. Nick Bromell, "'The Blues and the Veil': The Cultural Work of Musical Form in Blues and '60s Rock," *American Music* 18, no. 2 (Summer 2000): 199.

14. Cynthia Mahabir, "Wit and Popular Music: The Calypso and the Blues," *Popular Music* 15, no. 1 (1996): 60. Finally, Mahabir links both calypsonian and blues players to their West African archetype, Legba: "the ultimate trickster."

15. Born Joel McGhee in Cleveland in 1919, Seneca was a noted New York–based rhythm and blues songwriter and singer as well as actor; he died in 1996. Comments in various forums confirm the film's unpopularity with many blues aficionados, for example, "I enjoyed *Crossroads* in the same way I enjoyed *Porky's.*" Dennis Roger Reed, posting, *Acoustic Guitar Forum*, January 13, 2003, http://

www.guitarseminars.com/ubb/Forum1/HTML/000055.html (accessed November 8, 2009). Mainstream film critics, however, gave it a tepidly positive rating: rottentomatoes.com ranked it 79 percent successful on April 4, 2010, on their "Tomatometer," http://www.rottentomatoes.com/m/1004995-crossroads/ (accessed November 8, 2009), and Walter Goodman calls it an "awkward mix of *Huckleberry Finn*" and "*The Devil and Daniel Webster.*" *New York Times*, March 14, 1986, http://www.nytimes.com/1986/03/14/movies/the-screen-walter -hill-s-crossroads.html?scp=2&sq=crossroads%20movie%201986&st=cse (accessed November 8, 2009).

16. Prior Hill/Cooder collaborations in which roots music played a key role include *Last Man Standing* (1996), *Southern Comfort* (1981), and *The Long Riders* (1980).

17. The most famous Satanic references are in Robert Johnson's corpus of songs, including "Crossroads Blues" but also "Hellhound on My Trail" and "Me and the Devil Blues." Other noted blues players, most particularly Peetie Wheatstraw ("The Devil's Son-in-Law / The High Sheriff from Hell") and Tommy Johnson, who is referenced in *O Brother, Where Art Thou?* likewise understood the self-promotional value of the devilish connection. Other blues players (most notably Son House) also gave lip service to the claims of Robert's natal legend.

18. Johnson had met the talent scout H. C. Speir in Jackson, Mississippi; Speir had in turn arranged the San Antonio sessions, which yielded the epochal "Come On in My Kitchen," "Kind Hearted Woman," "I Believe I'll Dust My Broom" and "Cross Roads Blues."

19. Quoted in Peter Doyle, *Echo and Reverb: Fabricating Space in Popular Music Recording, 1900–1960* (Middletown, Conn.: Wesleyan University Press, 2005).

20. W. R. G. Horton, "God, Man, and the Land in a Northern Ibo Village-Group," *Africa: Journal of the International African Institute* 26, no. 1 (January 1956): 17–28. The following title credits themselves are framed with a visual montage of seminal LP covers. Hamilton discusses the emphasis in blues studies in the fifties and sixties on "realness," as reflected in both aural and visual media; for his comment describing "realness" as iconic, see "Blues," 31–32.

21. "Crossroads (1986) Duel," *YouTube*, http://www.youtube.com/watch?v=DoQKbnCDW94 (accessed April 4, 2010).

22. Alessandra Stanley, "TV Weekend: Holding Fast to Dreams in a Destitute World," *New York Times*, February 11, 2005, http://tv.nytimes.com/2005/02/11/arts/television/11tvwk.html?scp=1&sq=&st=nyt (accessed February 9, 2007).

23. Brewer's film also resembles *Black Mama, White Mama* (1972), a remake of *The Defiant Ones* (1958), with Pam Grier and Margaret Markov taking the roles originated by Sidney Poitier and Tony Curtis. *Cleopatra Jones* (1973) and its sequel, *Cleopatra Jones and the Casino of Gold* (1975), are blaxploitation films on the *Shaft* model, also featuring Pam Grier.

24. Craig Brewer, Scott Bomar, Stephanie Allain, and John Singleton, "The Black Snake Moan" and "Rooted in the Blues, " *Black Snake Moan*, DVD, directed by Craig Brewer (Los Angeles: Paramount, 2006).

25. John Singleton, "Conflicted: The Making of Black Snake Moan," *Black Snake Moan*, DVD.

26. A. O. Scott, "Chained to the Radiator? It's for Her Own Good," *New York Times*, March 2, 2007, http://movies2.nytimes.com/2007/03/02/movies/02blac.html (accessed May 5, 2007).

27. Ibid. Son House, at 00:16 in the *Black Snake Moan* DVD, says, "Ain't but one kind of blues, and that consistses [*sic*] between male and female that's in love. In love. Just like I sing one of them songs while ago and I put her face in that. Say that love hide all fault; make you do things you don't want to do. Love sometime will leave you feeling SAD and blue. I'm talkin' about the blues now; I ain't talkin' about no monkey junk. And it consisted between male and female, and that means two people supposed to be in love when one or the other deceives the other'n through their love."

28. Rob Nelson, "Hussy and Flow," *Village Voice*, February 27, 2007, http://www.villagevoice.com/2007-02-20/film/hussy-n-flow/ (accessed April 4, 2010); italics added.

29. Spike Lee's *Bamboozled* (2000) does a far more sophisticated job of engaging, and problematizing, not only the noxious stereotyping but also the transcendent virtuosity of blackface performance than does Brewer's film.

30. A wonderful signifyin(g) moment comes in the climactic scene when the cartoonish racist Homer T. Stokes hurls a double-barreled accusation at the bearded "Soggy Bottom Boys": "These boys are *not white*! Hell, they ain't even old-timey!"

31. See Peter Guralnick, *Sweet Soul Music: Rhythm and Blues and the Southern Dream of Freedom* (Boston: Back Bay Books, 1999), probably the best book-length treatment of the cultural and social implications of 1960s rhythm and blues.

32. A similar conflation occurs in the character of Charles Durning's "Governor Menelaus P. 'Pappy' O'Daniel," the name of a historical Texas governor, but whose character's charlatan nature recalls later Louisiana politicians epitomized by such as Earl Long.

33. Brackett cites the murderous rednecks at the climax of *Easy Rider* (1969) as an archetypal filmic portrait of the "Devilish South," referencing "a world of Jim Crow laws, racism, illiteracy, and in-bred psychosis"; see "Banjos, Biopics, and Compilation Scores: The Movies Go Country," *American Music* 19, no. 3 (Autumn 2001): 254.

34. Roger Ebert, "*O Brother, Where Art Thou?*" *rogerebert.com*, http://rogerebert.suntimes.com/apps/pbcs.dll/article?aid=/20001229/reviews/12290301/1023 (accessed October 26, 2009). The Coen brothers also refer to Ebert's characterization; see William Rodney Allen, *The Coen Brothers: Interviews* (Jackson: University of Mississippi Press, 2006), 179. The scene is also consistent with the intentionally revisionist "magic realism" of the screenplay, and the liminal nature of the blues, that at this climactic moment, the damned musician would find himself rescued by a slapstick trio of mask-wearing tricksters ("The color guard is colored!") and that the cyclopean Klan leader John Goodman should finally be crushed by his own fiery cross.

35. This quote commemorates Handy's first experience at hearing the blues, at a train station in Tutwiler, Mississippi, in 1913; see "Yellow Dog Blues," *Father of the Blues* (New York: Da Capo, 1991), 74.

Revamping the South

Thoughts on Labor, Relationality, and Southern Representation

Tara McPherson

During the 2006 Oscar telecast, Academy Awards president Sid Ganis commented on Hollywood's efforts to help rebuild New Orleans post-Katrina, citing the production of several films in the region. Subsequently, a good deal of film and television production moved to Louisiana, particularly to Shreveport. While the rise of "Hollywood South," as Louisiana is now sometimes known, might seem an act of good will on the part of the film industry toward a storm-ravaged region, the seeds for this change were planted before Katrina wreaked havoc along the coast. In July 2005 Louisiana State House Bill 731 took effect, providing healthy incentives for media production companies to move to the state.[1] Production numbers for film, television, and commercials made in Louisiana increased dramatically, with the Bayou State emerging as second only to the Los Angeles area for total annual film production in the United States.[2]

A case in point is *True Blood*, one of several media projects at least partially produced in the South, part of what many in Hollywood lament as "run-away" production. This essay takes up this morphing pattern of production alongside other southern-tinged shifts in the global economy, including the Walmart empire, to query the very stakes of studying representation. Although my education trained me to produce close textual readings—that is, at the level of narrative and image—I have come to wonder if such readings sometimes distract us from analyzing the workings of capital, particularly in moments of intense economic reorganization. While *True Blood* exhibits an interesting reworking of several standard southern myths, might the real action actually be taking place offscreen, as capital reconstitutes itself in an era of networked globalization? Tweaks on southern imagery might actually be part and parcel of this new economy, offering a little something for everyone in keeping with the logics of niche marketing and mass personalization.

In fall 2008 I experienced some trepidation as I cued up the first epi-sode of *True Blood* on my TiVo. I had enjoyed executive producer Alan Ball's *Six Feet Under* a great deal, but here Ball was trudging not only into southern territory but also into vampire tales. The threat level for cliché and stereotype seemed enormously high. I feared the worst. As the series opens, we see a speeding SUV swerve into a "GrabbItKwik" mart, unloading a drunken college couple seeking to spice up their white frater-nity lives with a little bit of the forbidden—in this case, a taste of some-thing vampirish. They encounter a black-clad, goth-y convenience store clerk who seems exactly what one might expect as he scowls at the pair and threatens to bite them, while the whole minidrama is observed by a character in camouflage lingering at the beer coolers, clearly meant to signify "redneck." Yet these comfortable clichés are almost immediately undone by the viewer's realization that the clerk is a fraud. The real vam-pire is none other than the redneck, perhaps the first vampire in hunting gear to ever grace the genre.

From this opening sequence of the first episode, something feels a bit different in points south. *True Blood* is southern gothic gone more than a little goth, with heavy doses of sex, sensuality, blood, and gore. While the show revels in its soapy sentimentality, taking up television's recent turn to the serialized and melodramatic with a vengeance, it does so with a smirk and a wink. In adapting Charlaine Harris's series of southern vampire novels, Ball takes several familiar stereotypes firmly in hand, reworks conventions of the southern gothic, and unfolds both new and tired patterns of representing sexuality, class, and race in the region. The southern imaginaries mapped by *True Blood* point to an emerging shift in televisual representations of race and other markers of difference. *True Blood* and recent serialized dramas such as *The Wire* map distinctive fig-urations of human relations, staging scenarios that would not have been imaginable on television in the 1990s and pointing toward nascent forms of sociality. I am intrigued by these changes as shifts at the textual level, but I am perhaps more interested in how we might reconcile these seem-ingly new tales with broad changes in the production contexts of an in-creasingly global media market.

Revamping the South: Beyond Lenticular Logics

In the opening of *True Blood*, we learn a good deal more about the series' fictional world than the perhaps surprising fact that vampires can wear camo. As the college students enter the convenience store, the clerk is watching television. In a nod to *True Blood*'s own production contexts on HBO, the show he is watching features HBO's Bill Maher as himself, interviewing Nan Flanagan (Jessica Tuck), the spokesperson for the American Vampire League (AVL). She has taken to the airwaves to campaign for civil rights for vampires, presenting these creatures of the night as just another misunderstood minority. Throughout the series' first two seasons, Nan will intermittently reappear, often on television, frequently debating representatives of fundamentalist religious groups, such as the evangelical Fellowship of the Sun. In urging the passing of the Vampires' Rights Act, with its echo of the ERA, Nan and the American Vampire League call to mind a host of groups arguing for mainstream civil rights for oppressed minorities, from women to African Americans to gays and lesbians. An exchange between vampire Bill Compton and human Jason Stackhouse further drives this home:

> JASON: A lot of Americans don't think you people deserve special rights. . . .
>   I'm just saying there's a reason.
> BILL: It's called injustice.

As this dialogue makes clear, the series fairly blatantly foregrounds issues of rights. It doesn't take a PhD in media studies to discern that *True Blood* positions these historical civil rights struggles as isomorphic with the battle by vampires to, in the words of the AVL, "be part of mainstream society." In particular, fans and journalists were quick to point out that, in *Variety* critic Brian Lowry's words, the show depends on a "vampires-as-downtrodden-minority gay metaphor." (While many viewers and critics seemed to take this in stride, Ken Tucker smirks that "[Ball] makes so many heavy-handed comparisons between vampires and homosexuals that you wonder if he's really never seen *Buffy the Vampire Slayer* or *The Lost Boys*.")[3]

Still, *True Blood* began airing during the lead up to California's vote on Proposition 8, an anti-gay-marriage initiative heavily funded by evangelical and Mormon organizations, so the series' engagement with the "gay vampire" trope has a particularly pointed edge. In claiming that vampires "just want to be treated like everyone else" and in sketching the Christian right as corrupt and bigoted, the series firmly lodges its vampires-as-gay characterizations within a critique of fundamentalist religions with a strong southern presence. From the "God Hates Fangs" billboard that flashes by in the opening credit sequence to the frequent and scathing critique of TV ministry, *True Blood* deploys its vampires at least partially to enter the fray over debates about gay rights. The often campy tension between the vampires and an evangelical Christianity builds with particular force in the second season, when Jason Stackhouse, brother to series' heroine Sookie Stackhouse, is recruited into the Fellowship of the Sun Church.

Despite the AVL's savvy and telegenic media presence, the vampires of *True Blood* are hardly portraits of a model minority. While the synthetic blood substitute "Tru Blood" has apparently freed vampires from *needing* human blood, most of the vampires still very much *want* it. And while the AVL preaches a kind of tame assimilation, these vampires are delighted to whip their fangs out at just about any moment. Across the first two seasons, Bill Compton seems the only vampire much interested in "acting human," while his compatriots happily engage in a sensual, sexual, and often violent carnality, actively converting (or "turning") humans into their own kind (enacting the paranoid fantasy of the far right that imagines gays to themselves be demons of conversion). While Bill and Sookie occupy a kind of moral high ground in the series, its affective and libidinal energies are invested elsewhere. The visual and aural design of the series pulses with excitement whenever packs of vamps are about. Fangtasia, *True Blood*'s vampire nightclub set in Shreveport, Louisiana, shimmers with desire and decadence, a strong lure for many of the series' humans and for its viewers, as fan blogs make evident.

Ample scholarly writing has debated the vampire metaphor in literature and popular culture, and it is not the task of this essay to enter far into that fray. Suffice it to say that scholarship of the past decade or so has drawn out pointed parallels between the role of the vampire and the role of gays and lesbians in the popular imaginary. In her lively 1997 study, *Our Vampires, Ourselves*, literary critic Nina Auerbach notes that each generation pretty much gets the vampires it deserves and observes that, following the emergence of the AIDS crisis and the patriarchal resurgences of the Reagan administration, vampires had "learned identity politics," becoming clannish and self-enclosed. Her early 1990s vampires are fatigued and drained of a vital energy, in need of a "restorative sleep."[4]

This fatigue is much less in evidence among the denizens of Fangtasia (even as it is quite palpable in our "moral" vampire, Bill). Instead, the vampires of *True Blood* seem to be pushing beyond an identity-based self-enclosure toward another mode of sociality. While, at the level of the story line, the vampires are often represented as morally ambiguous (if not blatantly evil) and as clannish, the aesthetic and affective registers of the series invest them with a lifeblood of their own. The most convincing moments of feeling and vividness in the series emerge from the vampires' lively nightlife and, more importantly, from the friction-laced interactions between vampires and humans. While vampire blood might be addictive, it is also intensely pleasurable, opening the rather lifeless humans roaming about the fictional town of Bon Temps, Louisiana, to new sensual and tactile relations to everyday life. They feel *better* and *more* following contact with vampires, opening themselves to vibrant registers of experience.

In theorizing the role of cruising within gay culture, Leo Bersani writes that the practice might be understood to clear "the ground for a new relationality." Drawing on Georg Simmel, Bersani suggests that sociability is about a pure relationality, about the possibility "of being 'reduced' to an impersonal rhythm."[5] Gay cruising thus posits a kind of elsewhere, imaging an alternate form of community that recognizes "sameness" while relating "lovingly to difference," opening up the subject to "the pleasure of existing at an abstract level of pure being."[6] *True Blood*'s loving attention to the lives of vampires taps into this mode of pleasure and implicitly celebrates an ethos of cruising. While the series seemingly stages an argument for rights based on identity markers (hence the American Vampire League), the pleasures and appeal of the series more accurately reside in an expansive notion of relationality that pushes beyond a view of humanity predicated on group-based markers of difference.

Auerbach writes that "vampirism springs not only from paranoia, xenophobia, or immortal longings, but from generosity and shared enthusiasm. This strange taste cannot be separated from the expansive impulses that make us human."[7] If, for Auerbach, the vampires of 1990s U.S. popular culture had lost touch with this expansive quality, *True Blood*'s vamps begin to reanimate this relational possibility. Certainly, this animation draws a vital force from its mapping over queer being and temporality, but the series also actively investigates relationality along other registers. In creating the television show, Alan Ball took certain liberties with the original novels, particularly in relation to representations of blackness. For instance, Ball keeps the hustling, drug-dealing character Lafayette (Nelsan Ellis) alive (if barely) in season two and, perhaps more significantly, expands on the role of Tara (Rutina Wesley), changing the character from white to black.

If the series' representations of gayness (in the not-so-coded form of vampires) feel both familiar, even stereotypical (i.e., Fangtasia as a gay bar, gayness as camp, etc.) and also seem to gesture elsewhere (toward ideal forms of relationality), the same might be said of its images of blackness. Lafayette is a recognizable mixture of a grab bag of "gay black queen" traits. Tara often functions as the kind of wisecracking black sidekick ubiquitous from much late twentieth-century popular culture, serving as a convenient backdrop for Sookie's story, scaffolding the white character's exploration of her own interiority. Tara is brash, angry, and damaged, even while she is portrayed as hypersexual and animalistic (particularly in the second season).

Alongside these tired tropes of blackness, the well-tuned ear might also pick up a slight low-humming nostalgia for all things "old south," including Bill's Civil War memories. He was turned into a vampire in 1865 while a soldier in the Confederate army. While he casts the war as far from glorious, describing "starving, freezing boys killing each other so that rich people can stay rich," the series does indulge in a bit of southern mythmaking, particularly in its often languorous tone. The camera lingers on Spanish moss and broad front porches, tapping into variations on the southern gothic. Yet we also see Bill struggling to come to terms with his history, with what he is and has done, perhaps a parable that illustrates how a guilty whiteness might seek redemption. Bill's melancholia often works as an affective wedge, blocking his transition into a transformed subject who can feel southern in new ways, but his emotional struggles and his attempts to be a "good man" model for us week after week the work involved in redeeming our pasts and transforming subjectivity.

On various blogs and Web sites, viewers of the show actively debate the meaning of this range of representations, toggling between revulsion at certain images (the sassy black woman; the snappy queen; the embrace of a certain lost South) and a sense that Tara "is slightly different than the average sassy black girl character. I'm not sure what it is, but it's different."[8] One difference is that Tara frequently speaks to issues in the racial histories of the United States, particularly in the South, from her lament at her mother's decision to name her after the mythical plantation of *Gone with the Wind* to her frequent allusions to slavery and to Bill's Confederate past. (We will return to Tara's relation to labor as we proceed.) Mark Auslander argues that the series points toward "the enduring violent echoes of enslavement" and notes that "presumably, the impossibility of determining the precise analogues of slave-owner and slave in *True Blood* is precisely the point. . . . [A]re there mysterious traces of the Free and the Unfree in each and every one of us?"[9] Again, the contours of an expansive relationality emerge, even among the tired realm of stereotype.

At stake is the very terrain of the human and how we might conceive or know it. The pale, blonde Sookie is continually asked, "What are you?" particularly by the vampires. "You're something more than human," Bill tells her. Sookie, of course, is "special," with the capacity to tap into the inner thoughts of others. This supersonic hearing functions as a way to cut through social nicety to the often dark heart of the covert racism (and often sexism) of the post–civil rights era. Her ability to listen in on the thoughts of others reveals the scripts of hate running behind more civil faces, while moments of blatant hate speech and violence underscore that overt hatreds are still a prominent reality. As such the series might be seen to push into blatant visibility an understanding of the various codes of racial representation and racism that scholarly work like my own has been at pains to explicate and highlight. While vampires may finally be coming out of the coffin, not everyone's happy to have them around.

Integration isn't a done deal here, and bigotry (whether covert or overt) constantly rears its ugly head (as it recently did in the real Louisiana when a judge refused to issue a marriage license to an interracial couple). Yet the series not only offers this snapshot of the mechanisms of contemporary racism; it also actively points toward another mode of sociability in which even the living and the dead might structure new modes of being together.

Further, the series not only stages a compelling (and fun) exploration of these issues, it also pushes beyond the various "lenticular logics" tracked in my earlier research. Largely surveying southern representation through the close of the last millennium, *Reconstructing Dixie* charts the different racial logics of black and white that prevailed before and after the civil rights movement, especially in the U.S. South. The overt racial logics of the pre–civil rights era typically defined black and white in relation to each other to fix their meaning, while the more covert methods of the post–civil rights era tended to separate black from white, suppressing relation. For instance, *Gone with the Wind* defines Scarlett's whiteness in relation to Mammy's blackness, deeply intertwining the two while privileging whiteness, while *Scarlett*, the 1990s sequel, seemingly dispenses with blackness altogether, suppressing relation. Neither mode is better than the other: each supports racist representation and racism. They are simply different modes of organizing both the visual and epistemological fields. I deem the second, covert mode a "lenticular logic," defining the lenticular as the dominant mode of racial representation (and racism) in the latter half of the twentieth century. As I note in the book, "the lenticular often serves to secure our understandings of race in precise ways, fixating on sameness or difference without allowing productive . . . connection. . . . Such a move limits our ability to see association or relation."[10]

My book does offer several examples of cultural productions that short-circuit the various logics of the lenticular, considering works that interrogate the relationship of sameness to difference in southern identity and that explore the possibilities of alliance and relationality. However, these works tend to be either fraught with contradiction (such as the TV series *Designing Women*) or deploy more experimental forms (such as Octavia Butler's wonderful novel *Kindred*). But *True Blood* is popular television (if within the rarefied space of HBO), not a feminist novel or an activist memoir. During the second season, the show's average nightly audience was about 5.2 million, HBO's highest-rated series at the time.[11] The first season's DVD box set spent more than two months in the top five for TV DVD sales.

If Tara's character somehow feels "different" to the blog poster quoted earlier, *True Blood* also *feels* different to me. And, like that commentator,

I cannot fully name the difference. But I sense that a new form of representing and understanding race (and region) in the United States is emergent, one signaled by a whole range of cultural shifts from the first black man elected U.S. president to a spate of popular television series featuring mixed-race casts, both developments that seemed very unlikely as I was finishing *Reconstructing Dixie* around 2002. This shift clearly does not have a single or a simple political valence (let alone an easily progressive one) but, like all moments of cultural shift, it offers new risks and possibilities.

Where might we look for other manifestations of this change or even for its potential causes? What other stories might rest below the surface of *True Blood*'s racy plotlines, visual excess, and expansive relationality? What else is changing in the South and beyond?

"A place called Premium Cable": Global Media and the Local

True Blood is partially shot in Louisiana, and the series' actors and crew have commented on the importance of the location work to setting the feel for the show. As Anna Paquin (who plays Sookie) told Baton Rouge television station WAFB's David Spunt, "Nothing really looks like the South, except the South. So our show is set in Louisiana and that's a big part of what works and what it is and it's important to come down here and capture it." Similarly, James Mangold, director of the 2005 film *Walk the Line*, a biopic about Johnny Cash, insisted that shooting in Tennessee allowed him "to capture part of our own culture." For the creative personnel involved in these productions, the southern location no doubt lends an air of authenticity to the work being made. Yet this authenticity would likely lose its appeal were it not for substantial tax credits available to media productions shot within the state. As Ilan Arboleda, the producer of *Bear Creek*, a film recently in production, observes, "The tax incentives in Louisiana are great. The great locations are an added bonus. It makes choosing Louisiana a no-brainer when it comes to choosing a place to film."[12]

In reviewing *True Blood* for the *Los Angeles Times*, critic Robert Lloyd notes, "The action may take place in the South, but the show itself is truly set in a place called Premium Cable."[13] While Lloyd was pointing to the high degree of sex and violence on the show in referencing paid cable channels, we might also push his comments toward another meaning. The "place called Premium Cable" is a peculiar location that simultaneously straddles Hollywood and a vast network of transnational capital. It is safe to say that one of the changes that make a complex show such as *True Blood* feasible is a dramatically different environment for media production in the postcable landscape.

In *Global Hollywood 2*, Toby Miller and others argue that Hollywood is no longer a "company town" but rather a "global factory."[14] The solidification of post-Fordist global capitalism has led to an increasing concentration of media ownership and distribution outlets, and advances in networked digital technologies have allowed for more geographically dispersed modes of production. "Hollywood" has always been a shared imaginary, much like the South, but today what we mean by Hollywood need hardly signify a specific place in southern California at all. Both the financial networks of Hollywood and the creative and postproduction processes of filmmaking are no longer tightly tethered to the region (or even to the United States). Information, media, and money are all one with the bitstream that sustains global capitalism.

In a recent article in *Geoforum*, Susan Christopherson observes that "The primary goal of the media merchants, then, is not production and distribution of products but identification of strategies to extract the maximum revenue from intellectual property."[15] One maximization strategy was fueled by the deregulation of media ownership rules, particularly in television. In 1995–96, when networks were still prohibited from producing their own shows, they had partial ownership in less than 20 percent of new series. By 2002 that percentage had grown to 77.5 percent. Large media conglomerates no longer need compete for expensive products; they simply create their own through their subsidiaries. Christopherson concludes that "the ability of the conglomerates to decrease their risks at the distribution end has enabled them to seek out and invest in alternative regional production sites and to squeeze producers to look for financing and production cost reductions from regional states."[16]

Louisiana's bid to become Hollywood South must be understood within these shifting machinations of global capital. The *Los Angeles Times* estimated that a hypothetical film that would cost $1,924,000 to produce in Los Angeles would accrue $1,041,997 in tax incentives in Louisiana, substantially lowering costs; the figure is likely higher.[17] The state's tax credits encompass not only individual productions but also infrastructure projects. An article in *State Tax Notes* describes the state's incentives:

> Investors in individual film projects are eligible for a credit of 25 percent as long as the total base investment for the project is more than $300,000. There's also a 10 percent credit for the amount of the base investment spent on payroll for Louisiana residents. The production credit is slated to be gradually reduced to 15 percent for all productions after July 1, 2012, while the payroll credit will remain constant. There is also a 40 percent credit allowed for infrastructure projects related to film, video, or television production, such as building new studios, postproduction facilities, and soundstages.[18]

Louisiana's system relies on private investment. Once producers are granted credits, they typically sell them to tax credit brokerage firms, and the state's taxpayers can then buy the credits to offset their own state taxes. Thus, in effect, the government is losing its tax revenue to benefit both global media companies and a small subset of (often wealthy) individual taxpayers, as well as the brokerage firms, which handle the transactions. Proponents of the scandal-plagued program argue that the incentives also generate other spending in the state, as well as new jobs for residents, but the chief economist for Louisiana's legislative fiscal office, Greg Albrecht, insists that "There's no way you can say this makes money for the public" treasury. He estimates that about 18 percent of what is spent by the state is recovered in taxes on new economic activity and notes that the state spent $121 million on the program in 2006.[19] In 2008 Louisiana credited the Brad Pitt film, *The Curious Case of Benjamin Button*, more than $27 million.[20]

Over forty states now have tax incentives for film production, setting up a scenario for intense competition for a fairly steady number of productions. And other states are not the only competitors Louisiana's nascent film industry is facing. Films are increasingly being shot in Eastern Europe, with an overall increase of production spending there of 927 percent from 2001 to 2005. It is easy to see this as a zero-sum game or a race to the bottom in which labor and public infrastructure are both losers. While film production is clearly not the same as many forms of outsourced manufacturing, this emergence of the South as an early mover in luring production away from other U.S. regions should strike a familiar chord with scholars of the South. From the brutal, union-busting practices that brought northern industry to the South in the middle of the twentieth century to the decimation of those very factories by the southern-born titan Walmart by the turn of the twenty-first century, the South has long been a site of global flows of capital and labor. (Of course, we might also recall the slave trade as an earlier manifestation of the South's long role in global economies.) If, as I have written elsewhere, "Wal-Mart's corporate model is coming to drive the world," we can now see the South as one node in a global franchise economy, one still tied to these older histories of exploitation even as it helps mint new ones.[21] In addition to the benefits of tax credits, media production has also moved to Louisiana in pursuit of cheaper labor, particularly given Louisiana's status as a nonunionized, right-to-work state. Simultaneously, Walmart has emerged as a powerful revenue stream for the studios themselves, particularly when the box-store giant pioneered the sale of movie and TV DVDs, decimating the movie rental market along the way. Thus, we see that the South continues to function within the global economy along a number of vectors.

To be clear, this is not a protectionist argument that film production should simply stay in Hollywood or that the South should not be in the business of media. Rather, it is a plea for flexible scholarly models that might more nimbly account for the shifting flows of capital. Miller and others point out that "newness is endemic to capitalism's propensity for continued disruption of production, a restless expansion-contraction-dispersion dynamic that sees companies move in concert with the revised social conditions they have helped to create." Put differently, capital will move and move on. The authors track this movement with some rigor and detail, offering the conceptual paradigm of the "New International Division of Cultural Labor" as a way to understand the changing roles of and for labor in a global, post-Fordist economy. They write, "Core and periphery are blurred, the spatial mobility of capital is enhanced, [and] the strategic strength of labor is undermined."[22] They offer a perspective firmly rooted in Marxist theories of labor.

There is much that is compelling here. There is also a fairly dismissive attitude toward textual analysis (the back cover announces that the book addresses the "vacuum left by textual analysis" in our understanding of Hollywood). While the book's early pages claim that "socio-economic analysis is a natural ally of representational analysis," the remaining three hundred–plus pages of text steer far from the representational.[23] In some ways, I'm quite sympathetic to such production studies and often find myself wondering if the world really needs another fine-grained analysis of some southern-tinged text (or any other). But, then again, I know that those texts have their own power in the world. Indeed, they are also documents of labor, of struggle, and of our own complex relations to capital just as surely as are Louisiana's tax credits. How can we truly understand the new forms of cultural labor if we distance ourselves from rich understandings of its products? What might we learn if we wedded an analysis of the economics of media production to a serious engagement with the narrative and visual force of cultural production? We might discern the modes by which complex economic and organizational structures are made meaningful at the level of lived experience or of narrative. While public policy and labor relations certainly are meaningful to daily life, how we understand them also happens at the surface of our screens.

Laboring Southern Style

Work like Miller's and Christopherson's continually underscores the weakened position of labor in this new global economy. Christopherson reports "high levels of worker dissatisfaction and a sense of increased risk" among those laboring in the media industries, with work harder to come by. She also observes that, while "below-the-line" employees are the hardest hit, the creative segment is also feeling the squeeze. She quotes a veteran filmmaker: "in cable, residuals (payments for each showing of the product) for writers, actors, and directors are a percent of the producer's gross. But if that producer is a network who self-deals the rights to their cable company . . . there is no compensation for that. Suddenly you discover that the 11% or 12% gross residual among the three guilds that has been fought over for so many decades is virtually meaningless, as rights are simply self-dealt among related entities."[24]

The frustration among workers is driven home in an early 2009 post on Nikki Finke's blog, *Deadline Hollywood*. In a column titled "Ship of Fools: MPAA Uses Oscars to Boast about Runaway Production," Finke posts an MPAA press release that concludes with the following: "The Red Carpet is just not big enough for the nearly 1.5 million people that comprise the motion picture industry. These workers range from truck drivers to set designers and caterers to animators. They earn more than $30 billion in wages each year. No wonder more than 40 states have enacted incentives to lure these 'Hollywood' productions to their cities and towns. So, as you watch Sunday night's awards show, keep in mind that there are more winners than those who take home a golden statuette." Finke introduces the press release by arguing that, now that more than forty states—including California as of 2009—have incentives for film production, the studios will just play them off one another to drive down costs. The posted comments on the column range from "That's capitalism for you, no one is owed anything, especially if others are willing to be more competitive" to "the industry will continue to 'outsource' production to the lowest bidders" to "Wow. Fuck them. Fuck. Them."[25]

These Hollywood workers are not the only disgruntled employees this essay has tracked. We might recall Tara, behind the bar at Merlotte's, only noticing the customers to tell them off. She is too busy reading a copy of Naomi Klein's *Shock Doctrine* to give service with a smile. As one commentator on Racialicious.com observes, "Okay, so I was actually inspired by Tara going 'This ain't rude. This is uppity!' and smacking the hell out of her manager in an awesome racial/retail revenge moment."[26] Or we might think of Lafayette serving up an "AIDS burger" to a homophobic customer. At one level, *True Blood* is a kind of workplace drama, a familiar form for television, a *Cheers* for the gothic set. Yet the show's engagement with labor is firmly rooted in the working class and in a pronounced resistance to performing unfulfilling labor. Work at Mulatte's is certainly not rewarding. The waitresses are harried, at risk, poorly paid, harassed. They *die* at work. Lafayette is working multiple jobs, as cook, on the road crew, as a dealer and prostitute. Even the vampires get stressed when their bosses are around. The series locates the risks and strains of labor as deadening and deadly.

In a special 2006 report on the world economy, the *Economist* reported that the average worker in a GIO country's "share of the cake" (of wages in relation to national income) is "the smallest it has been for at least three decades," while corporations' portion of the national cake have rapidly expanded. The weekly wage of "typical" U.S. workers fell even as their productivity increased. The report concludes that "most workers are feeling squeezed."[27] In other words, many workers feel a lot like the denizens of Bon Temps: overworked, underpaid, at risk. Perhaps we should read the stressed-out vampires busily trying to protect their territory and turf less as analogues for gay rights struggles (even if they are also that) and more as parables about the working conditions of television professionals in the era of global capitalism. These workers have descended on Louisiana much as the vampires have.

In *True Blood*, rewards and pleasures—such as Tara's gluttonous immersion in the hedonistic palaces of the maenad Maryann or Sookie's heightened attention to nature following sex with a vamp—do not emerge from hard work but from magical happenstance and access to alterity. The humans (and the vampires) most come alive outside of the constraints of work and the circuits of labor: in associations with the undead, through supernatural and mythical contact, and in the dark of night. Thus, the series actively stages the appeal of nonproductive leisure, of hanging about, of the "pure sociability" of Simmel and Bersani.[28] In pursuing ways of being not bound to work and labor, *True Blood* also sets into motion models of alliance that span differences of class, race, gender, and mortality. The pleasures of the show emerge as it maps an access route to elsewhere.

Bersani is pushing toward an otherness that is "unlocatable within differences that can be known and enumerated," a kind of pure otherness, an "identity-free contact." This "jouissance of otherness has as its pre-condition the stripping away of the self, a loss of all that gives us pleasure and pain in our negotiable exchanges with the world."[29] In this argument and in the related scholarship on cruising by Tim Dean, there is a sketching of a mode of otherness that relies on a "conceptual distinction between otherness and difference," a push beyond identity and identification. Dean goes so far as to argue that "identities of whatever sort remain incompatible with openness to alterity."[30]

Bersani and Dean unspool their arguments through a turn to psychoanalysis, but we might also suggest a more materialist reading and ask why these fantasies of a postidentity sociability are so compelling (to theorists, media workers, and television viewers alike)? Perhaps they express our longing to imagine a world that does not so tightly wed us to the machinations of global capital, a space where we can momentarily be free from the endless penetration of labor into the spaces of leisure, working harder and harder for less and less, plugged into an array of beeping devices. While setting such an elsewhere in a southern terrain might seem odd or even reactionary, this regional turn is actually deeply convincing. As the cosmopolitan vampires interact with the small-town South, moving beyond identity to rare moments of pure sociability, relationality, and pleasure, the fraught divides of urban/rural, black/white/brown, North/South, rich/poor, and gay/straight are temporarily suspended, even overcome. Given its long and complex role in the national imaginary, as well as its centuries-old relation to the networks of global capital, the South is a deeply reasonable mise-en-scène for these emergent yearnings. It is, of course, a fantasy, but in our imaginings of different worlds we also set the stage for other futures and perhaps begin to call them into being. While it is possible that the vampires of *True Blood* are simply distracting us from our deep imbrications in capital and from our alienated relationships to labor, they might also be animating other longings that can move us elsewhere. We will have to work through difficult and messy southern histories if we aim to get there.

NOTES

1. Louisiana State House Bill 731, Regular Legislative Session, *Motion Picture Tax Credit*, July 2005, HLS 05RS-1157, http://www.legis.state.la.us/billdata/streamdocument.asp?did=309228 (accessed April 17, 2010).

2. Louisiana has retained a solid share of film and television production since this time, although it jockeys between second and third place in the sweepstakes of the states with the most production (competing with California and New York).

3. Brian Lowry, "*True Blood*," *Variety*, June 5, 2009, http://www.variety.com/index.asp?layout=print_review&reviewid=VE1117940424&categoryid=32 (accessed September 7, 2009); Ken Tucker, "TV Review: *True Blood*," *Entertainment Weekly*, no. 1009, September 5, 2008, http://www.ew.com/ew/article/o,,20284276,00.html (accessed September 7, 2009).

4. Nina Auerbach, *Our Vampires, Ourselves* (Chicago: University of Chicago Press, 1997), 187, 192.

5. Leo Bersani, "Sociability and Cruising," *Umbr(a): A Journal of the Unconscious* 2 (2002): 20, 11.

6. Ibid., 17, 11.

7. Auerbach, *Our Vampires, Ourselves*, vii.

8. "Browne," comment to Tami, "True Blood: Tired Stereotypes," *Racialicious*, September 25, 2008, http://www.racialicious.com/2008/09/24/true-blood-tired-stereotypes/ (accessed August 19, 2009).

9. Mark Auslander, "Theorizing Race and Slavery in HBO's *True Blood*," *Cultural Productions*, December 11, 2008, http://culturalproductions.blogspot.com/2008/12/theorizing-race-and-slavery-in-hbos.html (accessed August 19, 2009).

10. Tara McPherson, *Reconstructing Dixie: Race, Gender, and Nostalgia in the Imagined South* (Durham, N.C.: Duke University Press), 2003, 27.

11. During the second season, each new episode was aired twice on the evening of its initial broadcast, at nine o'clock and again at eleven. The average audience across the two viewings was 5.2 million.

12. David Spunt, "*True Blood* Goes for True Louisiana Feeling," WAFB Channel 9 News, Baton Rouge, Louisiana, July 10, 2009, http://www.wafb.com/Global/story.asp?s=10709647&clienttype=printable (accessed September 7, 2009); "Director's Commentary," *Walk the Line*, DVD, directed by James Mangold (2005; Los Angeles: Twentieth Century Fox, 2006); Ilan Arboleda, quoted in Joshua Davidson, "True Blood Filming in Baton Rouge," *Tiger Weekly.Com Blogs*, January 28, 2009, http://www.lovingtruebloodindallas.com/2009/01/true-blood-filming-in-baton-rouge-hbo.html (accessed September 7, 2009).

13. Robert Lloyd, "Television Review: True Blood," *Los Angeles Times*, June 13, 2009, http://articles.latimes.com/2009/jun/13/intertainment/et-true-blood13 (accessed September 7, 2009).

14. Toby Miller, Nitin Govil, John McMurria, Richard Maxwell, and Ting Wang, *Global Hollywood 2* (London: British Film Institute, 2005), 133.

15. Susan Christopherson, "Behind the Scenes: How Transnational Firms Are Constructing a New International Division of Labor in Media Work," *Geoforum* 37, no. 5. (September 2006): 744.

16. Ibid., 749.

17. John Horn, "Hollywood's New Backlot? The U.S." *Los Angeles Times WPIX .com*, August 17, 2005, http://www.wpix.com/cl-na-louisana17aug17,0,245616 .story?page=3 (accessed September 7, 2009).

18. Matthew Bailey, "Hollywood South: Why Film Credits Are Good for Louisiana," *State Tax Notes*, June 2, 2008, 715.

19. Greg Albrecht's detailed financial report from March 2005 is available online. "Film and Video Tax Incentives: Estimated Economic and Fiscal Impacts," State of Louisiana Legislative Fiscal Office, http://lfo.louisiana.gov/files/revenue/FilmVideoIncentives.pdf (accessed September 7, 2009).

20. Michael Cieply, "States' Film Production Incentives Cause Jitters," *New York Times*, October 11, 2008, http://www.nytimes.com/2008/10/12/us/12incentives.html?pagewanted=1&_r=1 (accessed September 7, 2009).

21. Tara McPherson, "On Wal-Mart and Southern Studies," *American Literature* 78, no. 4 (2006), 696.

22. Miller and others, *Global Hollywood 2*, 127, 109.

23. Ibid., 6.

24. Christopherson, "Behind the Scenes," 745–46.

25. Nikki Finke, "Ship of Fools: MPAA Uses Oscars to Boast about Runaway Production," *Deadline Hollywood*, February 20, 2009, http://www.deadline .com/hollywood/mpaa-boasting-about-runaway-production/ (accessed August 13, 2009).

26. "Browne," "True Blood: Tired Stereotypes."

27. Mark Thoma, "Avoiding Protectionism," *Economist's View*, September 19, 2006, http://economistsview.typepad.com/economistsview/2006/09/avoiding_pro tec.html (accessed August 19, 2009).

28. Georg Simmel, "Sociability," in *On Individuality and Social Forms*, ed. Donald Levine, trans. Everett Hughes (Chicago: University of Chicago Press, 1971), 127–29.

29. Bersani, "Sociability and Cruising," 21–22.

30. Tim Dean, *Unlimited Intimacy: Reflections on the Subculture of Barebacking* (Chicago: University of Chicago Press, 2009), 206, 212.

Contributors

Deborah E. Barker is Associate Professor of English at the University of Mississippi. She is the author of *Aesthetics and Gender in American Literature: The Portrait of the Woman Artist* (2000). She has published articles in *African American Review, Mississippi Quarterly, LIT: Literature, Interpretation, Theory,* and *The Faulkner Journal.* Her recent publications are on postmodernism and the southern chick flick, and filmic adaptations of Faulkner's novels. She is currently working on a book about the southern rape complex in film.

Melanie R. Benson is Assistant Professor of Native American Studies at Dartmouth College. She is the author of *Disturbing Calculations: The Economics of Identity in Postcolonial Southern Literature, 1912–2002* (2008). She has published articles on Louis Owens, William Faulkner, Barry Hannah, and on Native Americans in southern literature.

Matthew H. Bernstein is Professor and Chair of Film Studies at Emory University, author of *Screening a Lynching: Leo Frank on Screen* (2009) and *Walter Wanger, Hollywood Independent* (2000) and editor of *Controlling Hollywood* (2000), an anthology on censorship and self-regulation. With Professor Dana F. White of Emory University, he is completing a study of moviegoing in Atlanta, during and after segregation.

R. Bruce Brasell received his PhD in Cinema Studies from New York University. He has taught film at Brooklyn College, New York University, Sarah Lawrence College, Vassar College, and Manhattan College and has published in *Wide Angle, Cinema Journal, Film History, Journal of Film and Video, Jump Cut, Film Criticism, Cineaste, Mississippi Quarterly, Southern Quarterly,* and the anthology *Out in the South.* He is in the process of completing two books: "Mediated Distinctiveness: Documentary Film, Race, and the American South" and "Sweet Are the Uses of Degeneracy: Southern Gothic and American Film."

Chris Cagle is Assistant Professor of Film and Media Arts at Temple University. He has published recent articles in the journal *Screen* and in the edited collections *Media Convergence History* (2009) and *Hollywood Reborn: Movie Stars of the 1970s* (2010). He is currently working on a book about the social-problem film and changes in the American film industry.

Ryan DeRosa has a PhD in Cinema Studies from New York University (2007) and has taught film at NYU and Ohio University. He is writing a book about the race integration film of the 1950s.

Leigh Anne Duck is Associate Professor of English at the University of Mississippi. She is the author of *The Nation's Region: Southern Modernism, Segregation, and U.S. Nationalism* (2006) and has written articles on William Faulkner, Zora Neale Hurston, and the Global South.

Briallen Hopper received her PhD in English from Princeton University. She is currently studying religion at Yale University and is working on a book about the ethics of emotion in American reform culture from abolitionism to the civil rights movement.

Robert Jackson is Assistant Professor of English at the University of Tulsa. He works in several areas of American cultural studies from the mid-nineteenth century to the present, focusing on interdisciplinary connections among literature, film and media, and social history. He wrote *Seeking the Region in American Literature and Culture: Modernity, Dissidence, Innovation* (2005) and currently is completing a book about the varied relations between black and white southerners and the motion picture medium from the silent era to World War II.

Kathryn McKee is McMullan Associate Professor of Southern Studies and Associate Professor of English at the University of Mississippi. She has published articles in *Legacy, Mississippi Quarterly, Southern Literary Journal, Southern Quarterly*, and *Studies in American Humor*, and she recently coedited with Annette Trefzer a special issue of *American Literature* called "Global Contexts, Local Literatures: The New Southern Studies."

Tara McPherson is Associate Professor and Chair of the Division of Critical Studies at the University of Southern California's School of Cinema-Television. She is the author of *Reconstructing Dixie: Race, Gender, and Nostalgia in the Imagined South* (2003), the coeditor of *Hop on Pop: The Politics and Pleasures of Popular Culture* (2003), and the founding editor of the online journal *Vectors: Journal of Culture and Technology in a Dynamic Vernacular*.

Sharon Monteith is Professor of American Studies at the University of Nottingham, UK. She is the author of *Advancing Sisterhood? Interracial Friendships in Contemporary Southern Fiction* (2000) and *Film Histories* (2006; with Paul Grainge and Mark Jancovich). She is the coeditor of *Gender and the Civil*

Rights Movement (1999; 2004), *South to a New Place: Region, Literature, Culture* (2002), and *The Encyclopedia of Southern Culture: Media* (forthcoming). Monteith has contributed to collections such as *Media, Culture and the Modern African Freedom Struggle* (2001), the *Blackwell Companion to Southern Culture* (2007), and *Poverty and Progress in the U.S. South* (2006). Her most recent book, *American Culture in the 1960s*, was published in 2008, and she is currently completing a manuscript titled "Civil Rights in the Melodramatic Imagination."

Riché Richardson is Associate Professor of African American literature at the Africana Studies and Research Center at Cornell University. Her scholarly essays have appeared in journals such as *American Literature, Mississippi Quarterly*, and *Forum for Modern Language Studies*. Her published and developing essays treat topics such as the role of the South in formations of race and masculinity in the African American context, African American film, southern rap, psychoanalysis, and global and diasporic perspectives in southern studies. She is the author of *Black Masculinity and the U.S. South: From Uncle Tom to Gangsta* and the coeditor, with Jon Smith, of the new book series, *The New Southern Studies*, at the University of Georgia Press.

Christopher J. Smith is Associate Professor and Chair of Musicology/Ethnomusicology and Director of the Vernacular Music Center at Texas Tech University School of Music. He is the author of *Celtic Backup for All Instrumentalists* (2000) and *Irish Session Tunes by Ear* (2005), as well as essays in *New Hibernia Review, The Renaissance in Ireland, Improvisation: In the Course of Performance*, and *Popular Culture and Postmodern Ireland*.

Valerie Smith is Woodrow Wilson Professor of Literature and Professor of English and African American Studies at Princeton University, where she directs the Center for African American Studies. She is the author of *Not Just Race, Not Just Gender: Black Feminist Readings* (1998) and *Self-Discovery and Authority in Afro-American Narrative* (1987). She is also the editor of *Representing Blackness: Issues in Film and Video* (1997).

Jay Watson is Professor of English at the University of Mississippi. He is the author of *Forensic Fictions: The Lawyer Figure in Faulkner* (1993) and the editor of *Conversations with Larry Brown* (2007).

Index

Friedman, Susan Stanford, 239, 250n59
From Mammies to Militants (Trudier Harris), 72
Frost, Frank, 322
Fugitive, The (1910), 35, 38
Fugitive Kind, The (1960), 9
Fun on the Farm (1905), 31, 33, 48n15

Gabbard, Krin, 332n1
Gaines, Ernest, 10
Gallagher, Tag, 132–33
Gates, Henry Louis, Jr., 254, 318, 320, 332n1, 333n13
Gathering of Old Men (1987), 10
Gator (1976), 221
Gaudréault, André, 110
gays, 52, 297, 301–2, 308–9, 312n5; Hollywood's avoidance of, 294, 302, 314; nihilism of, 312, 316n47; racial tension of, 56, 300, 307–8, 311; religious persecution of, 311, 338; in representations of vampires, 338–40, 348–49; within southern identity, 17, 294, 298–300, 303–4; and violence, 297, 302, 311, 314n28. *See also* gender; lesbians
gaze (white), 325, 328–29
gender, 6, 32, 52, 55, 297; in constructing southern identity, 59, 297–300, 304, 309, 312; as construction of cinema, 18, 60, 161, 300–303, 312n5, 338; economies of, 80, 89, 91; and heterosexuality, 90, 92–93, 160, 307, 309, 311; and homoeroticism, 294, 301–2, 307, 311; in queer social structures, 311–12, 339–40, 348; in race struggles, 156, 161, 163. *See also* gay; lesbian
General, The (1927), 126
Gentleman's Agreement (1947), 113
Geoforum (journal), 344
George, Cynthia, 61
George Washington (2000), 12
Geronimo, 256, 272n19

Geronimo Rex (Hannah), 256, 272n19
Ghosts of Mississippi (1996), 10, 180
Girl on a Chain Gang (1964), 16, 211; exploitation of civil rights activism in, 198–200, 210, 212; representations of sexuality in, 201–3, 205
Girlfriends (television show), 58
Glass Menagerie, The (1950), 9
Glazer, Nathan, 168–70
Global Hollywood 2 (Miller et al.), 344
Global South, 1, 13, 19n3, 243; defined, 3
Gone with the Wind (Mitchell), 53–55, 58, 61, 65, 73
Gone with the Wind (1939), 8, 124; constructions of antebellum South in, 8, 12, 54, 58, 61, 71; femininity in, 58, 64, 69–70; as guide to protocol, 53, 58, 62, 68; racial constructions in, 65–66, 73–74, 342; role of Mammy in (*see* Mammy)
Goodman, Andrew, 197–98, 200–201, 211
Goodman, Walter, 334n15
Gothic South, 4, 7, 18, 298, 337, 341, 347; in homoerotic media, 297, 300–301, 304; in Humid Time constructions, 310
Grady, Pam, 278
Graham, Allison, 313n18
Grapes of Wrath, The (1940), 139
Great Depression, 7, 12, 90; cinema during, 64, 67, 79; social effects of, 74, 81, 89, 91, 93
Great Train Robbery, The (1903), 22n13, 30
Great War (World War I), 27
Green, Al, 322
Green, David Gordon, 293, 303
Green Pastures (1936), 6
Greene, Graham, 257
Grier, Pam, 334n23

The New Southern Studies

The Nation's Region: Southern Modernism, Segregation, and U.S. Nationalism
by Leigh Anne Duck

Black Masculinity and the U.S. South: From Uncle Tom to Gangsta
by Riché Richardson

Grounded Globalism: How the U.S. South Embraces the World
by James L. Peacock

Disturbing Calculations: The Economics of Identity in Postcolonial Southern Literature, 1912–2002
by Melanie R. Benson

American Cinema and the Southern Imaginary
edited by Deborah E. Barker and Kathryn McKee